# Alentejo

WITHDRAWN

## the Bradt Travel Guide

**Alex Robinson**

edition
I

www.bradtguides.com

Bradt Travel Guides Ltd, UK
The Globe Pequot Press Inc, USA

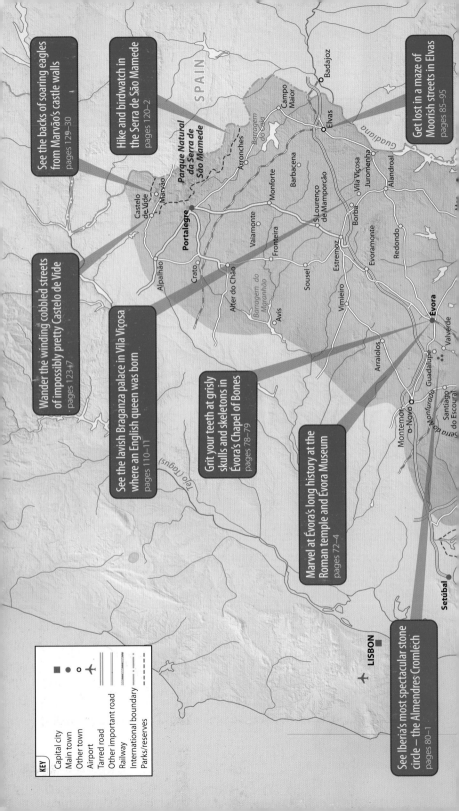

See the backs of soaring eagles from Marvão's castle walls
pages 129–30

Hike and birdwatch in the Serra de São Mamede
pages 120–2

Get lost in a maze of Moorish streets in Elvas
pages 85–95

Wander the winding cobbled streets of impossibly pretty Castelo de Vide
pages 123–7

See the lavish Braganza palace in Vila Viçosa where an English queen was born
pages 110–11

Grit your teeth at grisly skulls and skeletons in Évora's Chapel of Bones
pages 78–79

Marvel at Évora's long history at the Roman temple and Évora Museum
pages 72–4

See Iberia's most spectacular stone circle – the Almendres Cromlech
pages 80–1

SPAIN

Parque Natural da Serra de São Mamede

Badajoz
Campo Maior
Elvas
Arronches
Barbacena
Barragem do Caia
Guadiana
Monforte
S. Lourenço de Mamporção
Vila Viçosa
Juromenha
Borba
Alandroal
Portalegre
Marvão
Castelo de Vide
Valamonte
Fronteira
Estremoz
Evoramonte
Redondo
Alpalhão
Crato
Alter do Chão
Sousel
Vimieiro
Barragem do Maranhão
Avis
Arraiolos
Évora
Valverde
Montemor-o-Novo
Monfurado
Guadalupe
Santiago do Escoural
Serra do

Tejo (Tagus)

LISBON

Setúbal

KEY

Capital city ■
Main town ●
Other town ○
Airport ✈
Tarred road
Other important road
Railway
International boundary
Parks/reserves

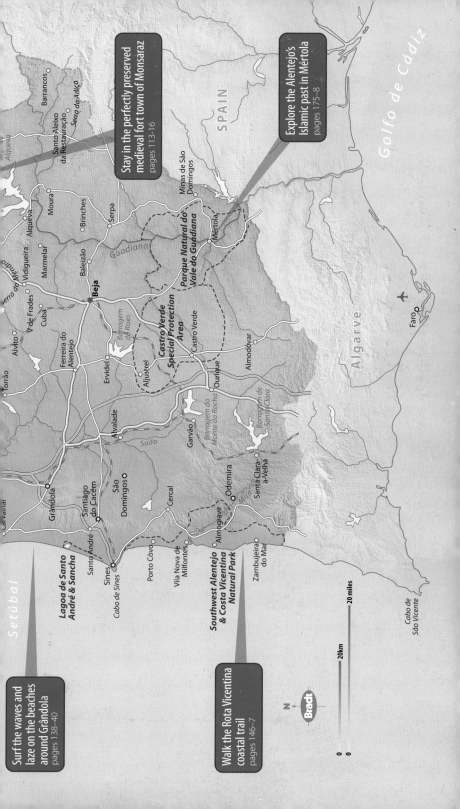

**Surf the waves and laze on the beaches around Grândola**
pages 138–40

**Stay in the perfectly preserved medieval fort town of Monsaraz**
pages 113-16

**Explore the Alentejo's Islamic past in Mértola**
pages 175–8

**Walk the Rota Vicentina coastal trail**
pages 146–7

SPAIN

Golfo de Cádiz

Algarve

Setúbal

Barrancos

Santo Aleixo
da Restauração

Serra da Adiça

Alqueva

Moura

Alqueva

Vidigueira

Marmelar

Brinches

Serpa

Minas de São
Domingos

Mértola

Guadiana

Baleizão

Beja

Parque Natural do
Vale do Guadiana

V de Frades

Cuba

Barragem
do Roxo

Castro Verde
Special Protection
Area

Faro

Alvito

Ferreira do
Alentejo

Ervidel

Aljustrel

Castro Verde

Almodôvar

Torrão

Alvalade

Garvão

Barragem do
Monte da Rocha

Ourique

Barragem de
Santa Clara

Sado

São
Domingos

Cercal

Santa Clara
a Velha

Grândola

Santiago
do Cacém

Santo André

Sines

Cabo de Sines

Porto Covo

Vila Nova de
Milfontes

Almograve

Odemira

Mira

Zambujeira
do Mar

Cabo de
São Vicente

*Lagoa de Santo
André & Sancha*

Carvalhal

*Southwest Alentejo
& Costa Vicentina
Natural Park*

N

Bradt

0    20km

0    20 miles

# Alentejo
# Don't miss...

### Elvas
The Manueline nave and
Baroque chancel of Francisco
de Arruda's Igreja de Nossa
Senhora da Assunção, one of
the many historic sights in this
UNESCO-listed town

(AR) page 93

### The Almendres Cromlech
This Neolithic monument, one of the
largest stone circles in the world,
is testament to the area's large
population in prehistoric times
(AR) pages 80–1

**Perfectly preserved medieval towns**
Built around a castle keep and encircled by [hi]gh walls, Monsaraz is [a] typical fortress town
(AR) pages 113–16

**The coast**
[A]lentejo's coastline is almost deserted for most of the year, and [w]alkers and swimmers can enjoy meadows of wildflowers and concealed coves
(AR) pages 131–51

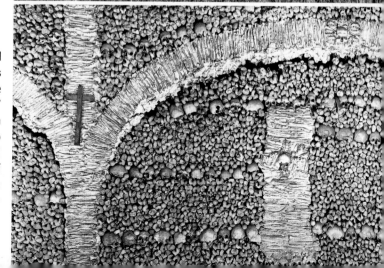

**Évora's Chapel of Bones**
'We bones wait here for yours to join us' [r]eads the inscription over the Capelo dos Ossos, lined with the remains of 5,000 skeletons
(S) pages 78–9

# Alentejo
# in colour

*left*   The Roman Temple that
dominates Évora's Largo
do Conde de Vila Flor is a
reconstruction of the only
remnant of ancient Ebora
(AR) pages 72–3

*below*   The Manueline-Mudéjar
pavilion known as the Ladies'
Gallery was once part of the
royal palace of King Manuel
I, but today hosts temporary
exhibitions and concerts
(SUS) page 79

*above*   The Praça do Giraldo, now thronged with locals sipping coffee and tourists come to see the sights, once had a more sinister past as the scene of the Inquisition's *autos-da-fé* (AR) pages 77–9

*below*   Évora's vast cathedral is a hodgepodge of Romanesque, Gothic and Baroque styles (M/SS) pages 75–6

# LISBON & PORTO

## THERE'S ONLY ONE WAY
## TO DISCOVER PORTUGAL

TAP PORTUG

with arms wide o

# AUTHOR

Alex Robinson has been a travel writer and photographer since getting lost in the Amazon with a soggy camera and a dozen rolls of slide film in the late 1990s. His work has been published in magazines including *The Sunday Times*, *Wanderlust*, *Budget Travel* and *Viagem e Turismo*, Brazil's premier travel publication. He is the only British journalist to win that country's prestigious Editora Abril journalism award, is the joint recipient of a US National Magazine Award, a Croatian Golden Pen

and a Friends of the Earth International Photography Award.

Long entranced by the Alentejo's empty beaches, crumbling castles and fine dining, Alex decided in 2014 that he was being selfish keeping the knowledge all to himself. He wrote this book as penance and hopes to meet you over a glass of Adega de Borba in one of Europe's finest and most forgotten corners sometime soon.

## AUTHOR'S STORY

I discovered the magic of Portugal through a handful of serendipitous moments. A free stop-over en route to Caracas – courtesy of the national carrier TAP – introduced me to the beautiful backstreets of Lisbon, with their cascades of cobbles, their *fado* cafés and their fabulous funiculars. A photography job in Tomar led to a chance encounter with an impossibly friendly professor who gave me a free guided tour of the occult sites of the Templar Knights in his rickety old Renault, before handing me the keys to his beach house in Nazaré. 'Post them back through the letterbox when you go tomorrow', he said, before leaving me on the doorstep and driving off back to Tomar.

And later on my way to Brazil I visited Évora, where I found myself in a brightly-painted café. As I sipped a thick *bica* espresso, the sweetest, saddest music began to play – lilting acoustic guitar, a harpsichord and a voice of tragic, limpid beauty which sent the hairs on my arms tingling. I had to know who was playing. And so delighted was the owner by my enthusiasm for *Madredeus* that she promised to show me Évora the next day – driving me to stone circles, the olive groves and a string of beautiful castles, the CD playing in the car stereo all the way.

I've been visiting the Alentejo ever since. And on every visit I've thrown myself into the present moment, planning little but a route and allowing the Alentejo to do the rest. It never disappoints. Every visit has brought some special serendipity – an invitation to meet a faith healer who reset the bones of my dislocated shoulder while chanting Ave Marias, a conversation in a bar leading to the discovery of a shipwreck on a lonely beach just as the sun melted into the sea, a meeting with an old widow sitting in a lonely village topped by a crumbling convent, its *azulejos* encrusted with vines, its roofless chapels echoing with birdsong. She pointed to the rocky hills around and told me in all earnestness that when she was a girl a family of werewolves lived there. Hidden behind a chicken coop at dusk when one of the brothers came out of his house, she'd even seen him change – twisted, deformed and then running, dog-like into the trees, salivating at the rising moon.

**PUBLISHER'S FOREWORD** *Adrian Phillips, Managing Director*

'Alan who?', I asked. I'm ashamed to say I'd never heard of Alentejo when it was suggested that Bradt publish the first guide dedicated solely to the region. But a few weeks later I was travelling around Alentejo myself, commissioned by *The Independent on Sunday* to write a piece about this glorious, little-visited area above the Algarve. I walked in cork forests and along windy beaches, climbed hilltop forts and explored Roman ruins; there was so much to enjoy and yet so few tourists there enjoying it. If you're interested, you'll find my article on the newspaper's website. However, Alex's guide is a far more compelling call to action. You only have to read his entertaining, inventive introduction on page vi to know you've bought a very special book.

First edition published January 2016

Bradt Travel Guides Ltd
IDC House, The Vale, Chalfont St Peter, Bucks SL9 9RZ, England
www.bradtguides.com
Print edition published in the USA by The Globe Pequot Press Inc,
PO Box 480, Guilford, Connecticut 06437-0480

Text copyright © 2016 Alex Robinson
Maps copyright © 2016 Bradt Travel Guides Ltd
Photographs copyright © 2016 individual photographers (see below)
Project Manager: Maisie Fitzpatrick

ISBN: 978 1 84162 568 3 (print)
e-ISBN: 978 1 78477 140 9 (e-pub)
e-ISBN: 978 1 78477 240 6 (mobi)

**British Library Cataloguing in Publication Data**
A catalogue record for this book is available from the British Library

**Photographers**
Alex Robinson (AR); Dreamstime: Jmammapac (J/DT); Shutterstock: Carlos Caetano (CC/SS), Tiago Ladeira (TL/S), Migel (M/SS), Inacio Pires (IP/SS), Vector99 (V/SS); Sunvil (S); SuperStock (SUS)
*Front cover* Mértola and the Guadiana River (AR)
*Back cover* Vila Nova de Milfontes (AR); streets in the old Jewish quarter of Castelo de Vide (AR)
*Title page* Vila Nova de Milfontes (AR); Arronches (AR); cork oak bark drying in the sun (AR)

**Maps** David McCutcheon FBCart.S; colour relief base map by Geographx

Typeset by Ian Spick, Bradt Travel Guides and Chris Reed, BBR
Production managed by Jellyfish Print Solutions; printed in Turkey
Digital conversion by www.dataworks.co.in

# Acknowledgements

Thanks to Rachel Fielding for commissioning this book, and to Hilary Bradt and Adrian Phillips for keeping the independent spirit of travel publishing alive. Thanks very much to Maisie Fitzpatrick for bearing with me cheerfully when a million deadlines converged, and for understanding the challenges of the freelance life.

And in Portugal thanks to all of the following: to TAP, to António and Ana at Turismo Alentejo for the wonderful trips, to Noel of Sunvil for the unwavering support and for profound knowledge and appreciation for the Alentejo. Thanks to João at the Casa do Terreiro do Poço for the great company, to Margarida Dias and her family for a wonderful time in Grândola and for sharing a passion for pictures, to Ana and António for coming round the northern Alentejo beaches with me, to Teresa at the Adega de Borba olive factory for showing me how you make the world's most delicious olive oil, to Jorge at the Hotel Rural Santo António for sharing the prehistoric monuments and rich culture of Arronches and to Gardenia and Raphael for supporting me while writing this book.

## FEEDBACK REQUEST AND UPDATES WEBSITE

At Bradt Travel Guides we're aware that guidebooks start to go out of date on the day they're published – and that you, our readers, are out there in the field doing research of your own. You'll find out before us when a fine new family-run hotel opens or a favourite restaurant changes hands and goes downhill. So why not write and tell us about your experiences? Contact us on ☎01753 893444 or e info@bradtguides.com. We will forward emails to the author who may post updates on the Bradt website at www.bradtupdates.com/alentejo. Alternatively you can add a review of the book to www.bradtguides.com or Amazon.

## FOLLOW BRADT

For the latest news, special offers and competitions, subscribe to the Bradt newsletter via the website www.bradtguides.com and follow Bradt on:

- f www.facebook.com/BradtTravelGuides
- ▼ @BradtGuides
- @bradtguides
- www.pinterest.com/bradtguides

# Contents

## LIST OF MAPS

## HOW TO USE THE MAPS IN THIS GUIDE

**KEYS AND SYMBOLS** Maps include alphabetical keys covering the locations of those places to stay, eat or drink that are featured in the book. Note that regional maps may not show all hotels and restaurants in the area: other establishments may be located in towns shown on the map.

**GRIDS AND GRID REFERENCES** Several maps use gridlines to allow easy location of sites. Map grid references are listed in square brackets after the name of the place or sight of interest in the text, with page number followed by grid number, eg: [64 A3].

## SEND US YOUR SNAPS!

We'd love to follow your adventures using our *Alentejo* guide – why not send us your photos and stories via Twitter (@BradtGuides) and Instagram (@bradtguides) using the hashtag #alentejo. Alternatively, you can upload your photos directly to the gallery on the Alentejo destination page via our website (*www.bradtguides.com/alentejo*).

# Introduction

The Alentejo is that bit of Portugal you'd do well to avoid. There's nothing here worth seeing. You're really far better off spending a few days in Lisbon and then whizzing down the motorway to those glorious, crowded beaches along the Algarve.

So off you go. And be sure to keep that foot hard on the accelerator pedal as you leave Lisbon airport, those eyes glued to the road. Firmly glued please. Don't look right or left. Ignore that castle on the hill, those crumbling Roman ruins, that palace hotel, those nesting storks, the soaring eagles, those lonely strands of empty sand.

Yes, and ignore the World Heritage Sites too.

In short, leave it all behind. As an expert on the region I can assure you that you'd be wise to do so. I've been wandering around the Alentejo for years now. Just for work, of course. And I can state with conviction that I can't stand those Baroque churches encrusted with gold and covered with intricately painted *azulejo* tiles. I am tired of the ground-breaking Renaissance art, the turbulent history, the Moorish forts and Phoenician towns, the winding rivers and cork oak forests where lynx and wild boar bask in the warm afternoon sun. And those medieval villages where you can hear a footfall on the cobbles, or the snore of an old man in a cloth cap dozing on his doorstep.

The meadows make me sneeze. The butterflies are too colourful. The air's too fresh, the stars too bright. And the wine is dreadful. So dreadful that the locals refuse to export it. 'We'll drink it all ourselves,' they say, 'to save foreigners the bother'. After all who wants rich, earthy reds, bursting with fruit, or tangy, crisp whites as fresh as a mountain stream?

And they keep those juicy fat olives and creamy cheeses for themselves too, those lightly toasted vanilla fragrant custard tarts, those gamey stews and seafood risottos. And those fish which are pulled straight from the sea and served before they've even been wrapped in plastic and sealed with a price label.

Unlike most of Mediterranean Europe the Alentejo is, I am afraid to say, positively underdeveloped. Even unspoilt. Rather than chain hotels with sparkling new wood veneer, accommodation tends to be in converted palaces and medieval castles filled with beautiful antiques and priceless paintings. Service is untutored – worryingly free of technical courtesy and filled with uncontrolled warmth. And the entire region is completely free of shopping malls. Instead, the cobbled streets that wind through whitewashed little towns and villages are lined with locally owned small shops where produce is made mostly by hand to centuries-old traditions.

It's all very off-putting. So follow your instincts – pass right through *en route* to busier places – to throw down your towel by the pool, sip that sun-warmed beer and enjoy those interminable tracts of purpose-built condos by the beach.

## ALENTEJO ONLINE

For additional online content, articles, photos and more on the Alentejo, why not visit www.bradtguides.com/alentejo.

# Part One

## GENERAL INFORMATION

## THE ALENTEJO AT A GLANCE

**Location** In the central south of Portugal

**Area** 31,551km², covering about a third of Portugal, which has an area of 92,212km²

**Climate** Mediterranean and maritime temperate

**Status** Republic

**Population** 749,000 (Alentejo), 10,825,309 (Portugal)

**Life expectancy** 77 years (men), 83 years (women)

**Capital** Évora (population 57,073)

**GDP per capita** €14,700

**Languages** Portuguese

**Religion** Catholic

**Currency** euro (€)

**Exchange rate** £1 = €1.35, US$1 = €0.87 (October 2015)

**National airline** TAP Air Portugal

**Nearby airports** Lisbon, Faro, Badajoz, Porto

**International phone code** +351

**Time** GMT +1

**Electrical voltage** 220–240V

**Weights and measures** Metric

**Flag** National: four fifths red on the right of the flag and a fifth grass green on the left. An armillary sphere emblazoned with the national coat of arms where the colours meet.

**National anthem** *A Portuguesa* (English: '*The Portuguese*') by Alfredo Keil and Henrique Lopes de Mendonça

**Public holidays** See *Public holidays and festivals*, pages 49–51

# 1

# Background Information

## GEOGRAPHY

The Alentejo covers some 31,550km² – a little over a third of Portugal – and sits in the central south of the country. It borders Extremadura in Spain to the east, the Algarve to the south and the Ribatejo and Portuguese Estremadura to the north. Lisbon lies about 50km northwest of the borders of the Alentejo – an easy drive. The landscape is characterised by flat or gently undulating plains, broken by steep rocky hills and rising in the north into the mountains of the Serra de São Mamede, whose highest peak, the Pico de São Mamede, is some 1,025m – a little lower than Snowdon. The region has around 300km of Atlantic coast fringed by long sandy beaches, backed by dunes, sandstone and rocky cliffs and broken by secluded coves and bays. The Guadiana River cuts through the Alentejo and has been dammed to form Europe's largest artificial lake, the Lago Alqueva – one of a handful of reservoirs that break up the overall dryness of the region.

For the purposes of this book we have chosen to divide the Alentejo into three regions (with a separate chapter for the capital, Évora, itself): the upper Alentejo extending northwards from Évora, the Baixo extending south from Évora to the Algarve, and the coast.

## CLIMATE

The Alentejo has a Mediterranean climate with hot, dry summers, mild autumns and winters (with changeable, rainy weather and snow only in the Serra de São Mamede mountains), and warm, sunny springs.

### AVERAGE TEMPERATURES IN ÉVORA (°C)

|         | Jan | Feb | Mar | Apr | May | Jun | Jul | Aug | Sep | Oct | Nov | Dec |
|---------|-----|-----|-----|-----|-----|-----|-----|-----|-----|-----|-----|-----|
| **Maximum** | 14 | 16 | 19 | 21 | 25 | 30 | 34 | 33 | 29 | 23 | 18 | 15 |
| **Minimum** | 6 | 6 | 8 | 9 | 11 | 14 | 16 | 17 | 15 | 13 | 9 | 7 |

## NATURAL HISTORY AND CONSERVATION

The Alentejo has a rich and diverse natural history that is explored in the main chapters of this guide. The coast – especially around the protected **Sado** estuary nature reserve and RAMSAR site and the **Santo André** and **Sancha** lagoon nature reserves – is an important nesting ground for migratory water birds and for marine mammals. Iberian lynx have been seen as recently as 2013 in the maquis forests and woodlands of the southern coast. The meadows and forests of the **Parque Natural do Sudoeste Alentejano e Costa Vicentina** preserve rare and endangered southern European plants and butterflies. The Rota Vicentina offers access.

There are two large natural parks in the Alentejo's interior. The **Parque Natural da Serra de São Mamede** in the north and abutting the Spanish border is home to more than 150 bird species including rare eagles and vultures and has colonies of threatened small mammals, amphibians and reptiles.

The **Parque Natural do Vale do Guadiana** and adjacent **Castro Verde Special Protection Area** in the Baixo Alentejo are home to important populations of great bustard, Europe's largest flying bird. The Parque Natural do Vale do Guadiana Natural Park, which protects the watershed of the Guadiana River, is one of the best places in Iberia to watch birds, has more than 37 reptile and amphibian species and is the only place in Portugal where the Iberian lynx (the world's second most endangered big cat) lives all year round.

For more information on the region's natural parks, contact the **ICNF** (Instituto da Conservação da Natureza e das Florestas) (*Avenida da República 16, Lisbon;* ☎ *213 507900; www.icnf.pt;* ⊕ *09.30–16.30 Mon–Fri*).

**HIKING IN THE NATURAL PARKS** The **Instituto Geográfico do Exército** (*IGEOE; Avenida Dr Alfredo Bensaúde, 1849-014 Lisbon;* ☎ *218 505300; www.igeoe.pt*) sells accurate scale maps for hiking for around €7 at its shop. These can be ordered through the post. Some of the maps are downloadable. For visiting natural parks with a tour operator see the main body of the guide and *Tour operators* (pages 40–1).

## HISTORY

Portugal's story is a fascinating *Game of Thrones* brew of intrigue, plotting and conquest rendered bittersweet with tragic love stories, ribald kings and romantic heroes. A little knowledge of it will ensure that you enjoy the Alentejo all the more.

Portugal was the keystone of Europe's development. This was the country that conquered Islam before Spain and then stole the trade routes from the Arabs. Portugal invented the fleet of conquest – the European hybrid of military might and mercantile savviness that would define the pre-industrial West. It opened up Asia and Africa, probably discovered Australia, and (if you believe the Portuguese) the Americas too. And Portugal was the first country to trade on a truly global scale – bringing Europe to the world and the world to Europe.

**THE NEANDERTHALS AND THE EARLIEST HUMANS** It all got off to a slow start. Proto-humans arrived in the Alentejo and in Europe as a whole surprisingly late. The earliest European site with abundant artefacts to have been reliably dated using modern techniques is Isernia La Pineta, a little to the southeast of Rome. At between 1 million and 700,000 years old, this is considerably later than Chinese and Southeast Asian settlement-making and some 3 million years later than the separation of proto-humans from other apes in Africa. For some 660,000 years – throughout the Lower and Middle Palaeolithic eras – these primitive Europeans were formed of at least two species: *Homo sapiens sapiens* – who are identical to modern humans, and *Homo sapiens neanderthalensis* – the Neanderthals – who were stockier, more muscular and with heavier jaws and brows.

Simple stone tools found along Portugal's central coast suggest that there have been humans here since around 500,000BC, though the oldest fossil is far more recent – some 100,000 years old, and is of a tooth belonging to a Portuguese Neanderthal man. It was unearthed in a cave in Nova da Columbeira in Estremadura.

The two human species interbred and eventually the Neanderthals died out due to competition and assimilation. This process was slowest in Spain and Portugal, where current knowledge suggests that Neanderthal humans lived alongside modern humans for the longest period of time anywhere in the world, as hunter-gatherers. In 1998 a 24,500 year old skull was discovered near Leiria, a little to the north of the Alentejo, which seems to have been of a Neanderthal-modern hybrid. Then in 2013 scientists found that it was by no means unique. All Europeans, it seems, are in part Neanderthals. Benjamin Vernot and Joshua Akey, population geneticists at the University of Washington in the USA, and Philipp Khaitovich of the Max Planck Institute of Evolutionary Anthropology, demonstrated that we have on average around 2% Neanderthal DNA for an area of the chromosome they measured associated with the metabolisation of fats. Iberians have around 20%. East Asians have less, and Africans have none.

Portugal at that time was a very different place both climatically and geographically. Huge ice sheets spread across northern Europe. France was tundra, central Spain park tundra (which is similar to the fenland of the contemporary mid-Arctic circle) and Portugal itself was a giant boreal forest interspersed with grasslands – a little like the taiga of today's Siberia. These stretched 40km beyond the modern Alentejo coast into a polar Atlantic. Neanderthals and modern humans foraged on the ancient shore and chased after auroch, boar, deer and wild horses in the forests. They also engraved and painted representations of these animals on the escarpment cliffs of the Côa Valley in Portugal's Beira Alta region, and (as recent dating studies from the University of Évora suggest) the caves of Alto Alentejo – around Arronches (pages 119–20).

The Escoural caves near Montemor-o-Novo are perhaps even older. They were probably used as a shelter by Neanderthal man as many as 100,000 years ago. The cave paintings of geometric figures and animals, including auroch, are more recent – made by modern humans in the Middle Paleolithic period.

After around 15,000BC the Portuguese climate began to change. By 9000BC it was roughly the same as today and a new more complex human population – entirely comprising modern humans – had begun to manufacture complex hunter-gatherer tools – liths (worked stones), set in grooved hafts, barbed spears for fishing, axes and stone knives. These Middle Stone Age (Mesolithic) communities were semi-sedentary, building seasonal shelters on the Alentejo shoreline, leaving behind middens. They buried their dead along with ornaments and offerings – of beads and shellfish – and lived easily and comfortably off the land for some 6,000 years, until the pressure of trade and conquest forced them once more to evolve.

**MEGALITHS, TRADE AND POTTERY** The Iberian Neolithic (literally 'new stone') Age saw a florescence of culture in Portugal. In the Alentejo this began in earnest around 4000BC, and was characterised by patchy forest clearance to make way for village settlements, the herding of animals, the production of stone tools and ceramics and perhaps most obviously the construction of Megalithic (literally 'large stone') monuments. These litter the Alentejo and comprise one of the largest concentrations of Neolithic structures anywhere in Europe. They include free standing menhirs (*menir/es*), some over 6m high, menhirs organised into groups of standing stones (*cromleque/s*) and dolmens (*anta/s*), which are stone slabs laid together to form table-like structures, some of which stretch into passage tombs.

It was once thought that the building of European megaliths began in the Aegean – following trends in the near Middle East, then spreading into the rest of Europe. Advanced chemical analysis over the last few decades has undermined this theory. Radiocarbon dating from sites in the Alentejo has shown that Portuguese megaliths are centuries older than anything in the Aegean and far older than other monuments in western Europe. The Almendres Cromlech, for instance – the largest and most spectacular of the Alentejo's prehistoric sites – is at least 3,000 years older than Stonehenge.

Little is known about the function of the megaliths or of their role in Neolithic life. We do know, however, that their presence is associated with increasingly ordered societies – capable of organising large groups of people to excavate and erect these massive monuments. As agriculture began, so did a more complex community life, based on the establishment of territories and dominions, led by an elite. It is likely that megaliths had cosmological religious significance – linking the determinate movements of the celestial bodies (notably the sun and the moon) with a determined ordering of events on Earth. These events certainly included the ritualistic burial of the dead. They probably also included the establishment of sacred space as a model of the cosmos or axis mundi, and a location through which communication with that cosmos was mediated by a priestly elite who used it to order the temporal and spatial in everyday life – the planting of crops, the engendering of fertility and so on.

Megalith construction continued into the Chalcolithic or Copper Age, which began gradually in Portugal. Silver, gold and copper had been used in the Alentejo since around 2500BC. Copper was abundant in the Baixo Alentejo and was cold hammered to produce ornaments from very early times. Perhaps inspired by ceramics technology, this evolved into annealing (moulding soft heated metal) and eventually smelting. In around 2000BC copper was mixed with tin to produce bronze, which was used to make weapons to protect increasingly large and well-organised communities of several hundred. Farmers used animal traction, produced woollen garments and beautiful bell-shaped pots that were traded between communities across the Alentejo and the whole of Iberia. They may also have ridden horses and used simple ploughs. They still buried their dead in dolmen tombs and established sacred space with the erection of huge menhirs, such as the Menhir da Meada near Castelo de Vide.

**PHOENICIANS, CELTS AND CARTHAGE** By the late Bronze Age (c1500BC) villages were trading not just across Iberia but across Europe, and with that trade came new religious ideas relating to the Earth, and in some cases mother goddesses and eye idols probably associated with sun or moon cults. Communities were divided between agricultural settlements on the lowland plains (which had large grain storage tanks built below ground) and militarised hilltop forts called *castros* which almost certainly controlled the agricultural villages through force of arms. Small seaports dotted the coast, including at Alcácer do Sal. It was around this time that the Portuguese first began the seafaring that would make them powerful, with villagers building *saveiros* – keelless wooden boats powered by a single sail attached not to a mast but to an L-shaped frame. These are still built in Maranhão state in Brazil today, making them one of the oldest continually manufactured nautical vessels on the planet.

By the first millennium a warrior cult had emerged in the Alentejo, based around the *castros*. Stele and elaborately decorated funeral urns have been unearthed throughout the region. Both depict stylised warriors, often brandishing bronze 'carp tongue' swords. By contrast, digs on the lowlands have shown that the warriors' agricultural subordinates were still using stone, wood and bone tools, indicating that Portuguese Bronze Age society was markedly divided.

Great change came to the Alentejo in around 700BC with the Iron Age and the Phoenicians – the Mediterranean's first nautical empire – who arrived along the Guadiana River and founded a port there, called Myrtilis (now Mértola). The Phoenicians introduced iron, nautical technology and the alphabet to Mediterranean Europe, including Portugal, which was producing its first written inscriptions (on funerary stele and ceramic vases) by the 5th century. The Celts followed them shortly afterwards from the north, and the intermingling of peoples and cultures brought new localised tribal civilisations to Portugal. These included the celticised Lusitani, who would give their name to the Roman province, and the Turduli, who were based in the Algarve and Alentejo. Many of these tribes were warlike and the original inhabitants of the Alentejo fortified themselves against them behind increasing numbers of *castros*. These developed into *oppida* – fortified towns that produced, stored and traded their own goods and were run by a military elite.

Concurrent with the rise of the *oppida* was the growth of the kingdom of Tartessos – around Huelva in Spain – just across the modern Portuguese border in the eastern Algarve. This trading empire was probably stimulated economically and culturally by both the Phoenicians (whose influence became ever stronger until the collapse of the Assyrian empire in 612BC) and later the Greeks. Tartessian influence was strong over the mining communities of the southern Alentejo, and their objects have been found all over southern Portugal.

From about the 6th century BC the Phoenician colony of Carthage began to establish itself as a new Mediterranean power, initially as traders and then as military imperialists. In the late 3rd century a Carthaginian army under Hamilcar Barca invaded and conquered southern Iberia. The conqueror brought his ten-year-old son, Hannibal, who grew up in Spain, married a Spanish woman and in 221BC expanded Iberian Carthage further, founding a new capital of Carthago Nova (New Carthage – now Cartagena) and annexing much of modern Portugal, including large chunks of the Alentejo. Hannibal attracted the attention of far-off Rome when he besieged and conquered the Roman outpost of Saguntum. When Rome demanded that his forces surrender, the general instead chose to invade Italy on elephants, kicking off the Second Punic Wars which would lead to the full invasion of Iberia by Roman forces, and the annexation of Portugal into imperial Rome.

## VIRIATUS AND SERTORIUS – HEROES AGAINST ROMAN DICTATORSHIP If it weren't for Hannibal, Rome may never have noticed Portugal. But the empire responded in kind after Hannibal's invasion. Carthago Nova itself fell in 209BC, and three years later the Carthaginians had been expelled from Iberia. The new conquerors established two new provinces – Hispania Criterior (or Nearer Spain, which stretched from the Ebro valley north through Murcia into Valencia) and Hispania Ulterior (or Far Spain, which covered modern Andalucía and southern Portugal). The rest of the peninsula was left in tribal hands. Hispania was of little interest to Rome beyond being a source of slaves, minerals, olives and tax, which the conquerors exploited so ruthlessly that they fomented first discontent and then open revolt. Tribal Iberia joined in, and when Rome decided to expand her territories further she was met by a long and protracted campaign of resistance from the hardy Portuguese tribes who lived in and around the *castros* of the mountainous interior. The principal irritant to Rome were the Lusitani.

Riding light and nimble Lusitanian horses and armed with short swords and bronze-tipped javelins, roving bands of Lusitani attacked the Romans with impunity and without mercy. Their leaders became so famous that they entered the histories of Strabo and Appian. Punicus raided deep into Roman territory in 155BC, laying waste to Roman forts and villas, and Caesarus defeated the Roman general Mummius in 153BC. But the outstanding leader of the Lusitanian resistance was **Viriatus**, who waged a humiliating campaign between 146 and 139BC, which included the defeat of a Roman army of 15,000 infantry and 2,000 cavalry at Beja. Unable to defeat Viriatus in battle, the Romans sued for peace, signed a treaty restoring land and liberty to the Lusitanian tribes and then had Viriatus assassinated while he was sleeping.

The subterfuge was partially successful. After the murder of Viriatus the Lusitanians continued their campaigns against the Roman settlements, but they were never as organised or successful, and their attacks amounted to little more than guerrilla strikes. Roman domination crept into southern Iberia through cultural and economic pressure. *Oppida* and agricultural communities were assimilated more than subjugated and the more bellicose Lusitani contained.

The tribes united again in 80BC under rebel general **Quintus Sertorius**, who like Hannibal before him had one eye and nearly overthrew an empire. The Sertorius of Plutarch's *Lives* sounds like an imaginary Ridley Scott hero. As a young soldier he swam across the Rhine in full armour, learnt the Celtic language and lived among the hostile Cimbri as a spy. He conquered a Celtic kingdom with only a few hundred men and ruled over Mauretania with an army of rebel legionaries and Cilician Turkish pirates. Caught up in the civil wars that troubled Rome in the decades between republic and empire, he sided against the victorious Roman dictator Lucius Cornelius Sulla, and was asked by the Lusitanian tribes to become their general and fight against the latter's oppressive regime.

With them Sertorius conquered all of Hispania, defeating a string of armies sent by Sulla, many of which were far greater than his own. They included armies commanded by the young Pompey – who would briefly rule Rome later in his life before being assassinated on the orders of Julius Caesar. For nearly a decade he ran Hispania as a parallel Roman state to Sulla's in Rome – but rather than being a dictatorship it was based on the old republican model – with a Senate, a disciplined army and a Roman system of schooling. Unable to defeat Sertorius in battle and fearing his rivalry and greater statesmanship, Sulla had him assassinated in 72BC – by one of Sertorius's supposed allies, Marcus Perpenna Vento, at a banquet held in Sertorius's honour. Pompey was then able easily to conquer Hispania for Rome, but disgusted by the treachery against his old enemy he had Perpenna Vento executed. Pompey assumed governorship of Hispania and was followed by a young Julius Caesar who founded Pax Iulia (Beja), renamed Ebora (Évora) Liberalitas Iulia, and Scalabis (Santarém) Scalabis Iulia, and established a Roman stronghold at the old Phoenician river port of Myrtilis Iulia (Mértola).

**IMPERIAL ROME AND THE CREATION OF LUSITANIA** After Sulla's retirement and death, Rome was briefly ruled by the triumvirate of Crassus (the richest man in Rome), Pompey and the young Julius Caesar. Crassus was killed by the Parthian Persians, supposedly by having molten gold poured into his mouth. Pompey was assassinated by Caesar, and his sons then fled to Hispania. After assuming the dictatorship of Rome (which marked the end of the Roman Republic and the beginning of the Roman Empire), Caesar pursued them, and in the process he further consolidated his subjugation of the Lusitani tribes. But it was his descendant Caesar Augustus who finished the job between 24 and 19BC. Augustus divided Hispania into three provinces (replacing the old divisions of Hispania Citerior and Ulterior and adding new conquered territory) – Hispania Terraconensis in the north and east, Hispania Baetica in the west and Lusitania, which covered much of the south of modern Portugal and had its capital at Emerita Augusta (Mérida) in present-day Spanish Extremedura.

Lusitania had a governor and under him was further subdivided into three convents or regions – Emeritensis (with its capital of Emerita Augusta), Scalabitanus (governed from Scalabis Iulia – Santarém) and Pacensis (governed from Pax Iulia – Beja). And these convents were further subdivided into towns (*populis*), many of which were old *oppida* and which included Salacia (Alcácer do Sal), Myrtilis Iulia (Mértola), Liberalitas Iulia (Évora) and Miróbriga (near Santiago do Cacém). The *castro* fort towns were romanised and became useful military bases and the accoutrements of Roman life spread throughout Lusitania – from the language, architectural styles and music to the temples, triumphal arches, the baths and the roads. These ran between the cities, the convents and the provinces, linking to roads in Gaul and running to Rome. *Latifundia* villas sprang up along them. Derived from *latus* (spacious) and *fundum* (estate), these were large areas of privately owned land producing the agricultural goods that fed the colony and Rome itself. They were run by an overlord (often a retired soldier granted land as privilege) and administered and worked largely by slaves. Slaves drove the economy of Roman Lusitania – at the time of Christ it is estimated that a third of the population were slaves.

It could be argued that Roman Lusitania's infrastructure formed the basis of Portugal's – and that of her colonies – into the late 20th century. Many of Portugal's main towns were its Roman towns, and the main roads that connect them follow Roman lines. Land and even whole towns were granted to Portuguese nobles by the crown until the proclamation of the Republic, and forced indentured labour running through generations continued on *latifundios* in the Alentejo until the late 20th century. It is painfully portrayed in José Saramago's *Raised from the Ground*. *Latifundios* exist in the northeastern and northern regions of Brazil to this day.

By the 3rd century a substantial number of slaves and freedmen had converted to a new religion – Christianity. This faith spread quickly across the Roman world and caused great problems for the Empire. Guided by the teaching of Early Church fathers like Tertullian and Origen, many (though not all) of these early Christians refused to pay homage to the Empire. They regarded trade as sinful and, perhaps most worrying for Rome, they were resolute pacifists. 'Christ in disarming Peter ungirt every soldier,' argued Tertullian, urging converted legionaries to resign from soldiering, avoid fighting and suffer martyrdom.

Imperial Rome saw only one way out of the problem. Under Constantine (AD272–337), it made Christianity the state religion thus taking control of doctrine and hierarchy and turning Christianity into a political institution at the heart of a powerful empire based in a new capital – Byzantium, or, as it was re-christened by the Christian Emperor, Constantinople. Constantine's conversion was the inevitable consequence of a critical mass of Christian practitioners within the Roman Empire threatening the power balance. Constantinople became the de facto capital of a new Roman Empire or Byzantine Empire, and the shift of power made Iberia even more distant from the heart of decision-making and ever more vulnerable to attack.

**THE GERMAN TRIBES** The attack came suddenly. In the autumn of AD409 a group of Vandals, Suevi (Swabians) and Alans broke through the Roman defences in the Pyrenees and entered Iberia for the first time. By 411 they had overrun the entire peninsula, Hispania and Lusitania were out of Roman control and the Germanic tribes were dividing the spoils, literally by lot. Lusitania went to the Alans. According to contemporaneous Roman historians, the tribe turned their swords to ploughshares. For five years Lusitania was at peace.

But then new waves of invaders swept in – led by Visigoths and Vandals, who waged war on the other tribes and each other. By the time the dust had settled in the 420s two remained – the Suevi and the Visigoths – who were Arian Christians (denying the divinity of Christ). Lusitania was divided between them for a little more than a century, after which the Visigoths dominated. Society became divided along different lines. A new military elite ruled and took over the towns and *latifundios*. A rural population made up of former Roman slaves (freed only in name under the Visigoths) and conquered free Lustianian Romans worked the *latifundios*. A large Jewish minority controlled trade.

**THE ARRIVAL OF ISLAM** Even the Germanic tribes who had ransacked Rome had some sense of common heritage and affiliation with the Roman Empire. They had adopted Byzantine Romano-Greek customs and habits, and they traded and made treaties with the Byzantine world. In short, they were part of the Graeco-Roman (Hellenistic) world, rooted in the language, politics, culture and history of the classic world, marked but not yet substantially altered by the new imperial religion of Christianity.

While the people who conquered Iberia in the 8th century were influenced in their religious outlook by early patristic Christianity and prophetic Judaism, they shared nothing of the Hellenistic cultural traditions of Greece and Rome. To the Iberians they conquered, the Muslims were far more alien than the Romans or Goths who preceded them. The conquest of Jerusalem, of Iberia, and later of Constantinople itself would see Europe unite in opposition, and increasingly conflate Christianity with Graeco-Roman culture in opposition to Islam.

The Muslim conquest came as rapidly as the Germanic invasion had done. In 711 an expeditionary force of Berber Muslims led by the warlord Taric ibn Ziyad landed in southern Spain. Taric was a subordinate of the Damascus-based Umayyad caliphs, in the employ of their provincial governor in Morocco. Sweeping north, Taric took Córdoba followed by the Visigoth capital Toledo. By 716 the Umayyads had conquered all of Iberia south of Galicia and León, including Lusitania.

The conquest was brutal. Based on the Quranic hadith 9:29, cities were given a choice – surrender and pay the *jizya* tax (ranging from 20% to 80% of income or goods), or be conquered and see all adult males executed and women and children enslaved. Many Christians fled to the mountains and then into France, where the Islamic invasion was finally checked.

**AL-ANDALUS** The Muslims called their new territory 'the country of the Vandals' – al-Andalus. Lusitania was Gharb al-Andalus – Western Andalus. Like the rest of Muslim Iberia it was administered from Syria, via Kairouan in Tunisia and the local capital at Córdoba. This complicated chain of command endured until the 740s, when the Umayyads were overthrown by the Persian Abbasid dynasty, who shifted the capital from Damascus to Baghdad and hunted down and murdered all of the Umayyad family, but for one prince, Abd al-Rahman, who fled to al-Andalus and set himself up as emir of an independent Umayyad state.

The al-Andalus Umayyads reigned until the late 10th century, first as emirs and later as self-proclaimed caliphs. Their rule was remarkable for its prosperity and patronage of the arts. This was particularly true under the rule of the Abd al-Raḥman III (AD891–961), who between military campaigns against the Christian kings of León and the Arab Christian rebel Umar ibn Ḥafṣūn, rebuilt Córdoba's magnificent mosque, erected a new city and palace and allowed Christian and Jewish communities to grow and flourish throughout al-Andalus.

The caliphate in Gharb al-Andalus was administered civically by *walis* or governors who resided in local capitals or *kuwar*. In the Alentejo these were Beja and Alcácer do Sal. Kuwars governed smaller settlements called *madinas*, and even smaller villages called *aldeias* and *alcarias*. Towns were heavily fortified around a

## THE JEWISH GOLDEN AGE

Jewish scholars disagree over whether the Umayyad, Almoravid and Amohad caliphates represented a golden age for Jewish life in Europe. What is certain is that under the Umayyads Jewish worship, culture and scholarship were allowed a relatively free reign. The Jews and Christians were protected under Islamic law as *dhimmis* – conquered people who paid the *jizya* tax and were thus afforded protection providing they did not proselytise. Jews rose to powerful positions. Hasdai ibn Shaprut was physician to the caliph and Joseph ibn Naghrela a *vizier* in Granada. The great Jewish philosopher Rabbi Mosheh ben Maimon (Maimonides) was born in Golden Age Córdoba and the Zohar of Moses ben Shem Tov de León was written just as al-Andalus was lost to Christian Spain and Portugal. However, what is also certain is that the 1066 Granada massacre – which occurred when the Umayyad caliphate began to collapse – resulted in the death of many more Jews than contemporaneous pogroms in Christian Europe, and that many Jews fled to Christian Spain and Portugal after the arrival of the Almoravids and Almohads. Moses Maimonides himself would later write of the latter dynasty 'Never has there been a nation that hated, humiliated and loathed us as much as this one.'

citadel (*alcaçova*) and defended by a military protectorate based out of Badajoz and a network of castles and *atalaias* (watchtowers). These were set up to defend the caliphate against Viking raids along the coast and Christian attacks from the north. And these were frequent. In 913, for instance, the supposedly vassal king of Galicia, Ordoño II, sacked Évora and massacred its Muslim population.

After the autocratic rule of al-Mansur (*hajib* or prime minister to the 12-year-old caliph) in the early 11th century, the Umayyad caliphate collapsed into anarchy. Al-Andalus subsequently became a patchwork of separate warring kingdoms or *taifas*, with Gharb al-Andalus lying within the *taifa* of Badajoz (ruled by a family of wealthy Berbers). Lacking the unity of the caliphate, the *taifas* were increasingly powerless against the Christian kings of the north. In a reversal of the *jizya*, the *taifa* lords were humiliatingly reduced to paying tribute to the Christians to stave off attack. Then in 1085 Toledo fell to the Christians and Alfonso VI, King of Castile and León, made increasing advances into Muslim al-Andalus, helped by Portuguese bandits like Geraldo Sem Pavor (see pages 14 and 114). Increasingly desperate, the *taifas* appealed to the powerful Almoravid dynasty that had conquered Morocco for help, in the name of the defence of Islam.

The Almoravids had begun as fundamentalist reformers in mid-11th century Morocco, controlling the desert trade route to and from the wealthy city of Sijilmasa. As their dynasty matured they became less fundamentalist, establishing a complex legal system and encouraging the spread of ideas. The great philosopher and theologian Ibn Rushd – or Averrões – who is credited with bringing the philosophy of Aristotle to Christian Europe (stimulating the Renaissance) was an advisor to Almoravid court. Until the 1120s the Almoravids held off the Christian knights, only to face an even more urgent threat from the south in the form of the firebrand Almohads, a Berber movement seeking to purge Islam of impurities and re-establish the doctrine of the unity of God.

The Almohad movement had begun with a hellfire preacher, Ibn Tumart, who in North Africa had proclaimed himself the Mahdi – an infallible, Messianic figure who would lead mankind to righteousness. In Algiers Ibn Tumart beat men and women with sticks after finding them mingling together in the streets, and he and his followers firebombed shops selling alcohol, destroyed musical instruments and even assaulted the sister of the Almoravid emir Ali ibn Yusuf in the streets of Marrakech for appearing in public unveiled. The emir banished Ibn Tumart, but this only enabled him to gather an army of illiterate Masmuda tribesmen around him. In 1130 they attacked Marrakech. When Ibn Tumart was killed in the battle the Almohads only became stronger. Their leader had become a martyr, the movement grew and by late 1140s it had spread across Morocco and had taken al-Andalus.

The Almohads set up a new capital in Sevilla, from where they waged a campaign of *jihad*. Arab Christians and Jews from al-Andalus began to flee into reconquered Portugal, Castile, León and Galicia. In 1184 the Almohads built the great mosque in Sevilla, whose Giralda tower stands to this day, to mark the accession of caliph Abu Yusuf Ya'qub al-Mansur, who inflicted a crushing defeat on Alfonso VIII of Castile in the Battle of Alarcos. It would be the last. The Christians were slowly eating into Muslim al-Andalus and by the early 13th century the reconquest of al-Andalus had begun in earnest.

## THE GREAT PHILOSOPHERS – AVERRÕES AND IBN ARABI

Al-Andalus produced two of the medieval world's greatest philosophers, the Aristotelian Muhammad ibn Rushd, known to the West as Averrões, and the mystic Ali Ibn Arabi.

Both thinkers lived in the 12th century and were born in Spanish al-Andalus just as it was coming to the end of its golden age of tolerance. Averrões is better known to Europeans – immortalised by Dante in *The Divine Comedy* and Raphael in his fresco *The School of Athens*. The philosopher was Europe's first great Aristotelian. After his commentaries on Aristotle were translated into Latin, Aristotle's ideas – initially as interpreted by Averrões – spread and became dominant in Europe. Aristotelianism postulated that nature could best be understood by empirical observation and reason – thus, as Averrões stated, 'knowledge is the conformity of the object and the intellect'. This empirical-rational epistemology formed the foundation for Renaissance science and the modern scientific method that developed from it. Averrões could therefore be considered the father of modern European thought.

Ibn Arabi has only become known to the West in relatively recent times, but his ideas have been of considerable influence in the East. While he did not call himself a Sufi, the later Sufi tradition called Ibn Arabi *al-Shaykh al-Akbar* – 'the Greatest Master'. Few thinkers have been more influential within liberal, mystical Islam. Ibn Arabi's ideas are the polar opposite of those of Averrões. He teaches that as humans are not primarily rational, reason cannot lead to knowledge. Knowledge, he argues, is partial and limited, for the direct apprehension of being-in-itself must always precede it. The person who perceives correctly – the gnostic – does not confuse being with external forms, as 'knowing the kernel of all belief, he sees the interior and not the exterior'. Ibn Arabi likens being to light: 'Were it not for light, nothing whatsoever would be perceived, neither the known, nor the sensed, nor the imagined' (*Ibn 'Arabî, al-Futûhât*, 1911 edition, 3:276). And just as being is beyond reason, so it is beyond belief: 'If a gnostic is really a gnostic he cannot stay tied to any form of belief' (*Kernel of the Kernel*, 1:1). Being for Ibn Arabi is the Divine constantly and ineffably revealed in time.

**THE KINGS OF CASTILE AND LEÓN AND THE EARL OF PORTUCALE** If you believe Iberian accounts, the Reconquest began in 718, with the battle of Covadonga fought under the banner of the Spanish Visigothic nobleman Pelayo. In reality Covadonga was a guerrilla insurgency, propagated by a group of isolated tribesmen, for while the Moors may not have occupied much of northern Iberia – including the land north of the River Minho in Portugal – they left it ravaged. But the battle was crucial for more than its victory. Pelayo founded a kingdom – Asturias – which later became centred on the cities of León and the county of Castile. After the dust had settled, it was the Asturian kings descended from Pelayo who reorganised the Christian north under their escutcheon and began the Reconquest in earnest.

As they did so, a number of key strategic centres emerged – either as settlements outside Muslim dominion or as towns or regions taken one by one over decades of guerrilla insurgence. They included León and Castile (which became Asturian royal capitals) and the former Roman port town of Cale. Cale was of key strategic importance – a river crossing at the mouth of the Douro which gave access both to the Atlantic and the fertile Douro valley. It was taken from the Moors in 868, and with its position at the mouth of the estuary, it soon became known as the port of Cale – Porto Cale.

The Asturian kings used Porto Cale as a base for the reconquest of all the land south of the Minho. By the early 10th century the land of Porto Cale extended south to the River Lima and east into the mountains of the Beira Alta, and the Asturian kings had become the kings of Castile and León – named after their new capital territories. The Kings of Castile and Léon suffered a brief but major setback when Al-Mansur ransacked Santiago de Compostela and León in the mid 10th century, but they continued the march south after this violent interlude. By 1064 Porto Cale had reached Coimbra, and the area controlled by Castile and León had become sufficiently large for the Leonese King Alfonso VI to divide it up. In 1095 he created the Condado Portucalense, which now stretched to the outskirts of Olispo (Libson) on the Tagus, giving the territory to his illegitimate daughter Dona Teresa, whom he married off to Henry of the House of Burgundy. The Condado Portucalense or Portucale would become Portugal.

**AFONSO HENRIQUES, FIRST KING OF PORTUGAL** At an early age Afonso Henriques lost his father, Henry Count of Porto Cale. The young king-in-waiting was brought up as knight by Portucalenses. At an early age, and in opposition to his mother, he began to see Portucale as somewhere very distinct from Castile, León and Galicia, his neighbour to the north. At 18 years old he was already willing to defend Portucale militarily at the battle of São Mamede, where he fought against Alfonso VII of León, who wanted to dissolve Afonso Henriques' earldom into the territory of Galicia. By the age of 20 Afonso Henriques was calling himself not an earl, but a prince. And just before his 30th birthday a decisive victory against the Almoravids in Ourique in the Baixo Alentejo had Afonso Henriques declaring himself king of a new country, Portugal, with Coimbra as its capital. Afonso VII of León, meanwhile, had gone one better, declaring himself King Emperor in 1135, and the new King and King Emperor met in Zamora in 1143, in the presence of the papal legate Cardinal Vico, to recognise each other's status formally. However, they failed to agree on borders for the new kingdom of Portugal. This was a mistake that would echo down the centuries, as successive Portuguese monarchs sought to fight off Spanish claims to bits of the territory they regarded as their own.

**RECONQUEST** It took 110 years from Afonso Henriques' assumption of kingship for Portugal to complete the Reconquest. And it was a piecemeal affair – carried out by

1

13

kings, bands of Crusader Knights acting independently and outlaws on the make like Geraldo the Fearless. In 1147 Afonso Henriques took Santarém and Lisbon, the latter with the help of a passing Crusader band who included the Englishman Gilbert of Hastings, who Afonso Henriques appointed bishop of the city. From the 1150s the Alentejo had become the main theatre of war. Afonso took the formidable fortress of Alcácer do Sal in 1158, after which the king and his agents – both official and unofficial – retook a swathe of territory and towns. One of the most successful was Geraldo Sem Pavor – or Gerald the Fearless, the Portuguese El Cid. Despite his nickname Geraldo would attack towns by stealth in the dark of night, usually under stormy weather. His capture of Évora (in 1204) was particularly cruel, and Geraldo also took Serpa and Juromenha, before moving into the Spanish kingdom of León and taking Cáceres, Trujillo and, after a long siege, Badajoz. This was much to the chagrin of the Spanish monarch, who sided with Moors against the Portuguese.

Afonso handed the reins of reconquest to his son Sancho just as the Almohads were flooding into al-Andalus with their armies. The Almohads fought back vigorously, retaking all of the Leonese and Alentejo towns won by Afonso Henriques and his cohorts, but for Évora. By the time Afonso Henriques' grandson, Afonso II, had assumed the crown in Portugal, the squabbling Iberian monarchs had come together to meet the new foe. They finally defeated the Almohads at a decisive battle in 1212 at Las Navas de Tolosa in Jaén with the help of the Crusader orders (including the Portuguese Knights Templar).

Las Navas de Tolosa was the watershed, after which the Moorish towns of the Alentejo quickly fell, with the great fort at Elvas being one of the last to hold out – until 1230. By 1297 the Portuguese Reconquest was complete, some 200 years before Spain's. Portugal's borders now roughly covered the land they do today, from the northern frontier with Galicia to the Algarve in the south, united under a single Portuguese monarch, belonging to the House of Burgundy.

## DOM DINIS 'O LAVRADOR' AND THE COLLAPSE OF THE HOUSE OF BURGUNDY If his Burgundian predecessors had won Portugal from the Moors, it was Dom Dinis and his saintly Queen Isabel (see box, page 100) who built the nation and consolidated it against the Spanish. But for a lapse at the end of his reign (which saw Dinis deposed by his son Afonso IV), Dom Dinis was an astonishingly enlightened and forward-thinking king by the standards of his age. He strengthened the *cortes*, or parliament, giving representatives of key towns and villages the right to vote on affairs that affected their governance, albeit only occasionally. He set up markets in Lisbon and the maritime exchange, probably the first insurance organisation for merchants in Europe. He founded universities, planted forests and rebuilt scores of castles in the neglected Portuguese interior – especially the Alentejo, stimulating the local agricultural economy and strengthening the borders with Spain.

Dinis's descendants proved less wise, forging a series of foolish alliances by love or marriage with Spain. The first occurred in 1355 during the reign of Afonso IV, Dinis's heir. Afonso's son Pedro had fallen in love with the Galician noblewoman Ines de Castro, who was pressurising him to claim the throne of Castile – which would have meant war for Portugal. Afonso IV had her murdered, resulting in a revolt by Pedro that nearly tore the kingdom apart. Pedro I had Ines crowned after her death. Their tragic story has been immortalised in art, from *The Lusiads* of Camões to Ezra Pound's *Cantos*, in ballet and 20 operas, most recently including *Ines de Castro* by the contemporary Scottish composer James MacMillan.

The spectre of Portugal being absorbed into Castile became even more acute under Pedro's son Fernando I. Rioting broke out when Dom Fernando married his lover Leonor Teles (known in Portugal as *a Aleivosa* 'the treacherous'). Leonor was already married. But Fernando was determined. He persuaded the Pope to issue an annulment and made her his queen. It was a disaster: not only did Leonor conduct a series of notorious affairs, but she disastrously persuaded her weak and fickle husband to marry off their daughter to Juan of Castile. This provoked a crisis.

After Fernando's death in 1383, Leonor acted as regent in the name of her daughter Beatriz, ruling Portugal with her lover, João Fernandes de Andeiro, the Count of Ourém and former ambassador to England. Desperate to avoid being absorbed into Spain, the Portuguese rose up in a popular revolt, led by an illegitimate son of Pedro I, João de Avis. Seeing his throne slipping away, Juan de Castile marched on Lisbon, but after a protracted campaign was defeated by Dom João de Avis, 'the plague' and the campaigns of the soldier-turned-saint Nuno Álvares Pereira. João de Avis personally killed the Count of Ourém (later passing the title to Nuno Álvares Pereira), Leonor was exiled and those nobles loyal to Castile were executed. Beatriz of Burgundy and her husband Juan of Castile continued to call themselves the King and Queen of Portugal until their death, but they had been deposed; Burgundy was no more. On 6 April 1385 the Portuguese *cortes* unanimously proclaimed João of Avis João I, King of Portugal and a new dynasty came to power – the House of Avis.

**THE HOUSE OF AVIS – FROM BOOM TO BUST** The collapse of the House of Burgundy may have looked like a disaster at the time, but it was the making of Portugal. Feeling precarious on his throne, the new king cemented what would become the longest alliance in Europe by signing the 1386 Treaty of Windsor with Richard II of England. To consolidate it, João married Philippa of Lancaster, the daughter of John of Gaunt – the real power behind the English throne. The treaty with England helped to secure 25 years of peace with Castile, and it was good for England too. King João in effect founded the British navy, agreeing to send Richard modern Portuguese battle galleys in return for English soldiers and bowmen.

Those galleys would be perfected and turned into the best ocean-going vessels in the world by João's third surviving son, Henrique – known the world over as **Prince Henry the Navigator**. The Muslims had only recently been expelled from Portugal, and determined to turn the Reconquest into conquest and gain plunder, Philippa of Lancaster persuaded the king to allow her children to attack Morocco. In 1415 – the year the queen died – they took Ceuta and Henrique was appointed the city's lieutenant. The prince returned to Portugal with a taste for exploration and the potential riches it could bring the kingdom. After King João made him the head of the Knights Templar order (or, as they had been rebranded, the Knights of the True Cross), the prince channelled his funds into building ships and sponsoring expeditions.

With the Templar Cross emblazoned on their sails, Henrique sent out fleet after fleet from Portugal in pursuit of gold and glory. Legend has it that he was a great man of science who founded a School of Navigation in Sagres. This probably isn't true. Nor did any of Henrique's expeditions establish the trade routes that would make Portugal Europe's most powerful nation. But that does not really undermine the prince's achievement. Without Henry the Navigator, it is unlikely that the House of Avis would have developed its yearning for exploration, or that Portugal would have made the strides in maritime technology that led to its invention of the maritime astrolabe and nonius and the ocean-going carrack and square-rigged caravel.

Portugal's first great discoveries occurred in the reign of **King João II**, who came to power 20 years after Henrique died. In 1487, under Dom João's direction, Bartolomeu Dias rounded the Cape of Good Hope, paving the way for the Golden Age, which occurred in the reign of Manuel I. In 1497 Vasco da Gama sailed around the Cape to India and opened up the spice markets of the Indies for Portugal (see box, page 150).

The expansion gained pace dramatically thereafter. In 1500 **Pedro Álvares Cabral** and his Florentine navigator Amerigo Vespucci landed in Brazil, claiming that country as 'A Terra da Vera Cruz', the Land of the True Cross, for Portugal. Vespucci would give his name to the Americas and Portugal would have a trading Empire that spanned the world from Brazilian Bahia to the farthest corners of Asia. From 1500 onwards a Portuguese fleet would sail east to the Indies in the spring of every year, and regularly west to Brazil. Portugal established colonies from the Amazon to the Argentinian border, and trading stations in Kerala, Mumbai, Macau, Colombo and Bangkok. In 1522 Fernão de Magalhães – known to the world as **Magellan** – completed the first circumnavigation of the globe.

Over the following century the Portuguese took Mombasa (controlling the Zanzibar spice trade), Hormuz (and with it control of the Persian Gulf), eastern and western India, and Malacca and Timor – and thus the spice markets of Indonesia. Their main base of Goa had by the late 16th century become so large that it was considered the second city of Portugal, complete with stately civic buildings and a magnificent cathedral. Goa became the base of the Jesuit mission to the Orient, from where the Portuguese launched expeditions to Japan, founding the port of Nagasaki and becoming the first and only Western nation to settle in that country until the United States in the 20th century. Adapted Portuguese guns played a crucial role in the 16th-century unification of Japan under Toyotomi Hideyoshi and Tokugawa Ieyasu. By the late 16th century Portuguese influence in Asia was so strong that Portuguese had become the de facto language of trade, as the widespread existence of Portuguese words in modern Asian languages attests.

The trade brought increasing prosperity to Portugal itself and a flowering of artistic life – the Manueline architectural style of the Arruda brothers, the poetry of Camões and the dramas of Gil Vicente. Like the rest of the country, Évora, a royal residence for the Avis kings, was packed with splendid palaces and peopled with elegant aristocrats leading luxury lifestyles. The capital, Lisbon, was even more lavish. Dom Manuel's court was the wealthiest in Europe – reportedly with 4,000 paid courtiers. But the boom was in reality a bubble. The 1496 expulsion of the Jewish people by **King Manuel I** (at the insistence of his bride-to-be, Isabel of Castile) deprived Portugal of much of its economic know-how and private economic wealth. And the establishment of a royal monopoly in 1506 ensured that everything depended on the king: royal consent was needed for even the smallest foreign commercial operation. Profit margins were slashed by the hefty taxes exacted by the monarch.

By the mid 16th century the bubble was becoming dangerous. Lisbon's population had escalated to some 100,000, yet there were just 800 entrepreneurs and 5,000 artisans. The rest of the working population were employed as bureaucrats and functionaries of the court.

With so little private capital, investment was nearly impossible, even for merchants. In the 16th century Portugal consumed a great deal, but it wasn't producing anything. The fine silks and luxury goods, guns, naval tackle and gunpowder were made elsewhere. By the end of the century Portugal's foreign debt became four times the internal debt and the country was broke.

The *cortes* government could do little to control the greed of the court. With all the wealth coming in from overseas, the king didn't need taxes from the land, so he paid no attention to the *cortes* parliament or the country as a whole. Squeezed by the monarchy, the landed gentry exploited their serfs and slaves mercilessly. In the backlands of the Alentejo, workers on the land must have wondered what the

Golden Age meant. They toiled under the sun on *latifundios* run by rich masters – just as generations before them had, stretching back to Roman times. The only difference was in the ethnicity of the slaves who were shackled alongside them.

Matters only got worse after the death of Manuel I in 1521. His son and successor **João III** came to power the year after the Pope excommunicated Martin Luther, prompting the Reformation. The response from the Vatican was reactionary and autocratic, and few royals were more loyal to the Pope than João and his Castilian wife Catherine of Austria. It was he who invited the Inquisition into Portugal, overseen by his brother, Cardinal Henrique of Évora and administered by the ultra-conservative and politically ambitious Dominican order. This resulted in further persecution of the Portuguese peasantry and of those Jewish and Moorish Portuguese who had remained in the country after Manuel's expulsion – many as forcibly converted, or 'new', Christians.

When João III died, leaving his three-year-old grandson Sebastião as his heir, Cardinal Henrique of Évora served as regent and the oppression worsened. Matters came to a head when the boy-king Sebastião attempted to revive Portugal's flagging economy with a new Moroccan crusade, which failed dismally, bankrupted the nation and left the House of Avis without an heir. **Philip II** – the Castilian Habsburg king of a new and united Spain – seized the opportunity, marched on Lisbon with a huge army and assumed the Portuguese throne.

**SPAIN TAKES OVER** Philip promised to respect Portuguese autonomy – for the *cortes* parliament, for the colonies and for the internal administration of the country. And for a while he did so and Portugal benefited from Spain's far greater prosperity – for while Portugal's fortunes had been on the wane since the wasteful and irresponsible reign of Manuel I, Spain's had been waxing. Its empire was the most powerful in the world and its fleet ruled the seas. It was said at the time that 'the sea was an emerald in the sandal of the king of Spain, the sun a topaz in his crown'. And England was a thorn in his side. Perfidious Albion had turned resolutely Protestant under Elizabeth I and her pirates were stealing the gold and silver that Philip had robbed from the Incas, Aztecs and Maya. As far as the Spanish were concerned, England had to be punished and the Catholic Mary Stuart crowned Queen in Westminster Abbey. In 1588 Philip prepared an Armada in the Tagus of 169 Spanish men-of-war and 31 Portuguese fighting galleons. Destroyed by Sir Francis Drake and the English weather, only 51 came back. The tide had turned and washed European power away from the autocratic monarchies of the Catholic south to the nimble Protestant merchant nations of the north. With Spanish power weakened, the Spanish and Portuguese colonies in the Americas and Asia became rich pickings.

'The Queen of England,' declared Elizabeth I, 'understands not why her or any prince's subjects should be debarred from the Trade of the Indies, which she could not persuade herself the Spaniards had any just title to … And this imaginary propriety cannot hinder princes from trading in those countries or from transporting colonies into those parts thereof where the Spaniards do not inhabit.'

By the time Philip II's grandson **Philip IV** had acceded the Spanish and Portuguese throne in 1621, the situation had changed dramatically. The English had settled in Virginia, taken Hormuz and were using the island of Jamaica to hound Spanish and Portuguese possession in the Americas. In the meantime, Dutch warships sacked the Iberian trading posts in Indonesia and their forces occupied Salvador and Recife in Brazil. And between 1623 and 1638 some 500 Portuguese vessels were seized by Spain's enemies. Like Portugal before it, Spain was broke, and its new subjects were deeply discontent. Revolt broke out in Évora and then throughout the Alentejo

## THE PORTUGUESE SLAVE TRADE

Enslaved by the Romans and sent all around the Empire, the Portuguese themselves became the biggest of all European slaving nations. Moors were enslaved after the Reconquest. Indians were enslaved in Goa. Japanese women were transported as prostitutes throughout Asia and those brought to Portugal are believed to be the first of their nation to see Europe. Guanche people from the Canary Islands worked the mills on Madeira and so many enslaved Africans were transported to Portugal that most modern Portuguese today have African genetic traces. The Portuguese enslaved so many indigenous Brazilians that entire tribes were wiped out along the Amazon and in the Cerrado forests of the southern interior. And between the 17th and 19th centuries Portugal (and its inheritor Republican Brazil) made some 30,000 slaving voyages between the Americas and Africa, transporting more than 4,650,000 people. This is more than double the number of voyages undertaken (and almost double the number of Africans enslaved) by the next largest trading county, Britain. Brazil received more than ten times the number of African slaves than the United States.

in 1637. By 1640 it had spread to Lisbon, Brazil and the African colonies. Spanish ministers in Lisbon were assassinated, Spain was forced to retreat, tail between its legs, and a new dynasty, the House of Braganza, took back the Portuguese throne when João of Braganza became **Dom João IV of Portugal**.

**THE BRAGANZAS** João IV was a cultivated and sophisticated man, with a great love of music and the arts, which passed to England through his daughter Catherine. Her marriage to King Charles II came with a handsome dowry which included the gift of Tangier and Bombay to the English, as well of the practice of attending the opera and taking afternoon tea. Charles II returned the favour by signing the Treaty of Alliance. English support also forced Holland to retract a Declaration of War and sign a peace treaty with Portugal which saw a partial end to hostilities between the nations in Asia and Brazil.

But Spain was still not placated and troubles with the old enemy were fought out in the Alentejo during the reigns of João IV's son Afonso VI and his grandson Pedro II, who fought a fierce war – the Portuguese Restoration War. This eventually led in 1668 to a peace treaty which finally recognised Portuguese sovereignty and returned the Alentejo cities of Elvas, Estremoz and Olivença to Lisbon.

By this time the Alentejo – like much of the Portuguese interior – was one of the most backward corners of Europe. Many of its oppressed workers had fled the country in search of a better life in an increasingly wealthy Brazil. In 1675, under the advice of his enlightened Chancellor of the Exchequer the Count of Ericeira, Pedro II became the first monarch in Portuguese history actively to promote and support manufacture and production in Portugal. Pedro's government fomented wool production and textile manufacture in the Alentejo and banned the importation of foreign cloth. A new crop from the Americas – maize – was planted in the Douro valley along with grapes. By the end of the 17th century wine was being produced in the Douro, fortified in Porto and shipped to England in huge quantities.

**GOLD AND THE BIRTH OF BAROQUE** Everything changed again in the late 1600s when gold was found in a little stream in southeastern Brazil and soon afterwards throughout the surrounding region. Discoveries became so prodigious that the region became known as Minas Gerais – or General Mines. Development of the Alentejo and the rest of rural Portugal was once more put on hold as the aristocracy sat back and enjoyed a fresh glut of wealth. By the early 18th century, when **João V** acceded to the throne, some 1,000 tons of Brazilian gold had been brought to Lisbon, alongside diamonds from the north of Minas Gerais and Bahia.

Like Manuel I before him, João V became inflated with his own importance. Determined to emulate Louis XIV of France, he spent millions on lavish buildings in the modish Baroque and Rococo styles – including a mini-Versailles at Mafra and a legion of glittering churches throughout the kingdom. And as Louis XIV did with France, he left Portugal bankrupt. He also inspired Portugal's first colonial revolution – the Inconfidência Mineira in Minas Gerais – the product of heavy Portuguese taxation and the cruelty inflicted by the Portuguese on the Brazilians. The Inconfidência was swiftly quelled, but it showed that the colony was increasingly independence-minded.

**THE 1755 EARTHQUAKE AND THE PROGRESSIVE REFORMS OF POMBAL** Things came crashing down in 1755 when Portugal suffered a catastrophic earthquake, whose impact was most greatly felt in Lisbon. The earthquake was one of the greatest natural disasters of modern historical times. It caused tidal waves so large that they swept across the Atlantic from Cornwall (which was hit by waves 10 feet high) to Barbados. The quake was felt as far away as Finland. Lisbon was almost razed to the ground, losing its lavish waterfront palace, cathedral and between 10,000 and 100,000 of its citizens. The towns of the coastal Alentejo were destroyed.

With the earthquake came a seismic shift in the balance of power in Portugal. The inept and corrupt monarchy of João V's son **Dom José I** was entirely ineffectual, and it was left to the former ambassador to Great Britain, Sebastião José de Carvalho e Melo, to clear-up the mess. De Carvalho e Melo, who later became known after his title, the **Marquis of Pombal**, was the kind of forward-thinking, politically progressive figure the Portuguese monarchy had been ignoring and suppressing for centuries. As the son of a lowly squire he was loathed by the court. But King José admired his efficiency, which became even more valued as he supervised the rebuilding of Lisbon. Over the following years Pombal assumed more and more control of the country as a whole, introducing a series of reforms which would drag the nation into contemporaneous Enlightenment Europe. He abolished slavery in Portugal and India, and ended the Inquisition and the associated *limpeza de sangue* (clean blood) legislation which had resulted in discrimination against Jewish people and the descendants of the Moors. Pombal instituted important economic reforms and political reforms which included the creation of Europe's first business school, the Aula do Comercio, a system of guilds and companies (modelled on those he had seen while an ambassador in London), the quality control of produce, and the awarding of coats of arms and titles to successful entrepreneurs. Pombal wrested educational control from the religious orders, who were expelled from Portugal, and set up state-funded primary and secondary schools and universities on Enlightenment European models, with departments devoted to the natural sciences and philosophy.

Those who opposed Pombal received short shrift. Under the new politics there was justice for all. Nobles were not exempt, and if they stood in the prime minister's way they were imprisoned. By 1776 Portugal's gaols were stuffed to the brim with the escutcheoned.

But Pombal went too far. The aristocrats rebelled, and when Dom José became ill his daughter Maria became regent, and then Portugal's first queen. Before lapsing into madness she had Pombal exiled and his reforms largely repealed. Portugal returned once more to the dark ages.

**NAPOLEON AND THE PENINSULAR WAR** Pombal's problem was that he was a man ahead of his time, a time which came in 1787 when the French tired of their monarchy and founded Europe's first modern republic. As the republic's great hero, Napoleon determined to carry its principles to Europe, with all the autocracy and self-assurance of a Pombal. Napoleon would rid the continent of monarchy, aristocracy and privilege. And his main enemy in doing so was Britain. Napoleon attacked Britain where it hurt most – trade. In 1806 he issued the Berlin decree which forbade the import of British goods into European countries allied with or dependent upon France. He formed an alliance with Spain, which had already invaded the Alentejo under a false pretext in a campaign which came to be called the War of the Oranges. Napoleon marched an army under General Junot into Iberia, installed his brother in Madrid and threatened to take the conflict to the next level. He would invade Portugal unless the Portuguese reneged on their neutrality and closed Lisbon to British ships, which were using the port as a waystation. Acting as regent for mad Queen Maria, João VI refused to comply, packed his bags and climbed on board a fleet of ships, together with the entire court of 10,000.

João had secretly petitioned the British prime minister William Cavendish-Bentinck, and British battleships escorted the Portuguese royal family away to safety in Rio de Janeiro. Lisbon was abandoned to the French and command of the Portuguese state handed to the British general William Carr Beresford. It was all in the nick of time. Junot and his army could still see the royal fleet on the horizon when they marched into Lisbon to set up court. Beresford did not oppose them. Instead he waited for an opportunity, and found it when Spanish unhappy about being ruled by Napoleon's brother began a concerted *guerrilla* campaign.

While Junot was busy suppressing them, British forces commanded by Arthur Wellesley (the future Duke of Wellington) landed in Coimbra and decisively routed the French who came to meet them. The French were humiliatingly shipped back to Napoleonic France in British warships and Beresford finally set up his military administration in Lisbon. From here the British coordinated their campaign against Napoleon in Spain. In 1810 Beresford's Portuguese troops and Wellesley's British defeated a massive French army of 65,000 near Almeida in the north of Portugal. It would be a decisive blow, enabling Beresford and Wellesley to base themselves right on the Spanish border at the garrison town of Elvas, which they used as a centre of operations against the French and their Spanish allies. Harried by Spanish guerrilla fighters and hounded by the British, the Napoleonic forces were chased across the Pyrenees in 1813. It was a great victory, but it came at huge cost for Portugal. In total, around 100,000 Portuguese had died, most of them civilians. And once again, the country was bankrupt.

**REVOLUTION AND REPRESSION** When João VI – as he had become with the death of Maria – felt all was safe he crept back to Lisbon with his court, leaving his son Pedro in charge in Rio. If he'd hoped all would be hunky-dory he had a nasty surprise. In his absence Beresford's Portuguese army had mounted a coup and written a liberal charter, which was a carbon copy of the Brazilian Constitution. The king could stay on, they said, but he and his inheritors would be subject to the *cortes* parliament, which would be elected by the people. Feudalism on the *latifundios* would be abolished, and the clergy would lose all their automatic rights.

João VI agreed to the liberals' demands, but died just a few years later in 1826. Once more the country entered crisis. João's heir Dom Pedro was now emperor of a newly independent, liberal Brazil whose government preferred him to stay.

Brazil saw itself as a modern state with a modern constitution and feared a return to absolute monarchy under Lisbon.

Pedro was forced by Brazil to compromise. He sent his daughter Dona Maria da Gloria back to Lisbon to take the Portuguese throne and rule as Maria II. She would accept all the parliamentary reforms and marry her uncle (Pedro's younger brother) Miguel, who would act as regent until she came of age. Miguel, however, was the figurehead for an absolutist movement led by aristocrats and *latifundiario* landed gentry who were loath to give up their privilege. They believed that what Portugal needed was to return to the good old days of Manuel I, and the absolutists would see to it that it would do so under Miguel. When the young pretender returned to Lisbon in 1828, he and his followers deposed Maria. Miguel declared himself supreme head of state, with absolute power, rejected parliament and all reforms and started to execute liberals. Thousands fled to Britain, which supported their cause, mounting an army in Plymouth and preparing for civil war.

In 1831 a liberal army led of some 7,000 Portuguese and British soldiers landed in central Portugal, initiating the War of the Two Brothers. They were led by Dom Pedro, who had abdicated his Brazilian throne to resolve the Portuguese crisis. The army took Porto, where they were joined by 10,000 liberal Portuguese. While 24,000 Miguelite supporters besieged them in the city, a smaller liberal army led by the Duke of Terceira sailed secretly from Porto to the Algarve. From here they marched overland through the Alentejo, where they garnered support. Occupied in Porto, the Miguelites could offer no resistance and in June 1833 the liberals took Lisbon. The following year a convention signed at Evoramonte in the Alentejo exiled Dom Miguel and all his descendants from Portugal on pain of instant death. He died in Bavaria in 1866 while out hunting boar.

The war had exhausted Dom Pedro, and he reigned as Pedro IV for just a few years before handing the throne to his daughter, Maria II.

**THE REPUBLIC** The Portugal of Maria II was in a dreadful state. It seemed as if the Civil War had solved nothing. The new constitution had abolished all tithes, privileges, monopolies and feudal obligations. But successive governments seemed unable to put anything in their place. While Portugal cried out for investment and industrial revolution, ministers plundered the state and lined their pockets. In 1834 the liberals confiscated the country's monasteries and convents and nearly a quarter of all the cultivated land changed hands. Yet the workers who tilled them were still feudal slaves in all but name. Illiterate and politically alienated, they were controlled by *caciques* in the employ of local landowners or politicians, who literally policed the populace's opinions – beating and imprisoning them if they dared to question what they were told to believe.

Nor did things change under Maria's son Dom Carlos, who came to the throne in 1889. Governments oscillated between Chartists and Constitutionalists, dictators and supposedly democratising 'Cabralists', Regenerators and Historicals, and all the while nothing changed. Portugal remained poor, indebted and undeveloped. The king was blamed and in 1908 assassinated together with his eldest son Prince Luís Filipe. His younger son ruled nominally for two more years before fleeing to Britain in 1910. The Portuguese armed forces gloriously declared a democratic Republic. They announced elections and banned all political parties but their own – the Republicans – and unanimously passed their own Republican constitution in 1911 before collapsing into more squabbling which was briefly interrupted by the First World War.

By 1918 the country's problems were so acute that it entered a state of semi-anarchy – riven by strikes, bomb detonations and insurrection and terrified by the spectre of Bolshevik communism, the military assumed power, initiating Europe's first fascist dictatorship. Aside from restoring law and order the military did little. By the late 1920s Portugal was desperate. Between 1910 and 1926 it had seen 45 governments come and go. The escudo had fallen to one-twentieth of the value it had against the pound after the end of World War I. It needed a solution. In 1928, in an attempt to solve the crisis General Carmona invited a professor of political economy from the University of Coimbra to take care of the public coffers and administer reform.

'I know very well what I want and where I am going,' declared Professor António de Oliveira Salazar in his inaugural address, 'but I cannot be asked to accomplish it in a few months.'

By 1932 Salazar had turned a budget deficit into a surplus – convincing the military to give him free reign. In 1933 Salazar became prime minister and the Estado Novo – or New State – began.

**FASCISM UNDER THE ESTADO NOVO**  For 42 years the Second Republic government was ruled under Salazar and briefly Marcelo Caetano as a dictatorship. The press was censored, communism outlawed, political parties other than Salazar's and trades unions banned or strictly controlled and the activity and morality of the population at large was under constant vigilance by the PIDE (Polícia Internacional e de Defensa do Estado). Government was merely legislative and answered directly to President Salazar without any dependence on parliament. Given the absence or suppression of political parties it was not surprising that Salazar won all the show elections.

Salazar implemented many structural and economic changes. The public purse was tightly controlled, allowing for the building of much-needed roads, bridges and civic buildings. Before Salazar law courts, hospitals, barracks and town halls were all accommodated in buildings appropriated from the church by the state in the 1830s. For the first time in its history Portugal became an urban country more than a rural, with a middle class instead of a dirt-poor majority and a tiny aristocratic minority. Portugal might have become prosperous had Salazar not decided to embark on a colonial adventure. When Angola, Mozambique, Cape Verde and Guinea Bissau agitated for independence Salazar refused. They were, he told the United Nations, overseas 'provinces' and not colonies – just like France's *départments*. Insurrection would not be permitted. Salazar sent in the army. This had a surprising counter-effect on the Alentejo. As the poor were drafted to Africa in huge numbers, the well of cheap indentured labour dried up. Desperate for workers, the *latifundio* landlords began to compete with each other – offering higher wages and shorter working weeks. By the mid 1960s wages were verging on fair, the working week had been reduced from dawn to dusk every day except Sunday to a 48-hour week. The indentured conditions which been in place since Roman times were finally becoming eroded. By the late 1960s once-poor farmers who had walked to school as children in bare feet with plastic sacking for coats and worked under debt peonage had begun to save enough money to buy modest smallholdings. Unplanned and unbeknown to the rest of Portugal, the Alentejo was undergoing a quiet rural revolution.

But the country as a whole was in a desperate state. By the late 1960s the economy was plummeting. More than 100,000 Portuguese had lost their lives fighting in Africa and the people were oppressed, mournful and melancholic. In 1968 Salazar suffered a brain haemorrhage when he slipped in the bath tub and hit his head, rendering him incapacitated and eventually leading to his death in 1970. Marcelo Caetano took over the dictatorial chair promising change that year. But he didn't deliver, and in 1974 the Armed Forces took over in a bloodless coup during which not a single shot was fired. It became known thereafter as the Carnation Revolution.

**DEMOCRACY AND MODERN PORTUGAL** With the Estado Novo gone, Portugal celebrated. The Communist party seized the moment, organising huge festivals, where rock music replaced Salazar's beloved *fado* and bands from the USA and Britain took to the stage. Stalls at street markets in Lisbon sold books which had been banned for half a century.

The wars were ended and Portuguese-speaking Africa gained its independence, followed shortly after by Goa. The PIDE secret police were disbanded, trade unions legalised, and as communists gained increasing influence industries and banks were nationalised. Furious arguments were waged over the question of common ownership of land and for the first time in history the workers of the Alentejo came into the spotlight. The communists championed their rights and appropriated 2 million hectares of land on their behalf – causing scores of *latifundio* owners to flee overseas, mostly to Brazil, which was at that time under a US-backed right-wing military regime. But the educated and urban communist elite had little grasp of the situation on the ground in the Alentejo. Those tenant farmers who only a decade before had begun to free themselves of debt peonage were treated as landowners. Their land was taken by the state and once more they found themselves with nothing.

In this atmosphere, Portugal's first ever genuinely democratic elections took place in 1975, for an assembly to draft a new constitution. The new constitution acknowledged full legal equality for women and the right of all Portuguese to vote, be they literate or illiterate. Previously only Portuguese men who could read and women with secondary education had been entitled to vote, albeit in the sham elections of the Estado Novo. The constitution of 1933 had proclaimed everyone equal under the law 'except for women' owing to 'the differences resulting from their nature and for the good of the family'. The 1976 parliamentary elections which followed the new constitution were the first in Portuguese history to grant universal suffrage. The communists were confident of winning.

But they lost, partly because of their campaign of ill-thought-out land reform in the Alentejo. The Portuguese opted for a soft socialist government. It was a compromise. Appropriated land was largely returned and agrarian and industrial workers given more rights. Portugal voted for Socialist or Social Democrat governments until 1986, when the Thatcherite Cavaco Silva came to power. Portugal entered the European Community that same year, and was a huge beneficiary of EC funds. The EC, and later the EU, built Portugal's first motorways. With European cash and know-how Portugal opened Europe's biggest copper and tungsten mines, and with a billion-euro European subsidy Volkswagen built a huge factory on the coast. The economy began to grow, although it was a fragile growth. Despite its fertile land, Portugal was decades behind Europe in agricultural technology and had to import food and fodder. Even in the 1990s the average hourly wage languished at €7 and some 200,000 children were working full adult hours, having left school at 14 with a poor education. Even with Thatcherite cuts, the state was bloated – burdened with an expensive, privileged bureaucracy left by centuries of monarchical monopoly and over half a century of dictatorship. Socialist and conservative governments did little to tackle the roots of the problem until the euro crisis of the 21st century when Pedro Passos Coelho came to office (with Cavaco Silva as president) and introduced austerity measures.

Since then there has been some reason for hope. Portugal's economy was the fastest growing in the EU in 2013. Tourism has grown steadily, particularly to Lisbon, which has successfully rebranded itself as a sophisticated, upmarket destination. And new industries have emerged, such as telecommunications and shoe manufacturing, whose foreign sales jumped 40% between 2011 and 2015. In 2015 the OECD predicted that Portugal's recovery would strengthen. But with unemployment at 13% (and around 35% for youths), low bond yields and a national debt at more than 100% of GDP, modern Portugal has significant problems.

## GOVERNMENT AND POLITICS

The Alentejo is a geographical rather than a political entity. Portugal is made up of 18 districts and two autonomous regions. These include the districts of Beja, Évora and Portalegre in the south, centre and north of the Alentejo respectively.

The four main departments of Portuguese government are the presidency, the prime minister and Council of Ministers (the government), the Assembly of the Republic (the parliament), and the judiciary.

Elections are by proportional representation. All Portuguese citizens (including those with dual nationality) over 18 have the right to vote. Candidates are voted into regional constituencies. These correspond to the 18 districts and the two autonomous regions, with two extra constituencies reserved for Portuguese citizens who live abroad. Thus the Alentejo has three constituencies. Candidates for these are nominated by the political parties.

Portuguese government is dominated by two parties – the social democratic Socialist Party and the liberal conservative Social Democratic Party. In 2015 the Prime Minister Pedro Passos Coelho of the Social Democratic Party governed in coalition with the right-wing conservative People's Party. Parliamentary elections took place in October 2015 with the Coalition holding on to power. Presidential elections are due to take place in 2016.

Portugal is a founding member of NATO and joined the EEC (later EU) in 1986.

## ECONOMY

For the economic history of Portugal, see *History*, pages 4–24.

Membership of the EC (since 1986), with associated investment, helped Portugal shift its largely agricultural economy towards mineral exploitation, small-scale industrial production, service industries and telecommunications. The Portuguese invented the pre-paid mobile phone and the MultiBanco teller machine, which enables customers to access 60+ functionalities, from bill payments to buying concert tickets.

The country experienced steady growth in the 1990s, but was hit badly by the 2008 crisis – a situation exacerbated by the country's unwieldy bureaucracy and bloated public sector. In 2011 Portugal became the third EU country after Greece and Ireland to ask for international financial assistance, receiving a €78 billion bailout from the EU and IMF tied to a commitment to cut spending and reduce the deficit in line with the EU target of 3% of GDP. The government achieved this and exited the programme in 2014, but still retains a significant national debt, low productivity, a minimum wage of €589.17 per month and GDP per head which is well under the EU average.

## PEOPLE

This complex, cultured people is one of Europe's most genetically diverse. Iberians and Phoenicians, Celts, Carthaginians and Romans, Goths, Moors, Jews, Japanese and sub-Saharan Africans make up the historical Portuguese. A diaspora of West Africans,

Chinese, Timorese and Brazilians have added to their variety. Studies of mitochondrial DNA carried out in the new millennium and published in *Human Biology* (77:2, April 2005) and the *American Journal of Human Genetics* (83:6 December 2008) concluded that Portuguese from southern Portugal have a 10.8% frequency of sub-Saharan African genes, that 36.3% of southern Portuguese descend from Sephardic Jews, and that Iberians as a whole have on average 10.6% North African DNA.

## LANGUAGE

Portugal is not to be confused with Spain. Non-Spanish travellers who speak Spanish in the Alentejo will find the locals as curt as a ticket collector. Speak Portuguese, however, albeit just a few words, and the world changes, locals are warm, welcoming and willing to do anything to help. There is a big contrast between the nations. The Spanish demand '*una cerveza*', without so much as a '*por favor*'. The Portuguese, *por gentileza*, mind their Ps and Qs, always say '*obrigado*' or '*obrigada*', dress well but not ostentatiously, speak quietly but emphatically, and firmly correct Brazilians (and other former colonials) on the proper use of Portuguese grammar.

Portuguese is a growing language; it is the eighth most spoken in the world and the third most spoken European language, ahead of French or German. More than half the population of South America speak Portuguese, it is widely spoken in Africa (with half a dozen countries using it as their lingua franca) and the Indonesian archipelago, and there are Portuguese speakers in excess of 100,000 in Canada, the UK, the USA, Spain (the Galician dialect is a form of Portuguese) and France.

Portuguese words have entered the vocabulary of myriad other languages. Examples include: *sekolah* (Indonesian, from Portuguese *escola* – school), *tempura, pan* and *iruman* (Japanese, from *tempero* – seasoning, *pão* – bread, and *irmão* - brother), *mesa* (Swahili, from *mesa* – table), *bendera* (Malay, from *bandeira* – tray) and *vindaloo* (Hindi via Konkani, from *vinha d'alho* – pork marinated in wine and garlic). The English words embarrass and marmalade are of Portuguese origin.

Like Spanish, French, Italian and Romanian, Portuguese is a modern Romance language – derived from Latin and changed over the centuries by exposure to other peoples. The Gothic tribes gave Portuguese words like *guerra* (war), the Celts *manteiga* (butter) and the indigenous Brazilians *abacaxi* (pineapple). There are many Portuguese words of Arabic origin, including *algodão* (cotton), *azeite* (oil), *oxalá* (God willing) and *xerife* (sheriff).

## RELIGION

As a country born of the crusades of the Reconquest, Portugal has long been Catholic and it remains so, with just over 80% of the population classifying themselves as such. The Alentejo's towns are replete with Catholic churches, many of them extremely beautiful, built in the Golden Age when Portugal was at the height of its powers or during the 18th-century Brazilian gold boom. Most of the Alentejo's lively festivals are also feast days, associated with a particular saint's day or an event in the Catholic Christian calendar.

Portugal has produced some 21 Catholic saints, of whom a handful are from the Alentejo (see box, page 26) and has one of the faith's most important pilgrimage sites in Fátima. This shrine was sacred before Christian times. Three children reported having had a vision of the Virgin there, and in 1917 70,000 people, including reporters and atheist academics, witnessed the 'miracle of the Sun', as promised to the children. An atheist reporter for secular newspaper *O Século* reported it thus:

One could see the immense multitude turn towards the sun, which appeared free from clouds and at its zenith. It looked like a plaque of dull silver and it was possible to look at it without the least discomfort. Before the astonished eyes of the crowd, whose aspect was Biblical as they stood bareheaded, eagerly searching the sky, the sun trembled, made sudden incredible movements outside all cosmic laws – the sun 'danced' according to the typical expression of the people ...

Of the 80% of Portuguese who call themselves Catholic only 29% attend church – the sixth highest in Europe. This compares with 39% in the USA and 12% in the UK.

Protestants of one form or another constitute 4% of Portuguese. There are some 35,000 Portuguese Muslims (mostly Sunnis from West Africa, 5,000 Ismailis and a small number of Indian Ahmadis), 7,000 Hindus, 600 Jews and 20,000 Buddhists. Many of the latter are Vajrayana and the Alentejo is home to one of the biggest Buddhist retreat centres in the world, **Tubthen Puntsok Gephel Ling**, in Santa Catarina near Alcácer do Sal (*Estrada Nacional 253, Herdade Corte Pereiro, Santa Susana, Alcácer do Sal;* ☎ *26 510 2162; www.gephelling.org*).

## CULTURE

While distinct geographically, and with its own cultural nuances, the Alentejo is nevertheless very much part of Portugal. In order to explore the culture of the Alentejo it is important to know a little of the culture of the country.

### ARCHITECTURE
**Pre-Roman and Roman** Aside from Palaeolithic middens and graves, Portugal's earliest buildings are the Neolithic and Copper Age megaliths of the

Alentejo (see *Megaliths, trade and pottery*, pages 5–6). These are quite different in scale and composition from the henges of northern Europe and the passage graves of Ireland and they come in three forms, all of which are well represented throughout the Alentejo. **Dolmens** (*Antas*) are made up of a large rock balanced on two others. Many of them serve as portico doorways to passage tombs and a number in the Alentejo were converted in later centuries to chapels (see box, page 81). The **Anta do Tapadão** (see box, page 119) near Crato is the second largest in Portugal. **Menhirs** are free standing stones, the largest over 6m tall. Some are decorated with abstract and figurative petroglyphs. The **Menhir da Meada** (see page 127) – the largest in Iberia – is in the northern Alentejo near Castelo de Vide. The Alentejo **cromlechs** or stone circles are smaller in scale than the famous stone circles of northern Europe, but they are far older and extend over a huge area. The most impressive in Iberia – the **Almendres Cromlech** (see pages 80–1) – is situated close to Évora.

The Bronze and Iron ages saw the building of hill top forts or *castros* throughout the Alentejo. They give towns like Castro Verde their names. Many of them were later adapted for Carthaginian or Roman use, and they continued to be adapted up until Napoleonic times.

The Alentejo lay at the heart of **Roman Lusitania** and there are plenty of extant Roman buildings in the district, albeit ruined. They include the reconstructed temple in **Évora**, with fluted Corinthian columns, the ruined towns of **Miróbriga** (see page 141) and **Ammaia** (page 130), with mosaics, baths, civic buildings and fora, and the villas at **Pisões** (page 161) and **São Cucufate** (page 162) near Beja.

Portugal has had Christian bishops since Roman times and was settled by Arian Christian Germanics. The only remaining traces of the early churches are found in Beja's **Santo Amaro church and Visigoth Museum** (see page 159) where you can see the barrel vaulting and Corinthian capitals characteristic of Visigoth architecture.

Much more remains of Portugal's 500 years of Muslim rule, but only in macro. The winding labyrinths of whitewashed sugar-cube houses lining streets ringed by castellated walls and rising to heavy set castles are utterly Moorish. But little of Islamic Portugal's architectural detail remains, aside from a few remnants like horseshoe arches in Beja castle, a *mihrab* in a church in Mértola and artefacts in museums in that city, as well as Moura and Beja.

**Romanesque** Architecture in Portugal begins in earnest from the 12th century. After the Reconquest, Christians spread from France to Iberia, bringing with them the Romanesque style. This had developed initially at Charlemagne's palace in Aachen, but as Christianity consolidated in the face of the expansion of Islam the style expanded with the building of monastic churches associated with shrines. These needed to be far bigger and grander than small community churches, in order to speak in stone of the power of Christianity and to accommodate increasing numbers of pilgrims. These vast Romanesque monastic churches were the precursors of the great medieval cathedrals. They adopted a cruciform shape – which had the advantage of allowing more people to view sacred relics put on display in the centre of the church – where the arms of the cross met and incorporated huge naves and high ceilings illuminated by clerestory windows.

Stylistically the Romanesque monastic churches rediscovered Roman architectural tropes and recalled the great Hellenistic cultural empire which had been largely taken over by Islam. Buildings are characterised by a sense of geometric harmony and functional solidity – with heavy walls offset by rounded arches and vaults. Windows tended to be small as engineering techniques were not yet advanced enough to combine large windows with structural strength.

The Romanesque arrived in Portugal shortly after the Reconquest and lasted longer in the country than in northern Europe. The Alentejo's earliest pre-conquest churches, most notably Évora cathedral, are built in that style.

**Gothic and Manueline** The term Gothic was first used in the late Renaissance by writers like Vasari, and was initially meant to be contemptuous. Italians were obsessed with the geometrical harmony of classical and Romanesque architecture and they saw the high arches and soaring spires of the Gothic churches literally as barbarous – architectural vandalism whose destruction of the Neo-classical echoed the destruction of Rome by the German tribes.

The Gothic first emerged in northern France in the early 12th century, during the construction of the great cathedrals of Chartres and Notre Dame de Paris. Engineers discovered that pointed arches, ribbed vaults and buttresses were far stronger than the Romanesque rounded arches and thick walls, allowing for taller, lighter buildings with windows whose stained glass served as a vast mandala of light. Indeed, stained glass rose windows literally functioned as such – being used for a kind of visual meditation whose medium of fixed gaze put the prayerful in a trance-like state and in the symbolic presence of the divine.

In Portugal the Gothic was modified and later elaborated. Churches tend to have wide naves and low clerestories and to be ringed by ancillary chapels. Stained glass was less elaborate than in France or England. Instead the Portuguese Gothic incorporated elaborate decoration with motifs often borrowed from the buildings of al-Andalus. Church naves were flanked with cylindrical towers, windows became horseshoe arches and carved effigies were set in a whirl of abstract decoration. While Portugal's finest Gothic buildings are in Batalha and Santarém, the Alentejo has some notable examples – like the **Igreja de São Francisco** and **São Bras Hermitage** in Évora, **Alandroal** and **Beja** castles, the **Largo da Porta de Moura**, and the **Igreja Matriz de Nossa Senhora da Anunciação** in Mértola.

As the Portuguese Gothic style matured it became ever more elaborate, incorporating the Mudéjar (Christianised Islamic) and the high Gothic decoration of the Spanish *plateresque* (characterised by lavish reliefs that look like stamped silver plate) to produce an elaborate, uniquely Portuguese architectural style forever associated with the Golden Age of Dom Manuel I and called after that monarch, the **Manueline**. Manueline buildings were constructed with the wealth and confidence of empire and magnificently decorated with effigies, motifs, abstract patterns and

## THE DE ARRUDAS

Many of Portugal's remarkable Manueline and early Baroque buildings were designed by de Arrudas. Francisco de Arruda was responsible for the Torre de Belém in Lisbon – the monument to the great explorers that sits on the quay to this day – and the lower town of Elvas. His brother Diogo built the Convento de Cristo in Tomar, Evoramonte castle and the Igreja Matriz in Viana do Alentejo. Francisco's son Miguel worked on the Convento de Nossa Senhora da Graça in Évora, Batalha Abbey and the Sé cathedral in Portalegre. Between them, the family has contributed to or designed five UNESCO World Heritage Sites – more than any other architectural family in the world.

nautical flourishes in homage to the sea which had made that empire possible. Doorways and windows were framed with carved ropes and seaweed and capped with armillary spheres – symbols of astronomical navigation, and of Portugal's dominance of the seas and the globe. Portugal's most famous Manueline buildings are the castle in Tomar and the Jerónimos monastery in Lisbon, but there are many fine examples in the Alentejo, most of them in the Baixo. They include the **Real Mosteiro** in Beja (pages 158–9), the **Pousada de Alvito** (pages 162–3), the **Igreja Matriz de Nossa Senhora da Anunciação** (page 164) in Viana do Alentejo, the **Igreja do Carmo** (page 77) in Évora and the castle in **Evoramonte** (page 101).

## Renaissance Mannerism to Baroque
The gradual wane in Portugal's fortunes after the Golden Age came with a return to the sobriety of classicism and the adoption of the **Renaissance** style. Order was imposed on ecclesiastical architecture in buildings and on the delightfully organic Moorish streets of lower **Elvas** by rectilinear *praças* and stately Palladian houses. Later Renaissance buildings like the **Igreja de Santa Maria** in Estremoz were decorated in the Mannerist style that emerged in the 16th century as a reaction against the idealised naturalism and harmony of the Renaissance, sabotaging it with unnatural lines, distortions and geometric tensions. Buildings often featured embellishments intended to surprise or shock, with exaggerated or inverted lines, incomplete pediments and, in the case of the Igreja de Santa Maria, corbels that appear to be on the verge of falling.

By the early 18th century the Portuguese court was the richest in Europe, thanks to the gold and diamond mines of Brazil, and it celebrated it by building some of the continent's most exuberant palaces and churches in the new, highly decorated Baroque and Rococo styles. The Baroque was brought to Portugal by the German goldsmith J F Ludwig (known in Portugal as Ludovice), who arrived with the Jesuits in 1701 and was employed ten years later by King João V to build a modest convent at Mafra, as an offering to the church in the hope of producing royal heirs. As the gold began to flow in from Brazil, João's convent morphed into a vast palace built to rival Versailles. The building looks Italian from the outside, but the inside is early Portuguese Baroque, with a multiplicity of galleries, extensive use of white marble and large windows. Ludovice went on to work on the main chapel in **Évora cathedral**, spreading the Baroque style to the Alentejo.

As it developed, Portuguese Baroque became (like the Manueline before it) very much a national style. Inspired by Ludovice's craft background, Portuguese Baroque architects abandoned traditional architectural norms, drawing on a diversity of design sources for inspiration. Carlos Mardel (d. 1763) introduced Chinese curves and upturned roof edges, which were then incorporated into portico designs. Ribeiro Soares da Silva modelled the doorway of Braga Town Hall on chair leg designs. Other Portuguese architects copied themes from German jewellery and English furniture books. Rather than being dominated by vast domes and lavish facades, Portuguese Baroque buildings became characterised by a playful simplicity of often surprising form (with curves and octagons used for church naves as well as rectangles), offset with complex architectural adornments. Interiors were an overgrowth of organic *talha* carved wood. Grapevines and flying phoenixes (symbols of the Eucharist and eternal life) glittering with Brazilian gold leaf entirely cover altarpieces, often incorporating the framing for pictures or *azulejos*, and flowing into structural features like pulpits, painted statuary and elaborately carved marble sculptures. Ceilings were painted with *trompe l'œil* scenes depicting biblical events like the Assumption.

The economics of the later Portuguese Baroque period – after the 1755 Lisbon earthquake – created a new, less auric and ostentatious style that became known

1

as the Pombaline (after the marquis who rebuilt Lisbon), whereby gilt wood was substituted with extensive coverings of *azulejos* illustrating scenes from the lives of biblical figures or the saints.

The Alentejo is replete with buildings either built as or decorated in Baroque style. They include the main chapel in the **Igreja de São João Evangelista** and **cathedral** in Évora (pages 74–5 and 75–6), the interior of the **cathedral** and the **Igreja da Ordem Terceira de São Francisco** in Elvas (page 93), the **Hotel Convento de São Paulo** near Evoramonte (page 101), the **Paço Ducal** in Vila Viçosa (pages 110–11), the **Real Mosteiro de Nossa Senhora da Conceição** in Beja (pages 158–9), and the **Sanctuário Nossa Senhora d'Aires** in Viana do Alentejo (page 164).

## The 19th and 20th centuries
Portugal's lapse into poverty and relative obscurity after the Pombaline era, the chaos of the Republic and the oppression of Salazar saw a decrease in architectural production and quality. This was exacerbated by the loss of the monasteries and convents in 1834. After appropriation by the state, the buildings saw little use, and until some were taken over as hotels in the 20th century they were left to looters and decay. Many fell into ruins, alongside the palaces of fallen aristocrats and the crumbling castles of the Alentejo hills. The decline was briefly ameliorated by a momentary florescence of ornate Portuguese Art Nouveau in the early 20th century. While this occurred mainly in Lisbon and Aveiro, there are a few examples in the Alentejo, most notably the quirky **Café Águias d'Ouro** in Estremoz (page 98).

Portugal's integration into the EU in 1986 saw an injection of cash and an associated revival of architecture. The country now has one of Europe's top architecture schools, the Faculdade de Arquitectura (School of Architecture) of the University of Porto, whose alumni include Fernando Távora and two Pritzker prizewinners – Álvaro Siza Vieira and Eduardo Souto de Moura (both of whom have worked principally outside Portugal). Contemporary Portugal has some wonderful buildings – both public and domestic, including Porto's Casa da Música and Vodafone building, Lisbon's Calouste Gulbenkian Foundation, Expo 98 pavilion (by Álvaro Siza Vieira) and the Estação do Oriente. In the Alentejo, noteworthy buildings include the **Centro de Artes** in Sines (page 142) and the **Lar de Idosos** in Alcácer do Sal (page 136). These buildings were finalists in the Mies van der Rohe international architecture awards in 2007 and 2013 respectively.

## FINE ART
### From the Palaeolithic to the Golden Age
Some of the world's oldest paintings are Portuguese, preserved in the Foz valley in northern Portugal, and in the Escoural caves (near Montemor-o-Novo) and shelf caves (near Arronches) in the Alentejo. All show a mix of figurative and abstract art, and date from the middle Palaeolithic period. But little remains from Portugal's Roman, Visigoth and Moorish periods, and the story of art in the country thus begins in earnest with the reign of Dom Manuel I, when painting and sculpture were either religious or devoted to the aristocracy, as formal portraiture or posthumous monuments.

Unlike Spain, Portugal has no great early Renaissance painters. This is because art in Portugal was rarely an individual pursuit, and by and large – even for outstanding works – we don't know who painted what. Early Renaissance painting in Portugal was predominantly religious and was conceived as part of the whole decoration of a church. What was important was stylistic unity, rather than individual brilliance or innovation. This was a collective art, with works produced not by individuals but in a collaborative partnership (*parceiro*) by studios (*oficinas*). One artist would be responsible for the overall composition, another the skin tone, another the draperies. Works were not attributed to an overall master (although studios were generally run by a senior artist). Nor were they signed, dated or documented. The naming of individual works by an artist or studio is seldom better than an educated guess, and were determined according to a style thought to have been developed by a senior artist known to have been running a studio at that time, such as Jorge Afonso and Francisco Henriques (examples of whose work are in Évora Museum) around Lisbon and Gaspar Vaz and Vasco Fernandes around Coimbra and Viseu. Yet the paintings ascribed to these artists may not even have been painted by them.

In the Alentejo the situation was somewhat different. The famous panels of the high altar in the cathedral in Évora were painted by a group of unknown Portuguese artists probably trained in Bruges (you can see them in Évora Museum). But while we have no real idea of who they were or who ran their studio we do know the name of the Golden Age artist who followed them and who was influenced by their style – the Flemish-born Portuguese **Frei Carlos**. As Carlos was a monk (residing in the Hieronymite Espinheiro Convent in Évora – now an upmarket hotel, page 67) he worked as an individual and not as part of a studio. And his work, which combines the poise, clarity and tranquillity of the best Flemish religious art, met with great success in Évora. Sadly, but for a few paintings in Évora Museum (pages 73–4), little of Frei Carlos's work remains in the city today. Most of his pieces, including the main and lateral altars of Convento do Espinheiro and the Aparição de Cristo a Nossa Senhora (Apparition of Christ to Our Lady), are in the Museu Nacional de Arte Antiga in Lisbon.

The 16th century saw a florescence of sculpture in Portugal, spearheaded by the Frenchman **Nicolau Chanterene**, who became a master contractor at the Hieronymite (Jerónimos) Monastery in Belém, Lisbon in 1517. Chanterene was responsible for much of the figurative carving on the building, including effigies of Dom Manuel I and Dona Maria of Aragón. In later life he worked extensively in Évora too, where he developed a Mannerist style, as can be seen from the splayed perspective on his Tomb of Bishop Alonso (in Évora Museum).

**Mannerism** Mannerist painting anticipated expressionism, in that figures showed exaggerated expressions or postures, were caught in a moment of compositional tension, or were literally elongated by emotion (as in the work of Michelangelo or El Greco). The first artists to experiment with the style in Portugal were a triumvirate of friends and relatives from the Lisbon school of Jorge Afonso – Gregório Lopes, Cristóvão de Figueiredo and Garcia Fernandes.

**Gregório Lopes** never signed (and only once dated) his work. But he did include a ladybird insignia in his paintings, from which they were later identified. Most of his paintings decorated churches in Setúbal, Tomar and Lisbon. His masterpiece, the *Juizo Final* (*Last Judgement*), now in the Museu Nacional de Arte Antiga in Lisbon, anticipates Tintoretto and El Greco.

**Cristóvão de Figueiredo** was sworn in as the official Examiner of Paintings in 1515 and worked principally in Coimbra. He worked in partnership with both Lopes and Fernandes and is best known for his *Deposição no Túmulo* (*Entombment of Christ*) and *Trânsito da Virgem* (*Assumption of the Virgin*, in the Museu Nacional de Arte Antiga in Lisbon). Both have high emotional intensity, with ascetic, drawn faces and elements of *chiaroscuro* – the dramatic offsetting of dark and light which would be perfected by Zurbaran and Caravaggio.

**Garcia Fernandes** was the only one of the three painters to work in the Alentejo – in Montemor and Évora. Pieces by him survive in Évora's Igreja de São Francisco (pages 78–9).

Art in Portugal declined under the boy-king Sebastião and his uncle Cardinal Henrique and the Inquisition, and then disappeared altogether under the Spanish, when Portuguese painters chose to work abroad. It would pick up only when Portugal found wealth again under João V.

Linking the later Mannerists and Baroque art in Portugal are two painters indebted to the great tenebrist chiaroscuro painters of Spain (and in particular to Zurbarán), Josefa de Óbidos and Bento Coelho.

**Josefa de Óbidos** is one of the few (recognised) great women artists of the Renaissance. She was probably born in Seville to a Portuguese father, the painter Baltasar Gomes Figueira, and a Spanish mother, Catarina de Ayala y Cabrera, who was almost certainly the sister of a pupil of Zurbarán. Josefa learnt her art with her father, while painting in churches in Óbidos, and was stylistically influenced by him, by Zurbarán and by Rubens, whose work she copied as a child. Her work comprises mostly still lifes and religious scenes. Intricately planned and composed, they are characterised by intense local colour, fine detail, strong tenebrist use of light and shade, and sculptural values. One of her best works, *Supper of the Holy Family*, now in the Évora Museum, is a loving, intimate and deeply feminine portrait of Jesus, Joseph and Mary breaking bread together. The painting is one of a series that celebrates the life of Jesus and his parents in ordinary, everyday surrounds, for instance in a carpenter's shop, or resting together on the Flight into Egypt. Other paintings of the infant Jesus and Mary celebrate motherhood, showing Our Lady caressing the Christ child or the two of them sharing intimate moments. And as a body of work they are unique in Baroque art in depicting the Holy Family as a family, and Christ and his mother with such frank and tender intimacy.

Stylistically **Bento Coelho** was strongly influenced by Josefa, but he is her inferior. His bold use of colour, verve and intensity led to him becoming royal painter in 1687.

## The Baroque

Portuguese Baroque began with portraiture and court art in the reign of João V – after gold had been discovered and the royal coffers filled there was money once more to spend. João needed paintings to decorate his magnificent Mafra palace and to document his lavish life, so he called foreign artists to Portugal and sent promising Portuguese to hone their skills in Italy.

Frenchman **Pierre Quillard** arrived in Portugal in 1726 as royal artist, and with his etchings of royal parties – depicting fireworks and dances and his portraits of aristocrats dressed in robes and wigs and appearing in palatial surrounds – he introduced the French Rococo into Portugal. He was succeeded by **Francisco Vieira de Matos**, who had studied in Rome and whose use of colour was strongly influenced by Poussin, though his paintings are stiff and formal in comparison to those of the great Frenchman.

Other painters of the Baroque followed them and included **Francisco Vieira Portuense**, who studied in London with Bartolozzi, and **Pedro Alexandrino de Carvalho** – a Portuguese Tiepolo who specialised in *trompe l'œil* church ceiling paintings lively with angels and vivid with moving clouds. His *Última Ceia* (*Last Supper*) is in the Igreja de Santa Maria da Feira in Beja.

But these artists were a prelude to the great Portuguese master **Domingos António de Sequeira**, the Goya of Portugal. Sequeira was born the son of a fisherman but he became a gold medalist in Paris, beating Géricault, Delacroix, Lawrence and Gérard in a competition. His work is vast and varied, comprising portraits, historical allegories and religious paintings of great grandeur. Sequeira worked as a craftsman too, designing the silver service set that was presented by the Portuguese nation to Wellington after the Napoleonic wars. With paintings like the agonising monochrome *Morte de Camões* (showing the writer dying by candlelight) he challenged the contemporaneous vogue for strong colour, showed that he was a great master of chiaroscuro and anticipated modernism. His portraiture combines mastery of light and movement. But the great religious cartoons of his final years are his masterpieces. On seeing them, art critic Martin Soria wrote that 'a mood of transfiguration arises which touches on the supernatural.'

Twentieth-century Portugal saw the emergence of two internationally important female artists. The abstractionist **Maria Helena Vieira da Silva**'s (1908–1992) dense, abstract expressionist pieces like *The Corridor* (1950; currently in the Tate in London) resemble mazes and mix a Kafakaesque dystopian modernism with a sense of transcendentalism. London-based **Dame Paula Rego** (1935–) was an exhibiting member of the London Group together with David Hockney, and in 1990 became the first ever artist-in-residence at the British National Gallery. Her work, which is illustrative and imbued with a strong sense of narrative, explores the image of the feminine in the contemporary West, in opposition to the idealised or sexualised depictions produced by male artists throughout the history of art, as well as in contemporary broadcast and print media and advertising.

**LITERATURE** The Portuguese are a bookish people. And they have produced some fine writers – born of the country's turbulent domestic history, its adventures overseas, the gain and loss of glory and the mix of cultures and nations which have shaped Portugal and the Portuguese. Before Portugal was Portugal, al-Andalus had produced two of the greatest writers in Arabic – Averrões and Ibn Arabi – and two of the greatest in Hebrew – Maimonides and Moses de León. The troubadours and court of Asturias inspired early Portuguese lyric and comic poetry in the *cantigas d'amor* (love songs) and *cantigas d'escario e maldizer* (songs of scorn and insult), written by King Dom Dinis, among others.

But it was the Reconquest and the subsequent Golden Age of the Portuguese Discoveries that saw the birth of a national literature. This began in the 15th century with the histories of **Fernão Lopes**, *Crónicas de 5 reis de Portugal* (*Chronicles of Five Kings of Portugal*), the *Crónica dos sete primeiros reis de Portugal* (*Chronicle of the First Seven Kings of Portugal*) and the *Cancioneiro geral* (*General Songbook*), a compilation of national poetry by the Évora-born **Garcia de Resende**. Prosperity under Dom Manuel saw **Gil Vicente** present myriad elegant comedies and powerful autos (religious plays) at court. His rival **Francisco Sá de Miranda** rooted his dramas in the classical forms of Sophocles and Euripides. His great tragedy *A Castro* (the tragedy of Ines de Castro) immortalised King Pedro I and his Spanish mistress with all the sweet agony of Tristan and Isolde. It seemed as though the two great dramatists were heralding the birth of a national Portuguese drama. But in 1536 the Inquisition declared theatre a gross and unholy form of entertainment, thus killing the art.

**Luís de Camões** had more success as a poet. Deeply rooted in classicism and formal technique, he produced hundreds of sonnets, odes, elegies and songs, and in 1572 a Neo-classical epic, in the tradition of the *Aeneid* of Virgil. *Os Lusíadas* (*The Lusiads*), based on Vasco da Gama's first voyage to India, proclaimed Portugal the inheritor of the glory of Greece and Rome. Other writers chronicled the actual Portuguese voyages. In the *História da Vida do Padre Francisco Xavier* (*Life of Father Francis Xavier*) **João de Lucena** told of the Jesuit's journeys in Japan and India. And the anonymously written Descobrimento da Florida (Discovery of Florida) and *Tratado Descritivo do Brasil em 1587* (*Descriptive Treatise on Brazil in 1587*) by **Gabriel Soares de Sousa** described the new Portuguese colonies in the Americas. **Fernão Mendes Pinto**'s *Pereginação* (*The Travels of Mendes Pinto*) is arguably Portugal's first novel, mixing real travel accounts with picaresque romps on the high seas.

**Bernardim Ribeiro** developed the Portuguese novel with in *Hystoria de Menina e Moça*, a pseudo autobiography mixing love, melancholy and chivalry which adopted themes and emotions previously found only in poetry and was an influence on Cervantes.

The greatest writer of the Portuguese Baroque period was the Afro-Portuguese Jesuit **António Vieira**. His sermons castigating the Portuguese of Belém and São Luís in Brazil for their cruel and immoral enslavement of the indigenous Brazilians are masterpieces of oratorical writing and mark some of the earliest European campaigning literature. As a prose stylist his impact on the Portuguese language is as great as that of Camões and Saramago. Vieira was hated by the Portuguese colonial establishment and the Dominicans of the Inquisition, but favour at court protected him until the death of his friend Dom João IV, after which he was tried and imprisoned. His subsequent report on the Inquisition was so scathing that it prompted the Pope to ban any *autos-da-fé* for seven years, inspiring even more hatred from the Dominicans, who framed him for complicity in a murder. He was banned from preaching and died alone in Brazil in 1674. Vieira was not the only writer crushed by the Inquisition. The Dominicans executed **António José da Silva**, a Jewish writer forced to become a New Christian, who had attempted to revive theatre. His satirical plays met with double disapproval, both for their form and their content.

The first great post-Inquisition writer was the romantic visionary poet **Almeida Garrett**, who rediscovered Gil Vicente and drama for the Portuguese with a series of historical Romantic plays which included *Um auto de Gil Vicente* (*An Auto by Gil Vicente*), *O Alfageme de Santarém* (*The Swordsmith of Santarém*), and *Frei Luís de Sousa* (*Brother Luís de Sousa*). His counterpart in prose was **Alexandre Herculano**, who had fallen in love with the historical romances of Walter Scott while exiled in England and who wrote a series of Scottian Portuguese Romantic novels which included *Lendas e Narrativas* (*Legends and Narratives*). Herculano was succeeded by **Camilo Castelo Branco**, whose 600 or so books comprise everything from Gothic fantasies to social realism, and **José Maria de Eça de Queirós**, the Zola of Portugal – a master of the realist novel whose most enduring work is *Os Maias* (*The Maias*), a portrait of three generations of a Portuguese family.

The 20th century produced Portugal's two greatest writers since Camões. **Fernando Pessoa**, who was born in Lisbon and schooled in South Africa, was 50 years ahead of his time, anticipating post-modernism while writing contemporaneously with modernists like Eliot. He wrote principally in heteronyms – literary personas, each with their own pseudo-biography and style: Alberto Caeiro was an untutored country romantic who wrote in free verse, Álvaro de Campos a London-based engineer with a predilection for transcendentalism and the futurists, Bernardo Soares the writer of a fictional literary journal, and perhaps most famously Ricardo Reis, a doctor with a love of the classics and in particular Homer. In his examination of personal identity and insistence that identity was understandable only in its own self-referential narrative, Pessoa anticipated post-modernism. Ignored in his lifetime, the poet is gradually gaining an international reputation. In 1994 the critic Harold Bloom selected him as one of just 26 writers responsible for establishing 'the Western Canon' of great literature.

Also included in the canon is **José Saramago**, who was a great admirer of Pessoa. Saramago was born into a family of landless peasants, whose lives he immortalised in one of his early novels, *Levantado do Chão* (*Raised from the Ground*). Set in the Alentejo, the story exposes the suffering under servitude which had been the lot of his parents and generations of Portuguese. This set the tone for his later work, which is characterised by a plea for empathy and a preoccupation with alienation from each other and from the realities of our social and political condition. 'We are always more or less blind, particularly for what is essential,' he said in an interview in 2008, two years before his death. *Levantado do Chão* introduced Saramago's distinct way of narrating through a polyphony of voices and from multiple standpoints in time and place. In later novels like *O Ano da Morte de Ricardo Reis* (*The Year of the Death of Ricardo Reis*) he plays with literary form, with sentences free of punctuation in many of his later works and protagonists referred to by their behavioural characteristics rather than proper names (echoing Pessoa's explorations of the nature of identity). Saramago was awarded the Nobel Prize for literature in 1998.

**CINEMA** Portuguese cinema betrays a strong French and Spanish influence. The giant of Portuguese cinema is Manoel de Oliveira, who made his first film in 1927 and continued producing roughly one a year until 2014, the year before he died at he age of 106. He has won numerous awards including two Career Golden Lions, in 1985 and 2004, and an Honorary Golden Palm for his lifetime achievements in 2008. His best-known work is probably *Past and Present*, a social satire directed in 1971, which earned him international respect. He is the only filmmaker whose active career spanned everything from the silent era to the digital age.

Other key directors include Fernando Lopes, Paulo Rocha, António da Cunha Telles and António de Macedo (whose 1973 film *The Vows* was in competition for the Grand Prix at the Cannes Film Festival), who were part of the Novo Cinema movement of the 1960s and early 1970s, which was heavily influenced by Italian Neo-Realism and the French Nouvelle Vague.

Unlike its Iberian neighbour, Portugal does not dub international films.

## MUSIC
**Folk and contemporary music** Little demonstrates the difference between the Spanish and Portuguese temperaments quite so powerfully as the music. Spanish music is fired by pain and passion – it's demonstrative, extrovert – perhaps most obviously in the agonised cries, the clacking castanets and the flurry of rapid *rasgueado* guitar strums and strikes which characterise flamenco. Portuguese guitars are plucked slowly, lyrically and mournfully, and they are accompanied by voices of soaring sweetness and operatic depth. Nowhere is this more apparent than in the national musical style of *fado*, which in English means fate. *Fados* are a musical mix of melodramatic mournfulness and the sweet sorrow of absence known in Portuguese as *saudade*. When he appropriated the *fado* (and its greatest historical proponent, **Amália Rodrigues**) as a tool of cultural indoctrination Salazar almost killed the musical style. But since the end of the dictatorship it has seen a return to popularity championed by a series of mesmerising young *fadistas*, almost all of them women. They include **Cristina Branco**, whose greatest song is perhaps Ai Vida, **Ana Moura** and the Grammy-winning **Mariza**, whose deep, sonorous voice has earned her record sales in excess of a million copies worldwide.

*Fado* is most associated with the cities of Lisbon and Coimbra, but Portugal as a whole has a rich traditional heritage of folk music which include styles like Cante Alentejano (see box, page 158), Celtic bagpipe *danças* (dances) and *ranchos folclóricos* – collective dances. Under the Estado Novo, traditional folk was fused with western styles to produce a protest music called *canto livre* (free singing) sung by artists like **Zeca Afonso**. After the collapse of the dictatorship folk was reinvented by a series of innovative Portuguese artists who drew on *fado*, electronic music, classical, madrigal and folk to create a contemporary, purely Portuguese popular music. The most internationally successful of these innovators are **Madredeus**, whose best album is *O Paraíso*, filled with gorgeous lilting melodies on pizzicato strings, organ and plucked classical guitars. Tracks like 'O Sonho' ('The Dream') and 'A Andorinha Da Primavera' ('The Spring Swallow') are imbued with the sweet sadness of *saudade*, yet are as bright and warm as the Lisbon summer during which the album was recorded. After leaving Madredeus, keyboard player **Rodrigo Leão** carved a career as a kind of Portuguese Brian Eno, collaborating with artists like Portishead's Beth Gibbons and Neil Hannon of the Divine Comedy on a series of thoughtful, reflective albums which mix orchestral pieces with trip-hop and compositions inspired by film music. With a voice which mixes Edith Piaf and Maria Callas, **Dulce Pontes** is Portugal's greatest diva. She found fame with her operatic *Canção do Mar* and followed it with a string of albums imbued with powerful emotion and played by illustrious session musicians who include the likes of American jazz saxophonist Wayne Shorter and Ennio Morricone.

Concurrent with the renaissance of folk-inspired popular music in Portugal was a rise in Afro-Portuguese styles, spearheaded by a group of talented young artists, many of them born of parents from Cape Verde and Angola. The most internationally successful is **Sara Tavares**, whose mix of inventive song-writing, beautiful wistful singing and percussive, lilting guitar playing was best showcased on albums like *Xinti* and *Balancê*. Modern Portugal is replete with talented artists who have one foot in Lisbon or Porto and another in West Africa. They include singer-songwriters **Waldemar Bastos**, **Tito Paris** and **Lura**, many of whom play regularly at Clube B.Leza in Lisbon (Facebook: B.Leza Associação).

**Classical music** Portuguese classical music is little known outside the country. Scarlatti taught in the court of Dom João V. The Baroque saw composers like **João Domingos Bomtempo** produce religious music, including Bomtempo's nationally celebrated Requiem Mass. Romantic composer **José Vianna da Motta** studied with Liszt and wrote a patriotic symphony based on Camões' *Os Lusíadas*, **Sinfonia em Lá Maior 'À Pátria', Opus 13** (1894), in four movements, which includes a long and lyrical Adagio. Inspired by Vaughan Williams, **Luís de Freitos Branco** drew on folk music from the Alentejo and images of the region's countryside to inspire his two *Suites Alentejanas* – Alentejo Suites. He also wrote a symphony inspired by William Beckford's *Vathek* – *Vathek, poema sinfónico (a partir de Beckford)*.

Portugal's leading mid-20th century composers were **Fernando Lopes Graça** (who produced a series of beautiful works which included a number of concertos and his very Portuguese *Historia Tragico-Maritima* (*Tragic Sea Story*) for baritone choir and orchestra) and **Joly Braga Santos**, a pupil of Luís de Freitos Branco. Santos's Fourth Symphony was described by David Hurwitz of *Classics Today* as having 'a finale whose Allegro contains 10 of the most purely exhilarating minutes of orchestral writing that you will ever hear.' In later years Braga Santos turned to the avant-garde.

**ALENTEJO ONLINE**

For additional online content, articles, photos and more on Alentejo, why not visit www.bradtguides.com/alentejo.

# 2

# Practical Information

## WHEN TO VISIT

The Alentejo is best visited in spring, late summer and early autumn when temperature is in the 20s and low 30s and visitor numbers are at their lowest. Spring sees the meadows burst into multi-coloured bloom, storks nesting on telegraph poles and butterflies on the wing. In autumn the vines and olive trees are heavy with fruit, the leaves are beginning to turn golden brown and wispy mist floats over the Serra de São Mamede mountains. Wildlife lovers – especially birdwatchers – should also consider winter, when huge flocks of migrating birds arrive on the coast and around the lakes.

## HIGHLIGHTS

**ÉVORA** Stroll through Évora's streets and alleys, stopping for creamy coffees and souvenir browses, and wonder at the monuments to its turbulent history – its ruined Roman temple and Moorish walls, its remnant palaces, its fortified cathedral and its magnificent small museum. Grit your teeth at the grisly skulls and skeletons in the Chapel of Bones and remember the gruesome side of Iberian Christianity, which saw the viciousness of the Inquisition. See pages 61–80.

**ELVAS** Get lost in the maze of Moorish streets around Elvas castle, ducking under washing lines that span the narrow ways, chancing on magnificent marble-filled churches, forgotten chapels and sweeping views over the plains to Spain. See pages 85–95.

**MARVÃO** Walk the medieval walls of the old Islamic fort town of Marvão, and clamber up the castle to see the backs of eagles as they soar on the thermals over the flatlands below. See pages 127–30.

**CASTELO DE VIDE** Wander the winding cobbles of Castelo de Vide, past whitewashed houses pinked with bougainvillea, and discover the old Jewish quarter and synagogue built when more than 20% of Portuguese were Sephardim. See pages 123–7.

**THE NATURAL PARKS** Hike the craggy hills of the Serra de São Mamede (pages 120–2) and Vale do Guadiana (pages 170–3) natural parks, home to rare plants and among the most diverse range of birds and mammals in southern Europe, including the critically endangered Iberian lynx.

**VILA VIÇOSA** See the lavish Braganza palace where the English queen who brought tea and marmalade to the nation was born. See pages 108–111.

**GRÂNDOLA** Surf or spread your towel on the empty beaches that stretch north and south from Grândola town. See page 140.

**ALENTEJO COAST** Walk the Rota Vicentina coastal trail along deserted strands, over rugged cliffs and running through cork oak woods and flower-filled meadows. See box, pages 146–7.

**MÉRTOLA** Explore the Alentejo's Islamic past in the spectacular hill town, perched on a cliff above a bend in the Guadiana River in the heart of a natural park. See pages 175–8.

**ALMENDRES CROMLECH** See a stone circle far older than Stonehenge, imbued with a sense of the sacred and set in pretty olive woodlands just outside Évora. See pages 80–1.

**MONSARAZ** Stay in this bone-white and perfectly preserved medieval fort town on a rocky crag near the Spanish border, with jaw-dropping views over the Alqueva lake and olive groves of the Alentejo plain. See pages 113–16.

**BEJA** Put your feet up with a glass of fine Alentejo wine and watch the sun sink over the countryside at one of the Baixo Alentejo's *adega* wine hotels. See pages 153–61.

**EVORAMONTE** Stay in Baroque luxury at the Hotel Convento de São Paulo, a former Pauline Convent with a beautiful chapel covered in *azulejos* and palatial living quarters, and spend your days hiking in the countryside and visiting the dramatic castles at Evoramonte and Redondo. See page 101.

**THE ALENTEJO COUNTRYSIDE** Don't miss staying with a family in a traditional *fazenda* farmhouse, set in meadows grazed by Lusitanian horses or in a tiny beachside village. I recommend many in this book.

## SUGGESTED ITINERARIES

The Alentejo is small and it takes under two hours to get anywhere from anywhere, so it's possible to fit a great deal into a short trip. The problem is where to base yourself. There's such a choice of hotels – in beautiful palaces and converted monasteries, in castles and family homes, on vineyard estates and the farms of fallen landed gentry – that it would be a shame to choose just one location. I've tried to theme the itineraries below – grouping by location and by pursuit. They are intended for inspiration only; feel free to mix and match.

**LONG WEEKEND** Base yourself at the Espinheiro or Loios Convents in Évora. Eat at A Cartuxa and Fialho, take a day to explore Évora and a day to see the stone circles of Almendres and the castle at Evoramonte, with lunch at the Hotel Convento de São Paulo. Return to Lisbon airport armed with bottles of fine Alentejo wine bought from Louro or Ervideira.

**JUST A WEEK** Take the long drive to Castelo de Vide and stay there for two days, visiting Marvão, the Roman ruins of Ammaia and the megaliths. Dine in the Casa do Parque. Drive south to Elvas and base yourself in that city, Borba or Vila Viçosa and visit the sights in the region. Dine at A Cadeia in Estremoz and Narcissus Fernandesii in Vila Viçosa. Spend a night in Évora and finish up with a day or two in Vila Nova de Milfontes.

**THE ALENTEJO LOOP** Take in the whole Alentejo. Begin in the north, basing yourself in Castelo de Vide or Marvão. Visit the Roman ruins of Ammaia and the megaliths, the cave paintings and Reynolds winery near Arronches (taking lunch at the Santo António Hotel). Drive south to Elvas and stay in that city, Borba or Vila Viçosa and visit the sights in the region. Dine at A Cadeia in Estremoz and Narcissus Fernandesii in Vila Viçosa. Then overnight in Juromenha, visiting the atmospheric ruined fort and lake before heading south to see Monsaraz and the wine regions nearby. Then visit the southern Alentejo, arriving in Beja either via Moura or via Viana do Alentejo. Spend a night or two in a countryside hotel near Beja or Serpa, before driving south to Mértola and the Vale do Guadiana Natural Park. Spend the night there before finishing off with a few days on the beach at Vila Nova de Milfontes or around Grândola.

**WINE AND DINE** Begin in Évora with a stay in Cartuxa, the Convento dos Espinheiros or the L'and Vineyards Resort in Montemor-o-Novo, which has the only Michelin-starred restaurant in the Alentejo. Drive to the Torre da Palma Wine Hotel in Monforte and use it as a base to visit Elvas, Marvão and the Herdade Reynolds and Dom Borba wineries. Dine at Herdade das Servas in Estremoz and Narcissus Fernandesii. Continue south to Monsaraz and stay or dine in the Horta da Moura, enjoying Henrique Moura's fine food and visiting the Herdade do Esporão winery. Finish with a night or so in the Herdade do Vau, one of the finest wine hotels in the Alentejo, near Beja.

**BACK TO NATURE** Contacting local nature-based tour operators along the way, begin in Alcácer do Sal with a visit to the Sado estuary to see waterfowl and dolphins. Move on to the Herdade Barradas da Serra and visit the meadows and salt lakes around the Lago Santo Andre, which are rich in bird and butterfly life. Then drive inland for a few days at the Herdade Monte da Apariça, one of the best wildlife hotels in Iberia near Guadiana Natural Park and the Castro Verde Special Protection Area. Finish with a few days in Marvão, hiking in the hills of the Serra de São Mamede and spotting vultures and eagles.

**TAKE THE KIDS** Stay in the Herdade Barradas da Serra near Grândola for horse-riding, walks and plenty of time on the beach. Move on to Vila Nova de Milfontes for some of the best rock pools and long strands of sand in Portugal and be sure to seek out the dramatic shoreline shipwreck. Finish with a few days at Herdade Monte da Apariça, watching for wildlife.

**CASTLES AND PALACES** Stay in the pousada in Estremoz, housed in Dom Dinis's magnificent palace, and dine at A Cadeia restaurant, set in the old castle dungeons. Use the pousada as a base to visit the Bragança palace in Vila Viçosa and the fortified World Heritage city of Elvas. Drive north to stay in the Mosteiro de Santa Maria de Flor da Rosa – a haunted fortified monastery near Marvão. Visit the castles at Crato, Marvão and Castelo de Vide before driving south to Monsaraz, stopping off at Alandroal and Juromenha along the way. Spend a night in Monsaraz before driving south to see the castles at Moura and Beja. Stay a day or two in the Pousada de Alvito – the palace of the Alvito barons – before finishing at the Pousada dos Loios convent hotel in Évora, next to the palace of the Dukes of Cadaval.

**ON THE BEACH** Begin in Grândola and spend a few days walking the wild and empty beaches and watching for wildlife in the Sado estuary. Continue to Vila Nova de Milfontes for wind-surfing, surfing or kayaking on the Mira River. Spend a day or even more walking a section of the Rota Vicentina, south from Porto Côvo or around Cabo Sardão.

**ART AND ARCHITECTURE** Begin in Évora, staying in the Convento do Espinheiro – once the home of the city's greatest painter, Frei Carlos. Visit the museum to see the paintings of Josefa de Obidos, the Évora Flemish masters and Frei Carlos, and the sculptures of Nicolau Chanterene, before touring the churches. Don't miss the chapels and Baroque organ in Évora Cathedral and the paintings by Garcia Fernandes in the church of São Francisco. Use Évora as a base to visit the Manueline castle of Evoramonte and the towns of Alvito and Viana do Alentejo (with their fine Manueline buildings) before basing yourself in the pousada of Estremoz. Visit the church of Nossa Senhora de Assunção in Elvas and the palace museum in Vila Viçosa. Then drive south to Beja. Use the city as a base to see Mértola (visiting the Moorish church and the Islamic museum) and Beja's spectacular museum.

## TOURIST INFORMATION

The Alentejo has an excellent tourism infrastructure with tourist offices or posts in even the smallest towns. All are included in the main body of the book. The offices are well-signposted – look for 'turismo' with an 'i' symbol. Staff generally speak good English and offices offer maps of the locations, pamphlets with historical and architectural information and help with booking hotels.

For online resources look at www.visitalentejo.pt, the state tourism portal, which has a wealth of information on what to see and do, accommodation, restaurants, routes and tour operators.

## TOUR OPERATORS

### GENERAL OPERATORS
### UK
**Sunvil** See ads, inside back cover, 2nd colour section & page 60. \0208 758 4722; www.sunvil.co.uk. The best international operator with bespoke trips as standalone holidays or as part of a longer Alentejo or Portugal holiday. Very well thought out & thoroughly researched routes.

### USA and Canada
**Active Gourmet Holidays** \+ 1 203 732 0771; www.activegourmetholidays.com. Cooking & cycling tours in the Alentejo, with visits to adegas.
**Classic Vacations** \1 800 221 3949; www. classicvacations.com. Small group tours throughout Portugal & the Alentejo, including Évora & Arraiolos.
**Sceptre Tours** \1 800 221 0924; www. sceptretours.com. Selected upmarket packages in Portugal & bespoke trips to the Alentejo.

**Sunvil** See ads, inside back cover, 2nd colour section & page 60. Also offers to travellers from North America.

### Portugal
**CITUR** www.citur.pt. All manner of trips throughout Portugal, including nature & family holidays including walks & wildlife trips on & around the Rota Vicentina.
**Eco Tours Portugal** \+351 220 108096; www. ecotoursportugal.com. Group & private tours around the Alentejo with hiking, biking & nature options & visits to gardens.
**Portugal Nature Trails** www.portugalnaturetrails. com. Walking, hiking, cycling & light adventure throughout Portugal & guided or self-guided walks on the Rota Vicentina as part of a group or bespoke.
**Raides Vicentinos** \+351 219 432693; www. ridingholidaysinportugal.com. Horseback riding on multi-day trips or excursions throughout the Alentejo.

For trip reports and first-hand guides to the area's birdlife, see www.cloudbirders.com, http://fatbirder.com, www.birds.pt, http://birdingpal.org and www.wheretowatchbirdsandotherwildlifeintheworld.co.uk

**Tur Aventur** ☎+351 266 743134; www.portugalbestcycling.com. Active holidays around the Alentejo – cycling, kayaking, walking, visits to castles & wineries.

**Vicentina Travels** www.vicentinatravel.com. Rota Vicentina walks, road & mountain biking & adventure & active trips. The company is an Alentejo specialist & is based in the region. Guided tours & bespoke guided trips.

## Spain

**Tee Travel** ☎+34 986 565026; www.tee-travel.com. A Spanish-based operator offering Rota Vicentina walks, gastronomy & wine trips, & light adventure in Iberia.

### SPECIALIST TOUR OPERATORS

**Cellar Tours** ☎+34 91 521 3939; www.cellartours.com. An excellent wine tourism operator based in Spain who can get you into hard-to-visit boutique wineries such as Tapada dos Coelheiros & Herdade do Mouchão.

**Portugal Walks** ☎+351 965 753033; www.portugalwalks.com. Guided walks throughout Portugal, including in the Alto Alentejo. On its Alentejo trip, this company really gets into the back lands, including the Serra de São Mamede

National Park (see pages 120–2), & the stunning countryside around Monsaraz.

**Run Portugal** www.runportugal.com. Scheduled runs in beautiful areas throughout the Alentejo.

**Walking Holiday** www.walkingholidayinfo.co.uk. An online directory of local tour operators who offer guided walks throughout Portugal, including the Costa Vicentina & the Serra de São Mamede.

### BIRDWATCHING AND NATURE TOURS

**Avian Adventures** www.avianadventures.co.uk. Small group tours throughout Iberia with options for wildlife photographers & excellent tour leaders.

**Birding in Portugal** ☎+351 283 933065; www.birdinginportugal.com. Birding trips & holidays based in a lovely lakeside lodge in the remote Alentejo near Santa Clara a Velha.

**Visit Portugal Birdwatching** www.visitportugalbirdwatching.com. Bespoke birdwatching & wildlife photography tours around the Alentejo.

### CAR AND MOTORBIKE RENTAL

All the major European rental companies operate in Portugal.

**LX Rent** http://www.lxrent.pt. Motorbike, scooter & car rental throughout Portugal.

# RED TAPE

Citizens from EU countries, the USA, Canada, Australia, New Zealand, Mexico, Israel, South Korea, Argentina and Brazil do not require visas to enter Portugal. Nationals of Australia, Canada and the USA can stay for up to 90 days without a visa. EU nationals can stay for an unlimited period, but must register with the local authorities after three months.

# GETTING THERE AND AWAY

The Alentejo is easy to reach. Lisbon is served by regular direct international flights with **TAP** (*see ad, 1st colour section; www.flytap.com*) from destinations in North and South America, Asia and European capitals. Australasians will need to change planes in London or another European capital. There are flights into Faro from UK, German and Irish airports, and Badajoz in Spain (which is just 15km from Elvas) has connections to other destinations in Spain.

**Lisbon Airport** has car rental offices on the ground floor of Arrivals. Buses 208 and 705 connect the airport to the Estação Oriente railway station for trains to Évora and Beja (see pages 45, 63 and 154 for specifics on train times and prices).

**Badajoz Airport** has connections only with other cities in Spain and is linked to Évora and Elvas (see page 89) by regular buses.

There are car rental booths in **Faro Airport** but no buses from the airport to the Alentejo. You will need to take a taxi to Faro bus station (*rodoviária*), from where there are onward connections to cities in the Alentejo.

For further specific information on bus and train times and connections see www.cp.pt (trains), www.rede-expressos.pt (buses) and local transport entries for the relevant town in the main chapters of this guide.

## HEALTH

There are no serious health issues to worry about, and no endemic diseases. Insect bites are perhaps the biggest risk in rural areas so it is worth taking an insect repellent. It is wise to be up to date with the standard UK vaccinations including diphtheria, tetanus and polio which comes as an all-in-one vaccination (Revaxis), which lasts for ten years.

If you do have an accident or fall ill, the level of healthcare is on a par with much of the rest of Europe. Residents of EU countries including the UK and Ireland should obtain a **European Health Insurance Card** (EHIC) before travelling, as this covers the costs of any standard medical treatment you may require. Everyone, including holders of an EHIC, should also take out travel insurance that includes medical costs, as the EHIC doesn't cover all eventualities, such as repatriation to your home country following an accident. This is available in the UK by calling ☏ 0845 606 2030, or online at www.ehic.org.uk.

**EMERGENCY CARE**  In a medical emergency, dial ☏ 112 to call for an ambulance. The major hospital in the region is the Hospital da Misericórdia in Évora (*Recolhimento Ramalho Barahona, Av Sanches de Miranda 30;* ☏ *266 760630; www.hmevora.pt*).

**TRAVEL CLINICS AND HEALTH INFORMATION**  A full list of current travel clinic websites worldwide is available at www.istm.org. For other journey preparation information, consult www.nathnac.org/ds/map_world.aspx (UK) or http://wwwnc.cdc.gov/travel/ (US). Information about various medications may be found on www.netdoctor.co.uk/travel. All advice found online should be used in conjunction with expert advice received prior to or during travel.

## SAFETY

Portugal is a safe country with low crime rates. Pickpocketing and theft from cars occur in the more heavily visited areas. Be especially vigilant on public transport at the airport and at the busy railway station in Lisbon. If you must leave items unattended in a car, then be sure to hide them in the boot. Hire cars and foreign-registered cars are often targeted by thieves.

If your passport is stolen, report it immediately to the local police. You will need the report for insurance purposes and to obtain a replacement travel document from the British Consulate.

## WOMEN TRAVELLERS

Portugal is a safe country for women travellers. Adopt the same common sense principles you would at home: avoid empty streets late at night and watch out for being followed; keep doors and windows closed and locked when you sleep; beware of accepting invitations from people you are not certain you can trust; and let people know of your whereabouts if you go hiking or on a trip.

## TRAVELLERS WITH DISABILITIES

Facilities for travellers with disabilities in Portugal are similar to those in the UK or USA. Lisbon and Faro airports have disabled toilets and can provide special wheelchair assistance by prior arrangement. Transport vehicles have specially reserved seats for disabled people, but few have wheelchair spaces. The Cartão de Deficiente – Caminhos do Ferro Portuguesas (CP Disability Rail Cards) can be obtained from CP ticket offices and are valid for two years. They entitle cardholders to a 25% discount on services run by the state railway operator CP. Forms to apply for a CP card for the disabled are available from ticket offices. The applicant will need to supply two passport-sized colour photos and a disability card valid within the EU.

UK Blue Badge drivers can use their permits in Portugal and while there are no roadside concessions, some car parks allow vehicles displaying a Blue Badge to park free of charge. Disabled spaces in car parks are marked with a wheelchair symbol. Avoid those that are also marked with a registration number. It is worth leaving a piece of paper next to your Blue Badge with the following translation printed out:

Cartão de estacionamento para pessoas com deficiência. Este cartão autoriza o portador a beneficiar das facilidades de estacionamento no Estado membro no qual o titular se encontre. Quando em utilização, o cartão deve ser colocado no interior do veículo, no seu vidro dianteiro, por forma a que fique visível. Modelo da Comunidade Europeia.

Some hotels and public buildings have disabled toilets and access ramps.

**ORGANISATIONS AND SOURCES OF INFORMATION** Disability Travel (*www.disabilitytravel.com*) is a comprehensive US site written by travellers in wheelchairs who have been researching disabled travel full-time since 1985. There are many tips and useful contacts (including lists of travel agents on request) and articles, including pieces on disabled travelling worldwide. The company also organises group tours. **Global Access News** (*www.globalaccessnews.com/index.htm*) provides general travel information, reviews and tips for disabled travellers. The **Society for Accessible Travel and Hospitality** (*www.sath.org*) provides some general information. **Enable Holidays** (*www.enableholidays.com*), **Disabled Holidays** (*www.disabledholidaydirectory.co.uk*), **Access Travel** (*www.access-travel.co.uk*) and **Disabled Access Holidays** (*www.disabledaccessholidays.com*) offer trips to Portugal.

## GAY AND LESBIAN TRAVELLERS

In southern Europe Portugal is perhaps the country most tolerant of gay and lesbian travellers. Legislation is some of the most tolerant in the world. Same-sex marriage was recognised in 2010 and there are wide-ranging anti-discrimination laws. **World Rainbow Hotels** (*www.worldrainbowhotels.com*) and **Purple Roofs** (*www.purpleroofs.com*) list gay- and lesbian-owned and friendly accommodation in Portugal and gay- and lesbian-friendly travel agents and tour operators.

## TRAVELLING WITH KIDS

Travel with children is straightforward in Portugal. Portugal is a very family-orientated country and kids are never expected to be seen but not heard. Even expensive restaurants provide children's seats and most have children's menus. Many hotels offer a discount family rate, don't charge for children under five and can provide an extra camp bed for a double room. Children under three generally travel for 10% on internal flights and for 70% until 12 years old. On tours children under six usually go free, and it may be possible to negotiate a discount rate. Bring Kwells or Stugeron from Europe or the US for motion sickness.

## WHAT TO TAKE

The Alentejo can be very hot in summer, with cooler evenings. Bring light (in colour and material) trousers, shorts, one long-sleeve shirt, skirts, sunglasses, sunhat, a shawl or light jacket for evenings and sandals/flip flops, smart-casual comfortable shoes and light goretex walking shoes or boots if you intend to trek. Thin cotton fabrics or a modern wicking artificial fabric are best. While the Portuguese are casual dressers, the better hotels expect smart casual wear for evening meals. Sun protection, antiseptic creams and pharmaceuticals are available easily and cheaply in the Alentejo's towns.

For spring and autumn bring a jumper and jacket, thicker trousers and a raincoat. In winter you will need a thicker jacket or coat and a warm hat and gloves if you intend to go into the mountains.

You will need a UK/US to European socket adapter.

## MONEY

Portugal uses the **euro**. There are seven different denominations of euro banknotes: €5, €10, €20, €50, €100, €200 and €500. The first series of notes is gradually being replaced by the Europa series, which started circulating in 2015. See page 2 for the exchange rate at the time of going to print.

**ATMs** are ubiquitous (be aware before you use them of charges incurred by your bank back home). Cash can be exchanged in banks and Casa de Cambio moneychangers. Travellers cheques are no longer widely accepted.

Portuguese **banks** are generally open from 08.30 to 15.00 Monday to Friday. Certain banks extend opening hours until 16.00 on Fridays and some open for a limited time on Saturday mornings. Portuguese banks are part of a national grouping of banks called Multibanco. Account holders may use a Multibanco debit card in ATMs across the country, and for buying most goods. These cards offer a huge range of banking services through ATMs. You can also use international bank cards in these machines.

To open a **bank account** in Portugal, residents of EU countries need an identity card or passport, a NIF number (available from the local finance office, or *finanças*), a residency card and proof of residence (eg: a utility bill).

## BUDGETING

The Alentejo is a little cheaper than most western European areas, including the Algarve to the south and Lisbon. If you book online, hotel prices in early spring, autumn and winter can be up to 50% cheaper than the summer high season prices.

Those on a tight budget can get by on €20–30 a day by staying in hostels, eating in cafes or supermarkets and using local buses. €60–80 will get you a room in a two-star hotel and meals in modest restaurants. €90–120 will get you more comfortable rooms in a homestay in the countryside or a modest town hotel, a simple lunch and dinner with wine, and a hire car. €120–200 will enable you to live well staying in *pousadas* and eating at the better restaurants.

## GETTING AROUND

**BUS** The Alentejo has an extensive intercity and local bus network. Intercity buses are run by **Rede Expressos** (*www.rede-expressos.pt*), whose site has timetable and price information in English. Local buses run on weekdays only, on an extensive network that covers even the smallest villages. Information is available from **Rodoviária do Alentejo** (*Avenida. Tulio Espanca, Terminal Rodoviário, Évora;* \ *266 738120; www.rodalentejo.pt*). The website, while in Portuguese only, is easy to use. Click 'Ver Horarios' to see PDFs of timetables. Bus prices are less than half their equivalent in the UK for a similar level of comfort. Some buses have toilets.

**TRAIN** Évora, Alcáçovas, Alvito, Cuba and Beja are connected to Lisbon's Oriente station by four *intercidade* (intercity) trains daily. For information contact **Comboios de Portugal** (\ *707 210220; www.cp.pt*). Tickets are available through travel agents or in railway stations and do not need to be booked in advance except on public holidays. First class (*primeira/conforto*) is more spacious with better seating and more storage space than second class (*segunda/turística*). Fares are low, with a ticket between Lisbon and Évora costing around €17 one way/€30 return in first class and around €13 one way/€22 return in second class.

**CAR** The best way to get around the Alentejo is by car, as this affords access to the smaller villages, the beaches, and out-of-the-way castles and natural attractions. Portuguese roads are excellent and far emptier than those in the UK. Motorways have toll booths, so be sure to carry loose change with you. Streets in Alentejo towns were built for people or horses by the Moors and can be very narrow. Avoid driving in town centres if possible.

With 9.7 road traffic deaths per 100,000 in 2012, Portugal is statistically safer for drivers than China (with 20.5) and the USA (11.6), but less safe than Italy (6.2), Canada (6), Australia (5.6), France (4.9), Ireland (4.2) and the UK (3.6).

Drive on the right-hand side of the road, giving way to the left at roundabouts. Speed limits are 120km/h on motorways, 90–100km/h on highways, and 50–30km/h in towns. The legal alcohol limit when driving is 0.05mg.

Child safety restraints are mandatory for all children up to 12 and under a height of 1.5m, who are permitted to travel in the front seat only if the proper restraints are in place and the airbags switched off. Cars with no seat belts in the back seats can't carry children under three years old.

It is mandatory to carry your driving licence, vehicle registration document (V5) and certificate of motor insurance. Fines have to be paid on the spot; most police vehicles have a portable credit/debit card machine. Failure to pay on the spot will result in the retention initially of the documents (for which you will receive a receipt), and if the fine is not paid in three days, of the vehicle.

**Car hire** Rental costs start at around €240 per week and are often cheaper midweek off season when booked ahead online. The major players all work in Portugal and have offices in the airport at Lisbon, which is the best place to hire for choice and prices. There are also car rental offices in Évora and Beja.

## ACCOMMODATION

Whether you're lording it in luxury in a palace or royal castle, staying in a traditional farm house set in flower-filled meadows or settling in to a Baroque, *azulejo*-bedecked bedroom in a converted 17th-century monastery, the Alentejo is replete with delightful accommodation options. Rates in Portugal include breakfast unless stated otherwise by the hotel.

***POUSADAS*** After the collapse of the Estado Novo, the Portuguese state sought to recuperate many of the beautiful monasteries and castles which had been left to crumble and decay after their appropriation by the republic in the 19th century. Converted into hotels, the *pousadas* were the Portuguese counterpart of the Spanish *paradores*, with luxurious rooms housed in some of the most beautiful historical buildings in Iberia. The *pousadas* have now been sold off to the private sector. Many are run by the Pestana group (*www.pestana.com*), and they sit alongside a handful of independently owned heritage hotels as the best accommodation in the region. Expect to pay anything from €75 to €170 per night.

***ADEGAS*** A number of the Alentejo's *adegas* (vineyard estates) have now opened their doors as hotels, offering accommodation in old *fazenda* houses or in modish purpose-built accommodation. Many of these vineyard hotels offer wine tours and tastings and have excellent restaurants.

***HERDADES* AND TURISMO RURAL** Concomitant with vineyard hotels are homestays in the countryside, either luxurious *herdades* (estates) or simple family homes. These are linked under the regional Turismo Rural scheme (TER – look for the signposts on the motorways and roads). A stay in a family home in rural Alentejo should not be missed. They offer a wonderful insight into traditional life, the opportunity to meet the warm and welcoming Alentejo people and to get the inside track on local secrets, be they hidden beaches, deserted Stone Age sites, small vineyards, olive producers or unique tours. We list many in the text. You can find more on the Alentejo Tourism website (*www.visitalentejo.pt*) and through Heranças do Alentejo (*www.herancasdoalentejo.net*) and Top Rural (*www.toprural.pt*).

**HOTELS** Alentejo hotels operate according to the international star system. Rooms come in different categories. Normally an *apartamento* is an apartment room with a separate living and sleeping area and sometimes cooking facilities. A *quarto* is a standard room – *com* *banheiro* is en suite and *sem banheiro* is with shared bathroom. The Alentejo has some small and well-appointed boutique hotels.

**PENSÕES** *Pensões* (singular *pensão*) are simple hotels offering excellent value and which often fall outside the star system. They can nonetheless offer comfort at a two or three star level, if not the business services required to earn them a star.

**ALBERGUES (HOSTELS)** Portuguese hostels or *albergues* offer the cheapest accommodation for travellers prepared to share a dormitory room (*dormitório*) with a group of strangers. Many also have double rooms. Almost all the hostels listed have internet, lockers, tour information and luggage storage. You can find out more about them on sites like Hostel Bookers (*www.hostelbookers.com*), Hostel World (*www.hostelworld.com*) and through Hostelling International (*www.hihostels.com*), membership of which offers discounted rates in scores of locations.

**COUCHSURFING AND AIRBNB** Couchsurfing (*www.couchsurfing.org*) and Airbnb (*www.airbnb.co.uk*) offer the latest alternative to hostelling or camping, with a homeshare exchange service whereby members offer their homes to other members visiting their city.

**CAMPING** The Alentejo has an extensive network of campsites. See www. eurocampings.co.uk, www.coolcamping.co.uk and www.campingportugal.org for details.

**BOOKING ONLINE** Aside from the usual online booking engines (which offer often excellent discounts), Wonderful Land (*www.wonderfulland.com*) is a good regional portal with a choice of mid-range rural and boutique hotels throughout the Alentejo and Portugal as a whole.

## EATING AND DRINKING

Most restaurants in the Alentejo offer Portuguese or regional dishes; international food can be hard to come by. But the Alentejo – which is known as the breadbasket of Portugal – is one of Europe's undiscovered gastronomic and oenological destinations, with a strong regional cuisine and some of Europe's finest wines. Alentejan food has more verve than most Portuguese fare, with a bolder use of herbs like coriander and a broad array of dishes. Dishes are full and strong flavoured, and are served in generous portions.

Alentejo cuisine developed out of local resources. With fertile soils, the region has been used for growing olives, vines, cork, wheat and barley since Roman times. Acorns form the cork and holm oaks, grains and the thin grass growing on the plains and slopes provide animal fodder for sheep, some cows and pigs, including the uniquely Alentejan black pigs that forage semi-wild. The Alentejo's woodlands, pastures

**RESTAURANT PRICE CODES**

Based on the average price of main course.

| | | |
|---|---|---|
| Expensive | €€€€€ | €30+ |
| Above average | €€€€ | €20–30 |
| Mid-range | €€€ | €15–20 |
| Cheap & cheerful | €€ | €8–15 |
| Rock bottom | € | <€8 |

2

and river valleys are home to game, including wild boar (*javali*), hare, partridge, quail and deer. The meadows are rich with wild herbs and gardens grow bushes of scented rosemary, thyme and lavender, alongside the reddest, plumpest tomatoes you'll ever see.

Thus the Alentejo is renowned in Portugal for its olive oil and bread, its goat and lamb and – perhaps most conspicuously – its pork. Many products are prepared from Alentejan pork or lamb. The *presunto* (cured ham) is as fine as Spanish *jamón serrano* or Italian Parma ham. *Chouriço* sausages are flavoured with the herbaceous fodder and nutty acorns upon which the black pigs graze. Dishes are rich and flavoursome, designed for feeding workers on the land. They include *carne de porco à alentejana* (pork marinated in garlic, coriander and white wine and served with clams), deliciously tender *bochechas de porco preto* (black pork cheeks) and *ensopado de borrego* (a kind of lamb stew). Other dishes are served with thick bready sauces, such as *migas* (made from fresh olive oil, breadcrumbs and herbs) or *açorda* (a garlicky bread-thickened, cilantro-infused soup served so hot that the eggs broken into it poach on contact). In the hills locals harvest chestnuts in autumn that are used to flavour soups and game dishes.

Towns and villages like Serpa, Niza and Évora are famous for their creamy sheep's milk cheeses. *Queijo da serra* is sweet, soft and delicious as an appetiser. *Queijo de Évora* is a stronger, more mature cheese, with a mouth-wateringly peppery taste that goes well with a rich Alentejo red. *Queijo de Serpa* is the best of the lot – rich and creamy with a full, nutty flavour. Alentejo cheese makes a wonderful accompaniment to thick tomato soups – bright broths thickened with a poached egg and simmered with bacon or *chouriço* – or icy gazpachos flecked with coriander and red and green pepper.

On the coast the seafood is as fresh as you'll find anywhere in Europe and it comes in great variety. Dishes include *ameijoas à bulhão pato* (clams in white wine and fresh herbs), *arroz de lingueirão* (a kind of risotto stew made with razor clams), *choco* (cuttlefish), delicately flavoured *dourada* (gilthead bream), and white fish like *pescada* (hake) and *robalo* (bass).

And then there are the convent desserts made in every other small town or village from recipes invented in the convents and monasteries. Such delicacies include *encharcada* (sweet chestnut mousses made from sieved egg yolks swirled into a skillet of boiling sugar syrup), *elvas da sericaia* (baked on a traditional tin plate and served with ripe plums), or *pão de rala*, a cake made with almonds and pumpkin, first made by the nuns of St Helena do Monte Calvário.

**VEGETARIANS AND VEGANS** Vegetarians are not well catered for in the Alentejo. Cooking is almost invariably regional and local cuisine is strongly carnivorous. Even vegetable dishes (like tomato soup) tend to be seasoned with meat stock, often bacon fat. Vegetarians may often find themselves resorting to egg- or cheese-based dishes or asking for *sopa 'sem tempero/caldo de carne'* ('without meat flavouring/stock'). Things are improving. Greater visitor numbers are leading to a greater awareness of vegetarian needs. Menus in the *pousadas* and larger hotels usually include a vegetarian option. Vegans suffer even more and may be restricted to buying noodles, vegetables and stock in supermarkets and self-catering.

**WINE** The Alentejo has some superb, inexpensive wines – from crisp, light whites that soften the summer heat to hearty, full-bodied reds for washing down those gamey autumn and winter dishes or sipping with a Serpa cheese.

Portugal has the second largest number of indigenous grape varieties in the world, many of which are grown in the Alentejo, and which impart their distinctive, regional character to the wines. They include Antão Vaz (perhaps the best white grape in the region, with good acidity and tropical fruit flavours), white Diagalves, Aragonez (aka Tempranillo, the most widely-planted red), Alfrocheiro, Castelão and Trincadeira. Blends are common, and one of the commonest is of Aragonez, Castelão and Trincadeira – producing a deep, fruity red.

There are eight designated wine regions (DOC) in the Alentejo: Borba, Évora, Redondo, Reguengos, Granja-Amarela, Vidigueira and Moura – covering the northern Baixo and southern Alto – and Portalegre, the eighth region, in the cooler regions of the Serra de São Mamede. Borba, Évora, Redondo and Reguengos are most typical of the Alentejo reds, made from grapes grown fat on the hot, long summers. Portalegre reds are fresher, grown in an area with higher rainfall, less sunshine and cooler nights.

Red wines fall into two varieties – complex bottles with full bouquets and a rich earthy undertone and intensely fruity bottles with a velvety richness which is almost New World in character. Many of the latter bottles are grown in the Granja-Amarela, Moura and Vidigueira regions using imported grape varieties that do well in the poor soils.

Alentejo whites are fresh, light and dry – the perfect complement to the hot weather. The best are made with the Antão Vaz grape.

## PUBLIC HOLIDAYS AND FESTIVALS

**PUBLIC HOLIDAYS** The Alentejo has some of the liveliest and most traditional festivals in western Europe. Most see very few visitors. The region also hosts a number of major arts and music festivals.

| | |
|---|---|
| January 1 | New Year's Day |
| Good Friday | Friday before Easter Sunday |
| April 25 | Freedom Day/Liberation Day |
| May 1 | May Day |
| Corpus Christi | Second Thursday after Pentecost. Not a public holiday until 2019 due to austerity measures. |
| June 10 | Portugal Day |
| June 13 | Feast of St Anthony (Lisbon only) |
| June 24 | Feast of St John the Baptist (Porto only) |
| August 15 | Assumption |
| October 5 | Republic Day. Not a public holiday until 2019 due to austerity measures. |
| November 1 | All Saints Day. Not a public holiday until 2019 due to austerity measures. |
| December 1 | Restoration of Independence. Not a public holiday until 2019 due to austerity measures. |
| December 8 | Immaculate Conception Day |
| December 24 | Christmas Eve |
| December 25 | Christmas Day |

**FESTIVALS** As well as regular festivals, the Alentejo hosts scores of one-off events every year, which include historic, cultural, music and food festivals. See www.visitalentejo.pt for details.

## January

**Elvas City Festival**  Music, arts and commemorations of the history of the city. 14 January.

## February

**Mardi Gras**  Carnival in Redondo, Viana do Alentejo, all very much influenced by Brazil with big street parties and parades. Takes place over the weekend and Monday before Shrove Tuesday.

## March

**Beja Agricultural Festival**  A celebration of all things rural, with music, food, handicrafts and agricultural shows. Dates vary – check with the tourist board.

## April/May

**Easter parades and procession**  Santiago do Cacém; takes place biennially on the fourth Sunday after Easter Sunday.

## May

**Mértola Islamic festival**  The most important Islamic festival in Portugal, with live music, film, arts and crafts, food and art exhibitions. Usually the penultimate weekend in May. Check the tourist office for precise dates.

## June

**Corpus Christi**  Religious parades throughout the region. Second Thursday after Pentecost.

**Tróia International Film festival**  One of Portugal's biggest film festivals, showcasing arthouse films from all over the world. Usually at the beginning of the month.

**São João**  This festival takes place throughout the region, featuring live music, craft and street markets, dances, dressing up and fireworks. The biggest celebrations are to be found in Évora, Beja and Elvas. Held during the last two weeks of the month.

## July

**Festival Évora Classica**  The equivalent of the British Proms, this is one of Portugal's most prestigious classical music festivals, with a focus on a particular composer or musical tradition every year, and work showcased in concerts throughout the city. Usually second week of the month.

**Festival of Monsaraz Museu Aberto**  Biennial (next in 2016) with *cante alentejano* (Festa do Cante nas Terras do Grande Lago), dance, parades, food and wine. Usually in the middle two weeks of the month.

**Marvão Music festival**  (*www.marvaomusic.com*). One of the best classical music festivals in Portugal, with concerts al fresco under the stars, at Marvão castle. Usually last week of the month.

**Festival Alentejo**  Évora. Rock and popular music with bands and artists from Portugal and the world over. Usually last weekend of the month.

## August
**Festival do Sudoeste** Portugal's Glastonbury and one of the biggest music events in Iberia, with big name bands from all over the world. Free camping. In Zambujeiro do Mar, usually in the first week of the month.

**Folklore Festival** Traditional dances, music and food in the village of Póvoa de Meadas near Castelo de Vide. 23–24 August.

**Freedom Festival** (*www.freedomfestival.eu*) Elvas. Biennial Psytrance dance festival next due in 2017.

## September
**Festival do Senhor Jesus da Boa Fé** Elvas hosts another series of religious and cultural events. 4–7 September.

**Aires festival** Viana do Alentejo hosts religious processions and cultural events. On the fourth Sunday of the month.

**São Mateus** Elvas is the venue for a traditional Portuguese festival with bullfights, street processions, live music and markets with traditional food. 20–25 September.

**Festa do Povo** The streets of Campo Maior are completely covered with brightly coloured paper flowers. Usually the last week of the month, but not every year.

## October
**Feira de Castro** Castro Verde. Music, dance and traditional parades.

## November
**All Soul's Day** Portugal's Day of the Dead, marked throughout the region. 2 November.

**Évora FIKE** Festival of short films with scores of shorts from all over the world, shown throughout the city. Usually in the first week of the month but dates vary.

**Feira da Castanha** A chestnut festival held in Marvão, usually around 14–15 November.

## December
**Christmas** The Portuguese celebrate Christmas on the evening of 24 December. Évora and Elvas are good places to be, with parties and midnight masses.

**New Year's Eve** Festivals throughout the region; the largest is in Évora, with street parties, fireworks and dancing.

## SHOPPING

The best buys are wine, olive oil, cheeses, jewellery and fashion (especially shoes). Most shops are open ⊕ 10.00–18.00 Monday–Saturday. Very few are open on a Sunday even in Évora.

**OLIVE OIL** Portugal produces some of the finest olive oil in the world, and it comes in astonishing variety. Here you can buy olive oil straight from the manufacturer, and most *adegas* sell their own oils. The younger the fruit, the spicier the taste. Herdade do Esporão 1267 from Reguengos de Monsaraz (page 116) won best in its class in the 2015 World's Best Olive Oils awards. Dom Borba (pages 107–8) has won numerous international awards. Both *herdades* also produce wonderful wines and can be visited prior to buying their best bottles at a discounted rate. Other excellent award-winning oils include Herdade da Ventosa, Azeite de Moura (Cooperativa Agrícola de Moura e Barrancos, CRL), and Cortes de Cima (Casa Agrícola Cortes de Cima, S A). Also look out for Portuguese olive oils that have won awards at the 'World's Best Olive Oils' competition but are not from the Alentejo; these include CARM Premium, Quinta Vale do Conde and the gold medal-winning Casa de Santo Amaro.

**WINE** For information on wine see pages 48–9. The best places to buy wines are the *adegas* themselves. We list many in the guide, but there are many more that can be visited for tastings and to purchase wine, some of which also provide meals. Road signs throughout the Alentejo signpost locations well known for wine and the *adegas* open to the public. For full information on their locations and what they have to offer see the excellent Rota de Vinhos do Alentejo wine route website: www.vinhosdoalentejo.pt.

The best **wine shops** are in Évora and are listed under the *Shopping* entries for that city (pages 71–2). Lisbon airport also offers a reasonable selection, albeit far less extensive and at a greater price than in the Alentejo itself.

**HATS AND WALKING STICKS** Portugal is one of the few European countries where you will still find hat shops, selling everything from boaters and big brimmed floppies to rakish fedoras, tweed walking hats and the cloth caps every other Portuguese man over 50 seems to wear. Even if you have no intention of buying, browsing the shops is a delight, and while you're there you can pick up a walking stick to tap along the dragon's tooth pavements.

**SHOES** Few know that fashionable Fly London shoes (*www.flylondon.com*) are in fact Portuguese. Or that Portugal produces some of the finest footwear in the world, from timeless brogues made from superb leather to super-soft, stylish and beautifully cut women's heels. The quality of leather and craftsmanship rivals Italy's, and footwear manufacture has as long and illustrious a tradition in Portugal as in that country, but shoes here cost a fraction of the price of those worn by the well-heeled in Milan. The best place to buy shoes in the Alentejo is Évora, though you might consider adding a Lisbon day to your schedule if you want to find that perfect pair. **Portuguese Shoes** (*www.portugueseshoes.pt*) and **Portuguese Shoes TV** (*www.portugueseshoestv.pt*) give an overview of the various manufacturers to search out.

**LEATHER** Portugal is one of the best places in Europe to buy well-crafted high quality leather goods at a competitive price. The country has a tradition of tanning and manufacture going back to Moorish times. Look out for high-end leather bags (especially the beautiful tan gentleman's briefcases in a contemporary-meets-1940s style), leather wallets, belts and accessories. Évora is the best location to buy leather, though the choice of what's on offer is small compared to Lisbon. For more information see leatherfromportugal.com

**CARPETS** Arraiolos has a history of carpet-making dating back to Moorish times, when artisans from Morocco, Turkey and Persia worked in the town. There are dozens of weavers in the little town proffering Portuguese carpets made to traditional Christianised Islamic designs from pure wool combined with petit point and cross-stitches. Price is determined by size and complexity. For more information see the box on page 105.

**JEWELLERY** Portugal has a long and noble tradition of goldsmithery and jewellery manufacture dating back to the Romans, enriched by the Moors and reaching its sophisticated height in the Baroque period. Quality and workmanship are extremely high. Portuguese gold has to be 19.2 carats minimum to be considered gold at all. Jewellers work the metal into elaborate filigree shapes. The most elaborate are plaques depicting scenes from stories, biblical passages or myths in meticulous stamping or moulding. Rings, earrings, necklaces and bracelets combine this craft skill with timeless design motifs rooted in uniquely Portuguese Baroque, Rococo and Art Nouveau expressions. Quality is exceptional and prices far lower than anything comparable you would find in France, Italy, the UK or North America. Évora has the greatest variety of jewellery shops. Lisbon has more.

**CORK** The Portuguese don't use cork merely to bung up bottles. In Évora you will find everything from umbrellas and handbags and ties made from the substance. While many of these items are interesting mainly as curiosities, keep an eye out for finely carved bowls and sculpted tablemats.

**COUTURE** Portuguese fashion is emerging from the long shadow cast by its more famous neighbour. And while Portugal does not yet have brand names as globally recognised as Loewe, Zara or Mango, many are of equal quality. Only a handful of the better labels have outlets in the Alentejo (see Évora), but if you make a Lisbon stopover, look out for Ana Salazar (Portugal's grande dame of fashion who created the first post-Salazar fashion house), Alexandra Moura (young, contemporary women's apparel), Casa Batalha (vintage-inspired costume jewellery), master bespoke tailors Rosa & Teixeira, luxury hosiers A J Gonçalves and the delightfully quirky Storytailors, who mix fairytale designs with brilliant tropical colours and pixellated patterns.

## SPORT

The country's national obsession is **football**, but the Alentejo is lacking in illustrious teams. Évora played in the Primeira Liga from 1953 up until 1966 and reached the semifinals of the Taça de Portugal cup twice, but now competes only in a district league. Benfica, Porto and Sporting are the country's top clubs.

## MEDIA AND COMMUNICATIONS

Portugal's top-selling **newspapers** are devoted almost entirely to football. There are four respectable broadsheets – the long established *Público* and its rival *Diário de Noticias*, plus the *Diário Economico* and *Jornal de Negócios*, which are the Portuguese equivalents of *The Financial Times* and *The Economist*. There are no English-language papers.

Portuguese **TV** has four main channels, two of them frowsty and state-run and the other two glitzy and independent. Ratings are dominated by games shows and soaps, the most popular of which either originate from Brazil or are modelled on the glossy Rio-based productions churned out by TV Globo. Nearly 70% of the country watch the evening soaps or *telenovelas*, making them even more of a national obsession than in Brazil itself. Films not in Portuguese are shown with subtitles.

**Post offices** (*correios*) are marked with a plaque showing a red horse and black lettering reading CTT Correios. Domestic post goes in red letterboxes; international post (*correio azul*) goes in blue boxes. Look out for the red stamp dispensers in the post offices (to save time queuing), or buy stamps in postcard shops. Allow seven days for international delivery and five within Europe.

**Internet cafés** are a rare find in the Alentejo, but broadband **Wi-Fi** usage in cafes and hotels is widespread.

If you have a GSM-compatible **mobile phone** you will be able to use your phone in Portugal. But it's far better value to buy a local SIM card. To buy a SIM, go to one of the network provider shops (Vodafone, Optimus and TMN are the key players). You will need to present ID and provide your home address. Credit can be topped up at any Agente Payshop or Agente Megarede shop, many of which are pharmacies or newsagents. Look for the signs or ask in the hotel.

## ARTS AND ENTERTAINMENT

The Alentejo's towns are so diminutive that arts and entertainment venues tend to be small, often doubling up as bars and restaurants. Évora and Beja have the best arts facilities, with the latter city having the Alentejo's best and most famous theatre. See the relevant town entries for details on specific venues. Many of the smaller towns, including Marvão, Porto Covo and Mértola, host lively music and arts festivals over the summer.

## CULTURAL ETIQUETTE

The Portuguese are relaxed and hospitable people and are not easily flustered. There are, however, a few points of etiquette worth noting.

**THE AULD ENEMY** First and foremost, do not confuse the Portuguese with the Spanish, Portuguese culture with Spanish culture or *fado* with *flamenco*. Doing so will illicit all the enthusiasm you might receive from a Scotsman asked if he'd like a cucumber sandwich, a glass of Pimms and a game of cricket. And unless you are from Spain, don't try and talk Spanish to a Portuguese person; address them in English if you have no Portuguese.

**SPEAKING PORTUGUESE** Most Portuguese will be surprised and delighted if you attempt to speak to them in Portuguese and even more delighted if you do so in a Portuguese accent (and not a Brazilian one). Foreigners speaking Brazilian Portuguese to the older generation should thank the mother country for giving Brazil its language, complain about 'the ridiculous' 2009 spelling reforms (which made the language closer to the Brazilian form), and stringently avoid the use of '*você*' (a form of 'you'), replacing it with '*o senhor/a senhora*'. See also pages 179–83.

**POLITENESS** The Portuguese mind their Ps and Qs as much as the English. Open doors for others, express gratitude and appreciation and use the correct form of address (see above).

**LIKING PORTUGAL** The Portuguese are diffident but proud. Any visitor who shows a real knowledge and appreciation of Portugal and anything Portuguese will themselves be appreciated. The more detailed that appreciation, the greater the reception.

**MEETING AND GREETING** Shake hands with those you do not know. Embrace those you know well and kiss women on both cheeks.

**PUNCTUALITY AND BUSINESS** Timing is often loose in Portugal, but not as loose as in Latin America. Expect people to arrive 15 minutes late, even for a business meeting. If you are doing business, do not rush to the nitty gritty. The pleasantries are important in Portugal; everything follows from relationship and this is established through camaraderie. And expect people to express their opinions strongly rather than try to seek out a common ground. Don't mix dinner with business!

**DRESS** Away from the beach the Portuguese dress more conservatively than in Mediterranean Europe – men tend to wear a shirt with a collar, women dresses or jeans with fairly modest tops.

**RELIGION** Be respectful of places of worship. Wear long trousers or tops with sleeves when entering a church and talk quietly. Don't stand in front of the altar for a long while taking pictures, and don't take any during a church service – especially with a flash. Be discreet if people are at prayer.

## TRAVELLING POSITIVELY

Increasing numbers of travellers are choosing to become more deeply involved in the destinations they visit. Rather than merely using them for beach, sun and a spot of adventure, they wish to learn more about them, interact more with local people and give something back to local communities. Much positive travelling is common sense, but here are a few tips, some of which are specific to the Alentejo or Portugal.

## BEFORE YOU GO

- Learn some Portuguese. Most Portuguese speak good English but will appreciate your interest in their language, and once you get beyond the basics, conversing in Portuguese, even simply, will ensure you get so much more from your visit.
- Read up on Portuguese history, culture and sport and listen to some local music. This will immediately earn you local friends.
- Learn something about the wildlife and visit areas where it is threatened, especially the raptors and lynxes.
- Consider supporting local NGOs that preserve the environment and protect wildlife like the critically endangered Iberian lynx and the region's rare raptors. These include the Liga para a Proteção da Natureza (*www.lpn.pt*), who do sterling work throughout Portugal. Many international NGOs like WWF support the LPN's work protecting the lynx.
- Plan ahead to visit local conservation or wildlife projects with local rather than international tour operator guides (these are indicated in the text).

## WHILE IN THE ALENTEJO

- The Alentejo is one of Europe's poorest regions. Help the local economy by buying the wonderful wines, cheeses, olive oil and arts and crafts, as well as local everyday produce (rather than imported goods): insect repellent, soap, shampoo, flip-flops, bathing costumes and so on are available at the same or better quality in Portugal as they are back home.

### ECOTOURISM: SOME POINTERS

Here are a few things to consider when choosing a tour operator or place to stay. The more these questions are asked, the more awareness is increased in Portugal.

- Does the establishment or operator have a written policy regarding responsible activity towards the environment and local communities?
- What exactly do they do to support the local community? How do they measure it?
- How many of their employees are locals?
- Do they train locals to enable them to work as guides or management?
- If the hotel is based in natural surroundings, do they have a species list for birds or mammals? What endangered or threatened species live in their area? How aware of these are they?
- What exactly do they do to support the environment? How do they measure it?
- Do they recycle? How do operators deal with rubbish, and do they make an effort to work with hotels that recycle? Do hotels recycle water and/or rubbish, and how do they treat their sewage?
- Do they use solar power or make an effort to work with those that do? Ask them what percentage of produce and services are sourced from within 25km of the lodge.
- What percentage of their food and chattels are locally sourced?
- How do they help tourists to become more involved in local conservation or community projects?

- Stay in a small local hotel rather than a big international chain. The Alentejo is replete with charming rural guesthouses and homestays, many of which are family-run and offer a far more intimate experience of Portugal and its people than a corporate-owned city hotel.
- Bring your rubbish in and out of national parks.
- Book tours through local operators rather than one central office in Lisbon. This distributes income more evenly.
- Always ask about the local wildlife, addressing specific questions to local guides and requesting a species list from hotels and operators that package themselves as practising ecotourism. This greatly increases awareness and the sense of economic importance of the wildlife itself. Hunting is widespread in the Alentejo and farmers often indiscriminately kill raptors. Showing an interest will help encourage locals to see animals as key to tourist interests, ensuring their preservation.
- Don't pick wild flowers.

# Part Two

## THE GUIDE

find the real Alentejo

There is plenty to whet your appetite in Portugal's undiscovered Alentejo region. Deserted beaches, amazing landscapes, medieval ruins and cultural gems – plus the most delicious fresh food and local wines.

A taste of the real Portugal, from the tailor-made holiday specialists.

7 nights B&B from just **£470pp**, including flights & car hire*.

call **020 8758 4722** or visit **sunvil.co.uk**
*Terms and Conditions apply, please contact us for details.

**Sunvil**

find the real country

# 3

# Évora and Around

*In Évora it's true there's an atmosphere impossible to find anywhere else … History's continual presence on its streets and squares, in every stone or shadow.*

José Saramago

Nowhere in the Alentejo is more redolent with history than its capital, Évora. Rising in narrow, winding Moorish streets to a central *praça*, crowned with a magnificent ruined Roman temple, ringing with the peal of bells from an array of Portuguese Golden Age churches and littered with stately mansions and monuments, the city has been protected as a UNESCO World Heritage Site since 1986. Its listing as such owes as much to its architectural unity as it does to its magnificent churches and small museums, for while Lisbon was levelled by the 1755 earthquake, Évora retains its medieval and Renaissance buildings. Nowhere in Portugal better preserves the country's architecture of Empire.

Évora is large enough to lose yourself in over a long summer day – idly wandering the cobbles, pausing to visit the Roman Temple, the cavernous cathedral and the beautiful churches of the Convento do Carmo and the Igreja de São Francisco (with its grisly chapel of bones). There are countless cafés serving local cakes, pastries and thick coffee, and fine restaurants dishing up traditional cooking from the area. The shopping is the best in the region – not just for souvenirs, but for everyday items like shoes, clothes and hats, which are so much better value in Portugal than back home, and for fine food and drink, including wonderful Alentejo wine, aromatic cheeses, pastries and cakes.

But Évora is more than a historic monument. It is a bustling community too. And while many of the smaller villages in the Alentejo feel abandoned by the younger generation, Évora is eternally youthful, its streets rejuvenated annually by the arrival of fresh batches of students rushing to attend lectures at the Alentejo's biggest university, gathering to gossip under the arcade in the Praça do Giraldo and nursing weekend hangovers over thick, steaming coffees in the town's myriad cafes.

## HISTORY

Before the Romans settled here, the hill that became the city of Évora was surrounded by Megalithic settlements. Their remnants include the Almendres Cromlech (pages 80–1), now regarded as one of the largest and most important prehistoric sites in western Europe. Évora hill itself was probably settled in Neolithic times, growing under the wave of **Celtici tribal migration** around 400BC and during the Lusitanian war of 155–139BC, led by Viriatus, who is nowadays regarded as the first national hero against the Romans. It became a town proper after the **Roman conquest of Lusitania** between 139 and 133BC, when it was formally established as Ebora – possibly named after the original Celtic settlement. Ebora means 'yew' in one of the Celtic languages. Ebora never became an established Roman colonial capital – only Caesar's Scallibus

Praesidium Lulium (Santarém) and Pax Lulia (Beja) were significant enough to earn this stature. Nonetheless, Évora played a pivotal role in the development not only of Lusitania (which covered around a quarter of the Iberian peninsula and included much of what is now Central Spain), but of Hispania as a whole. Between 80 and 72BC Ebora was the headquarters of **Quintus Sertorius**, seen by some as the Lusitanian Hannibal. Sertorius rebelled against the Roman dictator Sulla, who had waged a merciless and bloody campaign in Lusitania. He defeated a string of Sulla's generals and conquered much of the Roman territory of Hispania. Sertorius came within a whisker of overwhelming the great Roman general Pompey and establishing a free Roman republic in Hispania, but was assassinated in 72BC at a banquet ostensibly held in his honour by Marcus Perpenna Vento, one of Sulla's agents. According to Plutarch, Sertorius's favourite deity was Diana, a claim which may have led to the Roman ruin that still sits at the heart of modern Évora being erroneously dubbed 'O Templo de Diana', a name that has stuck to this day.

Between 60 and 44BC Sertorius's Ebora – together with the remaining Lusitanian rebels – was conquered and crushed by another great Roman dictator, **Julius Caesar**. Caesar swept across the Alentejo from his headquarters in Scallabis (Santarém), took Ebora and rechristened it Liberalitas Lulia. The Roman Temple dates from this later Roman period, as do parts of Évora's city wall, and the 16th-century Aqueduto da Água de Prata, an aqueduct that still towers over the rooftops of Évora, was probably built on the site of an original Roman construction.

The city was conquered briefly by the Visigoths after the fall of Rome and then occupied as 'Yabura' by the Moors, who expanded the town and consolidated it as an important economic and cultural centre within western Al-Andalus. The poet Abd al-Majid ibn Abdun al-Yaburi (1050–1135), a chronicler of the Berber Aftasid dynasty, hailed from Évora. In the 12th century Évora became an outpost of the **Almoravid Empire**, which stretched from its capital in Marrakech over the Maghreb and Al-Andalus. Évora's present-day layout, with narrow winding streets lined with whitewashed houses, dates from this period, and the city fortifications show the remains of the original Moorish wall and an ancient kasbah. In the mid 12th century it was taken by the Almohad dynasty, who battled with the crusaders. In 1159 the Christians took the city, only to lose it once more to the Almohads in 1161. The city was finally reconquered by the Portuguese El Cid, **Gerald the Fearless**, in 1165. Gerald was a bandit turned soldier who captured many key towns in the Alentejo and Spanish Extremadura, including Beja and Badajoz. But it is for his capture of Évora that he is most remembered – largely because Camões wrote about it in *The Lusiads*, describing Gerald sneaking into the city by night, killing the elderly Arab watchman and his daughter as they slept and opening the city gates to his companions while brandishing their heads. His representation – as a knight swinging his sword, with the severed heads of the watchman and his daughter – remains on the city's coat of arms.

Évora was never retaken and it grew in importance and prosperity under the Portuguese. The cathedral dates from the medieval period, when the city was growing in influence. It reached its zenith in Portugal's **Age of Discovery** under the Avis Dynasty (1385–1580), when Évora became the seat of the court and the epicentre of a power struggle between the royal family and the nobility. Portugal's most important noble – Fernando II, the third Duke of Braganza (whose descendant Catherine would marry Charles II of England) – was executed in one of Évora's handsome public squares. **Vasco da Gama**, who was born in Sines on the Alentejo coast, probably studied mathematics and navigation in Évora. His voyages made the monarchy and Évora wealthy. The city became one of the most cosmopolitan in Europe – its streets filled with African, Indian and Chinese slaves, whose descendants mixed with the Portuguese and make up the townspeople today.

Under the **House of Avis** (1385–1580) Évora became an important cultural centre, attracting the French sculptor Nicolau Chanterene (the master stone-carver whose work decorates churches in Santiago de Compostela and who carved much of Lisbon's Mosteiro dos Jerónimos) and the dramatist Gil Vicente. Many of the city's more lavish palaces and religious buildings date from this period, including the Convento dos Lóios (now one of Portugal's most beautiful *pousadas*), the churches of São Francisco and the Convento do Carmo (with its superbly preserved Manueline door), and the Palácio dos Condes de Basto.

By the late 16th century the court was firmly established in Lisbon, and Évora had become more a centre of learning than of political influence. The Jesuits founded a university here in 1559 which for two centuries rivalled Coimbra for learning. But it was disbanded in 1759 after the Marquis of Pombal expelled the Jesuit order from Portugal under pressure from slave traders in Brazil. Évora went into decline, remembered chiefly as the site of a key battle in the Peninsular War (1807–14). By the 19th century it was little more than a market town, known for hosting one of the biggest markets in the Alentejo. In the 20th century the city's historic buildings, which were slowly crumbling into dust, were finally remembered and gradually restored. The university re-opened in 1973, giving the city new life. In 1986 it gained World Heritage status, bringing the first trickles of tourism.

## GETTING THERE AND AWAY

Évora has good **road connections** with Lisbon and the rest of the Alentejo. Lisbon is 135km from Évora on the E90 and E1 motorways – just under two hours' drive. Beja is 80km south on the E802 highway (around 90 minutes' drive). Faro is 225km further south along the same road – about three hours' drive: Castelo de Vide is 122km north on the E802 highway – just over two hours' drive. **Parking** is best beyond the city walls and is largely free. There is little parking in the historic centre, where streets are very narrow. Take a cab into town or walk – the centre is roughly ten minutes' walk from anywhere along the city walls.

Europcar (*www.europcar.pt*) has **car rental** offices in Évora, but you'll have more choice and better prices hiring in Lisbon.

The **railway station** [65 E8] (*estação de caminho de ferro; www.cp.pt*) is just over 1km south of the Praça do Giraldo, beyond the city walls and along Rua da República. Trains run to Lisbon (Oriente station) via Casa Branca (*4 daily, 90–100 mins*), and to Beja (*4 daily, 2hrs 10mins–2hrs 20mins*). For more details and the most accurate prices see www.cp.pt. A taxi from the railway station to hotels in the historic centre costs €3–5.

The **bus station** [64 A4] (*terminal rodoviário*) is also beyond the city walls and just under 1km west of the Praça do Giraldo along Rua Serpa Pinto. Buses run to Lisbon, Beja, Borba, Elvas, Estremoz, Moura, Portalegre (change for Castelo de Vide and/or Marvão), Reguengos de Monsaraz (for Monsaraz) and Santarém. For the latest and most accurate bus journey times and prices see www.rodalentejo.pt and www.rede-expressos.pt.

## ORIENTATION

Évora is small enough to negotiate on foot. The old town is surrounded largely by its old city walls and is spread across a low hill. It clusters around two principal central

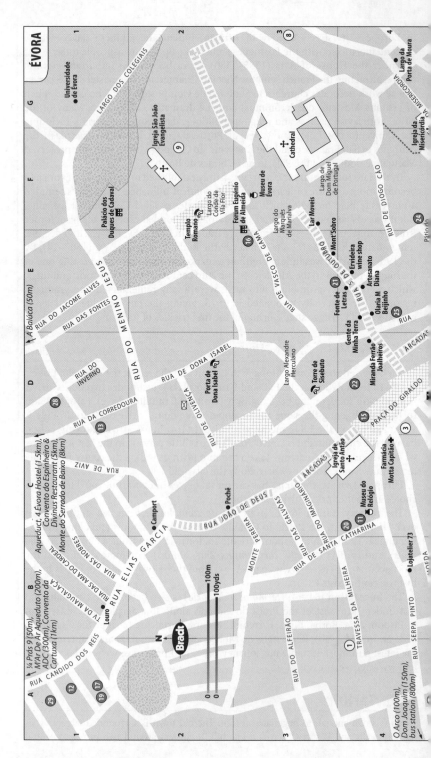

# ÉVORA

- Universidade de Évora
- Largo dos Colegiais
- Palácio dos Duques de Cadaval
- Igreja São João Evangelista (9)
- Largo da Porta de Moura
- Igreja da Misericórdia
- Cathedral
- Largo de Dom Miguel de Portugal
- Templo Romano
- Largo do Conde de Vila Flor
- Forum Eugénio de Almeida (16)
- Museu de Évora
- Largo do Marquês de Marialva
- Lar Moveis
- Rua de Diogo Cão
- Pátio do (24)
- Mont'Sobro
- Ervideira wine shop
- Artesanato
- Olaria M Diana
- Fonte de Letras (21)
- Beijinho (23)
- Rua
- Gente da Minha Terra
- Miranda Ferrão Joalheiros
- Torre de Sisebuto (22)
- Largo Alexandre Herculano
- Porta de Dona Isabel
- Arcadas
- Praça do Giraldo (15) (3)
- Igreja de Santo Antão
- Farmácia Motta Capitão
- Poché
- Museu do Relógio (11) (20)
- Lojatelier 73
- A Baiúca (50m)
- Rua do Jacome Alves Jesus
- Rua das Fontes
- Rua do Inverno (28)
- Rua do Menino
- Rua da Corredoura (13)
- Rua de Aviz
- Aqueduct, 4 Évora Hostel (1.5km), Convento do Espinheiro & Divinus Restaurant (5km), Monte do Serrado de Baixo (8km)
- Rua Elias Garcia
- Camport
- Rua João de Deus
- Rua Pereira Alves
- Rua das Galvões
- Rua de Sarva do Imaginário
- Rua de Santa Catharina
- ¼ Prás 9 (50m), M'Ar De Ar Aqueduto (200m), ADC (300m), Convento da Cartuxa (1km)
- Rua Cândido dos Reis
- TV da Magualaça
- Louro
- Rua das Ama do Cardeal
- Rua das Nobres
- (29) (12) (17) (19)
- Monte Pereira Alves
- Travessa da Milheira
- Rua do Alfeirão
- Rua Serpa Pinto
- O Arco (100m), Dom Joaquim (150m), bus station (800m)
- Bradt
- N
- 100m
- 100yds
- 0

64

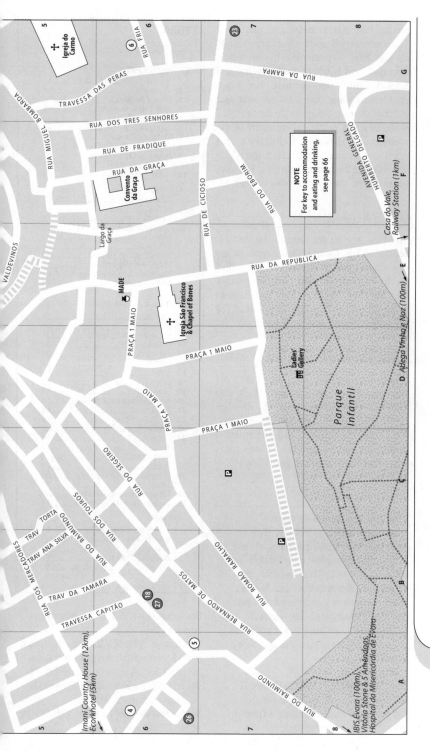

Igreja do Carmo

RUA FRIA

TRAVESSA DAS PERAS

RUA DOS TRES SENHORES

RUA DE FRADIQUE

RUA DA GRAÇA

Convento da Graça

Largo da Graça

RUA MIGUEL BOMBARDA

VALDEVINOS

RUA DA RAMPA

AVENIDA GENERAL HUMBERTO DELGADO

Casa do Vale,
Railway Station (1km)

RUA DO EBORIM

RUA DE CICIOSO

RUA DA REPUBLICA

**NOTE**
For key to accommodation
and eating and drinking,
see page 66

MADE

PRAÇA 1 MAIO

Igreja São Francisco
& Chapel of Bones

PRAÇA 1 MAIO

PRAÇA 1 MAIO

PRAÇA 1 MAIO

Ladies'
Gallery

Parque
Infantil

D. Adega Vinha e Noz (100m)

RUA DO SEGEIRO

RUA DOS TOUROS

RUA DO RAIMUNDO

TRAV TORTA

TRAV ANA SILVA

RUA DOS MERCADORES

TRAV DA TAMARA

TRAVESSA CAPITÃO

RUA ROMÃO RAMALHO

RUA BERNARDO DE MATOS

RUA DO RAIMUNDO

Imani Country House (12km),
Ecorkhotel (5km)

IBIS Évora (100m),
Vitória Stone & 5 Amêndoas,
Hospital da Misericórdia de Évora

*praças*, one monumental and one civic. The monumental *praça* – the Largo Conde de Vila Flor – crowns the hill on which Évora sits and is where the Cathedral and Roman Temple are situated. The Praça do Giraldo some 200m to the west and watched over by the Igreja de Santo Antão is the business centre, where many of the municipal buildings – including the tourist information office – are situated, and where you will find the central municipal bus stop, the main taxi stand and a string of cafes.

## GETTING AROUND

The best way to get around the historic centre is **on foot**. If you need to go elsewhere, **taxis** are cheap and easy to find on the Praça do Giraldo. Green Trevo **city bus number 34** runs every ten minutes or so around the centre, stopping at the Praça do Giraldo and the bus station.

## TOURIST INFORMATION

The tourist office [64 D4] (*posto de turismo; Praça do Giraldo 73;* ☎ *266 777071; www.visitevora.net;* ⏲ *Apr–Sep 09.00–19.00 daily, Oct–Mar 09.00–18.00 daily*) has free maps and information pamphlets and can help book hotels, tours and hire cars. Staff speak good English.

## TOUR OPERATORS

**AGIA** (The Association of Alentejano Interpretative Guides) ☎ 963 702392; www.alentejoguides.com. Daily guided tours of the historic centre leaving from in front of the tourist office at 10.00 & visiting Praça do Giraldo, the Cathedral, the Roman Temple, Portas de Moura square, the Igreja de São Francisco & the Capela dos Ossos. The tour takes 2–3hrs & costs €12. Children under 12 are free, & there is a minimum of 2 people. Bespoke tours are also available in & around Évora.

**Cartuxa** See page 74.

**Ebora Megalithica** ☎ 964 808337; www.eboramegalithica.com. Morning or afternoon half-day guided visits to the Menhir & Cromlech of Almendres & the Zambujeiro dolmen with local archaeologists. Pick-up anywhere in Évora. Excellent value.

**TukAlentejo** ☎ 925 905680. Tours of the historic centre & the Megalithic sites by motor rickshaw, aka tuktuk. Tuktuks on the Praça do Giraldo [64 D4], in front of the Sé, outside the Igreja de São Francisco in high season (Apr–Sep).

**Tur Aventur Outdoor Escapes** ☎ 266 743134; m 966 758040; www.portugalbestcycling.com.

### EVORA

*For listings, see pages 67–71*

**Where to stay**

1 Best Western Santa Clara.......A4
2 Évora Inn.......D4
3 Hostel Santantão.......D4
4 M'Ar De Ar Muralhas.......A6
5 Moov.......A6
6 Namaste.......G6
7 Old Évora Hostel.......A4
8 Pensão Residencial Policarpo.......G3
9 Pousada Convento de Évora dos Loios.......F2
10 Solar de Monfalim.......F4

*Off map*

4 Évora Hostel.......D1
ADC.......A1
Casa do Vale.......F8
Convento do Espinheiro.......C1
Ecorkhotel.......A6
IBIS Évora.......A8
Imani Country House.......A6
M'Ar De Ar Aqueduto.......A1
Monte do Serrado de Baixo.......C1
Vitória Stone.......A8

**Where to eat and drink**

11 Art Café.......C4
12 Bistro Barão.......A1
13 Botequim da Mouraria.......D1
14 Café Alentejo.......D4
15 Café Arcada.......D4
16 Cartuxa.......E3
17 EME.......A1
18 Évora Wine Bar.......B6
19 Fialho.......A1
20 Maria Severa Casa de Fado.......C4
21 Momentos.......E3
22 Mr Pickwick.......D4
23 Pão de Rala.......G7
24 Passion.......F4
Pousada de Évora Convento dos Loios.......(see 9)
25 Praxis.......E4
26 Sabores de Alentejo.......A6
27 Salsa Verde.......B6
28 Taberna Típica Quatra Feira.......D1
29 Tasquinha do Oliveira.......A1

*Off map*

¼ Prás 9.......A1
5 Amêndoas.......(see Vitória Stone)
A Baiúca.......D1
Adega Vinho e Noz.......E8
Divinus.......(see Convento do Espinheiro)
Dom Joaquim.......A4

Mountain bike rides, half-day & day hikes, & jeep tours in & around Évora. Locations include the aqueduct & surrounding countryside, the Megalithic sites, Estremoz (& the cork oak forests & marble mines), Monsaraz & Alqueva lake.

## WHERE TO STAY  *Map, pages 64–5.*

### LUXURY

🏠 **Convento do Espinheiro** (92 rooms) 📞266 788200; www.conventodoespinheiro.com. Set in a 15th-century Hieronymite convent nestled in rolling countryside 10mins' drive from Évora's historic centre, this hotel offers peace, quiet & colonial heritage garnished with 5-star luxury. Amenities include an indoor & outdoor pool, a plush full-service spa & one of the best hotel restaurants in the region. Opt for rooms in the old convent itself (rather than the modern annex). The convent is most famous in Portugal for once being the home of one of Iberia's more illustrious church artists, the Flemish monk Frei Carlos (see page 31), some of whose paintings can be seen in Évora Museum. A room in the hotel bears his name. €€€€€

🏠 **M'Ar De Ar Aqueduto** (64 rooms) Rua Cândido dos Reis 72–78; 📞902 270127; www.mardearhotels.com. Stylish, contemporary rooms with modern 'designer' touches – Starck-inspired drapes, mood lighting, combination colours, iPod stations & contemporary furniture in a modern building close to the aqueduct on the northern edge of the city. Spa, excellent restaurant (with international & Asian options, including a sushi bar), plenty of parking & good, 24hr service. €€€€€

🏠 **Pousada Convento de Évora dos Loios** (32 rooms) Largo Conde Vila-Flor; 📞266 730070; www.pestana.com. Magnificent historical convent in the heart of Évora, overlooking the Roman temple & next to Évora Museum. Rooms are palatial, many of them decorated with *azulejos*, & the restaurant is one of the best in town. There's a pool & gardens, & the concierge can organise a range of tours, guides & excursions. The church (St John the Evangelist, pages 74–5) is perhaps the most beautiful in the city. €€€€

### UPMARKET

🏠 **ADC** (Albergaria do Calvario) (22 rooms) Travessa dos Lagares 3; 📞266 745930; www.adcevora.com. Small hotel in a good position in the historic centre, set in an attractive 500-year-old town house which once housed an olive oil shop. Rooms are well appointed & modern, set around an attractive medieval central courtyard with a large olive oil grinding stone at its centre. The best (in the premium category) have small balconies & come with their own kitchens & amenities. Service is excellent, with a range of local tours & guided trips on offer, & the hotel serves a generous b/fast, for which much of the menu comes from locally sourced organic produce. €€€€

🏠 **Ecorkhotel** (56 rooms) Quinta da Deserta e Malina, Évora; 📞266 738500; www.ecorkhotel.com. This eco-hotel generates its own electricity, heats its twin swimming pools, spa & rooms through solar power, & boasts that it is the first in the world to be faced with cork, which acts as insulation throughout. Rooms are all suites (&, with separate living & bed areas, are good for families), in a series of 70m² cubic villas sitting in fields under a blazing sky a short drive from Évora. The décor is minimalist, space-age & bright white throughout, offset by muted greys & chiselled staff in sharp uniforms. €€€€

🏠 **Imani Country House** (7 rooms) Quinta de Montemuro, Guadalupe village; 📞925 613 847; www.imani.pt. Set in lawned gardens fringed by apple orchards & olive groves a stone's throw from Évora's prehistoric sites & a 20min drive from the city, this hotel is perfect for those who want to wander Évora by day & return to a home from home with starry nights & morning birdsong. Rooms & huge suites are housed in beautifully converted medieval stables & come with roaring fires, rugs, raw wood & playfully painted antique furniture. There's a small pool & a decent restaurant specialising in local cooking, & the helpful & welcoming owners can organise excursions & walks. You'll need your own hire car. €€€€

🏠 **M'Ar De Ar Muralhas** (91 rooms) In a good location just 5mins from the Praça do Giraldo, this modern neo-Art Deco low-rise building is the sister hotel to the M'Ar De Ar Aqueduto (see left) & offers a similar level of service, with 24hr reception & a fine restaurant serving Alentejo food. There's a pool & spacious gardens, & the business facilities include conference rooms. €€€€

## MID-RANGE

🏠 **Best Western Santa Clara** (41 rooms) Travessa da Milheira 19; ☎266 704141; www. bestwesternhotelsantaclara.com. A modest little 3-star with rooms so small that you can sit on the end of the bed while writing at the desk. The best are on the upper floors, with balconies overlooking a tiny backstreet & a huddle of terracotta roofs. Quiet, a couple of minutes from the Praça do Giraldo & with a generous b/fast. €€€

🏠 **Casa do Vale** (27 rooms) Quinta de Vale Vazios; ☎266 738030; www.casadovalehotel.com. Sitting on the main Lisbon–Spain road 5mins' drive from the city centre, this is a great option if you have your own car & are on a budget & flying visit. There's on-site parking, tennis courts, a small pool & a trampoline for kids. The building is ungainly & motel-like, but rooms are modern, with chunky soft furnishings, soft tones & plenty of natural light. The best are those facing south (& catching the sun) at the back of the complex away from the road. Those on the lower floors have larger balconies. €€€

🏠 **Évora Inn** (10 rooms) Praça da República 11; ☎266 744500; www.evorainn.com. This stylish small, budget boutique hotel is situated in the heart of the old city off the Praça do Giraldo, in the house where the Portuguese republic was proclaimed in 1910, & is decorated with *objets d'art*, paintings & photography. Rooms are individually themed & decorated with modish wallpaper, moulded faux-60s furniture & anglepoise lamps. Those on the higher floors have views over the whitewash, terracotta & belltowers of the historic centre. €€€

🏠 **Monte do Serrado de Baixo** (4 rooms & a private cottage for up to 8) Quinta do Serrado; ☎966 758940; www.montedoserradodebaixo. com. In the countryside 8km northwest of Évora, this farmhouse hotel offers peace & tranquillity with the convenience of Évora's restaurants & sights within a short drive. The muted off-whites & terracottas of the rooms are in perfect harmony with the traditional cottage architecture, & there's a flower-filled garden with a small pool. €€€

🏠 **Vitória Stone** (48 rooms) Rua Diana de Liz 5; ☎266 707174; www.vitoriastonehotel.com. An ugly beige concrete block on the outside, but a

fashionable boutique hotel on the inside, where modernist design meets Megalithic stone interior, with vast granite basins, sinuous slate tables & slick rooms conceived by celebrated Portuguese interior designer Nini Andrade Silva. See also the entry for 5 Amêndoas restaurant, page 69. €€€

## BUDGET

🏠 **4 Évora Hostel** (5 rooms) Rua Alfredo Henrique da Silva 1; ☎266 043943; www.4evorahostel.com. Hostel meets boutique hotel at this swish out-of-town property. Rooms & dorms in the modernist main building are walled with modish grey polished concrete & dark wood panelling. Quadruples are good for families or groups, & there's a swimming pool & a comfortable main lounge area with soft sofas & TVs. €€

🏠 **IBIS Évora** (87 rooms) Rua de Viana 18; ☎266 760700; www.ibis.com. Standard corporate-designed 2-star 10mins walk from the centre with small, no-nonsense budget rooms & standard Accor Ibis services (b/fast between 04.00 & noon, 24hr reception, etc). Heating & a/c are centrally controlled & cannot be overridden in the rooms. €€

🏠 **Moov** (80 rooms) Rua do Raimundo 99; ☎266 240340; www.hotelmoov.com. Set in a large curvilinear concrete building, this hotel's appeal rests largely in its location, a stone's throw from the historic centre & the Lisbon road, & with extensive on-site parking. Rooms are small & businesslike, with laminate flooring, fitted furniture, muted tones & modern facilities. The best are on the upper floor overlooking the inner courtyard. B/fast is extra. €€

🏠 **Solar de Monfalim** (26 rooms) Largo da Misericórdia 1; ☎266 703529; www. solarmonfalim.com. One of the city's oldest hotels with simple rooms (with red terracotta floor tiles, sturdy hospital beds & leather sofas), & public areas decorated with all manner of old bric-a-brac, including antique radios & telephone equipment. €€

## SHOESTRING

🏠 **Hostel Santantão** (5 rooms including dorms) Praça do Giraldo 83; ☎963 789142. Smack in the centre of town on the Praça do Giraldo & with very simple dorms & dbls (some with balconies), this hostel is run by helpful local Nelson & his family. Staff can organise tours around town

& to the Neolithic sights & the b/fast area on the roof has great views out over Évora. €

🏠 **Namaste** (4 rooms) www. hostelnamasteevora.pt. Bright, clean, furnished with chunky furniture, colourful rugs & scatter cushions, & decorated with contemporary art, pithy quotes & attractive faux-Asian wall paintings, this hostel sits a stroll from the key sights inside the city walls. Individual rooms & dorms. No b/fast. €

🏠 **Old Évora Hostel** (4 dorms) Travessa do Barão 4 (off Rua Serpa Pinto); ☎934 734493; www.oldevorahostel.blogspot.co.uk. A stroll from both the bus station & the Praça do Giraldo & sitting on a quiet street, this hostel – situated in a 150-year-old townhouse – couldn't have a better location. Rooms are spruce & spartan but the beds are a snip at under €15, & they are the same price in a twin room as a dorm. Book ahead in high season & through the hostel website for the best rates. €

🏠 **Pensão Residencial Policarpo** (19 rooms) Rua da Freiria de Baixo 16; ☎266 702424; www. pensaopolicarpo.com. Cosy & brightly decorated rooms, many with views in a historic building in the centre replete with 18th & 19th-century *azulejos*. Rooftop terrace with sweeping views, decent b/fast & plenty of trips & activities on offer from the helpful staff. €

# ✖ WHERE TO EAT AND DRINK *Map, pages 64–5.*

## EXPENSIVE

✖ **Cartuxa** Rua Vasco da Gama 15; ☎266 700839; www.restaurantecartuxa.com.pt; ⏱ 12.30–14.30 & 19.00–22.00 Tue–Sun. One of the best restaurants in the Alentejo, with a menu of contemporary Alentejano & Mediterranean cooking by chef Bouazza Bouhlani (also of Divinus at the Convento do Espinheiro (see below) & formally of the W Hotel, Barcelona), served in a bright, elegant dining room next to the Roman Temple, & including traditional Portuguese rock cod with clams cooked in coriander, & pork loin stuffed with sausage meat & creamed potato. Superb wine list. €€€€€

✖ **Divinus** Convento do Espinheiro (see page 67); www.divinusrestaurante.com; ⏱ noon– 15.00 & 19.00–22.30 daily. For one of Évora's most romantic dinners, book a low-lit table under the arches of the medieval cloister in this converted convent 10mins' cab ride from the city centre. The food is contemporary Alentejano by chef Bouazza Bouhlani (who also works at Cartuxa), whose signature dishes include sea bass with Alentejo herbs, clams & bread broth. €€€€€

✖ **Pousada de Évora Convento dos Lóios** Largo Conde Vila Flor; ☎266 730070; www. pestana.com; ⏱ noon–15.00 & 19.00–22.30 daily. With tables & chairs covered in high thread-count cotton, candlelit & sitting under the cloisters next to an orangery, this restaurant (like its competitor Divinus) is at its most romantic in the evenings. The menu is diverse, with local dishes like Alentejo lamb sitting next to tiger prawns & a string of vegetarian options. Excellent wine list featuring regional varieties. €€€€€

## ABOVE AVERAGE

✖ **¼ Prás 9** Rua Pedro Simões 9a; ☎266 706774; www.restaurante14pras9.pt; ⏱ noon– 15.00 & 17.00–22.00 Thu–Tue. Unostentatious, tucked away in a quiet backstreet & courting neither fame nor fortune, over the years this intimate Évora eatery has nonetheless established a reputation for running one of the finest kitchens in the country. The dining room is dominated by Portuguese in the know, eager to keep the secret & not to mention the restaurant on TripAdvisor. Few tourists make it here. Dishes like house specialities *arroz de tamboril* (monkfish & rice) & *pescada frita com arroz de camarão e amêijoas* (fried hake with prawn rice & clams) are prepared with the freshest ingredients, exquisitely cooked & in portions fit for a glutton. €€€€

✖ **5 Amêndoas** Vitória Stone Hotel (page 68), Rua Diana de Liz 5; ☎266 707174; www.vitoriastonehotel.com; ⏱ noon–15.00 &19.30–22.00 daily. Contemporary Portuguese cooking with a menu rich with local dishes including pork cooked in a Moscatel & green apple sauce & served with stuffed tomatoes & green beans, & a range of rich Alentejo soups. Those looking for something lighter will find a range of seafood dishes (including delicious tiger prawn *gratinade* served with creamed spinach). Beyond soups, side dishes & salads there's little for vegetarians. €€€€

**X Salsa Verde**  Rua do Raimundo 93a; ☎266 743210; www.salsa-verde.org; ⏱ 11.00–15.30 & 19.00–21.30 Mon–Fri, 11.30–15.00 Sat. One of the few vegetarian restaurants in the Alentejo with a wide buffet choice of comfort café food – pastas, salads, very lightly spiced curries & myriad tofu-based dishes. Takeaways are available & there's free Wi-Fi. €€€€

**X Tasquinha do Oliveira**  Rua Cândido dos Reis 45a; ☎266 744841; ⏱ noon–15.00 & 17.00–midnight daily. The tiny 14-seat dining room & exuberant, friendly husband-&-wife hosts make dinner here feel like a home visit. Manuel runs the dining room & acts as sommelier, while Carolina attends to the kitchen, dishing out delicious Portuguese *petiscos* (marinated artichokes with ham, bean & chorizo salads), breaded miniature lamb chops, & regional plates like roast partridge, black pork & monkfish & rice accompanied by a wide choice of Portuguese wines. €€€€

## MID-RANGE

**X A Baiúca**  Rua das Fontes 67; ☎266 704782; ⏱ noon–15.00 & 19.00–22.00 Tue–Sun. Hearty local food served in a rustic dining room decorated with Alentejo crockery & accompanied most evenings in high season by live acoustic music. €€€

**X Adega Vinho e Noz**  Rua Ramalho Ortigão 12; ☎266 747310; ⏱ 10.00–midnight Mon–Sat. Regional & international home cooking by the owner's mother, with excellent *gazpacho* served with fried mackerel, mixed grill, wild boar stew & boiled quinces with walnuts. €€€

**X Bistro Barão**  Rua da Zanguela 8; ☎963 007760; Facebook: BistroBarão; ⏱ 12.15–15.00 & 19.00–midnight Thu–Tue. One of the few restaurants in Évora serving international dishes like peppered steak & stuffed mushrooms. Accommodating to vegetarians. €€€

**X Café Alentejo**  Rua do Raimundo 5; ☎266 706296; www.cafealentejo.com; ⏱ 12.30–15.00 & 19.30–23.00 Mon–Sat. A traditional Portuguese tavern with simple but beautifully prepared Alentejo food served on chunky oak tables. Specialities include roast lamb & kid, & *bochechas de porco preto com migas de espargos* (black pork cheeks with asparagus *migas* – a mixture of asparagus & bread with olive oil). €€€

**X Dom Joaquim**  Rua dos Penedos 6; ☎266 731105; www.restaurantedomjoaquim.pai.pt; ⏱ noon–15.00 & 19.00–22.45 Tue–Sun. One of Évora's most popular weekend eateries serving elegantly prepared, simple Alentejo home cooking by local boy Joaquim D'Almeida. Serves dishes like *almofada* (literally, 'cushion' – a generous pork pie), roast kid goat & *arroz de lebre* (rice with hare) to an enthusiastic dining room of local families & couples on an evening out. Quiet mid-week. €€€

**X Fialho**  Travessa do Mascarenhas 16; ☎266 703079; www.restaurantefialho.com; ⏱ noon–16.00 & 19.00–23.00 Tue–Sun. One of the best regional restaurants in the Alentejo. The dining room is formal without being stuffy, with heavy white tablecloths, walls covered with commemorative plates & awards, & waiters in bow ties gliding to & fro & speaking in whispers. Menus, perused over a cover of superb regional cheeses, olives & hams, is meat-heavy, with lamb, beef & pork cooked in regional styles. There are some seafood & fish options. The wine list, which is predominantly regional, is extensive & excellent. Mains from €12. €€€

**X Momentos**  Rua 5 de Outubro 61b; ☎925 161423; ⏱ noon–15.30 & 19.00–22.30 daily. Serves an expansive menu of Portuguese & international dishes whose diversity & exuberant presentation somewhat exceed the quality of what is at heart comfort food. The fish dishes (which are very fresh & well prepared) are a safe option. Extremely attentive service & a decent wine list. €€€

**X Mr Pickwick**  Rua Alcárcova de Cima 3; ☎266 706999; www.evora.net/mrpickwick-mrsnob; ⏱ 11.00–15.00 & 19.00–23.00 Mon–Sat. A little hole-in-the-wall tucked in an alley right off Praça do Giraldo. Vaulted brick ceilings, copper pans on the wall & a tall, dark wood bar with rows of dark Alentejo reds (sold by the glass or bottle) give a cosy feel, complemented by warm service & Alentejo home cooking. Regional dishes include lamb, *migas de bacalhau* (cod cooked with bread & served with fresh orange & coriander) & a range of puddings. The restaurant is named in honour of the owner, who loves Dickens & as a self-proclaimed *bon viveur* identifies with Pickwick himself. €€€

**X Sabores de Alentejo**  M'Ar de Ar Muralhas Hotel, Travessa da Palmeira 4/6; ☎266 739300; ⏱ 12.30–15.00 & 19.00–22.00 daily. A busy open-plan dining room next to the main bar means that meals in this hotel restaurant are accompanied by hubbub & rushing waiters rather than the intimacy of candles. The food is good, however, with local dishes like quail eggs cooked with dry Alentejano ham & Portuguese roast lamb. €€€

**✕ Taberna Típica Quarta Feira** Rua do Inverno 16–18; ☎ 266 707530; ⏰ 13.30–15.00 & 19.30–21.30 Mon–Sat. A rotating menu of Portuguese home-cooking served in generous portions in a traditional tavern set in a small townhouse in the old centre. Specialities include grilled hake & fried pork steak. €€€

## CHEAP

**✕ Art Café** Museu do Relógio, Palacio Barrocal, Rua Serpa Pinto 6; ☎ 266 751434; ⏰ 14.00–17.30 Tue–Fri, 10.00–12.30 & 14.00–17.30 Sat–Sun. This lovely little café – set in a handsome colonial courtyard outside the Watch Museum (page 78) next to Praça do Giraldo — is the perfect place to relax, book in hand, & thick coffee & snack (including delicious Alentejo pita bread stuffed with olives) on the table. €€

**✕ Botequim da Mouraria** Rua da Mouraria 16a; ☎ 266 746775; ⏰ noon–15.00 & 18.00–22.00 daily. Alentejo home-cooking from welcoming owners Domingos & Florbela, with a menu overflowing with local dishes including *migas, lombinhos de porco preto* (black pork loin), cheese pastries & quince jelly – all made locally sourced & washed down with Alentejo whites, reds & liqueurs. €€

**✕ Café Arcada** Praça do Giraldo 7; ☎ 266 741777; www.lusitana.com; ⏰ noon–22.00 daily. As much a bar as a patisserie – serving ice-cold draught beer, steaming Portuguese coffee, steaks & comfort food, & delicious snacks & cakes (including *pastéis de nata*). Great for watching the world go by on the Praça do Giraldo. €€

## ROCK BOTTOM

**✕ Pão de Rala** Rua do Cicioso 47; ☎ 266 707778; ⏰ 07.30–20.00 daily. Excellent coffee & local cakes, including *pão de rala* itself (see page 186). €

# BARS, NIGHTLIFE AND ENTERTAINMENT *Map, pages 64–5.*

Évora is the only town in the Alentejo with any nightlife beyond bars and restaurants. Options are nonetheless limited.

**♀ Maria Severa Casa de Fado** Rua Santa Catarina 25; ☎ 968 351100; Facebook: restaurante. mariasevera; ⏰ 23.00–03.00 Tue–Sat. The only location in the Alentejo where you will hear authentic live *fado* music, often performed by top acts from Lisbon & Coimbra, who in the past have included Celeste Rodrigues, Soraia Branco & Ana Moura. Decent food, petiscos & a lovely tavern space.

**☆ EME** Praça Joaquim António de Aguiar 18; ☎ 927 133869; ⏰ 23.00–03.00 Wed–Sat; from €4. Bar & club with a lively ladies night on Wed & music from DJs like Peter Beats & Curto. Mostly house music.

**♀ Évora Wine Bar** Rua do Raimundo 93; ☎ 266 735625; ⏰ 18.30–midnight Tue–Sat. Cosy little tavern bar with a good choice of Alentejo wines (& some beers). Occasional live music.

**☆ Praxis** Rua de Valdevinos 21a; ☎ 266 708177; www.praxisclub.com; ⏰ 23.00–03.00 Fri–Sat & some weekdays in high season; from €5. The city's biggest club with DJs like Enigma & Moreno, & big, very popular parties usually filled with students from the university.

**☆ Passion** Patio do Salema s/n; ☎ 925 613006; ⏰ 23.00–03.00 Fri & Sat; from €2. One of Évora's most popular bars/clubs with house, trance & hip-hop from Portuguese DJs like Fernando Alvim & Grouse & Miko.

# SHOPPING

Most of the best souvenir shops are on Rua 5 de Outubro running north from Praça do Giraldo to the cathedral. Évora is the best place in the Alentejo to shop for general items, especially shoes and clothing. Shops throughout the city sell myriad items made from cork, from the expected – tablemats and bottle stops – to the unexpected – umbrellas, handbags and ties. Shops generally open from Monday to Friday from 09.00 or 10.00 to 19.00, and from 09.00 or 10.00 on Saturday until 17.00 or 18.00.

**Ana Sousa** [64 D4] Praça do Giraldo 80; ☎266 741991; www.anasousa.com. One of Portugal's better mid-range designers, offering fashionable, smart casual & evening wear for women. Excellent value.

**Artesanato Diana** [65 E4] Rua 5 de Outubro 48; ☎266 704609; montsobro.com. Together with their sister shop Mont'Sobro a little further up the street (see below), this has the best choice of cork souvenirs in Évora, with bags, shoes, slippers (lined with sheepskin), tablemats & even bow ties.

**Camport** [64 C2] Rua José Elias Garcia 22; ☎932 116060. One of a handful of excellent shoe shops selling well-made, modish men's & women's footwear made in soft & supremely comfortable leather.

**Ervideira wine shop** [64 E4] Rua 5 de Outubro 56. A broad selection of Portuguese & Alentejo wines.

**Fonte de Letras** [64 E4] Rua 5 de Outubro 51; ☎266 899855; www.fontedeletras.blogspot.pt. Arty local book & music shop with a range of high quality Portuguese CDs (which you can listen to), Portuguese & English language books & a small café serving organic coffees, teas & snacks.

**Gente da Minha Terra** [64 E4] Rua 5 Outubro 39; ☎964 956259. Brightly coloured, contemporary ceramics, wooden jewellery, scarves & general souvenirs, together with wines, jams & a small selection of Portuguese CDs.

**Lar Moveis** [64 F3] Rua 5 de Outubro 88; ☎266 743044. One of the largest shops on the street,

selling antique Portuguese furniture & ceramics, cork souvenirs & wine.

**Lojatelier 73** [64 B4] Rua Serpa Pinta 73. Contemporary, locally made handicrafts including jewellery, aprons, ceramics & bags designed by shop owner Isabel Bilro.

**Louro** [64 B1] Rua José Elias Garcia 32; ☎266 702700; Facebook: lourowines. One of the best & longest-established wine merchants in the city, founded in 1951 & with a broad range of high quality Portuguese & regional wines & wine-related paraphernalia.

**Miranda Ferrão Joalheiros** [64 D4] Rua 5 de Outubro 28; ☎266 702209. One of the best traditional jewellers in the city, with a range of beautiful northern Portuguese rings (including some unusual wedding bands), & filigree gold brooches, earrings & pendants.

**Mont'Sobro** [64 E3] Rua 5 de Outubro 66; www.montsobro.com. A broad range of artisanal items crafted from cork, from fruit bowls & floor tiles to suitcases & umbrellas.

**O Arco** [64 A4] Rua dos Penedos 15. An antiques gallery selling beautiful curve-legged Portuguese furniture & contemporary painting, set in a 15th-century falcon aviary lovingly restored by owner Francisco Piteira.

**Pochê** [64 C2] Rua João de Deus 120; ☎266 703688. Hand-crafted, fashionable leather, cork & fabric bags.

## OTHER PRACTICALITIES

✚ **Farmácia Motta Capitão** [64 C4] Praça do Giraldo; ☎266 759170

✚ **Hospital da Misericórdia de Évora** [65 A8] Recolhimento Ramalho Barahona, Av Sanches de

Miranda 30; ☎266 760630; www.hmevora.pt

✉ **Post Office (Correios CTT)** [64 D2] Rua de Olivença s/n; ☎266 745480

## WHAT TO SEE AND DO

**AROUND THE LARGO CONDE DE VILA FLOR** Begin a wander around old Évora in the centre of the city, at the Largo Conde de Vila Flor. This attractive rectangular *praça* is surrounded by some of the best examples of the Roman, Gothic and Baroque architecture that earned Évora its World Heritage Site status.

**Templo Romano (Roman Temple)** [64 E2] At the far northern end of the Largo Conde de Vila Flor, with dark Corinthian columns stark against the sky, is the Roman Temple. It is the only significant remnant of the old Roman settlement of

Ebora. It once stood on one edge of the main public square, or forum, which would have served as the Roman town's principal meeting place and market. The building you see today is not original, but is rather a romantic reconstruction built in the late 19th century by the Italian architect Giuseppe Cinatti. Archaeologists have had to piece together clues as to the building's origin and purpose from its parts rather than Cinatti's whole. For many years the ruin was referred to as the Temple of Diana, but it is unlikely ever to have been dedicated to the goddess. The myth probably arises from associations with Sertorius – the 'Lusitanian Hannibal' – who had a headquarters in the city (see page 8) and who paid homage to Diana. Most Roman forum temples were dedicated to Jupiter or to the cult of the emperor, and it is likely that this building was no exception. According to research by the Portuguese archaeologist Maria da Conceição Lopes, the original building probably dates from the reign of Claudius I in the first century AD, when Ebora was known as *Liberalitas Lulia*. The architectural style is unique to Iberia and North Africa. The 14 fluted columns, topped with intricately carved Corinthian capitals in Estremoz marble, are built from carved granite. Excavations around the building have exposed a 5m wide water tank. This would have run around the base of the temple, possibly being used as a public bath. Steps would have led up the podium to a main door behind the columns. This would have led in turn to the temple sanctuary. The architrave would have been topped by a frieze, cornice, pediment and a roof, the latter almost certainly made of terracotta tile.

The temple has had a long and not always distinguished history. The original building was ransacked by invading northern European hordes during the decline of the Roman Empire in the 5th century, further dismantled by the Moors, and then served briefly as an arsenal after the Reconquest. In the 15th century its remaining superstructure was preserved when it was incorporated into a castle tower, with the columns and architraves kept as part of the new building's walls. The tower served as a slaughterhouse for a brief period and then formed part of a series of structures used during the bloody Portuguese Inquisition. The tower was finally demolished by Giuseppe Cinatti, who reconstructed the temple as we see it today, making use of the remnants and various other bits of masonry distributed around the *praça* and the wider city to create a romantic ruin, a semblance of the original temple.

## Museu de Évora (Évora Museum) [64 F3] (*Largo Conde de Vila Flor s/n;* ☏ *266 702604; museudevora.imc-ip.pt;* ⊕ *09.30–17.30 Tue–Sun; admission €3, free on the first Sun of the month; ticket price includes entry to the cathedral*) The city's museum sits immediately opposite the temple, 30m to the south, housed in a 17th-century former episcopal palace. It's a fine small museum with some beautiful sculpture and painting. The ground floor is devoted to the former (with pieces from the Roman period through to the Renaissance). Look out for the Roman funerary stelae and several pieces by Portugal's most important late Renaissance sculptor, Frenchman Nicolau Chanterene – notably the Cenotaph of Bishop Dom Afonso, the tomb of Álvaro da Costa (ex-governor of Brazil) and a tender statue of a very young Virgin and Child from an altarpiece in the palace of Dom Luís da Silveira, Count of Sortelha. Chanterene is most famous for his Manueline work on the Mosteiro dos Jerónimos in Lisbon, but he lived part of his life in Évora.

The first floor of the museum is devoted to curiosities (a narwhal horn, a Mongol shield, some ornate Baroque silver and gold ecclesiastical pieces) and to Flemish, Portuguese and Italian painting – most of it religious or portraiture. The grandest and most illustrious work is the 17th-century polyptych of the life of Our Lady, made up of 13 paintings showing scenes from Mary's life and painted by a group of unknown Flemish artists. The lesser-known works may prove even more interesting to visitors. These include a wonderful depiction of the *Supper of the Holy Family* by Josefa de Óbidos, one of the few prominent female artists of the Baroque period. Josefa was born in Seville to an Andalusian mother and a Portuguese father – the painter Abílio de Mattos e Silva – under whom she learnt her craft. She worked with him from childhood, and at the age of 14 produced a remarkable representation of St Catherine in Coimbra, where her father was working on the Convento da Graça. She is best known for her still lifes, but her religious paintings are more remarkable for their exquisite creative control, especially in the use of light to create a feminine intimacy, exemplified by the strong sense of family love in the painting displayed here.

Other paintings to look out for include a portrait of Catherine of Braganza at the age of 12 by Avelar Rebelo. After she became Queen of England in 1662 Catherine was unpopular with the English aristocracy, largely because she was a Catholic in a virulently anti-Catholic court. She was never crowned queen, as Catholics were forbidden from attending church. She was repeatedly betrayed by Charles II, who had numerous mistresses (one of whom Catherine was forced to accept as a lady–in–waiting), was portrayed as dowdy by court artists like Sir Peter Lely and is largely remembered by the English for being less than glamorous and for introducing tea and port wine to Britain. The Évora portrait shows a very different Catherine – proud, regal, rather beautiful and clearly a good deal happier than she would be in England.

### Fórum Eugénio de Almeida [64 F3] (*Largo do Conde de Vila Flor;* \ *266 737145; www.fundacaoeugeniodealmeida.pt;* ⊕ *10.00–18.00 Tue–Sun; admission €4, free Sun*) This contemporary art space hosting temporary shows is housed in the former Palace of the Inquisition. Some of the original rooms – including the inquisitor's office – have their original Baroque ceiling paintings. Look for the seal of the Inquisition on the oak ceiling of the Courtroom – a cross flanked by an olive bush and a drawn sword. The houses in the garden next to the Fórum are decorated with unusual 16th-century murals depicting many-headed dragons, leopards, peacocks and bizarre phantasmagorical figures.

### Cartuxa [64 E3] (*Largo do Conde de Vila Flor;* \ *266 748300; www. fundacaoeugeniodealmeida.pt;* ⊕ *10.00–18.00 Tue–Sun; admission €4, free Sun*) The Cartuxa, or former charterhouse, is next door to the Fórum, and now houses a wine and olive oil tasting centre and upmarket restaurant (see page 69). The centre offers wine tastings, sells Alentejo bottles and organises wine and olive tours of the region.

### Convento de Lóios e a Igreja de São João Evangelista (Lóios Convent and Church of St John the Evangelist) [64 F2] (*Largo do Conde de Vila Flor;* \ *967 979763;* ⊕ *10.00–13.00 & 14.00–17.30 Tue–Sun; admission €3, or €5 with a combined ticket which also includes admission to the Palácio dos Duques de Cadaval*). The convent and church lie opposite the Roman Temple, immediately to the east. They were built on the site of the old Moorish castle. Bits of it remain intact in the towers of the next door palace, and its influence is felt in the art and architecture of the buildings. The convent is now a *pousada* – one of Portugal's state-run luxury hotels (page 67). It's well worth popping inside for coffee or a meal, if only to see the beautiful 15th-century Manueline cloisters, where the restaurant is now situated (page 69). Their double, curvilinear arches show a clear Islamic influence.

The church itself became in effect the private place of worship for the dukes of Cadaval – scions of the Braganza family whose title was created in the 17th century by John IV. Its interior is covered with stunning *azulejo* tiles telling the life story of Saint Lawrence Justinian, an Augustinian friar who became the first patriarch of Venice and who negotiated the city's relations with the Ottoman Empire after Constantinople fell to Muslim forces in May 1453. His story is one which resonated with the clergy of 15th-century Évora, and Portugal as a whole. They were painted by one of the Alentejo's most illustrious artists, Antonio de Oliveira Bernardes (c1686–1732), whose art decorates myriad Portuguese churches, including the magnificent cathedral in Braga and the Jesuit church in Lisbon. The church has a grim ossuary, a hidden Moorish cistern and is thick with tombs – including those of Dom Francisco de Melo (descendant of Rodrigo de Melo, the founder of the church), attributed to Nicolau Chanterene (page 31), and many of the Cadaval dukes.

## Palácio dos Duques de Cadaval (Palace of the Dukes of Cadaval) [64 F1]
(*Largo do Conde de Vila Flor;* ⏰ *10.00–13.00 & 14.00–17.30 Tue–Sun; admission €2.50, or €5 with a combined ticket that also includes entrance to the Igreja de São João*) In life, the dukes spent their days in the Cadaval Palace next door to the Lóios Convent. The palace is a building flanked by heavy towers and topped by a castellated wall. Wander inside to see the temporary art shows, the eclectic collection of manuscripts, formal portraits (mostly of the Cadavals), jewellery, and the view of the Roman Temple from the palace's inner courtyard.

## Universidade de Évora (Évora University) [64 G1] (*Largo dos Colegiais 2;* ✆ *266 740800;* ⏰ *no opening hours; free admission*) The university sits behind the Church of St John the Evangelist to the northeast of Cadaval Palace. It was founded as Portugal's predominant Jesuit theological school in 1559, after the order had been turned away from Portugal's great university city of Coimbra in favour of their rivals the Dominicans (who founded the College of Saint Thomas Aquinas in Coimbra in 1566). Technically the university is the second oldest in the country – though it was closed between 1759 (when the Marquis of Pombal expelled the Jesuits from Portugal) and 1973 when it reopened. It's an airy Renaissance building with two storeys of arcaded cloisters surrounding a central, lawned court, some attractive 18th-century *azulejos* and a central hall whose ceiling is made of the tropical red dye wood which gave Brazil its name.

## Sé (Évora Cathedral) [64 F3] (*Largo do Marquês de Marialva;* ✆ *266 759330;* ⏰ *09.00–noon & 14.00–16.30 daily; admission €2.50; Sacred Art Museum* ⏰ *09.00–11.30 & 14.30–16.00 Tue–Sun; admission €3.50*) The cathedral lies some 200m south of the museum. A vast stone hulk, it inelegantly fuses Romanesque, Gothic and Baroque. Its massive masonry and squat pinnacled lantern tower dominate the sky. It looks like a refuge in the shape of a church, built by a despot to fortify himself against any conceivable onslaught. And in essence this is what it was. Work first began on the building in 1186, a year after the death of Portugal's first king, the crusader Afonso 'the Conqueror'. Portugal's second king, Sancho I 'the Populator', lay the foundation stone on the rubble of a desecrated Moorish mosque, at a time when Évora was a Christian outpost torn from the heart of the Almohad Empire and still terrified that it would be swept away in dire reprisal from the powerful Al-Andalus to the east. Two years before work on the cathedral had begun, the great warrior king Abu Yaqub Yusuf had constructed a monumental mosque whose main minaret, the Giralda, could be seen for miles over the sweeping plains that surrounded his new fortified

capital Seville. Évora Cathedral was built in its shadow, the first major Christian temple of the Portuguese Reconquest in the Alentejo. In its massive militarised stone and mish-mash of architectural styles, it reflects the evolution of Portugal itself from fledgling Crusader kingdom to Europe's greatest colonial power.

When work began on the building, the prevailing architectural style was Romanesque. The side façades, cavernous, top-heavy lantern tower and huge, frowsty nave (with its massive, rounded rose granite arches) are in this style. The expansive cloisters (with Manueline flourishes and sculptures of the Evangelists), rose windows and entrance portico are later Gothic. The latter is particularly impressive – extending in six marble arches over corbels decorated with effigies of the apostles standing over rows of human and fantastical animal figures. St Peter (looking to heaven) and St Paul are immediately on either side of the doorway and were sculpted by master craftsman Telo Garcia, from Lisbon. They are flanked by the other ten (less of course Judas Iscariot) carved in a cruder style attributed to a less skilful, anonymous sculptor.

The most interesting features of the interior are the chapels, of which there are six, all of them Baroque or Rococo. The Lady Chapel (which is the oldest), Chapel of St Lawrence, Chapel of St Mantius (who is said to have served the Last Supper) and the Chapel of the Blessed Sacrament are dominated by fine Portuguese Baroque altar pieces, covered in glittering gilt. They surround the main chapel, which juts from the eastern end of the church, its white marble incongruous with the rose granite of the original building. It was commissioned by King João V in the early 18th century and executed by the royal architect, Johann Friedrich Ludwig (João Frederico Ludovice), a Lusitanian-German who designed the palace of Mafra in Lisbon, and like that building and João's lavish court, was funded by gold from the mines of Minas Gerais in Brazil. The chapel is a meditation in coloured marble, decorated with a beautiful cedar crucifix by Portuguese sculptor Manuel Dias and a painting of the Assumption by Agostino Masucci, an Italian who had also worked for João on the Palace of Mafra.

The cathedral's **sacred art museum** (*see page 75 for contact details and admission details*) is located in the old cathedral choir school next to the church. It contains an interesting 14th century French sculptural triptych of the Virgin (missing its original ivory head), which opens to reveal painted scenes from her life, vestments, monstrances and works by Portuguese artists including Diogo de Contreiras – one of the most important painters of the Portuguese Renaissance.

## AROUND THE LARGO DA PORTA DE MOURA [64 G4] The Largo da Porta de Moura, the old city gate since Roman times and now a busy traffic junction, lies 200m north of the cathedral and is reached along the steep and winding Rua de São Manços. The Largo is watched over by some handsome Renaissance houses with mudéjar-Manueline balconies (most notably Garcia de Resende's house, a national monument, on the corner of São Manços and Freiria de Baixo). A 16th-century water fountain sits at its centre – a rectangular marble tank topped by a marble ball inscribed with the words *Qui Convertit Petram in Stagna Aquarum et Rupem in Fotes Aquarum Anno 1556* ('he who turns stone into ponds and rock into fountains, 1556'). This is one of the oldest extant city fountains in the Alentejo and until the mid 20th century was one of Évora's great meeting places. Locals would gather to chat under the adjacent arcades. Travellers would water themselves and their animals as they came in and out of the city. Subjugated by the car, the fountain is now relegated to isolation on a traffic island, and is little more than a landmark. Use it to find the two more interesting churches (page 77) which lie in the immediate vicinity.

**Igreja da Misercórdia (Church of Our Lady of Mercy)** [64 F4] (*Largo da Misericórdia s/n;* ✆ *266 703864;* ⏰ *09.00–noon & 14.00–17.30 Mon–Sat; free admission*) This tiny church sits to the west along the Rua da Misericórdia, a handsome mannerist structure designed by architect to the archbishop Manuel Pires (who was also responsible for the church of Santo Antão). It has a richly carved mannerist portico and one of the prettiest naves in the city, covered with more beautiful *azulejos* by António de Oliveira Bernardes and crowned with a Baroque altarpiece.

**Igreja do Carmo (Carmelite Church)** [65 G5] (*Rua Dom Augusto Eduardo Nunes s/n;* ⏰ *09.00–noon & 14.00–17.30 Mon–Sat; free admission*) This church, one of the most peaceful and little visited in the city, lies due south of the fountain along Rua Dom Augusto Eduardo Nunes. Entrance is through an impressive Manueline doorway made up of carved ropes and knots and transposed from an original Manueline Braganza palace destroyed in a fire in the 17th century. The church interior has been largely renovated in recent years. The expansive, airy nave is flanked by chapels with towering gilt altarpieces which rank among the best in the city and whose exuberant carving seems inspired by the hope of Resurrection rather than the gloom of crucifixion and death so often expressed in Baroque church art in Iberia. There are some beautiful paintings in there too, including one of Our Lady looking down from Heaven to St Simon Stock (founder of the Discalced Carmelites, the most staunchly contemplative Carmelite order) and another of St Simon and St Teresa of Avila (the author of *The Interior Castle*, one of the greatest mystical treatises written in Iberia). Both paintings are masterpieces and were discovered by the current priest, Padre Joaquim, when he recently took over patronage of the church; they were rolled up in a pile and set aside to be thrown away as rubbish. Both are Italian, and as this book was going to press Joaquim was undertaking research to verify whether they are by an important Renaissance master.

The church's most striking painting tells the story of the death of the founder of the Carmelite order, Albert Avogadro (St Albert of Jerusalem). The saint is depicted in Heaven, standing next to the Virgin, with a wound in his side. Albert was stabbed to death by the Master of the Hospital of the Holy Spirit in Acre (now Akko), northern Israel, during the Lateran Council in 1215. Mary ignores Albert, instead looking down from heaven at the saint's murderer, who lies next to a discarded pack of playing cards (symbolising his dissolute life), prostrate and repenting, a dagger in his hand. A tongue of flame descends from the Virgin to his forehead, signifying that the importance of the murderer's repentance and forgiveness is greater even than Albert's sainthood. This reinforces one of the central beliefs of the Carmelite order – the need to make an existential choice to turn from attachment to the world to a life of prayerfulness and contemplation.

**THE PRAÇA DO GIRALDO AND AROUND** If the Largo Conde de Vila Flor is the spiritual heart of Évora, then the Praça do Giraldo [64 D4] is its secular heart. This is where the modern city meets, on the handsome Portuguese paving and under the cloisters of the buildings which line the square. It's where locals stop for a coffee al fresco at one of the tables next to the fountain, or indoors, newspaper in hand, at one of the numerous little cafés which sit around the *praça*. And it's where commuters and tourists leave and arrive in buses and taxis, making it as bustling as it was when the square was a market in Roman times.

The Praça do Giraldo had a more sinister secular life in older times. It was here in 1483 that the Portuguese monarchs of the house of Avis wrested control from the powerful barons of the Alentejo with the public execution of Fernando, the third

3

duke of Braganza, by King João II. And between 1536 and 1773, the Inquisition carried out its grizzly *autos-da-fé* here. These were initially clerical and involved the forced conversion of Jews and Muslims under the aggressive Dominican-dominated Portuguese church. Seeing its power, the Inquisition was rapidly taken over by the Spanish Habsburg monarchy (who ruled Portugal as a province between 1580 and 1640), and controlled thereafter by a landowning aristocracy who ruthlessly exploited their indentured workers and used the *autos-da-fé* to inflict grizzly punishments or executions, meted out to keep the poor in check. These included the burning alive of convicts on giant funeral pyres in 1573.

The square's relationship with politics continued into the modern age. The establishment of the first Portuguese Republic was proclaimed from a townhouse on the Rua da República in 1910, as was the fall of the Estado Novo in April 1974.

Even the **Igreja de Santo Antão (Church of St Anton)** [64 C4] (*Praça do Giraldo s/n;* ⊕ *09.00–noon & 14.00–17.30 Mon–Sat; free admission*) – a heavy early Baroque structure at the *praça's* northern end, dating from 1557 and designed by the Bishop of Évora's official architect Manuel Pires – has secular roots. It occupies the site of Roman Ebora's great Triumphal Arch, which was demolished to make way for the church. The Henriquina Fountain sits in front of the building, dating from 1571 and carved from a single slab of rose-coloured Estremoz marble. This was originally fed by the city aqueduct and was the city's main source of drinking water. Its eight fonts represent the eight streets which radiate off the Praça do Giraldo. These include Rua Serpa Pinto immediately to the west, where you'll find the **Museu do Relógio (Watch Museum)** [64 C4] (*Rua Serpa Pinto 6;* \ *266 751434; www.museudorelogio.com;* ⊕ *14.00–18.00 Tue–Fri, 10.00–12.30 & 14.00– 18.00 Sat–Sun; admission €2*), a delightful collection housed in a former Baroque palace and established by timepiece enthusiast António Tavares d'Almeida (1948– 2012). Together with its sister museum in Serpa, the museum protects more than 3,000 timepieces, including priceless carriage clocks and antique watches by Rolex, Piaget, Vacheron Constantin and Patek Philippe, some of the them dating from the 1700s.

The Rua da República runs south to Évora's most famous attraction, the **Igreja de São Francisco and the Capela dos Ossos (Church of St Francis and the Chapel of Bones)** [65 E6] (*Rua da República s/n;* \ *266 704521;* ⊕ *09.00–12.45 & 14.30– 17.30 Mon–Sat & 10.00–12.45 & 14.30–17.30 Sun; admission €2*). If the Carmelite Church (page 77) focuses on the spiritual, then its Franciscan counterpart is grimly material, built in the 17th century when the Inquisition was at the height of its powers and punishments and executions must have been a frequent occurrence in the nearby Praça do Giraldo. 'We bones wait here for yours to join us' reads the inscription over the chapel. Thousands are squeezed into the walls of the building, yellowing in the frowsty air. It's hard to know what's more horrible – the chapel itself or visions of it being built. One imagines the friars with a huge pile of remains in the middle of floor, arranging them neatly by size, fitting them into the gaps in the wall like pieces of a puzzle – a femur here, a tibia there, a small skull squeezed into the last small space between the top of a column and the ceiling. Popular mythology has it that the monks were trying to solve an overcrowding problem at the city's monastic cemeteries and that the bones are all of the clergy. In reality the friars robbed graveyards throughout the city, exhuming the dead from the city's cemeteries in a quest for morbid masonry. By the time they had finished their work the monks had consumed some 5,000 skeletons and were, it seems, so inured to death that they hung two desiccated corpses – one of them of a child – from the chapel walls for extra shock factor. A popular legend has it that they are the corpses of an adulterous husband and his son, cursed never to rot to bones by the betrayed wife on her deathbed.

The Church of St Francis itself is less morbid. But it's still grim – a vast, grey cavern of soaring Gothic arches. Its portico is strongly Mudéjar – with horseshoe arches – a hallmark of the Spanish architect Afonso de Pallos, who worked both on this church and the huge cathedral in Seville. The church was a royal chapel for the Avis kings John II and Manuel I, who have their coats of arms carved into the top of the portal. The huge nave is covered with Portuguese Renaissance paintings, including on the altar of the Senhor da Coluna (Lord of the Column) a magnificent Mannerist polyptych depicting the Passion of Christ, by Évora artist Francisco João.

Immediately to the north of the church of St Francis is **MADE (Museu do Artesanato e do Design – Museum of Arts and Design)** [65 E6] (*Praça 1 de Maio 3;* \ *266 771212;* ⊕ *09.30–13.00 & 14.30–18.00 Tue–Sun; admission €2*), with an eclectic collection of mostly Portuguese traditional arts, crafts and contemporary design.

Immediately opposite on the Largo da Graça, and worth a look in passing, is the early 16th-century Neo-classical **Igreja e Convento da Graça (Church and Convent of Our Lady of Grace)** [65 F6], now a military college, whose façade is topped by a lumpy bell tower and statues of seated, roaring giants, known to locals as the *meninos da graça* ('children of grace'), symbolising the four corners of the world dominated by the Portuguese Crown. They are reputedly by Nicolau Chanterene (page 31). The church itself is bare, secularised and last functioned as a primary school.

Immediately beyond the church of St Francis to the south are the city's leafy **public gardens**, set around a small lake with fountains in the grounds of the former royal palace of King Manuel I. A fire in the early 20th century destroyed all of the building except parts of a small turreted Manueline-Mudéjar pavilion with horseshoe arches known as the **Ladies' Gallery** [65 D7], which was later reconstructed. It now serves as a temporary exhibition and concert space. Close to the pavilion are a series of faux Renaissance ruins, constructed from the remnants of a former episcopal palace by Giuseppe Cinatti, the Italian architect responsible for the rebuilding of Évora's Roman Temple. Nearby is a **statue of Vasco da Gama**, the great explorer who became the first European to reach India by sea in 1499, thus opening the way for Portuguese expansion and the country's first imperial golden age. Da Gama is said to have been given the commission to make his voyage by King Manuel in the defunct palace.

**THE CITY WALLS AND BEYOND** Évora has two sets of city walls – one dating from Roman times, the other from the late Renaissance. Remnants of both still exist. The most impressive remnants of the early wall are the **Porta de Dona Isabel (Queen Isabel's Gate)** [64 D2] (*Rua de Dona Isabel s/n*), a very well preserved Roman arch and the **Torre de Sisebuto (Sisebuto Tower)** [64 D3] (*Rua Alcárcova de Cima s/n*) where bits of Roman wall are visible, together with the exposed ruins of a 1st century AD Roman house with simple glazed frescoes.

The city's outer walls, which are still largely intact in a number of places – most notably around the Porta da Lagoa gate (at the northern end of Rua Cândido dos Reis) – date from between the Middle Ages and the 17th century. Évora's **aqueduct** [64 D1] (*Rua do Cano s/n*) bisects the 17th-century walls between the Porta da Lagoa and the Porta de Avis gates in the city's north. It was built on the site of an earlier Roman construction, and dates from the early 16th century. A walking or bike trail follows its path, beginning on Rua Cândido Mendes (where houses and shops have been built into the aqueduct arches) and continuing for 8.5km past the 17th-century **Forte de Santo António (St Anthony's Fort)** (built by King João IV and not open to the public), to Metrogos, from where it is possible to catch a taxi back to Évora. The tourist office (page 66) has information on the route and some local tour operators (pages 66–7) offer it as a day excursion. Nearby is the **Convento do Calvário**, founded in 1570 by a minor Franciscan order (open to the public on request), with some fine gilt carving.

The attractive Baroque **Convento da Cartuxa (Carthusian Monastery)** [64 A1] lies just beyond the city walls near the Porta da Lagoa. It was built by the Carthusians between 1587 and 1598 and after the monks were expelled, served as a palace for the Kings of Braganza and subsequently as the Évora School of Agriculture, during which time the beautiful church was turned into a grain store. It is now once more a Carthusian monastery, owned and managed by the Eugénio de Almeida Foundation (page 74), through whom visits can be arranged. It is the only Carthusian monastery in Portugal.

The **Ermida de São Brás (St Blaise's Hermitage)** (*Praça de São Brás s/n*) is a striking, brilliant white Mudéjar building with Moorish turrets, castellated walls and a simple *espadaña* bell gable immediately south of the public gardens and just beyond the city walls. What you see today is largely a 1531 reconstruction of a late 15th-century building. The interior is simple Romanesque. The *azulejo* mural inside shows details from the life of St Blaise, an Armenian saint whose intercession is said to ward off disease.

## AROUND ÉVORA

**The Almendres and Zambujeira megalithic sites** Together with the cromlech of Vale de Maria do Meio (off the N370 road some 2km north of the A6 near Guadalupe), this group of mostly Neolithic monuments are the most significant in the Iberian peninsula and rank among the most important prehistoric remains west of the Pyrenees. Almendres Cromlech is one of the oldest and biggest stone circles in the world – with construction beginning around 6,000bc and continuing through to the structure you see today, which dates from around 3,000 years later. Almendres and the other monuments nearby are the best known of a scattering of some dozen stone circles and 800 menhirs in the Évora region – testament to the area's large population in prehistoric times. The monuments are of probable astronomical significance. Évora is situated on one of only two latitudes in the world where the full moon appears on the zenith on certain nights of the year.

*The Almendres monuments* A well signposted dirt road running off the N114 (which runs west out of the city) leads for some 5km to the village of Nossa Senhora de Guadalupe and thence to a clearing under a wizened almond tree. Look for signs for the Cromeleque dos Almendres and Menir dos Almendres. From here it's a ten-minute walk along a rivulet-worn track running between two fenced-off fields to the **menhir** – a worn shard of crystal encrusted granite. It sits sentinel over a plain of ancient cork oaks and lichen-splashed almonds, its ancient mystical presence profaned by fences and ugly grain stores. Évora's spires and roofs sit on the horizon, distant in the east.

The more famous and impressive Cromeleque dos Almendres (Almendres Cromlech, or 'Cromlech of the Almonds') is some 2km beyond the menhir along the same road. It's a huddle of more than 20 stones, smoothed into concaves by millennia and clustered in a cork oak grove on a hill, also looking out towards Évora. They look like spectral, shrouded children, frozen in time. Try to come during the week early or late in the day when the site is empty, the breeze plays in the trees and the grove is imbued with a sense of the sacred.

## PORTUGAL'S DOLMEN CHURCHES

Despite the rigours of the Inquisition, one of the Catholic Church's great strengths has been its ability to assimilate the sacred traditions of other faiths into its own, especially where the Jesuits and the Benedictines dominated. In Latin America the Maya of San Juan Chetumal use Christ and the saints as new symbols for ancient connections, and the saints of the Afro-Brazilians of Bahia and Pernambuco double up as Candomblé divinities or *orixas*. Many Catholics on the left wing of the church have long striven to protect this ability of the Church to preserve rather than destroy – an ability whose ultimate fruit was enunciated as *Nostra Aetate* and *Lumen Gentium* in the doctrinal documents of Vatican II.

This process of assimilation is an ancient one. It began with St Paul's invitation to the gentiles to enter the temple even though they were not circumcised. And its history can be traced from the Middle East into Europe. In Portugal it is most concretely seen in the Alentejo, where prehistoric sacred dolmens have been incorporated into chapels and churches.

The most famous of these is the **Anta de Pavia in Mora** – a tiny town 50km north of Évora. This 4m-high stone burial chamber sits in the town's central praça, capped with a tiny belltower, fronted with a Romanesque doorway and with a shrine to St Denis inside. Most visitors don't even notice it's there. There's a similar chapel at **São Brissos in Montemor-o-Novo** (page 104).

When Christianity came to Portugal with the Romans, this was a profoundly pagan country. And in its rural areas it remained so – at least formally – through the Gothic invasions, the Moorish conquest and even the Inquisition. Like the Irish, the old Portuguese were people deeply connected to the land and the seasons. They worshipped the spirits of trees and springs, and as Christianity became dominant, especially after the Reconquest, these traditions were transformed, even as their substance remained the same. Feminine spirits of springs or grottoes often became associated with the Virgin Mary and old places where the sacred imbued the Earth became new holy sites where the Madonna appeared to local people. Most were ignored by all but the locals – tolerated or ignored by priests, assimilated into daily Catholic life. One was championed by the Catholic Church's ecclesiastical hierarchy – at Fátima.

Nowadays most of these sacred sites are forgotten, consigned by modernity to old stories, separated from the land or any experience of being alone with it, under a full moon or canopy of stars free of artificial light. The sites are remembered only in legends of werewolves and witches associated with the hills around Arronches, or the *duende* of the woods.

But in the hills of São Mamede and the Vale do Guadiana, there are still silent places, and in the smaller towns and villages of the Alentejo you can find seers and bonesetters, and locals who pray to the Madonna of a spring or rocks. The dolmen churches of the Alentejo serve as a physical reminder of the ancient traditions these few unwittingly preserve.

**The Zambujeira dolmen** The great dolmen of Zambujeira lies 3km to the southeast (look for the turn-off a few hundred metres after the village of Valverde, which lies immediately south of Nossa Senhora de Guadalupe). At over 6m tall it's one of the biggest passage mounds in Europe and originally lay beneath a low hill covered with turf – like Maeshowe in Scotland. It is unique in Portugal.

**4**

# The Alto Alentejo

The Alto Alentejo is one of the most beautiful and romantic parts of Europe. As you drive north or east from Évora the remnant crags of ancient mountains burst from the vast flatness of the plains – islands in a sea of wind-waving wheat, gnarled and ancient olives or rindless cork oaks. Most are crowned with a castle – Moorish turrets and balustrades sitting sentinel in ancient anticipation of some encroaching Crusader or Spanish army. Medieval villages like Arraiolos, Evoramonte, Alandroal and Redondo cluster around their walls, a jumble of terracotta and whitewash. In places these villages have secondary fortifications, as in the hilltop strongholds of Castelo de Vide, Monsaraz and Marvão, where you can watch eagles from above as they soar on the thermals. In others the castles have grown to become towns, such as Estremoz, surrounded by the rubble of the marble industry, the royal capital of the Bragança dynasty at Vila Viçosa or the great fortress of Elvas, ringed with massive star-shaped walls and used as a base by Wellington in the Peninsular War.

But it's not all history. Large areas of the Serra de São Mamede mountains in the eastern Alto on the border with Spain are protected as a natural park, which is home to some of Europe's rarest birds. And like the Baixo, the Alto Alentejo's plains have long been Portugal's breadbasket and wine cask. Towns like Borba and Arronches produce some of Iberia's finest wines and olive oils.

## TOURIST INFORMATION

The regional tourism office is based in Évora (*Praça do Giraldo 73*; ✆ *266 777071*; *www.visitevora.net*; ⊕ *Apr–Sep 09.00–19.00, Oct–Mar 09.00–18.00 daily*). Municipal and local tourist offices are given in the section on each town. Those in Elvas and Estremoz have the most useful information.

### GUIDED TOURS

**Rota do Fresco**  Rua 5 de Outubro 20, Vila Nova da Baronia; ✆ 284 475413; www.rotadofresco.com. Art tours & excursions around the region, from half-day trips to week-long itineraries, focusing on the *azulejos*, frescos & murals within the region's castles, churches & national monuments. Locations include Évora, Alandroal, Borba & Vila Viçosa, & the agency runs courses on how to paint your own

fresco or mural, which can be incorporated into a tour.

**Tur Aventur Outdoor Escapes**  ✆ 266 743134; m 966 758040; www.portugalbestcycling.com. Mountain bike rides, half-day & day hikes & jeep tours throughout the Alto Alentejo. Offers visits to the cork oak forests & marble mines around Estremoz & Borba, Monsaraz & Alqueva Lake around Mourão.

## GETTING THERE AND AWAY

**BY AIR**  The nearest airports are at Lisbon, 134km from the regional capital Evora, and Badajoz (*Carretera Badajoz-Balboa s/n, 06195 Badajoz, Spain*; ✆ *+34 924 21*

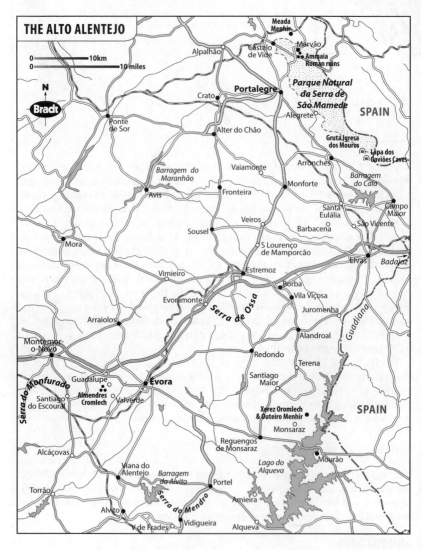

## THE ALTO ALENTEJO

0 ——————————— 10km
0 ——————————— 10 miles

N

Bradt

**Meada Menhir**
Alpalhão
Castelo de Vide
Marvão
**Ammaia Roman ruins**
**Parque Natural da Serra de São Mamede**
Portalegre
Crato
Alegrete
SPAIN
Ponte de Sor
Alter do Chão
**Gruta Igresa dos Mouros**
**Lapa dos Gaviões Caves**
Arronches
*Barragem do Maranhão*
Vaiamonte
Monforte
*Barragem do Cala*
Avis
Fronteira
Santa Eulália
Campo Maior
Veiros
São Vicente
Sousel
Barbacena
Mora
S Lourenço de Mamporcão
Vimieiro
Estremoz
Elvas
*Badajoz*
Borba
Vila Viçosa
Evoramonte
*Serra de Ossa*
Juromenha
Arraiolos
*Guadiana*
Alandroal
Montemor-o-Novo
Redondo
Terena
*Serra do Monfurado*
Guadalupe
Évora
Santiago Maior
Santiago do Escoural
**Almendres Cromlech**
Valverde
**Xerez Oromlech & Outeiro Menhir**
Monsaraz
SPAIN
Alcáçovas
Reguengos de Monsaraz
*Lago do Alqueva*
Mourão
Viana do Alentejo
*Barragem do Alvito*
Portel
Torrão
Amieira
Alvito
*Serra do Mendro*
V de Frades
Vidigueira
Alqueva

*04 00; www.aena.es*), fewer than 5km from Elvas and with flights to Madrid and Barcelona on Air Europa).

**BY CAR** To get the most from the Alto Alentejo you will need a car. While the larger towns like Elvas and Estremoz are well-connected to Lisbon, Évora and the other major towns of the Alentejo, getting to the smaller villages on public transport involves a great deal of time on long, slow local bus journeys. Many of the gorgeous rural hotels which make staying in the Alto Alentejo such a pleasure are unreachable without a car. The A6/IP7 motorway runs through the heart of the Alto Alentejo, connecting Estremoz, Elvas and the Spanish border at Badajoz with Évora and Lisbon. Smaller roads branch off this motorway, for Monsaraz, Evoramonte and the other minor towns and villages. The fast IP2/E802 trunk highway runs north off the A6/IP7 to Portalegre, from where it's a short drive to Castelo de Vide and Marvão in the far north.

**BY TRAIN** Évora is the only town in the Alto Alentejo with a railway station (page 63) (*www.cp.pt*), connecting the Alto Alentejo to Lisbon's Oriente station via Casa Branca, and to Beja (*4 trains on weekdays, 3 on weekends; €15*).

**BY BUS** Those travelling by bus will find Évora the best base for the region as it is a transport hub for much of the central Alto Alentejo. The city has the most frequent connections to Borba, Elvas, Estremoz, Moura, Portalegre, Reguengos de Monsaraz (for Monsaraz) and beyond to Santarém, Lisbon and Spain. Those travelling to the coast will find it quickest to go via Beja (which has twice daily connections to Grândola – from where there are services to Alcácer do Sal, Odemira and Sines), Setúbal or Lisbon. See www.rede-expressos.pt for precise details.

## GETTING AROUND

The best way around the Alto is with a hire car, picked up at Lisbon airport, or if arriving in the region overland from Spain or on public transport from another part of Portugal, then in Évora or Elvas. Europcar has offices in both cities and offers rates competitive with those at Lisbon airport. Roads are well paved and have good signposting, and parking is readily available even in town centres and extremely cheap by European standards.

## TOUR OPERATORS

For more locally based tour operators see the relevant sections of the chapter.

**AGIA** Praça do Giraldo 73, Évora; \963 702392; www.alentejoguides.com. Guided tours throughout the Alentejo including the historic centre of Évora, Elvas, Marvão & Monsaraz.

**Alentejo Retreat** www.alentejoretreat.com. Self-catering holidays in the Serra de São Mamede National Park for birdwatchers & wildlife lovers (pages 120–2).

**Birding in Portugal** Quinta do Barranco da Estrada, Santa Clara-a-Velha; \283 933065; www.birdinginportugal.com. Birdwatching in the Alentejo for dedicated birders & birding photographers, & those who want to include birdwatching as part of a more general holiday. The owners run a beautiful rural retreat, the Quinta do Barranco da Estrada inland from Odemira (page 145).

**Birds and Nature** www.birds.pt. Company that organises birdwatching tours throughout the region, including trips to the Serra de São Mamede.

**Gourmand Breaks** \+34 972 219640; www.gourmandbreaks.com. This Spanish company offers fine dining & wine tours of the Alentejo (including to L'and Vineyards in Montemor-o-Novo (page 103), the only Michelin starred restaurant in the Alentejo, with or without other locations in Portugal & Spain.

**Grekking** Rua D Nuno Álvares Pereira 163, Grândola; \927 403942; www.grekking.com. A broad range of excellent cultural, wildlife, trekking, birdwatching & conservational tourism trips throughout the Alentejo (& Portugal as a whole), including birdwatching, hikes & mountain bike excursions in the Serra São Mamede.

**Publibalão Ballooning** \912 207276; www.publibalao.com. Hot air ballooning – operators with more than 20 years' experience.

## ELVAS

This spectacular garrison town (and UNESCO World Heritage Site) crouches behind massive star-shaped fortifications a stone's throw from the Spanish border. Wandering the winding, whitewashed alleys, which run like mycelia around the old Moorish castle, is a delight. Old men in cloth caps snooze on doorsteps, cats meow as you pass, then rush up walls coloured with bougainvillea and scurry across the hot terracotta tiles. Washing sways gently in the hot summer air, next to peeling doors, which lead to the dark and cool interiors of gilt and *azulejo*-covered Baroque and Gothic churches. There are terrific views from the battlements of the old city over the plains and a succession of little forts built between the 17th and 19th centuries towards the city's fortified counterpart, Badajoz in Spain.

**HISTORY** The proliferation of Megalithic and Neolithic sites around Elvas shows that even before Rome or Islam had their empires, the fertile plains around Elvas were one of the most extensively settled areas of inland Iberia. There are some 22 prehistoric cromlechs, dolmens and tombs in Elvas municipality alone – most sitting forgotten in farmers' fields, and dating from the Chalcolithic (Copper) and Bronze ages between 4000 and 1800BC. By the Iron Age the strategic importance of the hill on which modern Elvas sits had led to the first fortifications. After the Lusitanian wars of 155–138BC, the Romans built a castellum here, complementing the larger fortresses they had constructed at Pax Augusta (Badajoz), Évora and Emerita Augusta (Mérida). After the fall of Rome Elvas was largely ignored by the conquering Visigoths and the town fell into decadence until it was taken by the Muslims, and expanded under Ibn Marwan from a Roman fortress to a medina or walled town, which they named Ialbax. Remnants of the Muslim walls still remain and the castle largely dates from this period.

Elvas's strategic importance grew after the Reconquest. It was taken from the Muslims in 1229–30 by Dom Sancho II, who gave the city its Latinised name, a coat of arms, reconstructed and strengthened fortifications and the first of Elvas's myriad churches. During a fresh campaign against the Moors in eastern Alentejo and western Spanish Extremadura and subsequent conflicts with the Spanish, Elvas was given a new set of walls, the 'Cerca Fernandina', with 11 gates and 22 towers, the principal of which was the Torre Fernandina. It still stands today. These withstood Spanish attack during a month-long assault in 1381, after which the city was re-enforced with troops and mercenaries from England under the command of Edmund of Cambridge.

In the early 16th century relative peace made Elvas increasingly prosperous. By 1513 it had grown large enough to be declared a city by Manuel I. A new main *praça* – surrounded by rectilinear European Renaissance streets – was built at the feet of the new Sé (now the Church of Our Lady of Assumption). These contrasted starkly with the medieval Moorish medina that lay up the hill around the castle. Water was brought right to the city centre across an impressive Neo-classical aqueduct, the Aqueduto da Armoreira, and the city gained a flurry of churches, monasteries and convents, including the Igreja da Misericordia (Church of Mercy) and Domínicas (Church of the Dominican Nuns), which survive to this day.

War began again in 1580 when Elvas was attacked and lost to the Spanish forces and then the Spanish crown after Philip II of Castile took the Portuguese throne. The revolt of Évora by the Duke of Bragança in 1637 signalled the beginning of the wresting of national power, and the control of Elvas, from the Spanish. The city would never be taken again. After Spanish attacks against Elvas in 1644, the city received even stronger walls and a series of outer star-shaped satellite forts, which make up most of what you see today. These were largely designed by Dutch Jesuit Johannes Augustijn Peter Cieremans (João Pascácio Cosmander).

By the 18th century Elvas was a fort as powerful and impregnable as its Spanish counterpart a few kilometres across the border, Badajoz. And in the 19th century the city became one of the principal bases of operations for the Duke of Wellington's

Peninsular War campaigns, during which time the joint British and Portuguese armies lay bloody siege to Badajoz, using Elvas as their base.

The local people – known as Elvenses – didn't begin to live beyond the fortification until the 1930s, when the Estado Novo built new neighbourhoods, a cinema, post

## DOUBLE DUTCH: COSMANDER AND THE OCCUPATION OF OLIVENÇA

The Jesuit engineer Father Joannes Cieremans (known in Portugal as João Pascácio Cosmander) was born in Hertogenbosh, Holland in 1602 and moved to Olivença in 1648 as part of a group of civil engineers contracted by the Portuguese to fortify their garrison towns and coastal cities during the early part of the Restoration War against the Spanish. Cosmander largely designed the outer fortifications at Elvas (including the minor forts), the citadel at Juromenha and the defensive walls of Olivença. In 1647, while returning to Elvas from Lisbon, he was captured by a small group of Spanish cavalry men who transported him to Madrid. Ushered into the presence of the Spanish monarch Philip IV, Cosmander was invited to pledge allegiance to Spain, something he may have been more than willing to do as Portugal was also at war with Holland at the time. Cosmander planned and led a successful attack on his adopted hometown of Olivença in June 1648, during which he was killed trying to force open the gate he knew to be most vulnerable to attack. It wasn't the last time that the Spanish would try to capture Olivença. In 1709 they lay siege to the town again under the Wars of Spanish Succession, destroying the Roman bridge, which remains in ruins to this day. In 1801 during the War of Oranges they finally occupied Olivença, renamed the town Olivenza and forced Portuguese king Dom João to sign the Treaty of Badajoz. They stipulated that Olivença would remain Spanish, and in return Spain would make no further claims on Portuguese territories. Six years later the Spanish – in league with Napoleon – reneged on that agreement, leading the Portuguese king to declare the Treaty of Badajoz *Ex justa causa* (invalid under its own terms). Over the following century the Spanish refused to hand Olivença back.

Spain and France of course lost the Napoleonic Wars – or, as they were known in Iberia, the Peninsular Wars. The Final Act of the Congress of Vienna (1815), signed between European powers including Spain to end the Napoleonic period and settle territorial disputes, specifically mentions Olivença. Article 105 states that Spain must return it to Portugal. But despite being signatories, Spain didn't give it back. Instead it tightened its grip. In 1840 the local population was banned from speaking Portuguese (even in church), a ban which was continued throughout the 20th century until the end of the Franco regime.

To this day, despite cordial relations between Spain and Portugal, the town remains a bone of contention. The Portuguese government does not recognise Olivenza as Spanish, and many Olivenses feel Portuguese. A visit to Olivenza by former prime minister of Portugal Admiral Pinheiro de Azevedo in 1981 prompted the Spanish to send a contingent of the civil guard to the town, in fear of riots against Spain. And as recently as 2014, 80 residents of Olivenza petitioned the Portuguese government to be granted Portuguese citizenship instead of Spanish. Some 100 further requests are still pending. Lobby groups including the Grupo dos Amigos de Olivença (*www.olivenca. org*) continue to lobby for the return of the town to Portugal.

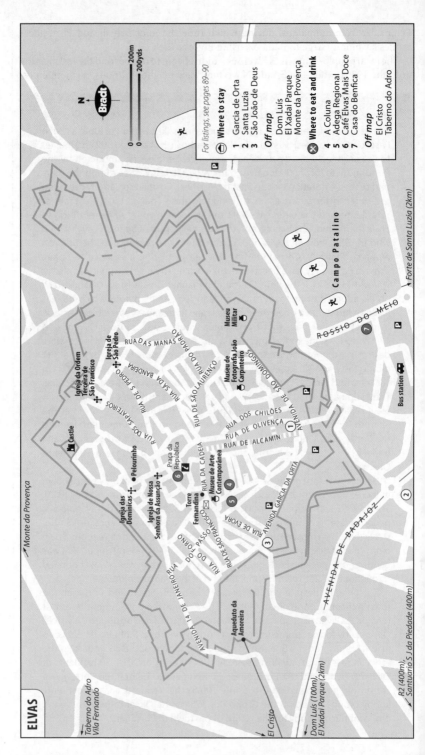

ELVAS

*For listings, see pages 89–90*

**Where to stay**
1 Garcia de Orta
2 Santa Luzia
3 São João de Deus

*Off map*
Dom Luís
El Xadai Parque
Monte da Provença

**Where to eat and drink**
4 A Coluna
5 Adega Regional
6 Café Elvas Mais Doce
7 Casa do Benfica

*Off map*
El Cristo
Taberno do Adro

Taberno do Adro
Vila Fernando

Monte da Provença

Igreja da Ordem
Terceira de
São Francisco

Igreja de
São Pedro

RUA DAS MANAS

RUA DE SÃO PEDRO

RUA DOS SAPATEIROS

Castle

Pelourinho

Igreja das
Dominicas

Igreja de Nossa
Senhora da Assunção

Praça da
República

Torre
Fernandina

Museu de Arte
Contemporânea

RUA DE S. DA BANDEIRA

RUA DE SÃO LOURENÇO

RUA DA CADEIA

RUA DE SÃO FRANCISCO

RUA DO TORNO

RUA DO PASSO

AVENIDA 14 DE JANEIRO

Aqueduto da
Amoreira

El Cristo

RUA DE SÃO LOURENÇO DO PADRÃO

Museu de
Fotografia João
Carpinteiro

Museu
Militar

RUA DOS CHILÕES

RUA DE OLIVENÇA

RUA DE ALCAMIN

AVENIDA DE SÃO DOMINGOS

AVENIDA GARCIA DA ORTA

RUA DE ÉVORA

Campo Patalino

ROSSIO DO MEIO

Bus station

AVENIDA DE BADAJOZ

R2 (400m),
Santuario S J da Piedade (400m)

Dom Luís (100m),
El Xadai Parque (2km)

Forte de Santa Luzia (2km)

Bradt

0    200m
0    200yds

office and the first pousada in Portugal, the Pousada de Santa Luiza, which remains the city's foremost hotel to this day (see below).

## GETTING THERE AND AWAY

**By car** Elvas lies off the main IP7/A6 Lisbon–Évora–Badajoz motorway which extends into Spain as the E90 passing through Mérida and eventually running to Madrid. Madrid is 420km, Lisbon 206km, Évora 84km and Badajoz international airport 15km from Elvas (with flight connections from the latter to Madrid and Barcelona).

**By bus** The *rodoviária* is 1km outside the old city, just off the A6 motorway. There are buses to Badajoz (*10 daily with Grupo Ruiz and Rodoviária do Alentejo; services go on to Évora; 30mins*), Borba (*6 daily; 30mins*), Estremoz (*5 daily; 45mins*), Évora (*4 daily; 1hr 35mins*), Portalegre (*2 daily; 2–2½ hrs; change here for Castelo de Vide & Marvão*), and Vila Viçosa (*2 daily; 35 mins*). There are also buses to Lisbon and Faro. For more information see www.gruporuiz.com, www.rodalentejo.pt and www.rede-expressos.pt.

**By air** Elvas has no airport, but Badajoz Airport in Spain is 15km away and has connections to Madrid and Barcelona.

**GETTING AROUND** The best way to see Elvas is on foot. The old city is completely contained within the fortified walls and is easily negotiable on foot. On weekdays it is straightforward to park in Elvas city centre (around €0.25 per hour), though be wary of the very narrow, winding streets. At other times it's better to park outside the old city centre and walk into town.

**TOURIST INFORMATION** The city's **Posto do Turismo** (*Praça da República s/n; 268 622236; www.cm-elvas.pt; ⊕ winter 09.00–18.00 Mon–Fri, 10.00–12.30 & 14.00–17.30 Sat & Sun, summer 09.00–20.00 Mon–Fri, 10.00–12.30 & 14.00–19.00 Sat & Sun*) has helpful English-speaking staff and a series of useful pamphlets on the key attractions, annotated maps and lists of hotels and restaurants.

## TOUR OPERATORS

**AGIA** See *Tour Operators*, page 85. Offers guided walks of Elvas, usually on a Saturday. Contact for full details.

**Alentejo 2U** (Finogosto) Rua dos Quarteis 9-A; 268 628110; www.finogosto.pt. Cultural & gastronomic tours around Elvas & the Alto Alentejo, including Islamic Elvas, Elvas & Olivença, Elvas & Badajoz, the fortifications, museums & religious architecture.

⬆ **WHERE TO STAY** *Map, page 88.*

🏠 **Monte da Provença** (10 rooms) São Vicente village s/n; 912 799202; www. montedaprovenca.com. Set in beautiful countryside 7km from Elvas, surrounded by vineyards & gardens & offering spacious, tastefully decorated suites & rooms, this traditional 14th-century Portuguese *fazenda* house offers a mix of hominess & 4-star comfort. There's a luxurious pool in the grounds & the owners offer a huge menu of activities inc ballooning, horseback riding, birdwatching, grape & olive harvesting & wine visits. Excellent restaurant. €€€€

🏠 **Dom Luís** (50 rooms) Av de Badajoz s/n; 268 636710; www.hoteldluis-elvas.com. Ask for the newer rooms in this business-like town hotel (under 10mins' walk from the historic centre). They were gutted & completely renovated in 2014, in contemporary muted tones & with fitted work stations & new beds. Some have a view out over the aqueduct. The hotel has a pool & a modest restaurant. €€€

🏠 **Pousada de Santa Luzia** (25 rooms) Av de Badajoz s/n; 268 637470; www.slhotel-elvas. pt. With its half-cylindrical terracotta roof tiles &

curvy concrete walls, Portugal's first ever *pousada* is a fusion of Californian hacienda & Le Corbusier modernism. It was opened under the Estado Novo in 1942. The furniture has been replaced (comfy sofas, wicker chairs, chunky table lamps) but many of the 1940s fittings remain as if in aspic – imagine Esther Williams posing next to the sculpted fittings in the pool. Indeed, as a protected building the hotel cannot be modified, meaning that there are no lifts, so bags have to be carried up the stairs. Decent restaurant & helpful staff, who can help to organise guided tours of the city & forts. €€€

🏠 **São João de Deus** (56 rooms) Largo São João de Deus 1; ☎ 268 639220; www. hotelsaojoaodeus.net. Though the public areas are looking a little frayed nowadays, this hotel housed in a restored convent remains the best place to stay within Elvas's historic centre. Rooms vary in size and quality. The best have views from the windows & raw stone or *azulejo*-decorated walls. There's

a swimming pool & the hotel restaurant serves Alentejo dishes. €€€

🏠 **El Xadai Parque** (13 rooms, 15 apartments) Estra Nacional N4 km 179; ☎ 268 621397; www. orbitur.pt. A complex of apartments & rooms gathered around a large swimming pool on a low hill 3km from Elvas town centre. Views of Elvas & Badajoz cities from the hotel. There is a restaurant & tennis court, & rooms come with fully equipped kitchens. Staff can organise excursions including horseback riding, cycling & hikes. A good option for families. €€

🏠 **Garcia de Orta** (9 rooms) Avenida Garcia de Orta 3A, Elvas; ☎ 268 623152; www.rgarciadeorta. com. Modest though this little guesthouse may be (with tiny, but well-kept a/c rooms, some with attractive views), it sits in an excellent location – on the edge of the historical centre next to the city walls, 5mins' walk from a large car park & fewer than 10mins' walk from the bus station. €€

---

✗ **WHERE TO EAT AND DRINK**  *Map, page 88.*

✗ **Adega Regional**  Rua João de Casqueiro 22; ☎ 268 623009; www.adegaregional-elvas.com; ⏱ noon–15.00 & 18.30–22.30 Wed–Mon. With walls decorated with *azulejos* & a menu rich with dishes like *migas de coêntros com prezinhas de porco fritas* and *borrego asado no forno*, this popular local eatery is the best location for traditional Alentejo cooking. €€

✗ **El Cristo**  Av da Piedade; ☎ 268 623512; ⏱ noon–15.00 & 18.30–22.30 daily. If you've eaten your fill of black pork and *migas* & are craving seafood then this long-established immensely popular open plan (& strip-lit) dining room next to the Parque da Piedade on the western edge of town will satisfy your craving, with dishes like *bacalhau dourado*, grilled tiger prawns and *ameijoas à bulhão pato*, all of which are specialities of the house. €€

✗ **Taberna do Adro**  Rua de Elvas 96, Vila Fernando; ☎ 268 661194; ⏱ noon–midnight Thu–Tue. Charming little village restaurant 6km west of Elvas, with room for just a few tables, decorated with Alentejo arts & crafts & serving Alentejo home-cooking. €€

✗ **A Coluna**  Rua do Cabrito; ☎ 268 623728; ⏱ noon–15.00 & 18.30–22.30 Wed–Mon. Simple but well-located working man's dining room with basic Portuguese standards like *bacalhau* & pork & beans washed down with drinkable table wine in an attractive dining room covered in *azulejos*. €

✗ **Casa do Benfica**  Rua Rossio do Meio 16; ☎ 268 088791; ⏱ noon–15.00 daily. You don't have to be a member of the Benfica supporter's club to eat the great-value set meal (soup, bread & olives, meat/fish of the day, pudding & coffee – all for €8) in the clubhouse restaurant, the Restaurante Sabores Gloriosos, but you will be greeted like a celebrity if you arrive here with a club scarf. €

☕ **Café Elvas Mais Doce**  Praça da República 9a; ☎ 919 976098. Delicious snacks, coffee, *pasteis de nata* (custard tarts made by Aloma, awarded Portugal's best *pastel de nata* prize in 2013) & chocolate cake, which owner Rosario assures diners is not merely the best in Elvas, but actually the best in the world. €

## WHAT TO SEE AND DO

**Aqueduto da Amoreira (Amoreira Aqueduct)**  For many centuries the Elvenses had a problem with water. As the town crowns a hill, most of the water sources were wells and springs. Aside from the Poço d'Alcalá, a well which had survived since Moorish times, most of these lay beyond the city walls. With the population growth that accompanied Elvas's first wave of prosperity in the early 16th century the problem became grave – and was rendered still more acute by an increasingly bellicose Spain whose quarrels with Portugal posed a perennial threat to the town. There simply wasn't enough water for the increasing numbers of inhabitants to survive a prolonged siege. In 1498 Manuel I imposed a tax on Elvas – the Real d'Água – to raise the money for the construction of the city's magnificent aqueduct, an imposing Neo-classical structure which at 8km long remains the most extensive in Iberia. The structure was designed by the great architect Francisco de Arruda (see box, page 28), who was responsible for the city's cathedral (now the Church of Our Lady of Assumption). But the anticipated cost was so high that work on the project didn't begin until 1537, and wasn't completed until 1622, when water finally began to flow into the Fonte da Misericórdia fountain in the city centre. For 329 years the fountain was filled by the aqueduct, withstanding sieges, wars and droughts. But it couldn't withstand the petrol engine. By 1951 it had come to be seen as a hazard to traffic and was removed from its pride of place next to the Igreja da Misericórdia to a more modest position on Praça 25 de Abril, where it sits dry under the sun.

**Castelo de Elvas (Elvas Castle)** (*Parada do Castelo;* ⏲ *09.30–13.00 & 14.30–17.30 daily; admission €1.50*) Elvas's ancient fortress sits at the highest point in the city, commanding a sweeping view of the plains from the battlements. Like most Alentejo fortresses it's a hodge-podge of Roman, Moorish and Christian Reconquista. While the walls are Moorish, most of what you see today dates from between the 13th and 16th centuries, remodelled first by Dom Dinis and then by Dom João II, who commissioned the tower. The castle was also a residence for the *alcaide*, the chief noble in the city. Many of Portugal's important treaties were signed here, including the Treaty of Elvas in 1382, which ended John of Gaunt and Fernando I's attempts to claim the Castilian throne for England and Portugal and established the borders of Portugal itself. The castle also served as a military base for Arthur Wellesley (later the Duke of Wellington) in the Peninsular War. A number of the English soldiers who died in that war are buried in Elvas's English Cemetery, restored for the new millennium by the British ambassador to Portugal, Sir John Holmes.

Elvas's castle fell into ruin in the late 19th century but was renovated by local people, who lobbied the government to protect more of the country's national heritage. The castle became Portugal's very first protected national monument in 1906.

---

### MAY THE LEGEND LIVE ON: THE HERO OF ELVAS

Look out for the Elvas coat of arms on the side of the Aqueduto da Armoreira, depicting a rider carrying a flag on his lance. This commemorates a local hero, Gil Fernandes, who some time in the 14th century crossed the border into Badajoz and stole that city's standard. Carrying it back to Elvas, hanging from his lance, Fernandes was intercepted by a troop of Spanish cavaliers who chased him back to Elvas. Seeing so many armed Spaniards, the Elvenses refused to open the gates of the city. Gil Fernandes raised the standard to the walls of Elvas with his lance, turned to face his assailants and gave up his life shouting 'the man dies but the legend lives on!' ('*Morra o homem e fique a fama!*')

**Torre Fernandina and the city walls** (*Rua da Cadeia;* ⊕ *Apr–Sep 10.00–13.00 & 15.00–19.00 Tue afternoon–Sun, Oct–Mar 10.00–13.00 & 14.30–18.30, Tue afternoon–Sun*) Elvas's three sets of walls can best be seen from the top of the Torre Fernandina tower (see *History*, page 86, for a description of the tower and the evolution of the walls), reached by a winding staircase. Look out for the drawbridge, which still spans a ditch at the main gate, and the bastions, which surround it, further inside. A small permanent exhibition within the tower is devoted to the history of fortified Elvas. The city has a number of gates. Perhaps the most interesting is the disused **Temple Gate**, easily recognisable by its classic horseshoe arch (which has been carefully restored). This is the old pre-Reconquest entrance to the 12th-century Moorish citadel. It strongly resembles the fort entrance to Almohad Badajoz, comprising a double gate watched over by a tower and with heavy ashlar gateposts and horseshoe arches in *alfiz* frames. It is now part of a private residence.

## The forts

***Forte de Santa Luzia (Santa Luzia Fort)*** (*Avenida de Badajoz;* ⊕ *May–Sep 10.00–19.00 Tue afternoon–Sun, Oct–Apr 10.00–17.00 Tue afternoon–Sun; admission €2*), **Graça Fort** (*not formally open to the public*) and the **Wellington Fortresses** (*not formally open to the public*) all sit on the edge of Elvas city and were built at various stages. The earliest, Santa Luzia, dates from 1641 and was designed initially by the veteran campaigner Matias de Albuquerque to garrison 300 soldiers. The fort was expanded by Italian Ieoronymo Roxeti and later Cosmander (see box, page 87) as part of the general city fortifications. Santa Luzia was completed in 1643, making it far older than the great forts built by the Frenchman Sébastien Le Prestre de Vauban, which Cosmander's Portuguese fortresses are sometimes said to emulate (all of Vauban's forts were built between 1667 and 1707). The fort has a long history: battered by the Marquis of Torrecusa's artillery during the Restoration War in 1644, and by the Marquis of Bay in the War of Spanish Succession in 1706 and 1711, it was finally occupied by the Spanish, the French and ultimately the victorious English during the Peninsular War of 1807–11. There's a secret passageway linking the fort to the centre of the city. The fort now houses a small museum.

It was during the Peninsular campaign that Wellington and William Carr Beresford (who commanded the Portuguese army between 1809 and 1820 when the monarchy had left for Brazil) further fortified Elvas with a series of **smaller fortresses**. These pock the countryside around the city and were used to garrison the huge army amassed by the English commanders. During the war entire villages between Badajoz and Elvas were looted for building material. Three of these fortresses survive to this day – the Fortim de São Pedro, the Fortim de São Mamede and the Fortim de São Domingos (which is in ruins). All can be visited but do not have set opening times.

Although it's crumbling and dilapidated nowadays, the finest of Elvas's forts is the **Forte da Graça**, which began life as the Hermitage of Our Lady of Grace, commissioned by Vasco da Gama's great grandfather. The current building (with its grand central governor's palace and elegant, carved main gate) was designed under the supervision of Wilhelm, Count of Schaumborg-Lippe by the French civil engineer Guillaume Louis Antoine de Valleré on the model of Vauban's French fortresses. The construction took just under 30 years, during which time it was the biggest military building project in the country. In 1763 there were 6,000 men and 4,000 animals working here – an enormous proportion of the population of Elvas.

## Igreja de Nossa Senhora da Assunção (Church of Our Lady of the Assumption)

(*Praça da República s/n;* ☉ *summer 10.00–13.00 & 15.00–18.00, winter 09.30–12.30 & 14.00–17.00; free admission*) Elvas's old cathedral was designed by the great Manueline architect Francisco de Arruda (see box, page 28), who had worked on the Torre de Belém in Lisbon. This was his chance to make a statement – to step beyond architecture into civic planning. The cathedral would be the jewel in the crown of a new Elvas, decorated with Manueline flourishes but replacing the Gothic with a fashionable new style, Renaissance Neoclassicism. Harmonious Renaissance proportions would impose order on Elvas's Moorish curves. A stately new *praça* (levelled by a team of workmen over many years) would be the centrepiece, and the city would have fresh running water here, right in its heart, brought by an elegant, Neo-classical aqueduct.

The church took rather longer than Arruda would have liked – opening its doors in 1537 after two decades of building but even then incomplete. Work continued on the decoration (under the guidance of master mason Diogo Mendes) until the end of the century, by which time it had become outmoded and further craftsmen incorporated the newly fashionable Baroque.

While the exterior of the building is undecorated Renaissance Classical (and much modified, having lost all its Manueline exuberance but for a Manueline circular window and a lateral doorway), the interior is particularly beautiful with pillars with Manueline corbels decorated with the Portuguese and Elvas coats of arms and the cross of the Order of Christ rising elegantly to an intricately painted vaulted ceiling capped with Manueline carved bosses and illuminated with clerestory windows. There's a beautifully carved Baroque chancel with a main altar (in multicoloured Estremoz marble) by Elvas-born mason José Francisco de Abreu (born 1753), who also worked on the Igreja da Lapa and the town hall in Villa Viçosa. The painting of the Assumption is by an unknown artist. At the opposite end of the nave is a Baroque organ by Pascoal Caetano Oldovini (aka Oldovino), a master organ-maker from Genoa who worked in the Alentejo between 1742 and 1785 and who renovated the organ in the cathedral of Évora.

The church's sacred art museum is worth a peek, with a collection of handsome golden era furniture, church art and ecclesiastical pieces.

## Igreja da Ordem Terceira de São Francisco (Church of the Third Order of St Francis)

(*Rua dos Terceiros;* ☉ *summer 10.00–13.00 & 15.00–18.00, winter 09.30–12.30 & 14.00–17.00; free admission*) It is an irony that in Portugal and its colonies the most lavish of all the churches tend to be those of the Franciscans (or their lay orders), who are so celebrated for championing asceticism. This church is no exception. Its interior is covered in priceless gilt and decorated with some of Elvas's finest *azulejos*.

The church was completed in 1716, on the site of the old Muslim tanneries. Then it was an empty shell – decorated over the following decades when the order's wealthy churchgoing patrons competed to sponsor ever-more-lavish ecclesiastical art. The gloriously ostentatious main altarpiece (an Aladdin's cave of glittering gold and carved wood), the marble pulpit and the chapels date from 1721. The sculptures are later still and are the work of the Genoese artist Giovanni Battista Maragliano (the son of the more famous Anton Maria Maragliano), who worked in Cadiz and Lisbon, where he was murdered during a robbery. The wonderful *azulejos* showing scenes from the life of St. Francis date from the late 18th century, as is the Franciscan coat of arms (with two crossed arms, Christ's right hand with the nail wound and Francis' left hand with the stigmata wound) above the main doorway.

**Igreja das Domínicas (Church of the Dominican Nuns)** (*Largo das Freiras –
Antigo Convento das Freiras de São Domingos;* ☉ *summer 10.00–13.00 & 15.00–
18.00, winter 09.30–12.30 & 14.00–17.00; free admission*) This church's exterior is
so modest it would be easy to walk past it without noticing it at all. Step inside
and you'll see one of the Alentejo's loveliest church interiors – an octagonal cupola
propped up with decorated pillars and covered entirely with intricately painted
*azulejos*. Beautifully carved wooden altarpieces covered with gilt fill the side chapels.

The church was built between 1543 and 1557 on the site of an even older Templar
church and was originally part of a convent which fell into disrepair (after the
religious orders were expelled from Portugal by Pombal in the 1830s) and which
was finally demolished in 1888.

You enter the building through a 16th-century Renaissance Neo-classical door
capped with two splendid medallions decorated with carved men's faces and a
Dominican cross. The interior decoration stands in contrast. It is a riot of 17th-
century Baroque, with ornate ribbons, garlands, gilt and tracery and striking
*azulejos*. The main chapel is topped by twin paintings of the Lamb of God carrying
an unusual standard decorated with an inverted star. Below is the coat of arms of
the powerful Silva family emblem.

The two side chapels are dedicated to the Virgin and St Thomas Aquinas, the
great Dominican friar and founder of the scholastic system of philosophy based on
Aristotle, which many argue paved the way for the Renaissance and the ideas of the
Enlightenment.

**Igreja de São Pedro (St Peter's Church)** (*Rua de São Pedro s/n;* ☉ *summer
10.00–13.00 & 15.00–18.00, winter 09.30–12.30 & 14.00–17.00; free admission*).
This modest little church is one of the city's oldest – built in 1230 immediately after
the reconquest of the city. While the building has an attractive Gothic doorway
(the only original feature of the church that survived extensive 15th- and 18th-
century modifications), it's remarkable principally for the superbly carved Baroque
altar pieces and ceiling stucco in the aisle chapels, and for its bell tower, which
incorporates one of the original Moorish fortress towers into its structure.

**Santuário Senhor Jesus da Piedade (Shrine of Our Lord of Mercy)** (*Rua da
Piedade s/n; summer 10.00–13.00 & 15.00–18.00, winter 09.30–12.30 & 14.00–17.00;
free admission*) This modest 18th-century Baroque church some 15 minutes' walk
outside the city centre is worth a visit to see more masterly carving by José Francisco de
Abreu (the chapel altars and the font are particularly beautiful) and the thousands of
ex-voto offerings that line the walls of the adjacent rooms. They range from centuries-
old paintings to early 20th-century photographs, embroidery, spooky wax castings
and even crutches, brought by pilgrims over the centuries as offerings to 'Jesus of Pity'.
And the pilgrims still come, especially at the annual September festivities.

**Museu Militar (Military Museum)** (*Largo de São Domingos;* ☏ *268 636240;*
☉ *10.00–12.30 & 14.30–19.00 Tue–Sun; admission €3*) This museum tells Elvas's
long military history in three themed sections – war medicine, war vehicles and war
weaponry – and has pieces dating from the earliest times, through the peninsular
war and into the 20th century.

**Museu de Arte Contemporânea (Museum of Contemporary Art)** (*Rua da
Cadeia;* ☏ *268 637150;* ☉ *14.00–18.00 Tue & 11.00–18.00 Wed–Sun; admission €1*)
Housed in an attractive 18th-century mansion house given to the city in 2007, this

museum focuses on modern Portuguese art, and is principally comprised of a collection amassed by Antonio Cachola.

## Museu de Fotografia João Carpinteiro (João Carpinteiro Photography Museum) (*Largo Luís de Camões s/n;* ☎*268 636470; www.museudefotografiaelvas. com.pt*) This museum houses a collection of old cameras and an archive of some 3,000 photographs charting the history of Elvas.

## Pelourinho (Pillory) This elegant, exquisitely carved Manueline stone column tucked away next to the Igreja das Domínicas (Church of the Dominican Nuns) at the gateway to the old medina dates from the early 16th century. Until the late 19th century it had pride of place on the Praça da República (or, as it was known in those pre-Republican days, the Praça Nova), and had like other pillories been used for public punishment. Prisoners were shackled here and whipped, or suspended in cages hanging from the metal struts on top of the pillory. On 2 October 1872, in the events which were eventually to lead to the establishment of a Portuguese republic, the pillory was taken down, smashed up, with its remnants locked in the municipal museum. What you see today is a partial reconstruction, based on a lithograph of the original by the artist Vitalino de Albuquerque, who in 1940 was just young enough never to have lived in an age when Portuguese were tied to a whipping post.

# ESTREMOZ

Built around one of the Alentejo's most romantic palaces, bristling with fine churches and perched prettily on a hilltop, Estremoz would be one of the most delightful towns in the upper Alentejo were it not for the untidy sprawl of suburbs and marble slag heaps which surround it. Don't let these put you off. Close your eyes as you pass through, enter old Estremoz through one of the magnificent medieval gates and forget all but the perfectly formed historical centre. This is focused on a regal castle keep and *praça*. Stepped streets drop down the steep hill from here to the new part of town, built around a large 18th-century square, the Rossio Marquês de Pombal, a mosaic of Estremoz marble dragon's tooth paving around which you'll find the town hall, tourist office, market stalls selling everything from cakes to leather belts, and parking spaces.

**HISTORY** Estremoz's palatial castle keep was founded in the 1280s by Dom Dinis and his wife Dona Isabel of Aragon, the 'Rainha Santa' ('Saintly Queen'). Dinis was known as 'O Lavrador' ('The Farmer') because of his love for the Portuguese countryside, and Estremoz's castle was one of his many projects to open up the Portuguese 'interior'. It was also a present for his new wife, who became inextricably connected with Estremoz and who was to die in the castle in 1336. When it was built it would have stood solitary on the hilltop. But a royal castle soon attracted courtiers, who built their own houses, and subsequently settlers.

By the 14th century Estremoz had grown from a castle to a fortified town, and continued to be used as a temporary home by a series of Portuguese monarchs. Dom Pedro I lived here until his death, and in 1380 Dom Fernando negotiated a secret deal with Richard II to consolidate the Anglo-Portuguese alliance, during which time his reviled queen, Leonor, became pregnant by her lover João Fernandes de Andeiro, second Count of Ourém.

By the 15th century Estremoz had began to lose influence to Évora (which became the new royal residence of choice) and later to Elvas (which was more important militarily) and Vila Viçosa, where the Bragança dynasty had made their palatial home.

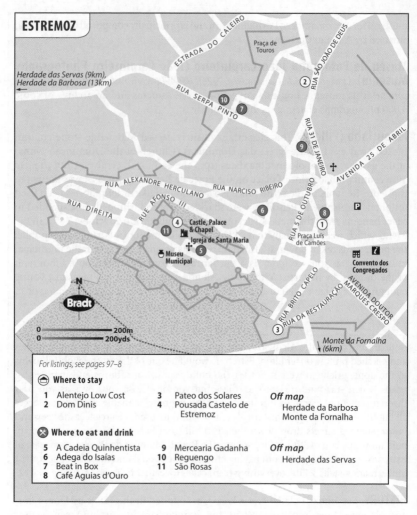

**ESTREMOZ**

Herdade das Servas (9km),
Herdade da Barbosa (13km)

Praça de Touros

ESTRADA DO CALEIRO

RUA SÃO JOÃO DE DEUS

RUA SERPA PINTO

RUA 31 DE JANEIRO

RUA ALEXANDRE HERCULANO

RUA NARCISO RIBEIRO

AVENIDA 25 DE ABRIL

RUA DIREITA

RUA AFONSO III

RUA 5 DE OUTUBRO

Castle, Palace & Chapel

Igreja de Santa Maria

Museu Municipal

Praça Luís de Camões

Convento dos Congregados

N

Bradt

0        200m
0        200yds

RUA BRITO CAPELO

RUA DA RESTAURAÇÃO

AVENIDA DOUTOR MARQUES CRESPO

Monte da Fornalha (6km)

*For listings, see pages 97–8*

🛏 **Where to stay**
1   Alentejo Low Cost
2   Dom Dinis
3   Pateo dos Solares
4   Pousada Castelo de
    Estremoz

*Off map*
    Herdade da Barbosa
    Monte da Fornalha

✖ **Where to eat and drink**
5   A Cadeia Quinhentista
6   Adega do Isaías
7   Beat in Box
8   Café Aguias d'Ouro
9   Mercearia Gadanha
10  Reguengo
11  São Rosas

*Off map*
    Herdade das Servas

**GETTING THERE AND AWAY** Estremoz is very well located, lying immediately off the main IP7/A6 Lisbon-Évora-Badajoz motorway. Évora, Elvas and Castelo de Vide are a short drive away. Borba and Vila Viçosa are on the doorstep. Lisbon Airport is at a distance of 168km, Évora 47km, Elvas 42km, Castelo de Vide 75km and Badajoz International Airport 57km (with flight connections from the latter to Madrid and Barcelona).

The bus station (*terminal rodoviário, Av Rainha Santa Isabel s/n;* ✆ *268 324266*) is 1km northeast of the old city. There are express **buses** to: Borba (*4 daily; 15mins*), Elvas (*5 daily; 45mins*), Évora (*3 daily; 45mins*), Portalegre (*3 daily; 50mins, change here for Castelo de Vide and Marvão*) and Lisbon (*7 daily; 2hrs*). There are also buses to Lisbon and Faro. For more information see www.rede-expressos.pt, and for local buses see www.rodalentejo.pt.

**GETTING AROUND** Estremoz is easily negotiable on foot. Do not drive in the old city, where the streets are extremely narrow and confusing. There are plenty of car parking spaces in the new part of town (around €0.25 per hour), from where it's under a 15-minute walk to the castle.

**TOURIST INFORMATION** The Estremoz Posto do Turismo (*Rossio Marquês Pombal 88A;* ☎ *268 339227; www.cm-estremoz.pt;* ⏰ *10.00–13.00 & 14.00–18.00 daily*) has a limited number of useful pamphlets and an annotated map of the city.

## WHERE TO STAY *Map, page 96.*
See also Borba, Vila Viçosa and the Hotel Convento de São Paulo in the Serra near Redondo, all of which are close enough to Estremoz to be used as an alternative base.

🏠 **Monte da Fornalha** (10 rooms) 6km outside of town – turn right off the N4 100m north of where it bisects the E90; ☎ 268 840314; www.wonderfulland.com. This rural retreat run by the affable Orlanda Alves is particularly lovely in spring, when the flowers are in bloom in the little garden & the sheep & cows fill the fields with the rattle of cowbells. Rooms & suites mix traditional Alentejo whitewash with modish modern minimalism, offset with colourful bedspreads, mosaics, tiles & rustic pastel colours. Spaces are broken by swaying cotton drapes & there's a lovely pine-tree shaded swimming pool with sun loungers. €€€€

🏠 **Pateo dos Solares** (41 rooms) Rua Brito Capelo; ☎ 268 338400; www.pateosolares.com. Elegant modern rooms in soft, muted tones set in an attractive 18th-century mansion house 5mins' walk from the castle. There's a large pool with sun loungers, a good restaurant (with an excellent wine list), & the hotel can organise wine-tasting tours around Estremoz & visits to Marvão, Évora & Castelo de Vide. €€€€

🏠 **Pousada Castelo de Estremoz** (33 rooms) Largo Dom Diniz s/n; ☎ 210 114433; www.pousadasofportugal.com. Not every hotel can boast that it was once a royal palace, but the Castelo de Estremoz can. A dozen kings & queens have slept in its weather-worn Manueline keep, & its walls have witnessed enough plotting & bed-hopping to satisfy a *Game of Thrones* audience. If this fails to intrigue then the castle can also boast wonderful views out over the plains towards Spain & Évora, rooms with regal beds (some 4-poster, others backed with coats

of arms), a fine restaurant & a jewel of a pool which is particularly lovely at dusk. €€€€

🏠 **Herdade da Barbosa** (4 rooms) EM 504, Estremoz–Sotileira road, São Bento do Cortiço; ☎ 966 305900. Scion of an old Anglo-Portuguese family who have grown cork & made wine around Estremoz since the 18th century, Maria Rita Reynolds is a wonderful host. Guests are welcomed to her beautiful historic farmhouse, set in lush hills a few kilometres north of Estremoz, where they can enjoy horseback riding, biking, boating or simply sunsets round the pool sipping Alentejo wine. Maria Rita is full of interesting stories & the food is first class. Be sure to see her hat collection & the farmhouse's eerie echo chamber. €€€

🏠 **Alentejo Low Cost Hotel** (12 rooms) Rossio Marquês de Pombal 13–15; ☎ 268 337300. Rooms may be simple & the fittings functional, but this little hotel is hard to beat for location & good value. Staff are friendly & keep everything spick & span, the tourist office is on the doorstep & the old centre 10mins' walk away. €

🏠 **Dom Dinis** (8 rooms inc dorms) Rua 31 de Janeiro 48; ☎ 268 333929; www.ddinishostel. blogspot.co.uk. Decorated in colours from a sweet packet, giant pictures of a violet-tinged Elvis, a peroxide blonde in sunglasses sitting on a leopard-print chair & a *Where's Wally* beach, this hostel-cum-guesthouse aims to attract the young traveller crowd. There's accommodation in dorms & private rooms. Staff can organise trips throughout the region & guests can enjoy free access to the nearby tennis courts & pool. The historic centre is 15mins' walk away. €

## WHERE TO EAT AND DRINK *Map, page 96.*
✖ **A Cadeia Quinhentista** Rua Rainha Sta Isabel, Castelo; ☎ 268 323400; www. cadeiaquinhentista.com; ⏰ noon–15.00 & 18.30–23.00 daily. This restaurant offers the

ultimate in gentrification – fine-dining in a former medieval dungeon set in the bowels of Estremoz castle. The dining room's gentle romantic lighting & coterie of cocktail-sipping, courting couples contrasts with the grim evocations inspired by the thick stone walls & heavy iron bars on the windows. Chef Alice Pôla's menu is modern Alentejo – crisp, well-prepared & bursting with flavour. It is particularly strong on seafood & game, with dishes like *perdiz suada em azeite* (partridge steamed in olive oil) & *pimentão da horta com amêijoas e migas de batata* (home-grown peppers with clams & puréed potato). The regional wine list is excellent. €€€

✗ **Herdade das Servas** EN4 km136, Rua de Estremoz 4; ☎268 098080; www.herdadedasservas. com; ⏱ noon–15.00 & 18.30–23.00 Tue–Sun. Sitting in a former wine cellar (with beautiful Romanesque arches), this restaurant combines fine Alentejo cooking with sommelier-matched fine Alentejo wines. Dishes include *bochechas do porco preto* (black pork cheeks), *sopa de tomate à alentejana* (Alentejo-style tomato soup) and *costeletas de borrego panadas* (breaded lamb chops), all cooked with aplomb by chef Fé Baía. €€€

✗ **São Rosas** Largo Dom Dinis 11; ☎268 333345; ⏱ noon–15.00 & 18.30–23.00 Tue–Sun. Elegant restaurant run by Margarida Cabaço & her family in a historic town house next to the Torre de Menagem in the heart of the historic centre. The menu is a fusion of international & modern regional cuisine, & includes *migas com entrecosto* (migas with rib-eye steak) and *costela de borrego no forno* (roast goat's ribs). €€€

✗ **Adega do Isaías** Rua do Almeida 21; ☎268 322318; ⏱ noon–15.00 & 18.30–23.00 Mon–Sat. Grilled meat & fish served in generous quantities & in rustic cellar surrounds – the dining room is decorated with huge ceramic wine containers & wall plates. There's often a lively crowd on weekends, especially when the restaurant hosts evenings of live Portuguese folk music. €€

✗ **Mercearia Gadanha** Largo Dragões de Olivença 84; ☎268 333262; www. merceariagadanha.pt; ⏱ noon–15.00 & 18.30–23.00 Thu–Tue. Alentejo & Portuguese standards with a modern touch (beautifully presented on big white plates) served on chunky wooden tables in a bright, rustic-chic dining room in an attractive town house just off the Rossio. The restaurant runs a wine shop stocked with a huge choice of local bottles & a delicatessen selling high-quality Alentejo products. €€

🗏 **Café Águias d'Ouro** Rossio Marquês de Pombal 27–29; ☎268 339100; ⏱ 07.30–18.00 Mon–Sat. This quirky brick-red art nouveau delight, topped with a Gaudiesque decorative balustrade & with every window built in a different architectural style, looks like it belongs in Barcelona rather than Estremoz. Just off the Rossio, it's a great place for a pit stop, a strong coffee & a *pastel de nata* before or after a wander around the town.

🍷 **Reguengo** Rua Serpa Pinto 87; ☎964 108247; Facebook: Reguengo Bar; ⏱ 19.00–02.00 Tue–Sun. Beer & *petiscos* followed by live music &/or DJs at the weekends. Young crowd.

☆ **Beat in Box** Rua Serpa Pinto 65; ☎268 322038; ⏱ 17.00–02.00 Tue–Sun. Bar turned after-hours club, attracting a mixed crowd of 20- to 60-somethings. Live music at weekends, including *fado*.

## WHAT TO SEE AND DO
### Castelo e Palácio de Estremoz (Estremoz Castle and Palace) (See also the listing in *Where to stay*, page 97.) While there has almost certainly been some sort of fortification on Estremoz hill since Roman times and a small Muslim settlement, the building you see today is purely Portuguese. The Tower of Three Crowns should more correctly be called the Tower of Five Crowns, as five kings built it. Sancho II (1223–1248) conquered Estremoz, taking the tiny citadel from the Moors and building the first fortress. Afonso III (1248–1279) expanded it and the current tower was built by Dom Dinis, who greatly expanded the castle into a wing of court, in honour of his wife Isabel of Aragon, around whom a cult of sainthood later grew (page 100). Dom Fernando (1367–1383) expanded the building further still at the beginning of his reign. In 1698, after the building was badly damaged in an explosion, Dom João rebuilt it in its current form (which is distinctly more Baroque than Dom Dinis's original), turning it into what was then the most famous armaments museum in Europe and greatly improving the adjacent buildings, including the church of Santa Maria do Castelo. The mix of architectural styles that

characterise the building, from Gothic and Manueline to Baroque, are testament to its chequered history.

The castle has a long and distinguished military history. Queen Isabel died in the palace in 1336 – exhausted after negotiating the end to a feud between her son Dom Afonso IV and the Castilian King Afonso XI. The castle was nearly lost to Castile in 1383 during the crisis of independence from Spain. But Nuno Álvares Pereira (the Portuguese hero eulogised by Camões, and the father of the House of Bragança), established a garrison here, wresting control from the Spanish and reclaiming Estremoz for Dom João (illegitimate son of Pedro I) and the first monarch of the House of Avis. And in another crisis of succession in 1580 Estremoz was the only Alentejo fortress to resist the Spanish invasion.

During the Restoration War Estremoz was an important garrison town, supporting Elvas. And after the British expelled French troops who had occupied Estremoz, the town performed the same role in the Peninsular War. In 1910 the castle and palace became one of the country's first national monuments and later a *pousada*. Non-guests polite enough to pay for a coffee or evening drinks will be rewarded on request with a discreet private view of the building and from the tower, looking towards Elvas, Portalegre and – on a really clear day – Badajoz in Spain.

## Capela de Rainha Santa (Chapel of the Saintly Queen) (*Castelo de Estremoz;* ⏲ *09.00–12.30 & 14.00–17.30 Tue–Sun; admission €2*) Only those in the know bother to ask for the key to this little chapel in the gallery of design across the square from the castle, and if they do so they're rewarded with a private view of one of the Alentejo's loveliest and most curious churches.

The building is a temple to the cult of the Saintly Queen (and wife of Dom Dinis), Dona Isabel, or St. Elizabeth of Portugal, as she is known to English-speaking Catholics.

Paintings and *azulejos* within the church tell the Queen's life story from her coronation and her intervention in the battle between her husband and son to the miracle of the roses and her death (where she can be seen prayerfully submitting her spirit to heaven). There is a modernist **statue of the Queen** on the *praça* – testament to the esteem in which she is still held by local people and the Portuguese as a whole.

The church was commissioned by Dom João IV's widow in 1659, supposedly in gratitude for victory against the Spanish at Elvas. The building was expanded in the 18th century, when it received its exquisite *azulejos*, attributed to Teotónio dos Santos (c. 1725) and André Gonçalves (c. 1730).

## Museu Municipal (Town Museum) (*Largo Dom Dinis s/n;* ☏ *288 329219;* ⏲ *09.00–12.30 & 14.00–17.30; admission €2*) Housed in an old almshouse on the square, this museum preserves a miscellany of items relating to Estremoz, from attractive 18th-century furniture, guns and antique crockery to figurines of local characters and types (think Mr Bun the Baker and Mr Mug the Milkman from Happy Families), an Easter pageant and a nymph of spring, all hand-crafted in clay.

## Igreja de Santa Maria (Church or Our Lady) (*Largo Dom Dinis s/n;* ⏲ *09.00–12.30 & 14.00–17.30 Tue–Sun, ask for the key from in the gallery of design across the square from the castle; free admission*) Estremoz's 17th-century parish church is small but perfectly formed – an exact 7m cube (if you ignore the chancel), with the spaces between the pillars a precise third of the length of the church, and the sacristy length an exact quarter of the length of the spaces between the pillars. By the time it was built, the exuberance of the Manueline had given way

4

Isabel (also known to English speakers as Elizabeth) was only 12 when she was betrothed to Dom Dinis of Portugal, but even at this young age she was extremely devout, attending mass daily, fasting regularly and giving alms to the poor. Dinis, by contrast, was anything but pious. He may have been a great king, but he was a rotten husband and both he and his court were notoriously concupiscent. Isabel's refusal to sink to their standards initially caused great conflict between the couple. They had two children – a daughter, Constantia, and a son, Afonso. Dinis also fathered others, whom Isabel raised as her own. Through great resentment at the favour Dinis showed to his illegitimate sons, Afonso rebelled. In the early 1320s he declared war against his father, and battle was only averted when Isabel placed her person between the two opposing armies, forcing them either mutually to kill her or to reconcile. They chose the latter and avoided a fight until 1325, when Afonso, disgusted with corruption at court and the failure of his father to consult parliament (the *cortes*), deposed him. After Dinis's death the queen averted war a second time when Afonso – furious at the treatment of his daughter Maria at the hands of the King of Castile – declared war on Spain. Isabel intervened and negotiated a peace agreement, but this exertion brought on the illness that led to her death in the castle at Estremoz. She was canonised by Pope Urban VIII in 1625, and Estremoz celebrates her feast day on 8 July.

A number of miracles are attributed to St Isabel, including – most famously – the Miracle of the Roses, which is said to have taken place in Estremoz. After Dinis discovered the queen was leaving the palace to take food to the poor he flew into a rage, threatening to lock her up and confine her to the palace. But she continued nonetheless, leaving the castle every day behind her husband's back. One winter morning the king caught her leaving with bread hidden in her dress. Asking her what she was carrying, she replied, 'Roses, my Lord.' He didn't believe her, and knowing it was winter when roses were not in bloom, he asked her to lift her dress. When she did so, the loaves had miraculously transformed into roses.

to a return to the formal. Santa Maria is Renaissance Neo-classical, decorated in the Mannerist style. Notice the corbels above the pediment on the facade – blocks that look like they could fall at any moment. These are typical of the Mannerist love of the surprising. The elaborate ecclesiastical decoration inside anticipates the Baroque.

**The Rossio and lower town** Daily life in modern Estremoz centres on and around this handsome square. On Saturday the square hosts one of the Alentejo's surviving weekly markets, with traders arriving from the villages all around, just as they have done for centuries, laden with everything from olives, cheeses and wine to fruit, vegetables and leather goods and souvenirs.

On the southern side of the square next to the tourist office is the **Convento dos Congregados and Museu de Arte Sacra (Sacred Art Museum)** (⊕ *09.00–17.30 Mon–Fri; free admission*), lower Estremoz's grandest church, built in the early 18th century and now home to the town hall. The building is unusual in having a curved front. Inside are some excellent *azulejos* of scenes from everyday life in the 18th century which are well worth a look. It is possible to climb to the bell towers (with permission from the staff in the town hall) for impressive views of Estremoz. The adjoining Sacred Art Museum (⊕ *09.30–noon & 14.30–17.30 Tue–Sun; free admission*) preserves a small collection of mostly Baroque statuary and ecclesiastical pieces.

## EVORAMONTE

Perched romantically on a barren hill in the Serra de Ossa, high above the surrounding plains, the massive round towers of the **Castelo de Evoramonte (Evoramonte Castle)** (⊕ *10.00–13.00 & 14.00–19.00 Tue–Sun; admission €2*) are visible for tens of kilometres. The castle has been an eyrie watching out for attack and invasion since the time of the Reconquest. The views from the battlements are breathtaking, and wandering around the tiny village that spreads around the castle's feet, within the secondary walls, is a delight.

A fortress was built here shortly after Gerard the Fearless – the liberator of Évora – expelled the Moors from the hill in the 12th century, but it was Dinis who commissioned the construction of the first castle proper in 1306, after building his palace in nearby Estremoz. The building was further fortified by Dom Manuel I, who employed one of the great architects of the Manueline era, Diogo de Arruda – brother of Francisco (see the box on the Arrudas, page 28), and the architect of Tomar's Templar castle and Viana do Alentejo's magnificent Igreja Matriz. De Arruda gave the castle its cylindrical towers, and within the keep you can see his trademark lavish decoration and embellished piers.

**GETTING THERE, AWAY AND AROUND** Evoramonte is a short drive from Évora (26km) and Estremoz (22km), lying a few kilometres north of the main IP7/A6 Lisbon-Évora-Badajoz motorway and at the highest point of the Serra de Ossa. There is very limited parking at the castle itself. Buses 8946 and 8104 run to Evoramonte on their way between Évora and Estremoz, as do buses 8956e and 8956pne, which run between Beja and Monforte via Évora, Evoramonte and Estremoz. Bus 8169 runs between Estremoz and Evoramonte. For more information see www.rodalentejo.pt. Evoramonte is tiny and easily negotiable on foot.

**TOURIST INFORMATION** There is a small tourist booth in the old town hall (*Rua de Santa Maria s/n;* ☎ *268 959227;* ⊕ *09.30–12.30 & 14.00–17.00 daily*). The nearest tourist offices are at Estremoz and Évora, and both have information about the castle.

**WHERE TO STAY, EAT AND DRINK** Evoramonte has a handful of simple guesthouses and Portuguese restaurants and cafés, though nothing to compare with Estremoz or Évora, both of which are under 30 minutes away, or the luxurious **Hotel Convento de São Paulo** between Evoramonte and Redondo (*N381;* ☎ *266 989160; www.hotelconventosaopaulo.com;* €€€€€). One of the Alentejo's most beautiful hotels, housed in a magnificent late 18th-century monastery rich with decoration, including very fine *azulejos* and Florentine fountains, and set in gardens in the heart of the Serra d'Ossa, the hotel has an excellent modern Portuguese restaurant, which is open to non-guests. Staff can organise all manner of tours.

## REDONDO

On the edge of the Serra d'Ossa and surrounded by lush vineyards, this little fortified town is worth visiting in passing to see its unusual castle – an ungainly

4

amalgam of Moorish walls, medieval whitewashed cottages and church bell towers. The parish church has attractive *azulejos* and a small sacred art museum. The town is also home to a **Wine Museum** (*Praça da República 5;* \ *266 909100;* ◔ *10.00–20.00 Tue–Sun*) devoted to the wines of the Alentejo in general, and Redondo in particular. The Convento de São Paulo nearby houses one of the most beautiful hotels in the Alto Alentejo (see page 101).

**GETTING THERE AND AWAY** Redondo lies at the junction of the N254 Vila Viçosa to Évora road and the N381 which runs north to Estremoz. Évora is 37km west, Estremoz is 26km north.

**Bus lines** 8558, 8917, 8919, 8976 and 8551 connect Redondo with Évora; routes 8558, 8976 and 8551 continue to Elvas. For more information see www.rodalentejo.pt.

**TOURIST INFORMATION** There is a tourist office next to the Museu de Vinho on Praça da República (\ *266 909039;* ◔ *summer 10.00–19.00 Tue–Sun, winter 10.00–18.00 Tue–Sun*).

## MONTEMOR-O-NOVO

With a population approaching 30,000, Montemor-o-Novo is a metropolis by Alentejo standards. It has a dramatic ruined castle right out of a Gothic novel, a crumbling convent and a Baroque church covered in fine *azulejos*, while the *fazendas* of its hinterlands are famous for their fine wines and olive oils, and the skeleton-filled Grutas de Escoural caves are Portugal's most impressive. If it were anywhere else than the Alentejo, where ruined castles and convents are two-a-penny, it would no doubt receive plenty of visitors. Yet very few people even pass through Montemor. It's worth doing so if you have an hour or two to spare, even if you are only in the area to dine in the Alentejo's only Michelin-starred restaurant and sample the fine wines in the *adegas* that lie within the region.

**HISTORY** Like many towns in the Alentejo, Montemor-o-Novo grew from a castle, and, as the name suggests, this castle was Muslim. The Montemor or Mountain of the Moors was captured by Afonso Henriques, the first king of Portugal, in 1166, making it – together with Beja and Évora – one of the first castle villages beyond the Tejo to be taken in the Reconquest. The castle and the settlement that lay within its extensive walls were adapted by the Portuguese knights and reconstructed in a more resolutely Portuguese style under Dom Dinis. By the 14th century Montemor had grown to become a prosperous trading town. It's said that Vasco da Gama visited in the late 1400s to plan his journey to the Indies. Shortly after, in 1495, João Duarte Cidade was born here to a Jewish family. In later life he would found the Brothers Hospitallers, becoming the father of modern nursing, for which he would eventually be canonised as St John of God.

Montemor's position of relative security far from the border with Spain and the threat of invasion led to the population gradually to abandon the hill and the steep old Moorish streets within the castle walls. They settled instead in a new town, close to their vineyards, cork plantations and olive groves. As it grew this town began to be called New Montemor – Montemor-o-Novo.

By the 18th century the castle, the streets of old cottages, the ancient churches and the old town hall had been abandoned. Over the following centuries they slowly fell into rack and ruin, which is how you will find them today.

## GETTING THERE AND AWAY

**By car** Montemor-o-Novo is very well connected, lying right off the IP7/A6. Lisbon airport is 100km away, Alcácer do Sal 47km, Évora 31km, Elvas and Beja 110km.

**By rail** Casa Branca and Vendas Novas railway stations are both 14km from Montemor-o-Novo. Both have four daily trains to Lisbon Oriente (*either 1hr 45mins or 80mins*) and Évora (*10mins or 25mins*). Casa Branca has onward connections to Beja.

**By bus** Montemor-o-Novo has many Rede Expressos fast bus services, including from Lisbon (*14 daily; 45mins*), Évora (*11 daily; 30mins*), Beja (*6 daily; 2hrs*) and Setúbal (*2 daily; 80mins*). Bus line 8555 connects Montemor-o-Novo with Alcácer do Sal and Grândola (*twice daily Mon–Fri; 2hrs 15mins and 2hrs 40mins respectively*), continuing on to Évora. For more information see www.rede-expressos.pt and www.rodalentejo.pt.

**TOURIST INFORMATION** There is a tourist office on Largo Calouste Gulbenkian (↖ 266 898103; ☉ *summer 09.30–13.00 & 14.30–18.00 Tue–Sun, winter 10.00–18.00 Mon–Sat*).

## WHERE TO STAY

🏠 **L'and Vineyards Resort** (22 rooms) Estrada Nacional 4, Herdade das Valadas Apartado 122, Montemor-o-Novo; ↖ 266 242400; www.l-andvineyards.com. The best resort in the Alentejo for wine & food lovers, with modish, minimalist modern rooms set in a garden of olive trees & wild flowers, surrounded by the *adega's* vineyards. Each is fitted in raw wood & decorated in muted whites & browns, & comes with a fireplace, wall-sized French windows (opening on to a patio) & (in the larger rooms) glass ceilings allowing clear views of the starry night skies. Decent pool, tennis courts, hammam & spa (with wine therapy), & the only Michelin starred restaurant in the Alentejo. Best rates through the hotel website. €€€€€

🏠 **Ameira** (60 rooms) Herdade da Ameira Aparatado 163, Montemor-o-Novo; ↖ 266 898240; www.hoteldaameira.pt. A sprawling family orientated resort with 2 child-friendly swimming pools, spacious rooms in modern annexes & a restaurant offering regional cooking. Wine-tasting tours & excursions can be organised through reception. €€€

🏠 **Monte de Chora Cascas** (6 rooms) Apartado 296, Montemor-o-Novo; ↖ 266 899690; www.wonderfulland.com. Pretty family-run hotel in a converted farmhouse amid leafy gardens (filled with butterflies in spring) on the outskirts of town. The owner is an interior designer & has decorated & furnished the hotel with rustic flair. Guests are treated like they're visiting a friend's home. Large pool, generous b/fasts. €€

## WHERE TO EAT AND DRINK

🍴 **L'and Vineyards** See *Where to stay*, above; ☉ 13.00–15.00 & 19.30–22.30, guests daily, non guests Wed–Sun; reservations essential. Portuguese cooking with an Asian twist & Alentejo traditional food reinterpreted as contemporary haute cuisine by Michelin-starred chef Miguel Laffan. Sommelier-matched Alentejo wines with every dish. €€€

## WHAT TO SEE AND DO

**The castle and the ruined old town** The castle and the remains of the old town sit on the hill, clearly visible from the motorway and from anywhere in the town that sprawls in a criss-cross of terracotta at its feet. You can drive right into the ruins, but it's more fun to park below and climb the hill on one of the little dirt paths, leaving the noise of the streets and the cars behind you for birdsong and the sound of the wind ruffling the grass. The ruins are very romantic: Manueline arches (with their characteristic knotwork embellishments), fragmented battlements, palace walls and church towers are encrusted with lichen, set in what has now become a wild flower meadow. And Montemor-o-Novo has so few visitors that you'll almost certainly have them entirely to yourself. You'll see a flag flying above the only part of the castle with any infrastructure – the 14th-century church of São Tiago (✆ 266 898103; ⊕ Nov–Mar 09.00–12.30 & 14.00–17.30 Tue–Sun, Apr–Oct 10.00–13.00 & 14.30–18.30 Tue–Sun; admission €1), where there's a small museum telling a little of the story of Montemor. The semi-ruined church itself is covered in attractive 17th- and 18th-century murals.

**The modern town** The lower town has a handful of interesting churches, although they can't compare to what you'll see in Évora a little to the east. The 16th-century **Convento de São Domingos** fell into ruin after the religious orders were expelled from Portugal, but was renovated in the 1970s and now houses a collection of small, quirky exhibition rooms with Stone Age artefacts (including menhirs), Roman remnants (including dozens of amphorae), toreador outfits, old sewing machines and a smattering of Baroque sacred art. The church itself has lost all its decoration but for the Mudéjar *azulejos* which still cover much of its interior.

The **Terreiro de São João de Deus** has a statue of the town's famous saint as well as a convent devoted to the saint, the **Convento de São João de Deus**, whose church has some exquisite *azulejos* telling the story of John of God's life. There is another fine church on the Terreiro, the **Igreja da Misericórdia**, with a Manueline door, vaulting, a rare 18th-century organ by Oldovini (one of a handful left in the world – see page 93) and a beautiful marble *Pietà* from the 15th century.

While in the lower town be sure to visit the **town market** (*Largo Bento Jesus Caraça s/n*), decorated with some very fine *azulejos* depicting scenes from rural life in the Alentejo in the late 19th century, including the back-breaking work on the *latifundos* so graphically described in Jose Saramago's *Raised from the Ground* (see page 190), and which amounted to slavery.

**Santiago do Escoural and the caves** (*Office at Rua Dr Magalhães de Lima Rocha 48, Santiago do Escoural;* ✆ *266 857000;* e *grutadoescoural@cultura-alentejo. pt;* ⊕ *09.30–12.30 & 14.00–18.00 daily; the caves can be visited at 10.30 & 14.30 Tue–Sat only, & exclusively on tours pre-booked through the office, €3*).The village of Santiago around 12km south of Montemor sits in a landscape literally strewn with prehistoric sites. The most fascinating of these are the Anta de São Brissos (aka the Anta-Capela de Nossa Senhora do Livramento) and the Grutas do Escoural. The former is an extraordinary 17th-century chapel built into a 3m-tall, 3,000-year-old dolmen complete with tiled roof, whitewashed walls and shrine. The latter is a honeycomb of caves whose 30 chambers are littered with calcified human remains and walls painted with prehistoric rock art of horses and aurochs. The remains date from the middle Palaeolithic (40,000–50,000BC). Outside the cave is an overgrown domed chamber or tholos (with the largest number of slate plaques so far found in Iberia). Look for what appears to be a pile of stone rubble about three quarters of the way up the hill. A Neolithic fort saddles the hill itself.

# ARRAIOLOS

Famous for carpets and an unusual round castle, Arraiolos fringes a low hill just off the main Montemor-o-Novo to Estremoz N4 highway, making it easy to visit *en route* to or from Lisbon. The castle is little more than a shell nowadays and a whistlestop tour of town, with a stop-off to browse for carpets, will take less than an hour. There's little reason to linger longer, unless you want to base yourself here at the beautiful *pousada*, which is housed in a converted convent.

## GETTING THERE AND AWAY
**By car** Arraiolos lies on the N4 Montemor-o-Novo to Estremoz highway. Lisbon airport is 122km away, Alcácer do Sal 69km, Évora 22km, Estremoz 42km, Elvas 85km and Montemor-o-Novo 22km.

**By bus** Arraiolos has Rede Expressos fast bus services to Lisbon (*1 daily, 1hr 35mins*) and Estremoz (*1 daily, 40mins*). On weekdays, bus line 8940 connects Arraiolos with Setúbal (*2 daily*), Montemor-o-Novo (*2 daily*), Estremoz (*1 daily*) and Elvas (*1 daily*). Line 8007 runs between Évora and Estremoz via Arraiolos (*4 daily, Mon–Fri*), lines 8016 and 8205 run between Évora and Arraiolos (*4 daily & 2 daily respectively, Mon–Fri*), and line 8913 runs between Mora and Évora via Arraiolos (*2 daily Mon, Tue, Thu & Fri, 1 on Wed*). For more information see www.rede-expressos.pt and www.rodalentejo.pt.

**TOURIST INFORMATION** There is a tourist office on Praça do Município (✆ *266 490254;* ⊕ *10.00–13.00 & 14.00–18.00 Tue–Sun*), which distributes leaflets on the history and monuments in the town and runs a modest centre (*Antigo Posto da GNR, Praça do Município 19;* ✆ *266 490240*) devoted to the story of Arraiolos carpets, and worth a visit for those interested in their design and manufacture.

**WHERE TO STAY, EAT AND DRINK** The **Pousada Convento Arraiolos** (*32 rooms; Nossa Sra da Assunção, Arraiolos;* ✆ *266 419340; www.pestana.com;* €€€€), is set in the 16th-century Convent of St John the Evangelist, with rooms in the original monks' cells (now turned from Spartan to luxurious). There's an excellent restaurant, a pool and tennis courts, and the chapel is decorated with gorgeous *azulejos*.

---

### THE CARPETS OF ARRAIOLOS

Gothic novelist and early industrialist William Beckford visited here on his travels in 1787 and recorded that the carpets of Arraiolos were 'of strange grotesque patterns and glaring colours.' They may have been exotic then, but nowadays they look familiar, with designs clearly drawn from Islam and specifically from Moroccan *kilims* and Iranian carpets. Moors living in Portugal would have imported carpets from throughout the Islamic Empire, and villages across the Alentejo made their own imitations. While Persian rugs remained popular at court (and were even commissioned from artists in Iran by Portuguese noblemen), persecution of the Moors after the Reconquest all but killed the art within Portugal itself. The number of carpet manufacturers in Lisbon diminished from more than 100 in the early 1400s to fewer than ten a century later. But in Arraiolos – an area replete with sheep farms – the tradition continued, in part perhaps because the local people adapted Islamic patterns and shapes, and then argued that rather than being Islamic, they were folkloric 'Portuguese' – a belief that is indulged to this day.

**SHOPPING** There are myriad carpet shops in Arraiolos and as all the carpets in the town are made by a cooperative, they all have much the same contents. The tourist office has a full list; otherwise it's worth walking along the streets around the castle.

**AROUND ARRAIOLOS: NOSSA SENHORA DA GRAÇA DO DIVOR** A tiny back road, the N370, connects Arraiolos with Évora via the village of Nossa Senhora da Graça do Divor. The village is barely a hamlet, but it nonetheless has some interesting sights. These include an eccentric 16th-century church fronted by a marble portico, prehistoric monuments (menhirs, cromlechs with ancient petroglyphs, and some 17 dolmens) and just outside the village, the **Casa da Sempre Noiva**. This beautiful 14th-century Manueline mansion covered with ornate Mudéjar motifs is not officially open to the public, though you can drive right up to it and take a look, and it is falling into ruins. More information on the village can be found at the Évora or Arraiolos tourist office.

## BORBA

Borba is famous throughout the Alentejo for wine, olives and marble – all of which are of the highest quality. And in Borba pretty much everything is orientated towards the pursuit of one of the three. The town seems to be made entirely of marble, from the dragon's tooth paving to the marble in the bus station urinals. And most of the townsfolk work in the quarries, on the *adegas* or in the olive farms that surround Borba, the most celebrated of which is Dom Borba itself – manufacturer of multi-award-winning olive oil and wine, and whose production centre on the edge of the town can be visited.

Borba is a sleepy little town that sees few tourists. This is an attraction in itself – a stay here in the town's only decent hotel (which is one of the loveliest in the Alto Alentejo) offers a glimpse of real Alentejo life. And Borba's location is hard to beat. The town lies within 20 minutes' drive of Estremoz and Elvas, 40 minutes from Évora and fewer than ten minutes from the great Bragança palace at Vila Viçosa.

**GETTING THERE, AWAY AND AROUND** Borba occupies a near-perfect position for exploration of the lower Alto Alentejo – a few hundred metres south of the IP7/ A6 Lisbon-Évora-Badajoz motorway. Elvas is 29km away, Évora 56km, Estremoz 14km, Vila Viçosa 6km and Monsaraz 53km.

The town is well-connected, with Rede Expresso **buses** to the following destinations: Elvas (*7 daily, 30mins*), Estremoz (*4 daily, 15mins*), Évora (*3 daily, 1hr 10mins*) and Montemor-o-Novo (*4 daily, 1hr*). There are also frequent local bus services to these and other destinations; for more information see www.rede-expressos.pt and www.rodalentejo.pt.

Borba is a very small town and is easily manageable on foot.

**TOURIST INFORMATION** There is a tourist office on the Praça da República (✆ *268 891630;* ⏱ *summer 10.00–19.00 Tue–Sun, winter 10.00–18.00 Tue–Sun*).

 **WHERE TO STAY** See also *Estremoz* (page 97) and *Vila Viçosa* (pages 108–9), which are both within 15 minutes' drive.

**Casa do Terreiro do Poço** (8 rooms), Largo dos Combatentes da Grande Guerra 12, Borba; ✆ 917 256077; www.casadoterreirodopoco.com.

João & Rita provide a warm welcome for guests to their lovely home in one of Borba's prettiest streets. Rooms are spacious & beautifully appointed, especially in the newly renovated wing, where each is individually decorated with a real sense of style – one with Balinese furniture & Java silks, another like an old Alentejo kitchen, complete with hanging dishes and an antique weighing scale. B/fast is sumptuous with genuine *mermelada* (made from the quinces grown in the garden), fruit & pastries, there's a lovely pool, & João & Rita can organise a host of activities throughout the region. €€€

🏠 **O Viajante** (11 rooms) Estrada Nacional 4 Maria Ruiva, Arcos, Borba 🖀 268 841363. Set

next to a big car park on the other side of the IP7/A6 from Borba (which is a 20min walk south), this ungainly guesthouse is built for overnighting truckers *en route* from Lisbon to the rest of Europe & after a cheap bed or a cheap meal. What it lacks in locational charm & convenience, it makes up for with well-kept rooms, each with firm beds, desks & private marble-faced bathrooms & a great-value on-site restaurant. Staff are friendly & can help organise trips & excursions. €

## WHERE TO EAT AND DRINK

🍴 **O Espalha Brasas** Monte das Naves de Cima, Alcaraviça, Borba; 🖀 268 891069; ⏲ noon–15.00 & 18.30–22.30 Tue–Sun. Regional cooking in a very popular restaurant set in the countryside 5km outside Borba. A big, open-plan dining room which buzzes with life at weekends, lovely views from the big windows & a menu strong on game (with hare,

rabbit & partridge) & typical Alentejo dishes like *bochechas de porco preto* (black pork cheeks). €

🍴 **Lisbeto** Rua Mateus Pais 31; 🖀 268 894332. Alentejo dishes like *porco preto* (black pork) & Portuguese & international standards (*bacalhau dourado*, steak & chips) served in generous quantities. Simple, unpretentious & good value. €

**WHAT TO SEE AND DO** Borba is under 10km from Vila Viçosa (see pages 108–11) and is best considered as a base for visiting that town, Estremoz and Elvas. While you are here it's worth popping in to the church of **São Bartolomeu** (*Rua de São Bartolomeu s/n*) to see its splendid Renaissance ceiling and some fine marble carving.

**Adega Dom Borba** (*Largo Gago Coutinho e Sacadura Cabral 25, Apartado 20, Borba;* 🖀 *268 891660; www.adegaborba.pt; admission €3; visits by prior appointment only*) The Adega Dom Borba winery is open for wine and olive oil tasting. The winery was established in the 1950s as a cooperative of local producers whose families had been producing first-class wine in the region for centuries. Today the *adega* comprises some 300 wine growers who harvest grapes from over 2,000 hectares. Their wine has won numerous awards. In recent years these include the gold medal at the Berliner Wine Trophy (2014) and several bronzes in the Decanter World Wine Awards and the International Wine Challenge (both in 2013). While oil can be

---

### UNEARTHING THE ALENTEJO'S TREASURES: BORBA AND ESTREMOZ

A rich seam of marble – the Estremoz anticline – underlies the entire municipality of Estremoz, from the villages to the north and Vila Viçosa to the south, and the area is pocked with quarries, some of which reach 400m deep. The marble is some of the best in the world with rich colours (most famously pink) and patterns, and has been used for building for thousands of years. The Roman theatre in Mérida across the border in Spain has columns of Estremoz marble, the rich chancel of Elvas' cathedral is carved from Estremoz marble, and many of Dubai's hotel lobbies and bathrooms are faced with the stone. At present some 30% of the 27km² that the marble occupies are exploited, with an output of some 400,000 tons, most of it taken from open cast mines between Borba and Vila Viçosa. At the current rate of exploration there is enough marble in the Estremoz seam to last 550 years.

sampled and bought at the *adega*, visits can also be made to the **Dom Borba Olive Oil factory** on the edge of town (by prior appointment – the tourist office or the Casa do Terreiro do Poço can organise visits). The olive oil is harvested on similar cooperative lines and it's fascinating to see it being processed from harvested fruit to storage and maturation in huge vats. The factory sells superb oil at good prices.

## VILA VIÇOSA

Today Vila Viçosa is a sleepy, unassuming little marble-producing town whose pretty streets are lined with orange trees. But between the 13th and 19th centuries it was one of the most important locations in the Alentejo, as the site of an imposing castle and a magnificent ducal palace, both built by the powerful Bragança dynasty, whose scions sat on the throne of Portugal and England. Both their castle and their palace can be visited today.

**GETTING THERE AND AWAY** Like Borba, Vila Viçosa occupies a near-perfect position for exploration of the lower Alto Alentejo – 10km south of the IP7/A6 Lisbon-Évora-Badajoz motorway. Elvas is 40km away, Évora 62km, Estremoz 21km, Borba 6km and Monsaraz 43km. The town is well connected, with Rede Expresso **buses** to the following destinations: Elvas (*3 daily, 35mins*), Estremoz (*no direct buses – go via Borba*), Évora (*3 daily, 1hr*), Montemor-o-Novo (*4 daily, 1hr 45mins*). There are also frequent local bus services to these and other destinations; for more information see www.rede-expressos.pt and www.rodalentejo.pt.

**GETTING AROUND** Vila Viçosa is manageable on foot. Taxis are plentiful and economical. Expect to pay around €5 between the castle and the Ducal Palace and around €10 one-way to Borba.

**TOURIST INFORMATION** There is a tourist office on the Praça da República (\ 268 889317; ⊕ 09.00–12.30 & 14.00–17.30 daily).

🏠 **WHERE TO STAY** See also *Estremoz* (page 97) and *Borba* (pages 106–7), which are both within 15 minutes' drive.

🏠 **Alentejo Marmoris Hotel and Spa** (45 rooms) Largo Gago Coutinho 11; \ 268 887010; www.alentejomarmoris.com. Though equally palatial, this modern hotel is the opposite of the understated *pousada*. Even if you don't stay here it's worth visiting for dinner to enjoy the wonderful contemporary cooking & see the lavish marble interiors & fittings. The most ostentatious of these wouldn't look out of place in a Dubai 5-star – a complete seam of crystallised marble sitting behind the reception desk. The spa is faced with luxurious caramel-coloured veined marble, the bathrooms are like jewellery boxes & the suites vast enough to hold a rock star. There are 2 luxurious pools & the hotel's restaurant (see page 109) is one of the best in the Alto Alentejo. The best rates are available through the hotel website. €€€€

🏠 **Convento de Vila Viçosa** (36 rooms) Convento das Chagas, Terreiro do Paço; \ 268 980742; www.pestana.com. This former *pousada*, housed in a former convent & run by the upscale Pestana group, oozes understated luxury. The convent itself is more than 500 years old & served as the school for the ladies of the Bragança household, including the Queen of England, Catherine of Bragança. Corridors, rooms & the chapel retain much of their original decoration, there's a fine restaurant & the service is as quiet, efficient & discreet as a Lusitanian Jeeves. The Ducal Palace is literally next door. €€€€

🏠 **Casa do Colegio Velho** (6 rooms) Rua Dr Couto Jardim 34; \ 268 889430; www. casadocolegiovelho.com. Set in a large, well-tended garden, decorated with antique furniture & housed in a 16th-century manor house, this hotel combines charm & romance with a great location just 5mins' walk from the Ducal Palace. Rooms in muted colours & polished wood are well kept & come with lovely bathrooms, some with standalone tubs & marble tiles & facings. It's worth upgrading to a suite for maximum luxury & space. €€€

🏠 **Solar dos Mascarenhas** (22 rooms) Rua Florbela Espanca 125; ☎ 268 886000; www.solardosmascarenhas.com. Modern, well-appointed rooms in a lovely 18th-century townhouse in the centre of Vila Viçosa. The hotel has a small swimming pool. The Ducal Palace & castle are a short walk. €€

🍴 **WHERE TO EAT AND DRINK** See also *Borba* (page 107) and *Estremoz* (pages 97–8).

✗ **Narcissus Fernandesii** Alentejo Marmoris, Largo Gago Coutinho 11; ☎ 268 887010; www.alentejomarmoris.com; ⊕ noon–15.00 & 18.30–22.30 daily. Dress well when you dine at the Narcissus. This restaurant unashamedly regards itself as a fine dining destination, & rightly so. The marble surrounds & gilt columns in this dining room wouldn't look out of place in a sultan's palace. Pedro Mendes's cooking is first class. Contemporary European & Portuguese dishes like *cação escalfado em caldo de algas sobre cebolada e molho de tomate com poejos* (rock cod steamed with seaweed with *cebolada* & reduced tomato & a garnish of pennyroyal) are beautifully prepared & presented, & complemented with sommelier-selected wine from a list of the best Portuguese bottles. Be sure to try the degustation of *semifrios* for dessert. €€€

✗ **Ouro Branco** Alameda das Varandinhas 43; ☎ 268 980556; ⊕ 12.30–15.00 & 18.30–22.30

---

### CATHERINE OF BRAGANÇA AND THE ENGLISH

Popular belief in England has it that Catherine of Braganza was a poor choice of wife for Charles II – dowdy, unsophisticated and ill-equipped to deal with life at the brilliant English court. The truth is entirely the opposite. Catherine was a trendsetter who changed England more than any other consort queen. As the daughter of João IV, king of a new and independent Portugal, she came from a court with refined European tastes. The English monarchy, by contrast, was severely damaged, near bankruptcy and culturally decades behind contemporaneous Europe. Catherine's dowry replenished the coffers and included the Bombay islands and free trade with the Portuguese colonies, among them gold-rich Brazil. And the new queen introduced tea (then a luxurious drink almost unknown in England), the fork and marmalade. She also brought European dancing and a trend for wearing trousers and shorter skirts. After installing herself in Somerset House she introduced modern European music too through the appointment Giovanni Sebenico (previously of St Mark's in Venice) as the master of music in her chapel. By the 1680s Italian opera had become the most fashionable music in London.

Yet Catherine is remembered unfavourably. This is largely because she was hated by the women of Charles' immoral court. Furious that the queen disapproved of the immorality of the court, Charles' myriad mistresses and sycophantic courtiers desperately tried to persuade the king to divorce her, fabricating stories of her treachery. He repeatedly refused. So they resorted to portraying her as dull and dowdy, and her reputation only began to improve after the publication of a 19th-century biography by the American historian Lillias Campbell Davidson, who famously wrote that 'Catherine lived in her husband's court as Lot lived in Sodom. She did justly, and loved mercy, and walked humbly with her God in the midst of a seething corruption and iniquity only equalled, perhaps, in the history of Imperial Rome.'

daily. A typical family-run restaurant serving Alentejo home cooking with dishes like *migas, porco preto* & homemade desserts. Excellent value. €

✗ **Dom João** Alameda das Piscinas 10; ☏ 963 820834; ☺ 09.00–midnight daily. Grilled meat, fish, seafood (inc delicious prawns) & Portuguese standards with an excellent value dish of the day for under €5. €

## WHAT TO SEE AND DO

### Castelo de Vila Viçosa (Vila Viçosa Castle) (*www.fcbraganca.pt*) The round

towers and battlements of Vila Viçosa's castle look down on the town from a small hill to the south of the Ducal Palace, surrounded by pretty gardens which burst into multi-coloured bloom in spring. The original building was founded by Dom Dinis in 1297, lost to the Spanish in 1383 and finally given to Nuno Álvares Pereira (see *History*, page 15) after the constitutional crisis of 1385. Nuno was at the time Portugal's wealthiest man. His only child, Beatriz, inherited all his wealth and married Afonso, the illegitimate son of King João I (who had been made the first Duke of Bragança by the Portuguese regent Pedro after the death of João I). The couple made the castle given to Beatriz's father their home, and with their wealth and aristocratic connections they founded the country's most powerful political dynasty.

Little remains of Afonso and Beatriz's castle. Used as a garrison in Portugal's perennial wars with the Spanish as well as a family home, the building was greatly expanded over the centuries. But it was too pokey and provincial for later Braganças. In 1502 Dom Jaime, the fourth duke commissioned an enormous palace for the family – the Paço Ducal. After the Bragança family left, the castle reverted to purely military use, becoming the only artillery garrison in Portugal and playing a key role in campaigns against the Spanish. It was adapted by Cosmander when the Jesuit military engineer was resident in Olivença (see box, page 87) and in 1662 by the German general-for-hire Friedrich Hermann, 1st Duke of Schomberg (who later became an English Knight of the Garter and died at the Battle of the Boyne), in preparation for its last great campaign – fuelling troops and guns for the battle of Montes Claros in June 1665.

It's fascinating to wander around the little settlement lying within the castle walls. With its overgrown gardens, butterflies and singing birds, and its rows of pretty little cottages, it seems more bucolic than bellicose. The castle rooms themselves are given over to two small museums: one of archaeology (with pieces from Stone Age and Roman Portugal, and Greek, Roman and Egyptian pieces from the private collection of one of the Portuguese kings), and the other of hunting (with lots of guns and stuffed animals, shot over the centuries by assorted Braganças).

### Paço Ducal (Ducal Palace) (*www.fcbraganca.pt; allow at least four hours for a

*visit to the palace. Guides are compulsory*) From the early 1500s the Braganças lived in this vast and monumental grey marble palace, set on an even vaster, bone-white courtyard. From end to end the three-storey building is longer than a football field and its frowsty rooms are stuffed full of antiques and priceless pieces collected by the nobles. Yet for all its grandeur, the palace feels gloomy. Perhaps it's haunted by the ghost of its first duchess, who was stabbed by her suspicious husband Jaime IV in an Othello-like rage of jealousy. The duke himself clearly suffered no punishment for the murder. He sits huge and majestic on a horse and plinth in the courtyard, a plume in his hat.

Jaime's original building was Manueline. Bits of it can still be seen, in rope-like carved embellishments over some of the lateral doorways near the adjacent convent. The current Neo-classical edifice was envisaged by his descendant Duke Teodosio in the 1550s and further augmented in 1566 by the sixth duke, by which time it had gone from grand to grandiose. A visiting papal legate reported that pages sounded trumpets whenever he lifted his cup to his lips.

Catherine of Bragança was born here in 1638. As a child she would have watched theatrical performances, firework displays, masques and bull fights in the great courtyard, and played blind man's buff: one of the palace rooms was reserved solely for playing the game.

When the House of Bragança finally acceded to the throne in 1640 the Paço became an official royal residence, and with only a few hundred rooms was once more deemed too pokey and further expanded. Two royal weddings took place here shortly afterwards, both at the same time, when the children of Dom João V and Maria I married the children of the King of Spain in a ceremony that later came to be known as 'the exchange of princes'. The palace was in use by the royals from then onwards, but for the hiatus when they took the entire court to Brazil, fleeing the country and leaving a British governor to fight off Napoleon. It finally fell into disuse when Portugal became a republic in 1910, but it is still managed by the Bragança family.

The upper floor of the Paço, the Andar Nobre, holds a series of rooms more remarkable for their decoration (there are some fine frescoes and 16th-century *azulejos*) than their furniture. The best stuff was moved to the main royal abode in Lisbon or to private collections. But the kitchen is fascinating – big enough to stage a concert and still kitted out with a bewildering array of utensils as if ready to prepare a feast.

The lower floors of the palace house collections: an armoury of medieval, Renaissance and 18th- and 19th-century weapons (including some grizzly pikes and fine English canons). There's a treasury with European ceramics like Philip II of Spain's travel water bottle, silver and gold plates and sundry items including an exquisite Goan ivory carving of the Infant Jesus as the Good Shepherd, with the child Jesus sitting on a three-tiered rocky mountain featuring scenes from his life and with the Tree of Jessé (a symbol of the Holy Trinity) fanning out as a background. The museum has one of the largest collections of carriages in Europe and a collection of priceless Chinese porcelain. The superb library has some beautiful rare illustrated books and manuscripts, and further galleries are devoted to temporary art exhibitions. Entrance to each of the collections is not included in the ticket price.

Between April and December the palace chapel hosts performances of Baroque and classical music. See the website for details.

**Convento das Chagas (Chagas Convent)** (see *Where to stay*, page 108) After disposing of his first wife, Dom Jaime Bragança was ordered by King Manuel I to do his penance by personally leading an army of 25,000 troops in a perilous expedition of conquest against the Moors of Azamor (now Az-Zammur in modern day Morocco). Bragança won easily, and after capturing the city sped home to a new wife, Joana de Mendonça, the daughter of the Baron of Mourão. Joana was either a devout and pious woman or in fear of her new husband, for in 1530 she founded this convent as a retreat, a burial ground for Bragança duchesses and a college for Bragança girls. The convent is now a *pousada*. The dukes are buried in the Mosteiro dos Agostinhos on the other side of the courtyard from the palace, a church usually closed to the public.

## ALANDROAL AND JUROMENHA

Alandroal sits in the heart of the rural upper Alentejo and takes its name from oleander, whose bushes colour the surrounding countryside pink in spring, offsetting the blue of the sky and the yellows, whites and reds of the meadows. Like so many of the region's smaller towns, Alandroal is dominated by a dramatic castle, within whose walls are a fortified parish church (dedicated to Our Lady of Conception, the patroness of Portugal), and a huddle of cottages. The castle and old centre can be wandered around at a leisurely pace in under an hour. There's little to detain visitors for longer, aside perhaps from a side trip to Cosmander's great ruined fortress at Juromenha 15km away, on the banks of the Guadiana River, looking across the water into Spain.

**GETTING THERE AND AWAY** Alandroal sits 8km south of Vila Viçosa on the N255 road (which runs to Reguengos de Monsaraz). Juromenha is 15km northeast of Alandroal on the N373 and 18km south of Elvas on the same road. Alandroal is 16km south of the IP7/A6 Lisbon-Évora-Badajoz motorway. Elvas is 48km away, Évora 70km, Estremoz 30km, Borba 15km and Monsaraz 51km.

The town is easily visited on a day trip from Vila Viçosa on **bus lines** 8931 and 8958 (Vila Viçosa only), and 8917 (Vila Viçosa, also connecting to Redondo and Évora). Bus line 8011 connects Vila Viçosa and Alandroal twice daily, then continues on to Juromenha.

Alandroal is so tiny a toddler could run through its historic centre in 10 minutes. Juromenha is smaller still.

**TOURIST INFORMATION** There is a tourist office on the Praça da República (☏ 268 440045; www.cm-alandroal.pt; ⊕ 08.30–12.30 & 13.30–16.30 Mon–Fri, 10.00–12.30 & 14.00–17.30 Sat–Sun). There is no tourist booth in Juromenha.

🏠 **WHERE TO STAY, EAT AND DRINK** Both Alandroal and Juromenha have places to eat that are open at lunch and dinnertime, but nowhere which stands out as being worth a special mention apart from the Casas de Juromenha.

🏠 **Casas de Juromenha** (5 rooms) Juromenha (well signposted as you reach the village); ☏ 268 969242; www.casasdejuromenha.com. Lazing around the pool or on the sun terraces of this snooze-inducingly tranquil country house it's hard to imagine that the area in which it lies was for centuries as ridden with conflict as the modern Middle East. The building sits on the banks of the Guadiana River, set in gardens filled with butterflies and the scent of lavender and rosemary, under night skies so unpolluted with light that they shimmer with millions of stars. The ruined fortress of Juromenha hulks on the hill above the guesthouse, and the captured Portuguese town of Olivença sits just across the river in Spain. It's easy to visit both by foot or boat (and bus) and the helpful staff can organise all manner of excursions – from bird-watching to kayaking, hiking and visits to the sights. €€–€€€

**WHAT TO SEE AND DO**
**Castelo Alandroal (Alandroal Castle)** (*Rua Diogo Lopes Sequeira;* ☏ *268 440045; free to wander around at any time*) Alandroal Castle sees very few visitors, which means you can wander along its battlements admiring the views out over the Alentejo at your leisure and almost certainly on your own even in high season. The building is Moorish in origin but rebuilt as Portuguese Gothic, with Mudéjar flourishes. It was commissioned by Lourenço Afonso, a scion of the House of Avis, in 1294 and expanded in grander form from the 17th century, when it became a bastion against Spanish incursion. It's a fascinating building. The architect of its construction was a Muslim stonemason known as 'O Mouro Calvo' ('The Bald Moor'). The Moor copied Muslim fortifications in Seville and Granada (as can be seen from the

shape of the towers and the horseshoe arches). He also daringly included a Latin inscription of the motto of the Nasrid kings of Granada 'LEGALI : BI :IL : ILLALLA', or 'Wa la Ghalib illa Allah'. His patrons were either careless or illiterate, for the stone inscription has lasted over centuries. The castle has a striking fortified church and there are wonderful views from the battlements out over the plains.

**Fortaleza de Juromenha (Fortress of Juromenha)** Be careful wandering through the decrepit churches and crumbling walls of this ruined hilltop fortress. The atmosphere is spectral, the spookiness enhanced by the whistling wind and the flap of birds disturbed from their roosts in the ruins. Locals tell of rumours of magic rituals being performed in the abandoned church on dark nights, and there's even an inverted pentacle carved into one of the ancient lichen-covered stones. But the real danger comes from the walls and ceilings, which are caving in, and the ground, which is pitted with holes – sudden drops in the meadow of poppy fields and daisies that now covers the old parade ground. Views over the bulwarks are wonderful – of the Guadiana River, inflated by flooded water from the Alqueva Dam, to Olivença in Spain and an endless horizon. Imagine this view from a bedroom or a dining table – the castle would be an unforgettable five-star hotel. There are even plans to make it one. But that would be a shame – it's already a world-class ruin.

The fortress is in small part the work of Cosmander (see box, page 87) and in larger part the work of the Frenchman Nicolau de Langres, and it stands on the site of an older medieval palace. Construction began in the 1640s, but in 1659 as the fortress was nearing completion an explosion in the arms store destroyed part of the new building and what remained of the old palace. Over a hundred soldiers were killed. Like Cosmander before him, Langres switched sides and in 1662 provided the information that resulted in a successful Spanish attack on the fortress he himself had designed. The attack was led by the son of Philip IV of Spain, John of Austria. It proved successful and Spain held the building until the Treaty of Lisbon was signed in 1668.

The fortress was partly destroyed in the 1755 Lisbon earthquake and fell into Spanish hands once again in the early 1800s during the War of the Oranges, the precursor to the Peninsular Wars. The fortress was recaptured by the British in 1808.

## MONSARAZ AND REGUENGOS DE MONSARAZ

Ringed by a perfectly preserved medieval wall, criss-crossed with cobbled streets and with whitewashed bell towers brilliant under the burning sun, Monsaraz is the kind of fortified hill town that should come with an Ennio Morricone soundtrack. It's all about atmosphere here. Try and come early, off-season and on a bright sunny day, when it's so quiet that your footfalls echo along the streets and you can hear the braying of donkeys kilometres away across the plain. There are no outstanding sights; Monsaraz itself is the destination. And the views of the tiny town are the reason for coming here: from below, looking up at its rocky hill; from its highest point, white against the golden plain; and from its castle battlements out over the Alqueva Lake and the grasslands of the high Alentejo.

Monsaraz is 18km east of Reguengos de Monsaraz, its modern counterpart and a provincial olive-, sheep- and wine-producing town with no sights of real interest. There are dozens of prehistoric ruins in the surrounding countryside and a few wineries open for visits.

**HISTORY** The plains around Monsaraz are littered with hundreds of stone circles, menhirs, cromlechs and dolmens, all testament to a Stone Age population that numbered many thousands. The Romans based in Évora claimed the area as part of their territory and may have built a fortress on the hill, though no remains have so far been unearthed. Monsaraz began with the Islamic invasion.

In fact, the town – like Marvão, its counterpart in the far north of the Alentejo – is so typically Moorish (built around a square castle keep and completely encircled by high walls) that you can almost hear the call to prayer echoing through its narrow whitewashed streets. It was taken from the Moors in 1167 by Geraldo Sem Pavor – Gerald the Fearless, the wayfaring brigand and mercenary who was also responsible for the recapture of Évora. After expelling the population, Gerald did little more than repair the damage he'd inflicted on the town, and then handed it over to the Crusaders, in the form of the Knights Templar, who established it as a small garrison against Spanish incursion.

In 1381 an English army led by Edmund of Langley, first Duke of York (and at the time Duke of Cambridge) and son of King Edward III of England, while waiting to attack Spain, turned on Monsaraz and ransacked the town. Edmund had come to Portugal as part of a scheme hatched by his brother John of Gaunt to mount a joint attack on the Castilian throne, which John of Gaunt claimed for himself. When Spain and Portugal made peace, Edmund's army of archers were sidelined and unpaid. The sack of Monsaraz was in reprisal. They were later captured by the Castilians and sent home in Spanish galleons.

Like so many of the border towns, occupation of Monsaraz oscillated between the Portuguese and Spanish over the centuries. By the early 20th century there was no longer any need for a fortress town and Monsaraz was slowly abandoned, in favour of Reguengos, which occupied a far more practical position on the fertile lowlands. The ossification continued until after the Estado Novo, when Monsaraz slowly returned to life as a tourist destination. But you're still more likely to see old men in cloth caps here and widows in black than young Portuguese – if you come early, that is, before the coach parties arrive.

**GETTING THERE, AWAY AND AROUND** Whether you drive here or arrive on public transport you will need to pass through Reguengos de Monsaraz, which has all of the transport facilities for the local area, and much of the infrastructure.

Reguengos de Monsaraz sits at the crossroads of the N255, which runs north to Alandroal, Vila Viçosa, Borba and the IP7, and the N256, which runs west to Évora and east to Mourão and Spain. Alandroal is 38km away, Vila Viçosa 46km, Elvas 83km and Évora 39km. There are two Rede Expressos buses a day between Reguengos and Évora (*35mins*).

There is no **parking** available within Monsaraz's walls, but plenty of car parking immediately outside. Two bus lines connect Monsaraz and Reguengos de Monsaraz: the 8174 (*4 daily, weekdays only, 30mins*) and the 8930 (*once daily from Monsaraz, twice daily to Monsaraz, weekdays only, 1hr*). A cab between Reguengos and Monsaraz will cost around €20 each way.

The only option for getting around Monsaraz is on foot. It takes around 20 minutes to walk from one end of the town to the other; it is only four streets wide.

**TOURIST INFORMATION** There is a tourist office on Rua Direita (❧ *927 997316;* ⊕ *09.00–12.30 & 14.00–17.30 daily*).

## WHERE TO STAY

**Casa Pinto** (5 rooms) Praça de Nuno Albares Pereira 10, Monsaraz; ☏ 266 557076; www.casapinto.es. This tiny guesthouse feels like a quirky home. Despite being Spanish-owned, rooms are named after former Portuguese colonies – Mombasa, Goa, Macau, Dili & Asilah – & are decorated in the style of each one. There's a gorgeous roof terrace with views of the Alentejo countryside. €€€

🏠 **Estalagem de Monsaraz** (19 rooms) Largo de São Bartolomeu 5, Monsaraz; 📞266 557112. A rustic country house with thick beams & a whitewashed façade on Monsaraz hill. There are wonderful views (over breakfast croissants & the edge of the pool) from the garden terrace & the best 2 rooms, the largest of which has a lovely Juliet balcony. €€€

🏠 **Horta da Moura** (25 rooms) Off the M514 road some 500m south of Monsaraz; 📞266 550100; www.hortadamoura.pt. This rural hotel tucked away in the countryside a couple of kilometres from Monsaraz & the Alqueva has suites of rooms in & around a converted old Portuguese farmhouse & is renowned for its excellent restaurant,

the Feitiço da Moura (see below), & the wine tours that Henrique Moura, the affable owner, conducts around the region. The grounds are extensive, with vineyards, cork oak trees, paddocks with horses & ponies & a luxurious infinity pool. €€€

🏠 **Casa Dona Antónia** (8 rooms) Rua Direita 15, Monsaraz; 📞266 557142; www. casadantonia-monsaraz.com. This little cottage right in the centre of town is unusual in combining homestay comfort & intimacy with hotel service. There are only a handful of rooms (simply furnished & with floor tiles & whitewashed walls), the best of which have balconies with views of the plains, but the guesthouse offers a rooftop terrace where b/fasts of local honey, jam & bread are served with a sweeping view & 24/7 reception staff who can organise tours of the Alqueva Lake, the wineries & Monsaraz itself. €€

✗ **WHERE TO EAT AND DRINK** See also page 116 for details of wineries in the Reguengos region.

✗ **Feitiço da Moura** Hotel Horta da Moura, M514 km 0.5 Monsaraz; 📞266 550100; www. hortadamoura.pt; ⊕ 12.30–15.00 & 19.00–22.00 daily. One of the finest restaurants in the region, serving contemporary Portuguese & Alentejo dishes like octopus with sweet potato, tomato & thyme, & Alentejo-style black pork. Chef Henrique Mouro is one of Portugal's most illustrious, having honed his craft in Belmond hotels in Peru and the Pestana group. He won first prize in Portugal's prestigious Chef of the Year Awards a few years back. €€€

✗ **O Alcaide** Rua de Santiago 18, Monsaraz; 📞266 557168; ⊕ noon–15.00 & 19.00–21.30 Mon–Wed & Fri–Sun. The best for local cooking, serving *bochechas de porco preto, ensopado de borrego, migas* & other Alentejo specialities in a

dining room hanging with agricultural & artisanal bric-a-brac. Excellent wine list. €€

✗ **Lumumba** Rua Direita s/n, Monsaraz; 📞226 557121; ⊕ noon–15.00 & 19.00–21.00 Tue–Sun. Local dishes inc *ensopado de borrego*, a mixed crowd of local people & visitors, & terrace tables with sweeping views over Alqueva Lake & the surrounding countryside. €€

✗ **Os Templários** Rua Direita 22, Monsaraz; 📞266 557166. Be sure to eat outside at this small, family-run restaurant in the heart of the old town. There are superb views out over the plains to the Alqueva Reservoir. The menu is of local dishes with Alentejo & Portuguese standards like *bochechas de porco preto* & *bacalhau com espinafres*. Decent wine list. €€

**WHAT TO SEE AND DO** Monsaraz is crowned with a castle and replete with churches. All are more beautiful from the outside than inside and preserve little of great interest either architecturally or historically. The parish church (**Igreja Matriz da Nossa Senhora da Lagoa**) dates from the 16th century, is decorated with *azulejos*, and has a gilt chancel (with statues of St Augustine and St Monica) and the marble tomb of the first Baron of Monsaraz, the Knight Templar Gomes Martins Silvestre. There is a small sacred art museum attached with a modest collection of monstrances, vestments and ceremonial items. The **Igreja da Misericórdia (Church of Divine Mercy)** (*Largo Principal s/n*), which dates from the 16th century, has some modest 18th-century gilt altarpieces and a statue of Senhor Jesus dos Passos (Christ bearing the cross), the patron of Monsaraz. The clerical wing of the church was once a hospital.

At the north end of town, there's a curious little domed hermitage, the **Capela de São João Batista (Chapel of St John the Baptist)** (*Rua de São João; not formally open to the public*) stuck on to the Baluarte de São João like a sugar cube with a marshmallow on top. The tiny door is usually closed and padlocked, but you can peek into the cell – which is covered in 17th-century murals – through the cracks. It's far older than the bulwark and may even be an old Moorish home or shop. The attraction here is the town itself and the atmosphere it engenders, if you visit early and off-season. And especially if you choose to wake early and wander the streets, or sip a glass of wine at sunset in a restaurant with a view like that of Os Templários and then walk to the battlements when it's dark to see one of western Europe's most star-filled skies.

**Wineries** The Reguengos region is renowned for fine wines, and a number of wineries are open to visits. **Enoforum Carmim** (*Rua Professor Mota Pinto, Apartado 3, Reguengos de Monsaraz;* \ *266 508200; www.enoforumwines. com*) is the largest wine producer in the Alentejo, producing some of Portugal's finest reds and fortified wines. Olive oils are produced here too. Visitors can see the olive press and take a wine and olive oil tasting tour. A visit with blind tasting of two wines costs €10, and reservations are essential. The **Herdade do Esporão** (*Apartado 31, Reguengos de Monsaraz;* \ *266 509280; www.esporao.com*) is a smaller producer making some very fine organic wines and an acclaimed Reserva. The staff can arrange a full half-day or day out, with birdwatching, cycling (including a picnic) or walking in combination with lunch and a tasting. A tasting costs €15, while lunch for two is €100, including a wine tasting tour and wine.

**The menhirs and megaliths** The countryside around Monsaraz is covered with prehistoric monuments that can only be visited on a tour (with Tur Aventur) or with a hire car. A prehistoric route is available from the Monsaraz tourist office, with GPS points for the monuments. These are not always accurate and you might have better luck the old fashioned way – using a good map and road signs.

The **Xerez Cromlech** (5km from Monsaraz – turn right off the M514 on to the Rua da Orada at the roundabout in the village of Telheiro), which consists of 50 standing stones around a central 4m menhir, is closest to Monsaraz. Its magic is only a little diminished by learning that it was moved to its present site after the flooding that produced the Alqueva Lake. The village of Xerez, outside which the stones originally stood, is now submerged.

The **Menir de Outeiro** lies a few kilometres or so to the north, just outside the village of Outeiro. At nearly 6m tall it's one of the largest freestanding menhirs in Europe, but was lying on its side when it was discovered in 1969. The **Menir da Belhoa** a few hundred metres to the west was broken when it was discovered in 1970, with only the top of the stone (which is covered in spiral cravings) surviving. The base is an imagined reconstruction in concrete.

A **Rocha dos Namorados** (Lovers' Rock), 8km east of Reguengos de Monsaraz after the pottery producing village of São Pedro do Corval, is a 2m-tall natural standing stone with Megalithic carvings on its sides. It has long been associated with fertility. The small stones littered on the top have been thrown there over the centuries. Local legend has it that every stone thrown by a single woman which lands on top and then falls signifies a year of waiting to find a partner.

# MOURÃO AND THE ALQUEVA LAKE

Out on a limb and a stretch of the N256 road as it cuts across the Alqueva Lake, Mourão is the last town before Spain. Being so close to the frontier, it is topped by the inevitable castle – a chunky, crumbling fortress with extensive bulwarks, parts of which incorporate a fortified early Renaissance church. Another bell tower is stuck on the keep like an afterthought. Mourão is a town that Spaniards and Portuguese pass through when travelling to each others' countries, or which tourists visit out of curiosity when exploring the countryside around Monsaraz. But if you happen to be here on a Friday or Saturday night, pop into one of the tavernas. You might just hear locals singing Cante Alentejano (see box, page 158). The town is a centre of the dying art. Mourão is a good place from which to take trips out on to the Alqueva Lake.

**GETTING THERE AND AWAY**   Mourão is reached on the N256 from Reguengos de Monsaraz, a 21km journey. A single Rede Expresso **bus** connects the town with Évora once daily via Reguengos (*50mins*).

**TOURIST INFORMATION AND TOUR OPERATOR**   There is a **tourist office** on Largo das Portas de São Bento (✆ *266 560010;* ⊕ *09.00–12.30 & 14.00–17.30 daily*).
   **PT Relax** (*Rua Alvará 199;* ✆ *961 628311; www.pt-relax.com*) offers boat and fishing trips on Alqueva Lake (with optional stops for sunbathing on beaches), boat hire, walks, mountain bike rides and jeep tours around eastern Alentejo, at modest prices. Longer trips include a decent picnic or restaurant lunch in Monsaraz (pages 113–16).

**WHAT TO SEE AND DO**   The Aldeia da Luz, a tiny settlement of identikit cottages, lies just outside Mourão. One of the tragic consequences of the flooding of the Alqueva Lake was the loss of a series of beautiful historic villages and prehistoric sites. The original Aldeia da Luz was one of them, lying submerged immediately offshore to the south of Mourão. The local population were moved from there into what they hoped would be a replica of their old village. The poignant village museum, the **Museu da Luz (Luz Museum)** (*Largo da Igreja de Nossa Senhora da Luz;* ✆ *266 569257; www.museudaluz. org.pt;* ⊕ *09.30–13.00 & 14.00–17.30 Tue–Sun; admission €2*) shows the real difference and tells the story of the relocation. For more information on Alqueva, see page 169.

# ARRONCHES

Werewolves and witches live in Arronches. On full moons mysterious figures haunt the crossroads on the deserted backroads that lead to Spain, and werewolves hunt in the hills around the Gruta da Igreja dos Mouros cave. Children are told not to go into the hills. 'One who did so was eaten. All that was left was his boots.' Or so the older locals say.
   Visiting when the moon is waxing or waning, Arronches feels like the sleepiest of places, sitting on the southern end of the Parque Natural da Serra de São Mamede, surrounded by prehistoric monuments and set in an area rich with wineries and olive plantations. It's a good place to base yourself for a day or two – to birdwatch in the Natural Park, see the Megalithic cave paintings and take a tour of the tiny castle towns that dot the region.

**GETTING THERE, AWAY AND AROUND**   Arronches sits on the N246 Elvas to Portalegre road around 10km from the Spanish border. Elvas is 32km away,

Portalegre 26km, Castelo de Vide 45km and Marvão and Estremoz 46km. There are no Rede Expressos buses, but **bus line** 8061 runs between Elvas and Portalgre via Arronches seven times daily from Monday to Friday.

Arronches has few attractions in its own right, so to get the most out of a visit here you'll need your own transport.

**TOURIST INFORMATION AND TOURS** The helpful Arronches **tourist office** is on Largo Serpa Pinto 10 (✆ *245 580085; www.cm-arronches.pt;* ⊕ *10.00–13.00 & 14.00–18.00 Tue–Sun*).

The **Hotel Rural Santo António** (see below) organises all manner of trips to the prehistoric sites, the Natural Park, birdwatching, visits to the castles and to wineries. It's worth staying in the hotel just to enjoy the trips.

## 🏠 WHERE TO STAY

🏠 **Torre da Palma Wine Hotel** (19 rooms) Herdade de Torre de Palma, Monforte; ✆245 038890; www.torredepalma.com. Set in extensive vineyards in the heart of the countryside 10mins' drive from Arronches, this 14th-century mansion house has been converted into a luxurious wine hotel. Rooms come with the kind of design flourishes you'd expect in an urban boutique hotel – silk screens, bedcovers & chaises longue in matching lilac silks. The restaurant is excellent, there's a beautiful spa & the hotel organises activities ranging from cycling, birdwatching & star-gazing to the raison d'être – wine-tasting tours. €€€€€

🏠 **Hotel Rural Santo António** (29 rooms) Bairro de Santo António, Rua A, s/n, Arronches; ✆245 589003; www.santoantoniohotel.com. Bulky modern hotel set in lovely countryside on the edge of town. Stunning views of the sun setting over Arronches from the balconies, & the sun rising over the Spanish border. Rooms are large, well appointed & modern with ample work spaces & big balconies, & the hotel has an excellent restaurant (see below) & a big pool. The staff can organise all manner of bespoke & package excursions. €€€

## ✗ WHERE TO EAT AND DRINK

✗ **Santo António** In the Hotel Rural Santo António; ⊕ noon–15.00 & 19.00–23.00 daily. Excellent regional comfort cooking from chef Andre Siverinho (formally of the Pousada dos Loios in Évora), with a menu featuring plenty of game (wild boar, venison, partridge & hare), & – unusually for the Alentejo – some decent vegetarian options. €€

## WHAT TO SEE AND DO
**Herdade Reynolds** (*Monte Figueira de Cima, Arronches;* ✆ *245 580305; www. reynoldswinegrowers.pt; visits on appointment only; tasting from €10, lunch from €40 with wine*) Robert Reynolds, the son of an English seaman, left Devon with his father in 1820 to make his fortune in Portugal, initially settling in Porto with the intention of producing fortified wines. But the market was already full with British companies like Taylors and Grahams, and the Reynolds family headed south to the Alentejo, initially to harvest cork oaks, and then to produce wine. Reynolds wines are still produced by the family and are named after Robert, his children and grandchildren. Gloria Reynolds, made from the Nelson Martins grape, is their most celebrated red and is available only to Reynolds Club members, at select restaurants and to those who visit the winery.

**The southern Serra de São Mamede** Arronches is a good alternative to Marvão and Castelo de Vide as a base for exploring the Serra de São Mamede (pages 120–2). The area around Arronches is particularly rich in birdlife – the low-lying rocky hills that lie on the border with Spain have large migrant populations of raptors, particularly vultures, and are now an important refuge for the European wildcat.

In the far south of the park near Esperança village, some 10km from Arronches, the mountains form low escarpments covered with Mediterranean pine and rich with roosting birds, caves and shallow valleys. Black and griffon vultures are a common sight here, especially around the **Gruta Igreja dos Mouros**, **Pinho Monteiro** and **Lapa dos Gaivões** – caves and low ridges covered with one of the greatest spreads of rock art in Portugal outside the UNESCO World Heritage-listed Côa Valley. For a century it was thought that these representations of horned figures, wild animals and geometric shapes were Neolithic, dating from around 3000–4000BC. But 2010 and 2012 studies carried out by the Laboratório de Arqueologia at the Universidade de Évora suggest they may be from the late Upper Palaeolithic (20,000–10,000BC),

## A TOUR OF THE CASTLE TOWNS

The region west of Arronches is dotted with half a dozen villages, whose ruined castles are open for visitors to wander in and out of at all times. While these are not attractions grand enough to merit a stay, they can be visited in a one- or two-day self-drive tour, or *en route* from Arronches to Castelo de Vide or Marvão. The best route would take them in as follows:

- **Monforte**, with a semi-ruined castle on the hill and a Roman bridge spanning the river.
- **Veiros**, with fewer than 500 inhabitants and an enormous round-towered granite and marble castle enclosing a tiny white-washed village.
- **Avis**, a pretty huddle of handsome whitewashed houses on the banks of the Maranhão River. Three towers remain of the castle founded by Dom João I (who went on to accede to the throne and found the royal dynasty of Avis, which he established in Évora). The monastery of São Bento has some fine interior decoration.
- **Alter do Chão**, with a chunky 14th-century Bragança castle. Horse-lovers should visit the **Coudelaria de Alter do Chão** (*Tapada do Arneiro, Apartado 80;* ✆ *245 610060; www.alterreal.pt;* ⊕ *twice daily visits at 11.00 & 15.00 Tue–Sun, €7.50*) outside the village, which is one of Europe's most magnificent horse studs, covering 800 hectares of countryside. It was founded by João V in 1748. Visitors can enjoy riding lessons and carriage tours, watch the mares and foals grazing and visit the riding schools, stables and museum, with displays of everything there is to know about how these horses are bred.
- **Crato**, a neat and tidy little village with a castle destroyed by John of Austria, which is literally falling to the ground. Around 2km from the centre lies one of Iberia's best preserved and most imposing fortified monasteries, the **Mosteiro de Santa Maria de Flor da Rosa** (⊕ *09.30–12.30 & 14.00–17.30 Mon–Fri, 10.00–13.00 & 14.30–18.00 Sat–Sun; admission €2*), now an extraordinary *pousada*. It is said to be haunted. The **Anta do Tapadão** dolmen, which is the second largest in Portugal, lies just outside Crato in the village of Aldeia da Mata.
- **Alegrete**, a village so small it barely knows it's there, with a romantic crag-top castle founded by Dom Dinis in 1319, and superb views out over the Serra de Mamede to Marvão from the battlements.

which would make them among the oldest in Europe, contemporaneous with those in the Côa Valley and Lascaux in France.

**Campo Maior** This town, 15km south of Arronches on the road to Badajoz, is topped with a massive Moorish castle and is famous in Portugal for its annual Festa das Flores (flower festival). This is the oldest and most traditional flower festival in the Alentejo. It takes place in July (on a different day every year – see the town hall website, www.cm-campo-maior.pt, for this year's date), when all the streets are carpeted with flowers. While you are here visit the ghoulish **Chapel of Bones** in the Igreja Matriz and the Olive Oil Museum in the **Lagar-Museu do Palacio Visconde d'Oliva** (*Rua de Olivença s/n;* ⊕ *10.00–18.00 Tue–Sun; admission €2*). A short drive further east is the tiny settlement of Ougela, where there is an impressive ruined fortress watching over the border to the dusty plains of Spanish Extremedura.

## PARQUE NATURAL DA SERRA DE SÃO MAMEDE

North of Arronches the Alentejo's plains become increasingly mountainous – the flat lands give way to low hills and then rugged country where rolling moors replace the plains, and crags become rocky ridges whose lower slopes are covered in woodlands of wild hazel, pine and oak perfumed with wild sage and interspersed with meadows of rock roses, silene, periwinkle and pimpernel. Prehistoric relics dot the fields – dolmens like crooked tables, the clustered circles of cromlechs and menhirs pointing skyward. Rivers and streams ripple through the hills and two big lakes dominate the lowlands, forming important havens for endemic amphibians and reptiles, as well as migratory water birds. Roads wind into the hills, to peaks and escarpments, some crowned with fortress towns like Marvão, Alegrete and Castelo de Vide, others bare and circled by soaring raptors. The land rises to the highest peak in southern Portugal, the Pico de São Mamede.

Most of the area is protected as the Serra de São Mamede Natural Park (*www.icnf.pt*). It is contiguous with the Parque Natural do Tejo and links with the ZEPA Sierra de San Pedro to form one of the largest protected areas in southern Iberia and an important refuge for otter, wildcat and Cabrera's vole, which is on the International Union for Conservation of Nature (IUCN) red list. The disused Cova da Moura mine has one of the largest bat colonies in Europe and the Serra has more reptile and amphibian species than anywhere else in Portugal, including the brilliant green emerald lizard, and European and Spanish pond turtles. But it is the **birds** that make the Serra truly spectacular, with some 150 recorded species, including big spectacular birds like short-toed and Bonelli's eagles, and black and griffon vultures, which are particularly abundant in the south of the park near Arronches. This is one of the few places in Europe where you can see raptors from above as they soar. Other species include black stork, lesser kestrel, red kite, great and little bustards, great spotted cuckoo, roller, azure-winged magpie, rock bunting, black wheatear and Spanish sparrow.

The Serra is great hiking and mountain biking country, and there are myriad opportunities for day walks or rides and longer treks, including walking from village to village. As elsewhere in the Alentejo, there are many rural homestays.

**GETTING THERE AND AWAY** The only practical access to the park is with your own transport, on an organised tour or a self-guided walk. The Serra runs along the border with Spain from Arronches in the south to Póvoas e Meadas in the north. The principal access road is the N246 running between Arronches and Castelo de

Vide via Portalegre, and the N359 running between Portalegre and Marvão. Base yourselves in one of these towns for access.

**GETTING AROUND** Dozens of little minor roads, not all of them well signposted, run off the N246 and the N359 and the roads around Arronches, Alegrete, Marvão and Castelo de Vide, cutting through the park. The wildest sections in the centre of the park – immediately northeast of Castelo de Vide, around São Julião, south of Marvão – and between Alegrete and Arronches in the south have no road access and you will need to take a map and a compass or a guide.

## TOUR OPERATORS

**Multi Aventuras São Mamede** ✆963 952926/ +34 633 732132; www.multiaventurassaomamede. com. This company offers light adventures in the Serra, inc mountain biking, horseback riding, climbing & rappelling, archery, photography, paintball & lots of guided day walks. Very good prices.
**O Poejo** See page 129. Offers walking & wildlife excursions throughout the Serra from the lovely boutique hotel in Marvão.
**Portugal Walks** ✆965 753033; www. portugalwalks.com. Includes the Serra in its week-long Alentejo trip & offers self-guided walking holidays throughout the region.
**Quinta Serra de São Mamede** See below. Offers mountain biking, walking, hot air ballooning & landscape painting to guests at the hotel.

**Walking Holiday** www.walkingholidayinfo. co.uk. Offers guided walks in the Serra de São Mamede with accommodation in self-catering cottages near the Pico de São Mamede.
**Quinta do Pomarinho** ✆965 755341; www. pomarinho.com. Guided, group & self-guided walking holidays in the Serra based in their rustic holiday homes at the foot of the park near Castelo de Vide. The Dutch owners' dream is 'to make Quinta do Pomarinho the hiking centre of the Alto Alentejo,' & they're enthusiastic fans of the park, knowledgeable about its flora & fauna & how it changes over the season. They have a list of 60 bird species recorded only within their grounds. Great for hikers & especially good for wildlife enthusiasts.

**TOURIST INFORMATION** The **tourist offices** in Arronches, Marvão, Portalegre and Castelo de Vide (see the individual town entries) can provide information on what to do and see in the Serra de São Mamede, and hand out maps.

Love Alentejo (*www.love-alentejo.com*) has downloadable self-guided walks on its website. The Portuguese forestry commission, the **ICNF** (*Instituto da Conservação da Natureza e das Florestas; Avenida da República 16, Lisbon;* ✆ *213 507900; www.icnf.pt;* ⊕ *Mon–Fri 09.30–16.30*) has detailed information on the park on its website (in Portuguese only).

The **Instituto Geográfico do Exército** (*IGEOE; Avenida Dr Alfredo Bensaúde, 1849-014 Lisbon;* ✆ *218 505 300; www.igeoe.pt*) sells accurate scale maps for hiking for around €7 at its shop. These can be ordered through the post. Some of the maps are downloadable from the website.

**WHERE TO STAY** In addition to the options listed below, **Alentejo Retreat** (*www. alentejoretreat.com*) organises self-catering holidays in the Serra São Mamede National Park for birdwatchers and wildlife lovers.

🏠 **Quinta Serra de São Mamede**
(2 1-bedroom villas, 1 2-bedroom villa) Ribeira de Sao Joao, Povoa de Meadas, near Castelo de Vide; ✆938 681201; www.quintaserradesaomamede. com. The real attraction here is the park itself. These rustic but well-appointed modern cottages,

decorated with bright splashes of colour from scatter cushions, spreads & pictures of nature, sit in the heart of the Serra close to the Spanish border, with walks & wonderful views literally on the doorstep. There's a pool, & the owners have a big menu of activities, including walking, canoeing, mountain biking, wine tours, horseriding, ballooning & golf. Cottages have fully equipped kitchens, dining rooms & sleep 2–4. €€€

🏠 **Quinta do Pomarinho holiday cottages** (4 houses sleeping 2–10 people) EN 246 km16.5, Castelo de Vide; ✆ 965 755341; www.

pomarinho.com. Houses, cottages or single rooms in converted rustic farmhouses on the 62-acre Quinta do Pomarinho estate just outside Castelo de Vide. The Dutch owners organise walking, rock climbing & wildlife-watching excursions. €€

## PORTALEGRE

The regional capital is a town you will inevitably pass by or through if visiting this part of the Alentejo by car or public transport, as it's a transport hub. It's pretty, too, climbing into the foothills of the Serra de São Mamede in higgledy-piggledy terracotta and crowding around a Moorish castle and an enormous 18th-century cathedral. However, as it's not nearly as charming as nearby Castelo de Vide and Marvão, it receives few visitors.

Cork and textile production helped the town to become rich between the 17th and 19th centuries, at least by Alentejo standards (you can still see the old industrial chimneys and factories in the suburbs). This left the town with a series of handsome public buildings and Baroque churches, many of them set around the town's large Rossio square. They are interesting to visit on an hour's diversion on your way north, perhaps after lunch in the excellent Tomba Lobos restaurant (page 123), but they aren't impressive enough to persuade many visitors to make the town their base for exploring the far north of the Alentejo and the Serra de São Mamede Natural Park.

### GETTING THERE AND AWAY

**By car** Portalegre is well connected to the rest of the Alentejo and to Lisbon by the IP2/E802 motorway, which joins the IP7/A6 at Estremoz. The N246 runs between the town and Arronches to the south and Castelo de Vide to the north, while the N359 winds into the hills to Marvão. Distances are as follows: Lisbon 232km, Estremoz 55km, Arronches 30km, Castelo de Vide 21km, Crato 22km, Marvão 21km, Évora 102km.

**By bus** Travelling between the rest of the Alentejo and Castelo de Vide and/or Marvão, you will have to change in Portalegre. The town has select services as follows: Rede Expressos to Estremoz (*3 daily, 45mins*), Évora (*2 daily, 2½hrs*), Lisbon (*6 daily, 2¾hrs*). In terms of **local buses**, line 8061 runs between Portalegre and Elvas via Arronches (*7 daily, 1hr10mins, weekdays only*), line 8903 runs between Portalegre and Marvão (*3 times daily, weekdays*), line 8012 runs to Castelo de Vide and Marvão (*1 daily*), and line 8068 runs to Castelo de Vide (*3 daily*). For more information see www.rodalentejo.pt and www.rede-expressos.pt.

**TOURIST INFORMATION** The **tourist office** is at Rua Guilherme Gomes Fernandes 22 (✆ 245 307445; www.cm-portalegre.pt; ⏰ 09.30–13.00 & 14.30–18.00 daily). Staff are very helpful and have a wealth of pamphlets, maps, route planners and advice.

🏠 **WHERE TO STAY, EAT AND DRINK** Consider staying in Marvão, Castelo de Vide or at the extraordinary Flor Blanca *pousada* in Crato, all of which are around 20km away.

In Portalegre, a reliable option is the **Rossio** (*19 rooms; Rua 31 de Janeiro 6;* ✆ *245 082218; www.rossiohotel.com;* **€€€**), with modern rooms and suites decorated with

*above*  Marvão's 13th-century castle offers views over the 15th-century parish church and medieval town, and further to the Serra de São Mamede (AR) pages 127–30

*below*  Mértola's castle has a Moorish keep that was enlarged by the Order of St James, which had its Portuguese headquarters here (SUS) page 177

*above* Longer than a football pitch, the Paço Ducal dominates the centre of sleepy Vila Viçosa; it was used by the Bragança dynasty until Portugal became a republic in 1910 (AR) pages 110–11

*left* The historic centre of Estremoz is a maze of stepped, cobbled streets and whitewashed houses (AR) pages 95–101

*below* The Herdade Reynolds winery near Arronches was founded in the 19th century and produces a number of celebrated reds (AR) page 118

*bottom* Castelo de Vide's castle offers wonderful views of the terracotta roofs, battlements and bell towers of the village below (AR) pages 123–7

*above left* The dining room at the Pousada de Beja, a restored 13th-century convent (AR) page 156

*above right* The Moors occupied Beja from the 8th to the 12th centuries, and many of its buildings combine Manueline and Mudéjar features (V/SS) pages 153–61

*below* The tiny town of Alcácer do Sal packs in a Moorish castle, a Romanesque chapel and striking views from both sides of the River Sado (CC/SS) pages 136–7

*top and above left* Typical Alentejo landscapes of undulating wheat fields, solitary cork oaks and vineyards: wheat, cork, wine and olive oil are the region's foremost products (AR and IP/SS)

*above* A shipwreck on a beach near Vila Nova de Milfontes (AR) pages 143–51

*left* The tiny Ilha do Pessagueiro lies just offshore from the Rota Vicentina coastal path and can be visited on a boat trip from Porto Côvo (AR) page 148

*right*     Due to building errors, the lighthouse at Cabo Sardão was built backwards so that it faces inland (AR) page 151

*below*     The Lago de Alqueva is the largest artificial body of water in Europe and irrigates thousands of acres of arid Alentejo land (TL/SS) page 169

*bottom*     The Parque Natural do Sudoeste Alentejano e Costa Vicentina is a 200km-long chunk of protected coastline featuring deserted beaches and striated cliffs (AR) pages 146–7

*above* Cante Alentejano, a style of traditional a capella singing by male voice choirs, can still be heard in various villages — here in **Arronches** (AR) page 158

*left* Carpets have been made in Arraiolos since Moorish times, and a town-wide cooperative sells traditional designs (SUS) pages 104–6

*below* Historical re-enactments marking the Alentejo's turbulent past take place all over the region — here in Beja (AR) pages 153–4

In September the streets of Campo Maior are decked with colourful paper flowers for the Festas do Povo (J/DT) page 51

You can't go far wrong with food in the Alentejo: the coastal villages offer up the freshest of fish, while cafés all over serve thick black coffee and fragrant vanilla custard tarts (AR)

*above* The fortifications of the Castelo de Marvão seem to emerge from the very rock, and it was once described as 'the most unconquerable in the entire kingdom' (AR) pages 129–30

Alentejo-themed art and photographs. It also has a little spa and fitness centre, and the staff are warm and friendly.

Portuguese come from kilometres around to sample the great local cooking from José Júlio Vintém at **Tomba Lobos** (*Bairro da Pedra Basta Lote 16 R/C, Portalegre;* ✆ *245 906111;* €€€), with dishes like wild boar, partridge, venison and woodpigeon, or favourites like *lombo de porco com amêijoas* and Alentejo black pig all served with a dash of gourmet technique and slick, contemporary presentation.

**WHAT TO SEE AND DO** Winding Moorish streets with attractive wavy dragon's tooth paving climb from the old town to Portalegre's imposing Baroque **cathedral**. The huge façade, flanked by massive twin towers, promises treasures within. Unfortunately, it doesn't deliver: the interior is positively Protestant in its starkness, at least by Portuguese standards, but for a painted gilt altarpiece in the chancel.

The **Mosteiro de São Bernardo (St Bernard's Monastery)** (*Avenida Jorge Robinson, Alto da Fontedeira;* ✆ *245 307400;* ◷ *10.00–noon & 14.00–17.00 Tue–Fri, 11.00–17.00 Sat & Sun; free admission*) is a national monument and far more sumptuous. Founded in 1512, it has a church filled with beautiful Estremoz marble statuary and carvings, including the fabulous Jorge de Melo tomb, probably by Chanterene (see page 31). The cloisters have exquisite *azulejos* dating from the 1730s. The tomb is of a bishop who – despite the sculptural beatification (with Mary waiting to welcome him to heaven) – was known in life to have fathered at least two children, one by a nun in the convent.

The **castle** is little more than a husk of honey-coloured bulwarks and battlements, worth seeing only for the views out over tiled roofs and church towers. The town has a small **Museu Municipal (Municipal Museum)** (*Rua José Maria da Rosa;* ✆ *245 300120; www.geira.pt/mmportalegre;* ◷ *09.30–12.30 & 14.30–18.00 Wed–Mon; admission €3*), mostly with statuary and church art, including countless images of St. Anthony, a statue of Nossa Senhora dos Dores with knives in her bosom that is almost grisly enough to be Spanish, assorted equally bloody statues of Christ, Chinese porcelain and some lovely lacy fans.

The private **Fundação Robinson** (*Rua Dona Iria Goncalves Pereira s/n;* ✆ *245 307463; www.fundacaorobinson.pt;* ◷ *10.00–13.00 & 14.30–18.00 Tue–Sun; admission €2*) housed in the old Franciscan church is a mini-Gulbenkian Foundation, with a fine little museum crammed with priceless sacred art, rooms for temporary exhibitions and a published journal. The Foundation was established by the Robinson family, whose ancestor George Robinson moved to Portalegre from Halifax in 1835 to make corks for the wine produced by his fellow countryman, Thomas Reynolds (page 118). The Foundation is slowly restoring many of Portalegre's historical buildings and works throughout the northern Alentejo. Lovers of decaying industrial architecture will enjoy a wander around the old Robinson cork factory on the edge of town – follow the chimneys.

# CASTELO DE VIDE

With sugar-white cottages, coloured pink and violet with hanging flower boxes and tumbling down a steep hill from a massive crusader castle, Castelo de Vide is one of the Alentejo's prettiest towns. Old widows wander the cobbles, men in cloth caps gather to chat idly on street corners and cats ooze out of open windows, with a stretch and a yawn, to lollop and laze in the sun.

Spring and summer late afternoons are particularly beautiful, after the monuments and museums close and Castelo de Vide returns to being a tiny provincial town, bathed in light as yellow and warm as melting butter and drifting into slow, sedate sleepiness. The views are lovely – terracotta roofs against the meadows and vineyards of the plain, furrowed with shadows by the sloping sunlight, the curves of medieval terraced houses rising to battlements or dropping to bell towers, the mantled coronet of Marvão's walls on a distant ridge. Around the castle meadow, butterflies fill the air like floating petals and in the narrow alleys of the ancient Jewish quarter the scent of dinner drifts out from half-open shutters.

**HISTORY** Castelo de Vide grew from a tiny settlement to a castellated village after it was fortified under Dinis I's campaign to strengthen the interior of Portugal in the 1300s. From the 15th century it had grown into a town of a few thousand, becoming a refuge for Jewish people fleeing persecution in neighbouring Spain.

Although it was of minor strategic importance compared to the larger Alentejo towns to the south, Castelo de Vide was attacked by the Spanish on countless occasions, leading eventually to further fortification and a new set of secondary walls in the late 17th century. After these walls had been completed, Castelo de Vide was able to resist a Spanish attack led by the Jacobite third Duke of Berwick (James II of England's grandson) – that is, until he threatened to put the locals to the sword and 'leave the women exposed to the brutality of the soldiers'. The locals dumped their arms and gunpowder in the castle well and surrendered, handing the town to the Spanish. The well later exploded, destroying much of the castle.

Castelo de Vide was occupied by the French and Spanish during the Peninsular War, and when it returned to Portugal it went into slow decline, re-emerging in the late 20th century with the advent of tourism.

## GETTING THERE AND AWAY
**By car** The N246 runs between Castelo de Vide and Elvas to the south via Portalegre. The N246-1 runs from Castelo de Vide to Marvão and then into Spain, where it becomes the N-521 to Caceres. Distances are as follows: Lisbon 226km, Estremoz 75km, Arronches 45km, Marvão 10km, Évora 120km.

**By bus** Travelling between the rest of the Alentejo and Castelo de Vide, you will probably have to change in Portalegre. The town has Rede Expressos buses to Lisbon via Portalegre (*2 daily, 2hrs 10mins*). Line 8068 runs to Portalegre (*3 daily*); line 8012 runs to Portalegre and Marvão (*1 daily*). For more information see www.rodalentejo.pt and www.rede-expressos.pt.

**TOURIST INFORMATION** The tourist office is at Praça D Pedro V (📞 *245 908227; www.cm-castelodevide.pt;* ⊕ *summer 09.00-19.00, winter 09.00–12.30 & 14.00–17.30 daily*).

🏠 **WHERE TO STAY** See also *Where to stay* in the Serra de São Mamede section, pages 121–2. It's worth staying a day or so in both Marvão and Castelo de Vide. Both villages are beautiful and each has a very different feel: Marvão is monumental but can feel as deserted as an empty museum after dark – stay here for contemplation. Castelo de Vide has more life.

🏠 **Casa Amarela** (11 rooms) Praça D Pedro V 11; 📞245 901250; www.casaamarelath.com.

One of the loveliest small hotels in the Alentejo – so much so that the Portuguese president

Aníbal Cavaco Silva stayed here when he visited the region in 2015. His room was number 102 – the largest & plushest of them all. All rooms have lovely, high quality antique walnut tables, dressers, Baroque mirrors & classy leather armchairs. The rooms have their original 18th-century heavy wooden doors. The house sits on Castelo de Vide's stately main *praça*. €€€

🏠 **Quinta das Lavandas** (7 rooms) Sítio de Vale Dornas (around 3km outside Castelo de Vide); 📞245 919133; www.quintadaslavandas.pt. This big blocky modern house is more attractive within than without. It has smart, modern rooms with colourful bedspreads & rugs offsetting the white walls & wispy drapes. The loveliest are coloured lilac, echoing the extensive lavender fields that the *quinta* maintains around the house. €€€

🏠 **Casa das Muralhas** (2 rooms) Praça Alta; 📞245 919116. A simple 1-bedroom historic house opposite the castle in the heart of Castelo de Vide. Kitchenette, sitting room & lovely views. €€

🏠 **Casa do Parque** (21 rooms) Av da Aramenha 37; 📞245 901250; www.casadoparque.net. On the edge of town 5mins' walk from the main *praça* & with one of the best kitchens in Castelo de Vide, this big 18th-century townhouse offers functional but well-maintained rooms with tiled floors at very good rates. The best on the upper floors are decked out with chunky old hardwood beds, raw-cotton counterpanes & have sweeping views from the Juliet balconies. Outdoor pool. Decent b/fast. €€

🏠 **Pensão Destino** (6 rooms) Estação de Comboios de Castelo de Vide; 📞966 852131; www.pensao-destino.webnode.pt. Rooms in the old Castelo de Vide station house, which is faced with beautiful *azulejos* by renowned secular artist Jorge Colaço, showing the views of the town. Rooms are bright with whitewashed walls, wood-panel flooring & rich blue shutters, & there are common areas with solid wooden tables & chairs, linen sofas & shelves of books for common use. Occasional goods trains rattle past *en route* between Portugal & Spain. €€

## ✖ WHERE TO EAT AND DRINK

✖ **Casa do Parque** See *Where to stay*, above; ⊕ 12.30–15.00 & 18.30–22.30 daily. The best restaurant in town, serving Alentejo dishes, game (hare, venison & partridge) & for local desserts such as *sopa dourada* (a sweet egg pudding with breadcrumbs & cinnamon), *farofas* & hazelnut mousse. Ask them to draw the curtains for views out over the pretty adjacent park. €€

✖ **Confraria** Rua de Santa Maria de Baixo; 📞914 116951; ⊕ 12.30–15.00 & 18.30–22.30 daily. A family-run restaurant with the husband acting as the sommelier & his wife as chef. Lots of Portuguese *petiscos* & local dishes including the famous hazelnut mousse (in season). €€

✖ **O Alentejano** Largo Mártires da República; 📞245 901355; ⊕ 12.30–15.00 & 18.30–22.30 daily. Decent regional cooking in a lovely setting in the historic centre, with views over the town. €€

**WHAT TO SEE AND DO** Like Marvão, Castelo de Vide is all about the atmosphere. The delight is to wander the streets and soak up the views and sense of local life. There are a few interesting sights to see in passing.

## Synagogue and Jewish Museum (*Largo do Dr José Frederico Laranjo;* 📞 *245 901361;* ⊕ *summer 09.30–13.00 & 14.00–18.00 Tue–Sun, winter 09.30–13.00 & 14.00–17.00 Tue–Sun; admission €1*). Castelo de Vide's Judiaria or Jewish Quarter is the prettiest part of town and is marked by stars of David on the pavements. One of the Alentejo's best small museums lies at its heart, in an old synagogue. It gives a real sense of how Jewish people lived in pre-20th century Portugal, what they suffered and what they contributed to the town. It also tells the story of the *Marranos* – Jews who practised their religion secretly at home, abandoning any practices which might identify them, such as circumcision, *mikveh* and the open celebration of scared days. Shabbat lamps were hidden inside clay pots, so those outside could not see the light burning, and Jewish women as well as men led prayer services.

When the Jewish people arrived in *Sefarad* (as they called the Iberian Peninsula) they were instrumental in the creation of Portugal, organising themselves into communities presided over by rabbis. While being subject to the laws of the kingdom they were granted administrative and judicial autonomy, freedom of worship and education. Jews numbered about 20% of the total Portuguese population, ascended to the highest levels of society and were instrumental in establishing Portugal's Golden Age.

Abraham Zacuto wrote mathematical tables that were crucial to Portuguese navigation, including those used by Vasco Da Gama on his trip to India. Guedelha was both a rabbi and a doctor and astrologer for kings Duarte and King Alfonso V. Jose Vizinho served as doctor and astrologer to King João II. Isaac Abravanel was one of Portugal's principal merchants – helping to boost the country's economy.

This began to change from 1492, when thousands of Jewish migrants fled from persecution and then banishment from Spain, initiated in part by the Inquisition. At that time villages in the interior of Portugal had populations in the low thousands and the country as a whole just over 1 million. The influx of an estimated 80,000– 150,000 Jewish immigrants fomented tension, prejudice and eventually severe persecution even by the state. In 1496, under pressure from Spain, Dom Manuel I gave the Jewish people of Portugal ten months to convert to Christianity or leave.

Most Jewish people converted, at least nominally. Like the Muslim Moors before them, they became Cristãos Novos – or 'New Christians'. Many continued to practise their religion in secret, as they did in Castelo de Vide, secretly observing the Sabbath at home while going to mass on Sunday. They practiced circumcision and observed Yom Kippur, calling it *Dia Puro*, or 'Pure Day'. Once again, they were nominally accepted into the state. Cristãos Novos were permitted to hold high office in government and the army, and could attain ecclesiastical positions. The great Portuguese saint John of God (page 102) was a New Christian.

But this only lasted a while. In 1506 two Dominican friars initiated a mob attack on Jewish people in Lisbon, in which some 2,000 Jewish people were killed over

**Castelo de Vide (the Castle)** The town's small castle is most remarkable for the views from its battlements. Inside it is bare but for two small museums – one dedicated to the prehistory of Portugal, the other to military architecture, which explores the history of the castle itself from the development of the first walls and towers under Dom Dinis up until the French invasions of the Peninsular War.

Of the original castle just two towers remain – the current building is mostly from the 18th century after an explosion precipitated by an invasion by Duke of Berwick destroyed much of the building.

**The churches** Architecturally and artistically, Castelo de Vide's churches are nothing special. The church of **Santa Maria da Devesa** (*Praça D Pedro V;* \ *245 901361;* ⊕ *no official hours; free admission*) in the main *praça* dates from the late 18th century, and has modest Baroque decoration and one of the largest facades in the Alto Alentejo. **São João** (*Rua de São João;* \ *249 312611;* ⊕ *no official hours; free admission*), which is plain inside, and **Santo Amaro**, with an attractive Baroque interior, are probably the oldest in town. **Nossa Senhora da Alegria (Our Lady of Joy)** next to the castle is covered top to toe with pretty Mudéjar *azulejos* and a Baroque chancel. Outside the town, 3km up a road which winds a vicious three-day pogrom, which later became known as the Easter Slaughter. King Manuel was absent from Lisbon at the time, and on his return the two Dominicans were tried and burnt at the stake, and 45 of the rioters were hanged.

Thirty years later the Domincans began their fierce and foul Portuguese Inquisition (page 17) and began persecuting the Cristãos Novos, just as they persecuted the peasants, and probably for the same reason – to extort money and free labour for them and keep them in check to the aristocracy who supported the friars against the Jesuits and Portuguese pressing for reform. Many Cristãos Novos fled for Brazil, Italy and England.

In 1773 the progressive Portuguese prime minister Sebastião José de Carvalho e Melo passed a law which led to the lists of Cristãos Novos being burnt and usage of the word Cristão Novo being banned in Portugal. The Inquisition was disbanded and the persecution came to an end.

In January 2015 the Portuguese parliament passed a law granting citizenship to all the descendants of Jews the country expelled in 1496. Applicants have to demonstrate a traditional connection to Portuguese Sephardic Jews through 'family names, family language and direct or collateral ancestry', and are vetted by Portuguese Jewish community institutions and government agencies.

In the early 1800s the Lisbon government began actively to promote Jewish migration back into Portugal. The first to come were British, as we know from the tombstones written in Hebrew and dating back to 1804 in the British cemetery in Lisbon. In 1892 the government repealed all restrictions on the Jewish people of Portugal, who began once more to build synagogues, the largest of which was the Shaare Tikvah in Lisbon. In 1912, the new Portuguese Republic reaffirmed the community's rights.

In 1988 president Mário Soares formally apologised to Portugal's Jewish community for the Inquisition, followed in 2000 by a public apology by the leader of the Portuguese Catholic church. A monument to the dead was erected in 2008 outside the São Domingos church in Lisbon, where the Easter Slaughter began.

up the adjacent hill, is **Nossa Senhora da Penha (Our Lady of the Rock)**, built on the site of a miraculous appearance of the Virgin and with beautiful views of the town, best seen at dawn.

**The Stone Age sites** The Castelo de Vide tourist office hands out leaflets with a route map of the many Stone Age sites around the town. These include the Menhir da Meada, which at 7m tall and 20 tonnes is the largest in Iberia, the Megalithic necropolis at Correleiros, and the Anta da Melriça, the Anta do Sobral and the Anta do Pombal (all dolmens), along with half a dozen others. These sites lie between the Póvoa e Meadas and the Baragem da Póvoa lake, and can all be visited in a long afternoon or morning from Castelo de Vide.

## MARVÃO

Ringing a high, rocky ridgetop in a castellated coronet of ancient bulwarked stone, capped with a fortress and latticed with a labyrinth of Moorish streets, Marvão could be a film set for *Game of Thrones*. It's astounding – a perfectly preserved medieval fortified town still set in stone, absent of even a hint of

4

concrete. Climb the steps up to the battlements and walk the walls to the castle to see across the mountains into Spain and over Portugal for tens of kilometres. You may spot the backs of eagles as they soar below, and drifts of cloud as they wisp across the high sierra.

For now Marvão is almost unvisited, at least at the best times of the year – in April and May when the wild flowers bloom, and September and October when the leaves turn yellow and orange and the air is scented with roasting chestnuts. The coach parties come, but it's in the heat and dust of the fierce Alentejo summer. Don't follow suit. There are no monuments here. It's all about the timing: save Marvão for the right moment.

It is worth noting that Marvão has some of the best festivals in the Alentejo (pages 49–51).

**HISTORY** Marvão's mountaintop location has been used for strategic purposes since pre-Roman times, by the peoples who built the prehistoric monuments that sprinkle the plains around Castelo de Vide. But it was the Romans who first built a settlement here – a hilltop lookout for the town of Ammaia that they built at the foot of the hill. Half-Galician Moorish noble Ibn Maruán built the first village on the hilltop itself. His name later became latinised as Marvão. Ibn Maruán was a rebel Sufi – a half-Galician renegade from the Cordoban Emirate who made a new *taifa* with a capital at Badajoz, extending his influence from there into the Alentejo. Fearful of reprisal, he built Marvão as an impregnable fortress to which he could retreat if threatened by Córdoba.

Ibn Maruán's state maintained independence from Córdoba for nearly 50 years, but was eventually absorbed into the Umayyad caliphate of Al-Andalus in the 10th century, and in the 11th century into *taifa* kingdom of Badajoz, ruled by a Slav called Sabur (a former serf to the second Caliph of Córdoba), the Berber Aftasid dynasty, and in the 1090s the jihadi Almoravid empire when it became the northern outpost of an African Muslim empire that stretched all the way to Mauretania. These fundamentalists were subsequently conquered by the equally fundamentalist Almohads, who in an unlikely alliance with Sufi fighting sect the al-Muridin founded a kingdom based in the Al-Garb (Algarve) that stretched into the northern Alentejo.

By the 12th century Muslim cities were falling like dominoes to the Portuguese kings and their Crusader armies. Marvão held out against King Afonso Henriques in 1160 but the town finally fell to Dom Sancho II in 1226. The fortress then fell under the auspices of the Knights Hospitaller who strengthened the castle and its walls in preparation for defending the Alentejo frontier against the Spanish. Many of the houses in Marvão bear their cross to this day and the castle has many Knights Templar traits developed at the Syrian castles like Krak des Chevaliers – the tall keep with outlying turrets, the huge cistern, curved entrances to slow down attackers and triplicate gates. The town withstood attack in 1641 and 1648, but like Castelo de Vide it fell to Spanish forces under the Duke of Berwick. The French governor installed by the Castilians imprisoned the entire population. Marvão returned to Portuguese hands, only to be lost again briefly during the Peninsula War.

**GETTING THERE AND AWAY** It's hard to reach Marvão without your own transport. Access to Marvão is from Portalegre or Castelo de Vide. The N359 connects Portalegre to São Salvador da Aramenha and Marvão. The N246-1 runs from Castelo de Vide to Marvão and then into Spain, where it becomes the N521 to Caceres. Distances are as follows: Portalegre 21km, Lisbon 236km, Estremoz 77km, Arronches 45km, Castelo de Vide 10km, Évora 123km.

**By bus** Travelling between the rest of the Alentejo and Marvão, you will have probably have to change in Portalegre. Line 8012 runs from Portalegre and Marvão (*1 daily*). There are more services from São Salvador de Aramenha, the small town at the base of the mountain. A cab from here to Marvão costs around €10. For more information see www.rodalentejo.pt

**TOURIST INFORMATION** The tourist office is at Largo de Silveirinha (at the entrance to the town) (↖ *245 909131; www.cm-marvao.pt; ⊕ summer 09.00–19.00, winter 09.00–12.30 & 14.00–17.30 daily*).

## WHERE TO STAY

**Casa da Silveirinha** (4 rooms) Rua da Silveirinha 1; ↖258 823789; www.casadasilveirinha.pt. Basic rooms in a historic house in the old town with a small garden & lovely views over the Serra. Big discounts out of high season on booking sites. **€€€**

**Dom Dinis** (9 rooms) Rua Dr Matos Magalhães 7; ↖245 909028; www.ter-domdinis.com. Simple rooms, simple food & simply wonderful views of the old town & the mountains from the roof terrace of this family-run hotel next to the castle in the old town. **€€€**

**O Poejo** (13 rooms) Av 25 de Abril 20, Santo António das Areias; ↖245 992640; www.a-opoejo.com. Tucked away in a converted townhouse in a village 5km from Marvão, this hotel has modern & comfortable rooms decorated in soft tones & with the kind of furniture you'd expect in a city boutique rather than a country retreat. Helpful staff organise excursions, inc self-guided or escorted walking trips into the Serra, self-drive tours of the prehistoric sites & *adega* visits for wine enthusiasts. The hotel has a restaurant & serves an excellent b/fast & dinner on request. **€€€**

**Pousada de Santa Maria** (31 rooms) Rua 24 de Janeiro 7; ↖245 993201; www.pousadasportugal.com. The best place to stay within the castle walls. Airy & breezy in summer & with roaring log fires in winter. Rooms have superb views out over the whitewashed walls & battlements to the rugged hills beyond, & the restaurant is excellent. **€€€**

**Sever Rio Hotel** (14 rooms) Estrada do Rio Sever, Portagem; ↖245 993318; www.severhotel.com. At the base of the ridge where Marvão sits & next to a rushing river, this hotel is a good option in the summer months for guests craving a pool. The restaurant is excellent, the rooms modern & well appointed, & the staff can organise trips into the Serra & around Marvão. **€€**

## WHERE TO EAT AND DRINK

**Pousada de Santa Maria** See above; ⊕ 12.30–15.00 & 19.00–22.30 daily. Come for dinner but arrive before the sun sets, for an aperitif with a sweeping view. Let the day fade & then dine romantically in the intimate low light with the stars twinkling outside. Food is excellent traditional Portuguese with a menu strong on fish & meat, & a superior wine list. Dishes are served in a lovely dining room with views out over the mountains, with discreet formality – a lovely experience. **€€€**

**Sever Rio Hotel** See above; ⊕ 12.30–15.00 & 19.00–22.30 daily. The best regional cooking in Marvão, served in a dining room right next to the Sever River at the base of the mountain. Loveliest in daylight – either at lunchtime or for an early evening summer meal. **€€**

## WHAT TO SEE AND DO

**Castelo de Marvão (Marvão Castle)** (⊕ *summer 09.00–21.00 daily, winter 10.00–19.00 daily; admission €2*) There can be few castles anywhere with a better strategic position than Marvão's. The fortifications seem to grow out of the rock, the walls perched on the edge of a ridge as it ascends to a peak affording 360° views running to scores of kilometres in every direction. In 1758, when Marvão's fort had reached its greatest proportions, the Portuguese chronicler Frei Miguel Viegas Bravo described the castle as 'the most unconquerable in the entire kingdom …

4

whose walls serve more for preventing those inside from falling than those outside from entering.'

Like most Alentejo castles, Marvão's is a composite building – walls upon walls, beginning with stones first assembled here before the Romans came. While some of the gates to the castle appear to be Roman in origin, the first great fort was built by Ibn Maruán, with many of the stones taken from the ruins of Ammaia. The castle keep and the walls were strengthened under the orders of Dom Dinis, who constructed an enormous cistern big enough to hold six months' worth of water for the entire town population in the event of a siege.

**Other sights in Marvão** The town has a handful of other places to visit. The **Casa da Cultura (Cultural Centre)** (*Rua 24 de Janeiro 1;* \ *245 909137;* ⊕ *09.30–13.00 & 14.00–17.30 daily; free admission*) preserves an old courtroom, the historical archive of the town and shows temporary exhibitions. The **Museu Municipal (Town Museum)** (*Largo de Santa Maria s/n;* \ *245 909132;* ⊕ *09.00–12.30 & 14.00–17.30 Tue–Sun; admission €1.30*) housed in the Igreja de Santa Maria church (the oldest church in the village, a simple 13th-century building with significant 16th- and 18th-century modifications) has a modest Baroque chapel with *azulejos* depicting pastoral scenes. The museum itself has archaeological finds from the prehistoric through to Roman and Moorish eras, mannequins in traditional Alentejo costumes and a collection of sacred art, including frescoes and images of St Bartholomew, St Sebastian and St Anthony, and dozens of images and effigies of the Virgin from the priceless collection of Rui Sequeira, one of modern Portugal's wealthiest art collectors. Outside the walls, the **Convento da Nossa Senhora da Estrela (Convent of Our Lady of the Star)** (⊕ *open by appointment only – contact the tourist office*) is one of the oldest Gothic buildings in the Alentejo, built by the Mendicant sisters in the early 15th century. It has a Manueline portal and marble crucifix and a tower with a vaulted Gothic cupola. The sacristy is covered with handsome *azulejos* and has a beautiful marble altarpiece. Despite being outside the walls, the convent is the spiritual heart of the village. Legend has it that when the Moors invaded, the Visigoth Christians buried a sacred statue of the Virgin before they fled. After the Reconquest a shepherd, guided by a brilliant star, found the spot where the statue was interred. The convent was built on the site, and was dedicated to the Virgin, who is the patron saint of Marvão.

**Ammaia** (*Estrada da Calçadinha 4, São Salvador da Aramenha, 5km south of Marvão;* \ *245 919089; www.ammaia.pt;* ⊕ *09.00–12.30 & 14.00–17.30 daily; admission €2*) The Roman ruins at Ammaia are impressive only in what they suggest was once here. The rubble of walls, pillars and pavements that sit behind the visitor centre litter the countryside around for hundreds of metres. In its heyday Ammaia was one of the largest Roman towns in the Alentejo. In AD45 it was already a Roman civitas – a client settlement recognised by Rome. By the end of the 1st century AD it had grown to become a *municipium* – a self-governing town integrated into the Roman Empire with a forum, temple, small bath and large villas for its wealthiest inhabitants. The town occupied an important position on the trade route between Lusitania and the city of Emerita Augusta in Spain, now Mérida. Like the rest of Lusitania it fell into decline, possibly after being partially destroyed by an earthquake. It was briefly occupied by the Visigoths and then left to ruin until it was unearthed by archaeologists in the late 20th century.

# 5

# The Alentejo Coast

The Portuguese are wise; they keep the best for themselves: their finest wines, their choicest olives, and the beaches of the Alentejo. Let the foreigners crowd the Algarve, they say, waving them south, while themselves choosing to linger in the Alentejo, lounging languidly on its vast empty beaches and quiet, concealed coves. From Alcácer do Sal in the north to Zambujeira in the south the shoreline is nigh empty, with meadows of wild flowers in place of evergreen golf resorts, and rural homestays rather than tourist towns of sugar-white villas. It's quiet here – not a place to party in, but to walk through, on the sinuous São Vicente coastal path that winds along the entire coast. Hikers come here to contemplate the edge of Europe as it drops in cliffs, bays and strands of sand into the seemingly infinite blue of the ocean. They come to watch birds and butterflies in a string of glorious national parks and protected areas; to eat catch of the day actually caught on the day; and to enjoy the hospitality of locals as yet untired of tourism.

It's worth spending a few days to a week on the coast, working slowly to or from Lisbon, basing yourself in one or several of the coastal villages – perhaps Alcácer for the Sado estuary, Grândola for the beaches and Vila Nova de Milfontes for the south. None are as spectacular as the towns of the interior; settlements on the coast take a back seat to nature. So check in, then grab a towel, suncream and walking shoes, and wander the meadows, the cliffs and the cork oak woodlands in search of a lonely beach.

## TOURIST INFORMATION

The **regional tourism office** is based in Grândola (*ARPT – Turismo do Alentejo, Rua Manuel Baptista Reis 6 R/C, 7570-284 Grândola;* \ *269 498680; www.visitalentejo.pt; Facebook: VisitAlentejoOfficial*). There are local tourist offices in many of the other towns, as listed in the chapter. The **regional website** (*www.alentejolitoral.pt*) is an excellent source of practical information on everything from public transport to walking along the Costa Vicentina.

See under the individual section headings in this chapter for information on guided tours.

## GETTING THERE AND AWAY

**BY AIR** The nearest airports are at Lisbon and Faro (in the Algarve). See *Getting there and away*, pages 41–2.

**BY CAR** From Lisbon take the E90 motorway across the Vasco da Gama Bridge and then join the IP1 Algarve motorway south, which runs parallel to the Alentejo coast some 40km inland, affording access to Grândola, Sines, Vila Nova de Milfontes and the coastal towns. There are car ferries from Setúbal to Tróia. The N261 runs

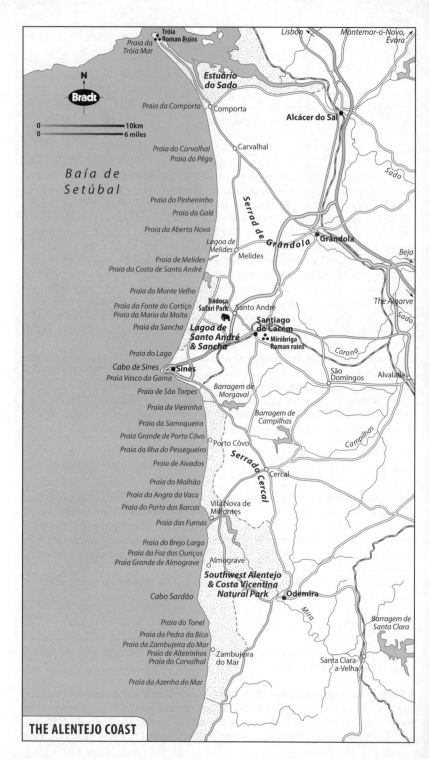

Lisbon

Montemor-o-Novo,
Évora

Tróia
Roman Ruins

Praia da
Tróia Mar

N

Bradt

Estuário
do Sado

0        10km
0        6 miles

Praia da Comporta    Comporta

Alcácer do Sal

Praia do Carvalhal    Carvalhal
Praia do Pêgo

Baía de
Setúbal

Sado

Praia do Pinheirinho

Praia da Galé

Praia da Aberta Nova

Serra de

Lagoa de
Melides

Grândola    Grândola

Beja

Praia de Melides    Melides
Praia da Costa de Santo André

Praia do Monte Velho

The Algarve

Praia da Fonte do Cortiço    Badoca
Praia da Maria da Moita    Safari Park    Santo André

Sado

Praia da Sancha    Lagoa de    Santiago
Santo André    do Cacém
& Sancha    Miróbriga
Roman ruins

Praia do Lago

Corona

Cabo de Sines    Sines
Praia Vasco da Gama

São
Domingos    Alvalade

Praia de São Torpes    Barragem de
Morgaval

Praia da Vieirinha

Barragem de
Campilhas

Praia da Samoqueira

Campilhas

Praia Grande de Porto Côvo    Porto Côvo
Praia da Ilha do Pessegueiro

Praia de Aivados

Serra de

Praia do Malhão    Cercal

Praia da Angra da Vaca    Cercal

Praia do Porto das Barcas    Vila Nova de
Milfontes

Praia das Furnas

Praia do Brejo Largo
Praia da Foz dos Ouriços    Almograve
Praia Grande de Almograve

Southwest Alentejo
& Costa Vicentina    Odemira
Cabo Sardão    Natural Park

Mira

Barragem de
Santa Clara

Praia do Tonel

Praia da Pedra da Bica
Praia da Zambujeira do Mar    Zambujeira
Praia de Alteirinhos    do Mar
Praia do Carvalhal    Santa Clara-
a-Velha

Praia da Azenha do Mar

**THE ALENTEJO COAST**

132

parallel to the coast south through Grândola. The N120 runs from here to Santiago de Cacém and south to the Algarve, never more than 10km from the coast.

Even if you enter Portugal by land, the best value option is to reach the Alentejo coast via Lisbon, having organised **car rental** from home with a pick-up at Lisbon airport, which is well served by public transport (see page 42). Car rental is far more difficult to organise and pricier on the coast itself, though bikes and motor scooters are available (see page 41 for more details).

**BY TRAIN** Four daily trains connect Lisbon's Oriente station with Grândola (*€10; 80mins*). There are also international trains to Grândola from Seville via Faro in the Algarve. This means that you can reach the coast by train from both Lisbon and Faro airports, with a short intra-city transfer. Other than Grândola there are no other railway stations on the Alentejo coast.

**BY BUS** The region is connected to Lisbon, the Algarve and other towns within the Alto and Baixo Alentejo by intercity buses that run to Alcácer do Sal, Grândola, Odemira and Sines. See www.rede-expressos.pt for intercity links and www.rodalentejo.pt for details of local bus lines within the region, where the search engine allows you to download pdfs of the routes and bus times.

## GETTING AROUND

To get the best of the Alentejo coast you'll need your own transport. Roads are well signposted both for towns, with blue plaques, and beaches (*praias*), with brown plaques. There are plenty of caravan and trailer parks and camping sites. See www.campingportugal.org and www.eurocampings.co.uk for fuller details.

For information on car rental, see above.

## TOUR OPERATORS

For more locally based tour operators see the relevant sections of this chapter.

**Birding in Portugal** Quinta do Barranco da Estrada, Santa Clara-a-Velha; ☏283 933065; www.birdinginportugal.com. Birdwatching in the Alentejo for dedicated birders, photographers & those who want to include birdwatching as part of a more general holiday. The company runs a dedicated birding lodge.

**Birds and Nature** www.birds.pt. Organises birdwatching trips throughout the region, including to the Sado River estuary, the Lagoa de Santo André and locations throughout the Costa Vicentina.

**Grekking** Rua D Nuno Álvares Pereira 163; ☏927 403942; www.grekking.com. A broad range of excellent cultural, wildlife, trekking, birdwatching & conservational tourism trips throughout the Alentejo (& Portugal as a whole), including birdwatching & wildlife watching on & around the Sado estuary.

**Iberian Wildlife** www.iberianwildlife.com. Offers excellent wildlife tours of the Sado estuary, run by the steadfast Teresa Farino.

## ALCÁCER DO SAL, TRÓIA AND THE BEACHES OF THE FAR NORTH

The Alentejo coast begins across the wild, wide Sado River estuary with the resort town of Tróia. The estuary is one of the best birdwatching sites in Europe and a herald for the wild coastal expanses that lie further south. Tróia is an anomaly on the Alentejo coast – a mini resort town complete with tower blocks and golf courses. But the beaches nearby, stretching along the Tróia Peninsula, are long, broad and empty out of season. The pretty, historical town of Alcácer do Sal is more typically Alentejan than Tróia, with Moorish streets spreading from a crag-top castle and a brace of historical churches.

## GETTING THERE AND AWAY

**By car** Alcácer do Sal can be reached from Lisbon, Faro and the rest of the Alentejo coast via the IP1/A2 motorway, which runs parallel to the Alentejo coast. Tróia is reachable directly from Setúbal by boat (see below), or via the EN261 highway, a circuitous road that leaves the IP1/A2 motorway at Alcácer do Sal and winds for some 25km around the Sado estuary before branching north along the Tróia Peninsula.

**By bus** There are frequent buses to Grândola (numbers 8943 and 8555), twice daily intercity buses to and from Lisbon (via Setúbal) and Évora (except on weekends for both destinations), as well as buses to Elvas, Beja and other towns within the Alentejo. See www.rodalentejo.pt for precise details on all services with timetables and full prices.

**By boat** Atlantic Ferries run car and passenger boats between Setúbal and Tróia (*www.atlanticferries.pt; hourly between 07.30 & 22.00 Jan–May, half hourly between 07.30 & 00.25, Jun–Sep, & almost hourly between 07.30 & 22.00 Oct–Dec; €14 for cars, €4 for foot passengers*).

**GETTING AROUND** There are no car rental offices on the northern coast. Bike hire and local tours can be organised through hotels. Bus 8319 runs between Alcácer do Sal and Tróia via Comporta four times daily between 06.00 and 18.00, taking just under an hour; for precise timetables consult www.rodalentejo.pt. Buses 8346pe and 8346pne run between Tróia and Grândola along the beaches seven times daily between them.

**TOURIST INFORMATION AND TOURS** There is a tourist office in Alcácer do Sal (*Largo Luís de Camões s/n;* ☏ *911 794685;* ⏰ *09.00–17.00 Mon–Fri, 09.00–13.00 & 14.00–17.00 Sat*) that provides information on the whole region, including the beaches and the Sado estuary. It offers useful maps and lists of recommended restaurants and hotels.

**Rotas do Sal** (*Estação dos Caminhos de Ferro 2, Apartado, Alcácer do Sal;* ☏ *967 066072; www.rotasdosal.pt*) offers kayaking, trail walking, dolphin-watching and birding on and around the Sado estuary.

🏠 **WHERE TO STAY** Note that Grândola (pages 138–40) is close enough to the northern beaches to serve as an alternative beach base to Tróia. It has some particularly good hotels.

🏠 **Blue & Green Tróia Design Hotel, Spa and Casino** (205 rooms) Tróia Marina; ☏ 265 498000; www.troiadesignhotel.com. A somewhat gimmicky design hotel whose extravagant exterior & swanky marketing belies the lack of attention to detail in the rooms & in the service, as well as the predominantly family clientele. Avoid rooms on the lower floors & opt for an ocean-view suite with a Jacuzzi above floor 10. See page 135 for restaurant listings. €€€€€

🏠 **Herdade de Montalvo** (102 houses) Km14.7 Estrada Nacional 253, Alcácer do Sal; ☏ 265 619441; www.herdademontalvo.com. A vast complex of private villas set in leafy, lawned gardens & with space for 2–8 adults (depending on villa). The largest have their own private swimming pools. All have well appointed kitchens. Tennis courts, sports facilities & a communal pool on site. €€€€

🏠 **Pousada Dom Afonso II** (35 rooms) Castelo de Alcácer, 7580-123 Alcácer do Sal; 📞265 613 070; www.pousadas.pt. This luxury hotel housed within the town's old Moorish castle is redolent with history, & its pool backs right on to the old Moorish walls. Rooms are housed in a modern building constructed within the shell of the old castle. Those at the corners afford the best views out over the town & the Sado River. The *pousada* has a good restaurant & can help organise tours around the region. Attractive online rates. €€€€

🏠 **Aqualuz Suite Hotel Apartamentos Troia Mar** (202 rooms) Tróia; 📞265 499000; www.aqualuztroia.com. This mega family resort's anonymity is ameliorated by the myriad facilities – a good spa, tennis court, indoor & outdoor pool, casino & kids' playground – & by the vast, well-appointed modern suites which come with 1 or 2 bedrooms, kitchens, living rooms & – on the upper floors – sweeping views. No in-room internet. €€€

🏠 **Soltróia Villa** (9 rooms) Urbanização Soltróia, Lote 419; 📞962 321199. www.albergariafozdosado.com. These big modern apartments set in villas a stroll from the beach are rented individually but are best booked ahead in a block – occupying a whole villa at a time –

making an excellent, good-value option for groups travelling together or large families. The villa has a private pool, kitchen, dining & living rooms and a large sun deck. €€€

🏠 **Tróia Residence – Apartamentos Turísticos Praia** (211 rooms) Carvalhal GDL; 📞265 499000. While the smaller rooms in this serviced apartment complex can feel pokey, the large modern suites are some of the best in Tróia, feeling more like a private villas, with a sundeck, kitchens (with laundry facilities), dining room & 1–3 bedrooms. The best have ocean views & private swimming pools. The complex is ideal for families on a beach break & is designed to feel more like a private condominium than a big resort, but it still lacks the authenticity & intimacy you'll get with the smaller hotels further south. Service can be sloppy. Well located for the beach & the marina. €€€

🏠 **Hotel Salatia** (9 rooms) Very simple, small air-conditioned rooms with en suites, beds & plain wooden desk, & little else. In an excellent location on the river bank, 10mins' walk from the *castelo* & close to a range of simple restaurants. Some street noise. €€

🏠 **Residencial Cegonha** (22 rooms) Largo do Terreirinho, Alcácer do Sal; Facebook: Residencial Cegonha. A simple but well-maintained family-run hotel with friendly staff but Spartan rooms. Well-located near the river in the heart of Alcácer. €€

## WHERE TO EAT AND DRINK

🍴 **Museu do Arroz** Sitio da Carrasqueira, Carvalhal; 📞265 497555; www.restaurantemuseudoarroz.com; 🕐 12.30–15.00 & 19.00–22.30 daily. Traditional Portuguese dishes with a contemporary twist, like *pasteis de bacalhau com arroz de tomate* (codfish pasties with tomato-infused rice) served in a smart dining room with an outdoor deck overlooking paddy fields. €€€

🍴 **B&G** Blue & Green Tróia Design Hotel, Tróia (page 134); 🕐 noon–15.30 & 18.00–22.30 daily. This slick, large resort restaurant dishes out well-presented modern Portuguese food to huge numbers of high-season diners. As you'd expect in a big resort restaurant, the quality of the produce & the consistency and care of the cooking are not what you'll find in the smaller restaurants beyond

Tróia, but this is nonetheless about as good as it gets in town. €€

🍴 **Porto Santana** Santa Maria do Castelo, Alcácer do Sal; 📞265 613454; 🕐 12.15–15.30 & 19.00–22.30 daily. Seafood & Alentejan specialities including delicious black pork, fried squid & clams, served in a homely dining room situated in a traditional whitewashed & terracotta-roofed bungalow. €€

🍴 **Comporta Café** Praia da Comporta, Tróia; 📞265 497652; 🕐 noon–15.30 & 19.00–late daily, closed Oct–Apr. Fresh seafood & Portuguese standards served in a big weatherboard building right on the beach. The best tables are on the shady sun deck, & in the evenings in high season it becomes a mood-lit beach bar. €

## WHAT TO SEE AND DO

**Tróia** The Alentejo coast begins immediately across the mouth of the Sado River with this little tourist town, which sits right opposite the town of Setúbal on the end of a finger-shaped peninsula of fine, golden sand. Today it's hard to imagine that Tróia was once the Roman outpost of Caetobriga. Its villas and forum were levelled by a giant tidal wave in the 5th century and what remained was later dwarfed by a spillage of resorts and condos from Setúbal. What's left of Roman Caetobriga today lies forgotten in the grounds of one of the skyscraper hotels that have made Tróia the nearest thing to a full-blown resort on the Alentejo coast – the only place with a marina, a golf course, tower block holiday flats, condos and modish hotels, all squeezed into the peninsula's narrow fingertip.

Like most resorts, Tróia is busy only in season, when a beach holiday and weekender crowd rolls in, predominantly from Lisbon. It feels post-apocalyptic between October and May, when its broad, gently sloping beaches (which stretch interminably south 20 minutes' walk southwest of the town centre) are busy only with wintering birds and dedicated surfers.

**Alcácer do Sal**  One of the Alentejo's oldest towns sits forlorn by the winding Sado River – sad that it sees most visitors only as they pass through. This is a shame. The tiny town has a wonderfully romantic castle (now a luxury *pousada* – see page 135), is replete with history and has far more character than Tróia. The bone-white cuboid Lar de Idosos da Santa Casa da Misericórdia nursing home just outside the town was a finalist in the 2013 Mies van der Rohe international architecture awards. Those not concerned about walking from their beach hotel direct to the sand might consider Alcácer as an alternative base for the far northern beaches. It's also a far better location from which to explore the Sado Estuary Reserve (see page 137). And even if you're in a rush to get to the coast, consider stopping for a break here, for lunch and a wander.

**History**  While there have been settlements in the area for 40,000 years, Alcácer itself is one of the oldest cities in Europe, founded as a Phoenician port and salt trading centre in around 1000BC, and important enough to mint its own coins. The port was conquered by the Romans in the 1st or 2nd century BC, when it was known as Salacia. Salacia was an important staging post between Mediterranean Rome and the colonies of northern Europe, and was used as a base for the conquest of Britain by the Emperor Claudius in AD43. Under the later emperors like Diocletian Salacia lost influence to Lisbon and later to Setúbal and Tróia.

The Roman fort was captured by the Umayyad Caliphate in 711. It was they who built the imposing castle which sits above the town and who gave Roman Salacia a new name – Al Qasr. Qasr was a word derived from the Roman *castrum* or fort, and it was around the new, heavily fortified castle that the Muslims built their new town, leaving the port area for the conquered Lusitanians. Al Qasr became a regional capital and a centre for the collection of taxes by the caliphate. The castle was expanded in the 9th century after Vikings began to raid the coast, extending its administrative and military influence as far north as Lisbon under the *alcaide* Banu Danis. The Muslim fleet that sacked Santiago de Compostela in AD997 left from Al Qasr. By the time of the Almoravid Empire, Al Qasr's influence stretched as far as Trujillo in Spain, and when Lisbon was re-taken by the Christians in 1147, the Moors retreated here. They briefly lost the city in 1160, capturing it again in 1191 under the leadership of Ya'qub al-Mansur and holding it until 1217, when Al Qasr finally succumbed after a long siege during which the Portuguese joined forces with a band of Crusaders anchored offshore, on their way to the Holy Land.

After the Reconquest the castle became an administrative seat for the knights of the Ordem de Santiago (Order of St James), who used Alcácer to control a vast territory stretching between Sesimbra and the Algarve. The knights stayed here until they moved their base to Mértola in the 13th century. The Moorish population of Alcácer remained high after the Reconquest, and until the Inquisition they were permitted to practise their religion under the protection of the king.

**What to see and do** There's an afternoon's worth of sights in Alcácer. The **castle**, which retains many of its Moorish features, is tacked on to a medieval Aracaeli convent which encloses a pretty Romanesque chapel. There is a **museum** in the crypt (*Castelo;* ＼ *265 612058;* ⊕ *Jul–Aug 09.30–13.00 & 15.00–17.30 Tue–Sun, Sep–Jun 09.00–12.30 & 14.00–17.30 Tue–Sun*) with artefacts from the region's long history. This includes the ruins of the old Phoenician, Roman and Islamic forts. Alcácer has two interesting churches. King Manuel I married Maria de Castile in 1500 in Alcácer's church of **Espirito Santo** (*Largo Pedro Nunes s/n;* ＼*265 610 040*). It is now a small archaeological museum and was closed for renovation as this book went to press. Look out for the early Manueline decorated window on the side of the nave. The interior of the **Church of Santiago** (*Rua do Outeiro s/n;* ＼*265 622213; 10.00–12.30 & 14.30–18.00 Tue–Fri, 10.00–12.30 Sat; free admission*), recognisable by its stunted twin towers, is covered with beautiful *azulejos*.

Like so many Alentejo towns, Alcácer is very photogenic. The best views are from the castle battlements (over a higgle-piggle of terracotta to the river), and from the far side of the Sado, from where you can see Alcácer's pretty waterfront of whitewashed houses mirrored in the gentle curves of the river. Both views are best at dusk and dawn.

## Reserva Natural do Estuário do Sado (Sado Estuary Reserve) The second largest estuary in Portugal and the first and arguably most important of coastal Alentejo's myriad protected wildlife areas stretches west from Alcácer do Sal. It covers some 24,000 hectares and is one of two RAMSAR sites in the Alentejo (the other being the Lagoas de Santo Andre e Sancha). It's an ancient landscape of rice paddies, wooden fishermen's huts and around Carrasqueira, colourful boats bobbing alongside clusters of time-worn stilted wooden jetties. Little seems to have changed but the clothes since the Romans turned up here to quell the Lusitanian peasants.

The estuary is a significant wildlife haven abutting the equally important Arrábida Natural Park in Setúbal and home to 300+ species of vertebrates. These include Spanish terrapins, stripeless tree frogs, western polecats, otters, the ultra-rare and pug-faced barbastelle bat and pods of inquisitive bottlenose dolphins. But it's the birds that are the main attraction. With a mix of woodland, heath and meadows, and expansive salt marshes, exposed mudflats, sandy beaches and tiny canals, this is one of the best places in southern Europe to see hill and woodland birds alongside waterfowl. There are significant populations of black-necked and great crested grebe, spoonbill, short-toed, Bonelli's and booted eagle, black-shouldered kite, waxbill and red and chestnut munia. The estuary is a breeding ground for purple heron, marsh harrier, black-winged stilt, little tern and white storks (who arrive in huge numbers in the spring). Birders can expect to see as many as 100 species a day – especially in winter when some 40,000 waders and ducks descend including hundreds of greater flamingo, occasional lesser flamingo and thousands of avocet, dunlin, gotwit, teal, pintail, shoveller and occasional long-tailed duck, green-winged teal and ruddy shelduck.

**Beaches** The beaches of northern Alentejo begin in earnest at Tróia. All have parking areas. The town beach is properly called **Praia Atlântica** and is the only place in the north with in-season crowds large enough to attract a market for watersports.

Surfing, windsurfing and kitesurfing along the beach can all be organised through hotels in Tróia, as can rounds of the adjacent golf course. Immediately south at the low-key condominium village of **Comporta** is Comporta beach – a long, broad stretch of golden sand immensely popular with families in season, and backed by dunes and a decent little restaurant, the Comporta Café (see page 135). Comporta village has a winery, the Adega de Herdade da Comporta (*www.herdadedacomporta. pt*), which is open to visitors on appointment only but whose wines are served at their sister institution, the **Museu do Arroz** (*see page 135;* \ *265 499950; Jun–Sep 10.00–13.00 & 14.00–17.00 Tue–Sun, Nov–Mar same hours, Fri–Sun; admission €2*), an old rice warehouse set behind working paddy fields, which tells the story of rice production in the area and doubles up as an excellent restaurant. A few kilometres south are the beaches of **Carvalho** and **Pégo**. The former is a delightful little bay sheltered by dunes, the latter a long sweep of broad sand with beach parasols and a decent chic-shack café restaurant, Sal (see page 140).

## GRÂNDOLA, SANTIAGO DO CACÉM AND THE CENTRAL BEACHES

While it has no standout attractions, the provincial town of Grândola is perfectly situated and well appointed with hotels and restaurants, making it the best beach base of any location on the central or northern Alentejo coast. There are sweeping stretches of sand on the doorstep, and lovely rolling cork-covered countryside. Tróia's least spoilt beaches are 15 minutes north, while the Lagoa de Santo André wildlife preserve and the Roman ruins of Miróbriga are just 20 minutes' drive south. Beyond these, the Alentejo coast grows ugly and industrialised for a bit around Sines, the site of one of Iberia's largest and smelliest oil refineries.

### GETTING THERE AND AWAY
**By car** Grândola sits right off the IP1/A2 motorway 115km south of Lisbon, 20km south of Alcácer do Sal and 170km north of Faro. A drive to the town from Lisbon's international airport takes around 70 minutes, and from Faro international airport about 100mins.

**By train** Grândola railway station (*Largo da Estação Ferroviária s/n;* \ *707 210220*) is reachable from Lisbon's Oriente station (*3 trains daily, 1hr12mins, continuing to Faro – 2hrs15mins*). Two trains daily run to and from Évora. See www.cp.pt for precise details.

**By bus** The bus station (*rodoviária*) (*Rua D Afonso Henriques;* \ *269 40240*) is 200m north of the Jardim Municipal in the town centre. There are four buses daily to and from Lisbon (*90mins*), four to and from Beja (*70mins*), a bus south to Lagos in the Algarve (for services to Faro and the airport), frequent connections to Sines (*50mins – be sure to avoid travelling via Setúbal*) and connections to Vila Nova de Milfontes, Almograve, Odemira and Zambujeira do Mar. See www.rede-expressos. pt for precise details.

### GETTING AROUND
**By car** There are no car rental offices on the northern coast. Bike hire and local tours can be organised through local hotels.

**By bus** Bus lines 8346pe and 8346pne connect Grândola six times daily with Tróia, running north along the beaches. The 8346pe stops at fewer beaches but does stop at Carvalhal. The 8346pne stops at Comporta, Pego and Carvalhal. Bus lines 8555 and 8943 connect Grândola with Santiago do Cacém. The bus station (*rodoviária*) is at Rua D Afonso Henriques (☎ *269 40240*), though many of these local buses pass through the neighbourhoods. Your hotel will tell you where to catch them. See www.rodalentejo.pt for details of times and prices.

**TOURIST INFORMATION** There is an excellent tourist office in Grândola (*Praça Marques de Pombal 1–3;* ☎ *269 750429;* ⊕ *09.00–17.00 Mon–Fri, 09.00–13.00 Sat*) with maps and information on the entire Alentejo, and a wealth of material on the Santo André lagoon, Miróbriga and accommodation and restaurant options in the entire region. The staff speak good English. The Alentejo regional tourist office is also in Grândola (*Rua Manuel Baptista Reis 6;* ☎ *269 498680;* ⊕ *09.00–17.00 Mon–Fri*). Staff here are extremely helpful and can provide detailed information on the whole of the Alentejo.

## LOCAL TOUR OPERATORS

**Herdade Barradas da Serra** See *Where to stay,* below. Horse-riding, self-guided walks, surf classes & rental, bike rides & bespoke tours – all organised by the friendly Elsa & her family at this lovely rural hotel.

**Passeios a Cavalo** ☎ 917 474865; www. passeiosacavalomelides.com. Horseback rides along the beaches, around Santo André lagoon & through the Serra da Grândola. From beginners to advanced.

**Passeios e Companhia** Rua 22 de Janeiro 2A, Grândola; ☎ 269 476702; www. passeiosecompanhia.com. Bike rental, bird- & wildlife watching at the Sado estuary & Santo André Lagoon, canoeing, rafting, walking & car & driver day trips around Grândola & to the Serra, the beaches, the Sado estuary & as far as Sines and Setúbal. Good value.

## WHERE TO STAY

⌂ **Monte do Giestal** (10 rooms) BRIC 801, Cova do Gato, Abela, Santiago do Cacém; ☎ 269 902068; www.montedogiestal.com. These modern villas with large, well-appointed kitchens in the heart of the countryside feel a little functional, but the suites of rooms, pool, games room & extensive menu of organised activities (including tennis, jeep tours, fishing, farm visits & handicrafts) make them good for families. The hotel is close to the IP1 Lisbon–Algarve motorway & a short drive from Santiago do Cacém. €€€€

⌂ **Serenada** (4 rooms) Monte da Serenada, Grândola; ☎ 961 758845; www.serenade.pt. A large, modern glass-fronted main house & rooms in a smaller annexe, overlooking a swimming pool & the Alentejo countryside. The owners produce their own wine & specialise in wine tourism with tastings from their well-stocked cellar, their own vineyards & wine-related excursions. €€€

⌂ **Monte das Faias** (8 rooms) Estrada Nacional 543, Grândola; ☎ 269 440003; www. montedasfaias.com. A row of whitewashed cottages, each furnished with chunky rustic furniture & set in a lawned garden in the countryside. The owners organise birdwatching

excursions & there is a tennis court & swimming pool in the grounds. €€–€€€

⌂ **A Toca Do Grilo** (17 rooms) Av 18 de dezembro 19A, Carvalhal; ☎ 968 059943. It's hard to beat this simple little hotel for value. Rooms sit above a (very popular) seafood restaurant (which is open until around 23.00) in Carvalhal village, 15mins' drive north of Grândola. They are simple, with space for a bed, a desk & bedside table that look like they were bought from a bargain catalogue, & chintzy bedspreads. But the beach is 15mins' walk away & there's a choice of simple restaurants on the doorstep. €€

⌂ **Dom Jorge de Lencastre** (34 rooms) Praça Dom Jorge, Grândola; ☎ 269 498810; www. hoteldomjorge.com. A modest 3-star in the centre of Grândola town with bright spacious, carpeted rooms with French balconies, some of which are looking a little frayed, & a decent b/fast. The beaches are a 10min drive west. €€

⌂ **Herdade Barradas da Serra** (8 rooms) Estrada EN 261-1 Tróia–Carvalhal s/n; ☎ 961 776610; www.barradasdaserra.com. Spacious, well-appointed rooms with chunky beds (covered with high thread-count cotton), gathered around a swimming pool & set in rolling countryside just outside Grandola. Elsa & her family are immensely helpful & knowledgeable about the area & serve a huge b/fast (with homemade produce) & delicious Alentejo dinners on request. €

## WHERE TO EAT AND DRINK

**A Coutada** Rua de São Sebastião 18, Grândola; ☎269 085439; ⏰ noon–15.00 & 19.00–23.00 daily. Game dishes like wild boar, hare & partridge served in a large dining room which buzzes with activity at lunchtimes. €€€

**Cais da Estação** Av General Humberto Delgado 16, Sines; ☎269 636271; www. caisdaestacao.com. It's worth stopping at Sines if only to take lunch or dinner in this delightful Alentejo restaurant, situated in a converted railway warehouse on the waterfront, a stone's throw from the pretty, *azulejo*-covered disused railway station. The food is some of the best in the Alentejo & includes award-winning *arroz de lingueirão com choco frito* (razor clams with fried cuttlefish) & petiscos like bell peppers stuffed with tuna & crab served with crispy Alentejo bread, both of which burst with tanginess. The wine list is local & superb, & service attentive but discreet. €€€

**Espaço Garrett** Rua Almeida Garrett 4, Grândola; ☎269 498087; ⏰ noon–15.00 & 19.00–23.00 daily. First-class Alentejo cooking & locally-sourced seafood served by an affable & ebullient host in cosy surrounds. The *bacalhau* &

*lombinho de porco preto com laranja* (black pig loin with orange sauce) come highly recommended. Much of the art on display in the restaurant is for sale; it is the work of local artist Maria do Rosário Fonseca. €€€

**A Talha de Azeite** Centro Comercial O Lagar Loja 17, Rua Dom Nuno Álvares Perreira ; ☎269 086942; ⏰ noon–15.00 & 19.00–23.00 daily. The best regional cooking in the area with dishes including beef in white wine with rice & beans & roast cod with coriander, garlic served with *migas* & sole cooked in mint tomato served with razor clams. €€

**Bife de Peru** Rua Dom Nuno Álvares Perreira 214, Grândola; ☎269 442946; ⏰ noon–15.00 & 19.00–23.00 daily. A rustic space serving Portuguese dishes with a modern twist, & with a menu heavy with meat. €€

**Sal** Pégo beach; ☎265 490129; www. restaurantesal.pt; ⏰ closed Nov–Apr & open weekends only Apr–Jun, otherwise 11.00–late daily. Chic beach shack restaurant & boho evening bar right on the sand, serving ultra-fresh seafood including clams, prawns, soups & salads. €–€€

## WHAT TO SEE AND DO

**Grândola** In Portugal this sleepy provincial town is famous for being emblematic of the Alentejo's stalwart socialist spirit. In the early 1970s the town was immortalised as 'Grândola, Vila Morena' in a song in the Cante Alentejano form (see box, page 158) by the Bob Dylan of Portugal, the poet and folk singer **Zeca Afonso**, who was strongly censured under the Salazar regime. Afonso used the townspeople as symbolic of the Portuguese fraternal spirit which stood in opposition to Salazar's fascist regime. '*Terra da fraternidade Grândola, vila morena, Em cada rosto igualdade, O povo é quem mais ordena*' he sung – 'Land of brotherhood, Grândola, the sun-burned town with equality in every face, where it's the people who give the orders'. The song was broadcast in 1974 by the Portuguese radio station Radio Renascença as the signal for the upsurge which became the carnation revolution. There's an iron monument in homage to the singer outside the town hall. It's about the only sight of interest in the town itself; Grândola, while pleasant enough, is not a destination in its own right, but it is nonetheless the best place to base yourself along the central and northern coast, positioned for easy access to the beaches north to Tróia and south to Sines. The wetlands and meadows around the Santo André lagoon and the Roman ruins at Miróbriga are on the doorstep, and Grândola boasts some of the best rural hotels and restaurants on the Alentejo coast.

**The serras** The Serras da Grândola e Cercal are a series of pretty hills covered in cork oak forest and meadowland, dotted with ancient windmills and scented with wild flowers and herbs, which roll gently east of Grândola town into the interior of the Alentejo. They are a good place for an early morning or late afternoon stroll when the light is low and the birds and butterflies at their busiest. The Herdade Barradas da Serra hotel (see pages 139–40) and Passeios e Companhia (page 139) organise visits and horseback rides.

**The lagoons** The coast immediately south of Grândola is pocked with extensive shallow saltwater lagoons, the largest of which is the **Lagoa de Santo André e Sancha**. It's an important bird refuge with similar species to the Sado estuary, including flamingos, purple herons, purple swam hens and western marsh harrier, while its extensive hinterland of meadows and pine woodlands are home to wild boar, otters, martens, Egyptian mongoose and myriad butterflies including spectaculars like swallowtails, hairstreaks and fritillaries. Self-guided boardwalks cut through the low forest and salt marshes just off the Sines–Lisbon coastal road 1km north of the hamlet of Vila Nova de Santo André; look for the signs. Maps can be downloaded from the Instituto de Conservação da Natureza e das Florestas (ICNF) website (*www.icnf.pt*). The Herdade Barradas da Serra hotel (pages 139–40) can also organise tours of the reserve.

Santo André lagoon can also be reached along the beach, which becomes two beaches immediately south of the access road running off the EN261 at the Aldeia de Bresco hamlet – follow the signs to the Eurocamping campsite. One beach faces the lagoon itself and offers gentle paddling and swimming. The other – 100m or so to the west, facing the open ocean – is pounded by powerful surf and has a strong undertow.

**Miróbriga** (*Herdade dos Chãos Salgados, Santiago de Caçém;* \ *269 818 460;* ⊕ *09.00–noon & 14.00–17.30 Tue–Sat; admission €3*) The Alentejo's most extensive Roman ruins lie scattered over a scrubby hillside a few kilometres inland from the Santo André lagoon, on the edge of the old Templar town of Santiago de Caçém. **Miróbriga Celticum** was built after Caesar's conquest on the site of an old Celtic trading town which dated to the 8th or 9th century BC. There are a few partially rebuilt houses (including one with the remnant of a Roman fresco), a ruined temple probably dedicated to Jupiter, an elegant Roman bridge, a forum and a complex of baths. These lie amidst large areas of rubble and the outline in brick of low walls, and the site is set on the side of a grassy hill that is coloured with wild flowers in spring. To reach Miróbriga take the Lisbon–Sines road out of Santiago. There is a sign for the ruins after 2km, reached via a right turn at a large windmill.

**Santiago do Cacém** This little town spreads around a hilltop Moorish castle (⊕ *Apr–Sep 09.00–18.00 Mon–Sat, 09.00–12.30 Sun, Oct–Mar 09.30–4.30 Mon–Sat, 09.30–12.30 Sun; free admission*) conquered and rebuilt by the Knights Templar. It's not one of the Alentejo's most distinguished localities. There's little inside now beyond the municipal cemetery, but there are views from the battlements out towards the coast to the west and the Miróbriga ruins to the east. The town itself holds little more of interest than a small **museum** that was once a prison under Salazar, and which today houses a collection of local furniture.

**Badoca Safari Park** (*IP8 between Grândola and Sines;* \ *269 708 850; www.badoca. com;* ⊕ *10.00–18.00 Mon–Fri, 10.00–18.30 Sat & Sun; adults €17.50, children aged 4–10 & seniors €15.50, families (2 adults & 2 children) €60*) This safari park is one of the best family attractions around Grândola, with an array of animals from lemurs (with whom kids can iterract), tigers and herds of antelope to Brazilian macaws and birds of prey. There's a small farm with fluffy livestock and ponies, picnic areas and activities including rafting. Allow at least a half day for a proper visit.

**Central Alentejo beaches** The coast west of Grândola is lined with magnificent beaches. They are mentioned from north to south here. Praia do Galé is a seemingly endless stretch of sugar-fine golden sand backed by crumbling, caramel-coloured sandstone cliffs and pounded by fierce waves. With powerful ocean waves and a calm lagoon, Santo André lagoon is good both for surfers and kids, and there's a small restaurant just off the sand. Immediately south of here are a string of lovely surfer beaches – Porto das Carretas, Areias Brancas and Moita, all of them with few people and no facilities. They and the beaches of Santo André lagoon are reachable off a small local road that branches west off the EN261 at the village of Aldeia de Brescos.

**Sines** The industrial town of Sines, home to a huge oil refinery, marks the division between the north and central and the southern Alentejo coast. It's an unprepossessing place, but it's worth stopping off on your way south for a couple of interesting local sights, to see a prize-winning modernist building and to eat in one of coastal Alentejo's best restaurants, the Cais da Estação (page 140).

*Castelo e Museu de Sines (Sines Castle and Museum)* (*Rua do Muro da Praia s/n;* ✆ *269 630600; www.sines.pt;* ⊕ *Sep–May 10.00–13.00 & 14.00–17.00 Tue–Sun, Jun–Aug 10.00–13.00 & 14.30–18.00 daily; free admission*) The town's medieval castle, which doubles up as the Sines Museum, perches on a crag above the main beach. Portugal's greatest explorer, Vasco da Gama (1469–1524), who was born in a house in the street which now bears his name, spent his childhood years here. Da Gama was given command of the Portuguese fleet in 1497 and became the first European to discover and chart a sea route to India via the Cape of Good Hope. *En route* he established contacts along the African coast, which would become trading posts and eventually towns and countries, whose names are Portuguese to this day. His voyages began the era of Portuguese expansion, during which the country was briefly the most powerful in Europe. Da Gama was given the town of Sines as a reward for his discoveries. The castle is of course much older. The present structure dates largely from the 15th century, although archaeological digs have found material dating back to Palaeolithic times, and the remnants of a Visigoth basilica. There is a statue of Vasco da Gama inside and the small museum is devoted to his life.

*Centro de Artes de Sines (Sines Arts Centre)* (*Rua Cândido dos Reis s/n;* ✆ *269 860080; www.centrodeartesdesines.com.pt;* ⊕ *exhibition space 14.00–20.00 daily; admission to building free but charge for performances and exhibitions – for details see the website*) Francisco and Manuel Aires Mateus's post-modernist **Sines Arts Centre** won the domestic AICA Ministry of Culture award and was a finalist for the 2007 Mies van der Rohe architecture prize. Its walls – with faux balustrades and monolithic rectilinear shapes – echo the towers of the Alentejo's Moorish castles, while its internal patios and narrow corridors are reminiscent of the streets of the villages in the interior and stand in contrast to the vast, stark internal exhibition and performance halls. The complex's smooth, polished stone is particularly beautiful when offset by the blue of the hot summer sky.

*Old railway station* Sines's disused railway station, situated a stone's throw from the arts centre, is worth a glance for the very fine 20th-century railway-age *azulejos* that adorn its façade. The Cais da Estação restaurant (see page 140) just across the square from here to the north is one of the best seafood eateries in the Alentejo.

**Tesouro da Igreja de Nossa Senhora das Salas (Treasury of the Church of Our Lady of Salas)** (*Largo da Nossa Senhora das Salas;* ☏ *269 632 237;* ⊕ *10.00–12.30 & 14.00–17.00 (Jun–Sep 14.30–18.00) weekends only; admission €1.50*) An inscription over the door of this lovely little church reads '*Esta Casa de Nossa Senhora das Salas mandou fazer o muito magnífico senhor Dom Vasco da Gama, Conde da Vidigueira, Almirante e Vice-rei das Índias*' ('It was the most magnificent Vasco da Gama, Count of Vidigueira and Admiral and Viceroy of the Indias who ordered the building of this house of Our Lady of Salas'). In fact, the church was built far earlier. Legend has it that in 1281 or 1282 a Byzantine noblewoman, Betaça Lescaris, travelling to Portugal to join the wedding party of the 12-year old Dona Isabel and 19-year-old Dom Dinis, found herself caught in stormy seas in the Atlantic. Praying to the Virgin Mary for rescue, she promised to build a church dedicated to her at the first safe port where she found shelter. The church of Our Lady of Salas is this church. Vasco da Gama expanded the building, and the Manueline flourishes that adorn it date from this later period. The gilt altarpiece and the beautiful *azulejos* (depicting scenes from the life of Our Lady) are 18th century.

Since its construction the church has been a Fátima before Fátima. Myriad miracles have been attributed to Our Lady of Salas over the centuries, and the church is an ancient place of pilgrimage. The museum is dedicated to this cult and preserves reliquaries, statues, jewellery, lavish robes and dresses, paintings and items of furniture, some of them priceless.

# VILA NOVA DE MILFONTES AND THE SOUTHERN COAST

South of Sines, the Alentejo coast gets windier and wilder, giving a real sense of the end of a continent and the beginning of a great ocean. The long sweeps of beaches around Grândola give way to broken cliffs and rugged rocks, interspersed with magnificent long bays and sheltered coves hidden under craggy heads. Storks nest on precipitous pinnacles along the capes and gulls soar and hover in the prevailing west wind. Walkers on the **Rota Vicentina** wend along the winding path as it climbs cliffs and borders bays, enjoying the most spectacular stretch of the route north. They are helping to spread the word about the area's beauty, and it is gradually becoming popular. The tiny fishing villages of **Porto Côvo**, **Vila Nova de Milfontes**, **Almograve** and **Zambujeira** have morphed into tiny tourist towns, with hinterlands of holiday homes, small hotels and camping parks. They are a long way from being the Algarve though, despite that region's immediate proximity. Odemira – the regional capital – is a pretty little whitewashed village scattered across the steep Rio Mira valley, which winds through the meadows, maquis and cork woods of the Vicentina Natural Park to the coast at Vila Nova de Milfontes. Its waters are some of the least polluted and most fertile of any river in Europe.

## GETTING THERE AND AWAY
**By car** All the towns of the southern Alentejo coast sit right off the IP1/A2 Lisbon to Algarve motorway. Distances from Lisbon/Faro airport to the main towns are as follows: Porto Côvo 170km/178km, Vila Nova de Milfontes 183km/172km, Odemira 202km/122km, Zambujeira do Mar 211km/148km.

**By bus** None of the towns have designated bus stations. Bus tickets are sold through local travel agents or hotels/hostels, all of whom can help with their purchases. Express services are listed below; see www.rede-expressos.pt for precise details.

**To/fromVila Nova de Milfontes:** Beja: 2 daily via Grândola (*3½hrs*); Évora: 1 daily via Setúbal (*4¾hrs; quicker to go via Beja*); Odemira: 3 daily (*20mins*), plus local buses; Lagos (for Faro): 1 daily (*2hrs10mins*); Lisbon: 3 daily (*3½hrs*).

**To/from Odemira:** Lagos (for Faro): 2 daily (*1½hrs*); Lisbon: 6 daily (*3¾hrs*).

**To/from Zambujeira do Mar:** Vila Nova de Milfontes: 5 daily (*30–45mins*); Lagos (for Faro): 1 daily (*1½hrs*); Lisbon: 5 daily (*3–4hrs*).

## GETTING AROUND
**By car** The nearest places to rent a car for a fair price are Faro, Lagos or Lisbon. Driving around the southern Alentejo coast is straightforward. There are two coastal roads – the quicker N120 which runs around 10–15km inland north to south, skirting the southwestern Alentejo and the Costa Vicentina Natural Park and cutting through Odemira and the far prettier N393 which runs along the coast through the park, with roads and tracks branching off to the beaches and village. Both roads are well signposted.

**By bus** Bus line 8964 connects Vila Nova de Milfontes with Almograve twice a day. See www.rodalentejo.pt for details on times and prices. Bus line 8214 runs between Vila Nova de Milfontes and Sines via Porto Côvo twice daily from Monday to Friday. Your hotel will tell you where to catch these buses.

## TOURIST INFORMATION
**Odemira** Praça José Maria Lopes Falcão; ✆283 320900; ⊕ 09.00–17.00 Mon–Fri
**Santa Clara-a-Velha** Alameda da Índia; ✆283 881358; ⊕ 10.00–13.00 & 14.00–18.00 Tue–Sat

**Vila Nova de Milfontes** Rua António Mantas s/n; ✆283 996599; ⊕ 10.00–13.00 & 14.00–18.00 daily
**Zambujeira** Rua da Escola s/n; ✆283 961144; ⊕ 10.00–13.00 & 14.00–18.00 Tue–Sat

## TOUR OPERATORS
**Aventur Activa** Hotel HS Milfontes, Vila Nova de Milfontes; ✆964 134643; www.aventuractiva. pt. Private tours, canoeing & sea kayaking, surfing, paintball, jeep trips, bike hire, tours & rappelling.
**Alentejo Surf Camp** Urbanização Alagoachos 143A, Vila Nova de Milfontes; ✆962 349417; www. alentejosurfcamp.com. Surf classes for all levels, plus accommodation (page 146) & surf packages.
**Costa Azul Surf Shop and Surf School** Praia Vierinha, Porto Côvo; ✆932 665269; www. costaazulsurf.com. Surf board rental & classes for all ages & levels, from beginners to advanced. Stand-up guaranteed.
**Ecoalga – Centro de Mergulho** Rua 25 de Abril, Porto Côvo; ✆964 620394; www.ecoalga.com. Diving trips over the rugged underwater scenery

around Porto Côvo & the Ilha do Pessegueiro. Clear waters. Abundant aquatic life.
**Fourwinds** Jardim de Porto Côvo, Porto Côvo; ✆967 561586; www.fourwinds.pt. Boat trips, hiking, Segway riding & children's activities (including pedalkarting, climbing & swimming with inflatable jackets).
**J Matias** Foros da Pouca Farinha; ✆965 535683. Boat trips around Porto Côvo & the Ilha do Pessegueiro.
**SudAventura** Rua Custódio Brás Pacheco 38A, Vila Nova de Milfontes; ✆283 997231; sudaventura.com. Surf board rental & lessons, boat trips, rock climbing & rappelling, mountain biking, horseriding & sea kayaking around Vila Nova de Milfontes.

## WHERE TO STAY
🏠 **Naturarte** (6 villas) Estrada de Vila Nova de Milfontes km1, Vila Nova de Milfontes; ✆913 619

939; www.naturarte.pt. Villas for up to 4 decked out with the kind of contemporary urban fittings

& furniture you might associate with a mid-range modish boutique hotel. It overlooks the Mira River & is surrounded by meadows & paddocks filled with horses. The beach & Vila Nova de Milfontes are a 10min drive away, & the hotel organises art, horseriding & walking excursions. €€€€€

🏠 **Herdade do Telheiro** (6 villas) Frequesia de Santa Maria, Odemira; ☎917 248126; www.herdadedotelheiro.com. The Alentejo is filled with lovely bucolic homestay hotels. This *herdade* is one of the very few whose accommodation is situated in original rural bungalows – lovingly restored & complete with their original terracotta roofs, shady *lareira* terraces & whitewashed facades & painted doorframes. Interiors are filled with rustic antique furniture & colourful rugs & bedspreads. The villas sit in a shady orchard garden in the heart of the countryside just east of Odemira (15mins' drive from the coast). €€€€

🏠 **Quinta do Barranco da Estrada** (10 rooms) Santa Clara a Velha; ☎283 933065; www.paradise-in-portugal.com. A country retreat on the shores of the Barragem de Santa Clara lake, with airy rooms in an annexe tiled with terracotta. Each is named in honour of local wildlife (Kingfisher, Wild Boar & Butterfly), fitting in with the spirit of the hotel, which focuses on an immersion in nature & specifically birdwatching. The hotel also offers walking in the hills, kayaking on the lake, fishing or simply soaking up the bucolic atmosphere. There's a sauna right on the shores of the lake & the hotel offers shiatsu & general massage. A good option for dedicated birders or those wanting a quiet country break or a tranquil spot to break the journey between the coast & the Baixo Alentejo. The owners can organise birdwatching throughout the Alentejo. €€€€

🏠 **Zambujeira House** (3 rooms) Rua da Saudade 9, Zambujeira do Mar; ☎918 524553; www.feelslikehome.pt. A holiday home housed in a 2-storey cottage in the village centre some 5mins' walk from the beach & with room for 6 with a shared living room, very small kitchen & a terrace. Restaurants are in close proximity. Note that the price is for the entire house & that the owners require minimum stays of around a week. €€€€

🏠 **Casa do Adro** (6 rooms) Rua Diário de Notícias 10-10A, Vila Nova De Milfontes; ☎283 997102; www.casadoadro.com.pt. Dona Idália's family have been in Vila Nova de Milfontes for hundreds of years, living in the heart of the village's historical centre. So the Casa de Adro is above all her family home, into which every one of her guests is welcomed with open arms & an array of complimentary cakes, juices & drinks. Rooms are cosy but modern – bright & airy with colourful bedlinen, balconies, little workstations & spotless bathrooms. B/fast & afternoon tea are delicious & ample, & Dona Idália, who is a fount of knowledge about what to see & do in the area, can organise anything from horse rides to river trips. €€€

🏠 **Monte do Zambujeiro** (6 villas, 5 suites) Estrada Longueira-Almograve; ☎283 386143; www.montedozambujeiro.com. A delightful rural retreat set in meadows overlooking the curves of the River Mira a few kilometres from the sea (& about 5km from Vila Nova de Milfontes). The large villas with well equipped kitchens, separate living areas & terraces are great for families or couples looking to cater for themselves. Some have suites of rooms. €€€

🏠 **Greenway Rooms** (4 rooms) Urbanização Brejo da Estrada Lote 14-A, Vila Nova de Milfontes; ☎916 464285; www.hostelworld.com. A recently opened B&B with very small but comfortable modern rooms with private bathrooms (for the price of the equivalent in many of the hostels), a shared patio & generous b/fasts in a private home 15mins' walk from the historic centre of Vila Nova de Milfontes & the beaches. €€

🏠 **Moinho de Asneira** (14 rooms) Apartado 128, Vila Nova de Milfontes; ☎283 990076; www.duneparquegroup.com. Attractive modern apartments & villas with kitchens, sitting areas (with cosy fireplaces & leather armchairs) & lovely river views. 5km from Vila Nova de Milfontes & the beaches. The hotel has a small spa & swimming pool & organises activities. There is complimentary use of the indoor pool, sauna & other facilities at the big Duna Parque hotel, a resort on the beach in Vila Nova. €€

🏠 **Ondazul** (9 rooms) Rua da Palmeira 1, Zambujeira do Mar; ☎283 961450. Small, functional rooms with tiled floors, a bed & a small work desk squeezed in. Some have balconies. The beach & local restaurants are 5mins' walk away. €€

🏠 **Walkers Milfontes Hostel** (6 rooms) Rua do Monte Vistoso 93; Vila Nova de Milfontes;

5

919 720509. This modest guesthouse aimed at Costa Vicentina walkers & situated just under a kilometre from Furnas beach is cosier than the hostel competition, & rooms rent for less or just a little more when shared as trpls & dorms for 4 with shared or private bathrooms. €€

**⌂ Alentejo Surf Camp** (6 rooms) Urbanização Alagoachos 143A, Vila Nova de Milfontes; ☏ 962 349 417; www.alentejosurfcamp. com. Friendly, party-orientated surfer hostel & home to local surfer Sergio & his pet dog. Service & security is very friendly but laidback, & there are surf classes for all levels. Sergio rents out boards. €

**⌂ Almograve Youth Hostel** (33 rooms) Av da Praia s/n, Almograve; ☏ 283 640000; www.hihostels.com. This big hostel housed in a whitewashed concrete building has simple, plain dorms & dbls (with & without private bathrooms) & modestly appointed kitchens. What it lacks in cosiness & conviviality it makes up for by being right next to the village beach & a few kilometres from Zambujeira, the site of the Sudoeste music festival. Busy in summer, cold in winter.

A Hostelling International membership card is required (€2) for stays. Max stay 6 nights. €

**⌂ Hike Surf and Lodge** (3 rooms) Rua São Sebastião, Vila Nova de Milfontes 24; ☏ 300 505996; www.hikesurflodge.blogspot.pt. Simple but tastefully decorated dorms, dbls & en suites aimed at holidaying surfers (& their families). The beach is a 10min walk away at the east end of the village, & the owners can organise surfing, cycling & hiking. Generous b/fasts. €

**⌂ Milfontes Beach** (28 rooms) Av Marginal s/n, Vila Nova de Milfontes; ☏ 283 990070; www. hsmilfontesbeach.com. The best appointed proper hotel in town sits right behind the main beach & offers modern rooms & suites with tiled floors, the best of which have expansive balconies with beautiful views out over Praia da Franquia, the Mira River & Praia das Furnas. Theses views are shared by the glass-fronted restaurant. The hotel has a decent-sized outdoor pool & can organise activities including river trips & surf classes. €

## WALKS ON THE ROTA VICENTINA

The Rota Vicentina is one of Europe's most spectacular coastal paths, running along deserted beaches, craggy clifftops and riverbanks, through meadows bursting with wild flowers, cork oak and pine forests and herb-scented maquis, and cutting through a string of magical little villages along the way. Almost all of the route lies within the Sudoeste Alentejano e Costa Vicentina Nature Reserve, a 200km-long chunk of protected shoreline.

The route takes in all of the Alentejo and western Algarve coast between Santiago do Cacém in the north and Cabo São Vicente (Cape St Vincent) – mainland Europe's westernmost point – in the south. Within the Alentejo there are two possible starting points.

The most popular route is the 120km **Fisherman's Trail,** which takes in the best stretches of the beautiful Alentejo coast and begins in Porto Côvo (page 148). From here the path hugs the coast south through Vila Nova de Milfontes (pages 148–9), where you can take the ferry across the River Mira, south to Almograve (page 151) and Zambujeira do Mar (page 151). The path continues along the shoreline from here to Odeceixe, after which it cuts inland, running parallel to the coast through the Algarve. Where the path is forced to cut inland there are circular loops around some of the prettiest coastal stretches. It eventually reaches Cabo São Vicente.

An alternative route, the 230km **Historical Way**, begins in Santiago do Cacém further north, running inland through the hills to Odemira, then crossing the River Mira and joining the Porto Côvo route at Odeceixe.

**HOW TO DO THE WALK** It is straightforward to organise a walk along the Rota Vicentina yourself. The Fisherman's Trail is clearly marked with blue arrows on very frequent

## WHERE TO EAT AND DRINK

✖ **A Barca Tranquitanas** Entrada da Barca, Porto Fiscal do Sardão, Zambujeira do Mar; ☎283 961186; Facebook: Restaurante a Barca – Tranquitanas; ⏱ noon–15.00 & 18.30–22.30 daily. Upmarket seafood restaurant (with an excellent Portuguese wine list), serving tiger prawns, monkfish & cuttlefish in an indoor wood-panelled dining room or al fresco with a view of the Atlantic. €€€

✖ **A Fateixa** Largo do Cais, Vila Nova de Milfontes; ☎283 996415. Alentejo dishes like *lombo de porco com amêijoas* & grilled squid, served al fresco with gorgeous river views on the quays next to the River Mira by António and his wife Fátima. The restaurant is one of the town's longest established. €€

✖ **Cervejaria** Rua Mira Mar 14, Zambujeira do Mar; ☎283 961113; ⏱ noon–15.00 & 19.00–22.30 daily, closed Sep–Jun. A seafood restaurant serving excellent clams with rice & a broad choice of fresh fish including standards like *sardinhas*, *dourada* & *robalo*. €€

✖ **Choupana** Praia da Franquia s/n; Facebook: Choupana; ⏱ 11.30–23.00 daily, closed low season. A beach shack restaurant right on the sand at the edge of Vila Nova & the beginning of the main town beach, Praia da Franquia. Friendly staff serve simple grilled seafood dishes (fresh in tourist season). The fabulous views, which are best at sunset, push up the price. €€

✖ **La Bella Pizza** Rua Casa do Povo 8 R/C, Vila Nova de Milfontes; ☎968 808569; ⏱ 19.00–23.00 Tue–Sun, noon–15.00 & 19.00–23.00 Sat & Sun. Those suffering from a surfeit of delicious black pork, *migas* & seafood or venturing out in search of something vegetarian should head for this Brazilian-style pizzeria & pasta restaurant. Aficionados of Brazilian pizzas firmly believe their pizzas are the best in the world. Be prepared for lots of cheese, puffy thicker-than-Italian pastry & gentle *bossa nova* plucked on the guitar by owner Jorge Soares. €€

✖ **O Marquês** Largo Marquês de Pombal 10, Porto Côvo; ☎269 905036; ⏱ noon–15.00 &

signposts. The circular routes are marked with orange arrows. The Historical Way is marked with green arrows. The www.rotavicentina.com site explains it all in great depth, breaks up the route into day-sized chunks and explains which stretches can be navigated on a mountain bike. The site is in excellent English and includes an interactive, printable map. Using the villages described in this guide as way-stations will give you plenty of accommodation and eating options, and the website has still more should you need them.

### TOUR OPERATORS FOR ROTA VICENTINA WALKS
#### Portugal
**CITUR** www.citur.pt. All manner of trips throughout Portugal, including nature- & family-oriented walks & wildlife trips on & around the Rota Vicentina.
**Portugal Nature Trails** www.portugalnaturetrails.com. Walking, hiking, cycling & light adventure throughout Portugal & guided or self-guided walks on the Rota Vicentina as part of a group or bespoke.
**Vicentina Travels** www.vicentinatravel.com. Rota Vicentina walks, road & mountain biking & adventure & active trips. The company are Alentejo specialists & are based in the region. Guided tours & bespoke trips.

#### International
**Sunvil Discovery** See page 40. The best international operator, with tailored trips as standalone holidays or as part of a longer stay.
**Tee Travel** www.tee-travel.com. Rota Vicentina walks, gastronomy & wine trips & light adventure in Portugal & Spain.

19.00–22.00 Tue–Sun. Portuguese Tapas & simple but very fresh seafood dishes served at tables on a little plaza in a restaurant close to the centre of the village. €€

✗ **O Sacas** Well-prepared fish standards (grilled bream, barbecued tiger prawns) & Alentejo seafood dishes like *arroz de tamboril* served in a rather scruffy open-plan shack whose simplicity is offset by the lively in-season evening atmosphere, generated by a buzzing crowd & occasional live Portuguese music. €€

✗ **Tasca do Celso** Rua dos Aviadores 34A, Vila Nova de Milfontes; ☏ 283 996753; www.tascadocelso.com; ⏲ noon–15.00 & 19.00–22.00 daily. The best restaurant in town & one of the best in the region, serving ultra-fresh seafood & Alentejo meat dishes, inc tiger prawns with rice & razor clams, & *carne de porco à alentejano*, in a big open-plan dining room furnished with fashionable distressed tables & chairs & decked out in raw stone, polished concrete & brightly coloured hangings & table mats. €€

✗ **Morais** Rua António José Almeida 1, Vila Nova de Milfontes; ☏ 283 996827; www.restaurantemorais.pai.pt; ⏲ noon–15.00 & 19.00–23.00 daily. Fish & seafood in enormous portions. So fresh that it needs no embellishment, it is served simply fried or grilled with condiments. For dessert try *farofias*, a local soft meringue infused with sweet lemon. €

## NIGHTLIFE AND ENTERTAINMENT

♀ **La Movida** Rua Conde Bandeira s/n (on the seafront), Vila Nova de Milfontes. Lively in-season bar serving cocktails, ice-cold beer & with DJs & dancing until the small hours.

♀ **Lua Cheia/A Barca Tranquitanas** Rua Antónia Mantas, Cerca do Arneirão, Vila Nova de Milfontes; ☏ 964 923571. Popular after-hours bar & mini-club with great value icy *mojitos* & *caipirinhas*, live music & DJs in the high season, & empty bar stools for the rest of the year.

## WHAT TO SEE AND DO

**Porto Côvo** The southern coast gets beautiful just as the industrial spires of Sines fade in the rear view mirror. The first village of any note is **Porto Côvo** – a sprawl of villas, caravan parks and bungalows spreading around the pedestrianised Rua Vasco da Gama and sitting behind a low clifftop. This affords wonderful views out over the ocean to the west and south to a rocky cove that serves as a natural harbour dotted with bobbing fishing boats. The Costa Vicentina path cuts up the cliff from here along one of its most popular stretches – a 2km path running next to the inky blue ocean, past a Bronze Age burial site, over dunes and beaches to the **Ilha do Pessegueiro** (Peach Tree Isle). This tiny island lies just offshore, like a flattened, minuscule St Michael's Mount, complete with the crumbling walls of a derelict fort. You could almost throw a stone on to its shores from the beach or reach it across the flats at low tide. Fishermen in Porto Côvo offer half-day trips here. The island sits opposite an exquisite white sand beach on the mainland, sheltered by dunes and watched over by a bulky 16th century fort, a car park and a café serving decent seafood and steaming coffee to huddles of coastal path walkers.

Porto Côvo's rugged scenery continues underwater in caves and arches, rocky reefs and swim-throughs, making it a popular spot for diving and snorkelling, both of which can be organised in the town.

**Vila Nova de Milfontes** The southern coast's prettiest seaside town lies a few kilometres further south. The town has no outstanding sights, although it still preserves the remnants of an old medieval fishermen's village, with a tiny church and a filigree of winding, whitewashed streets huddled in a hinterland of villas behind a crumbling castle. But it sits in a gorgeous location perched over the limpid, aquamarine Mira River and surrounded by myriad marvellous beaches, from sweeping strands of white sand to rocky coves with the rusting ruins of wrecked ships. The locals are warm and welcoming and there is a good choice of hotels and one excellent restaurant. The castle, or **Forte do São Clemente** (not open to the public), as it is properly known, was an important bastion against pirate raids from North Africa after the Reconquest of southern Portugal. It subsequently passed into private hands and was briefly opened as a luxury hotel and restaurant, although it appears derelict now.

## Odemira and the River Mira

The Mira begins its course some 145km from Vila Nova, in the Serra do Caldeirão. As most of its length lies within the Southeast Alentejo and Costa Vicentina Natural Park, it is one of the cleanest in western Europe and is rich with fish and bird life. Boat trips go from Vila Nova as far as the regional capital **Odemira** in the interior, which is sprinkled into a green valley like fallen sugar cubes. On the way you pass a working watermill and reedbeds busy with wading birds. The N123 road runs inland from here to the source of the Mira near the remote village of **Santa Clara-a-Velha**. In the village there is an atmospheric ruined church and an equally eerie ruined Roman bridge (look for signs to the Ponte de Santa Maria) running over a limpid stream and set in lovely surrounds. A few kilometres from here is the huge Barragem de Santa Clara lake, which almost overflows with fish and is surrounded by hills covered in woodland.

## Beaches

Vila Nova is all about the beaches. The town beach, the **Praia da Franquia**, is a half-moon of sand sitting immediately west of Vila Nova and with lovely views over a ripple of sandstone cliffs and a sweep of sandy coastline. Immediately to the north, beyond the lighthouse and across shifting dunes tied down with a loose lattice of cooch grass and wild flowers, is the **Praia do Carreiro das Fazendas** (also sometimes called Praia do Farol – or lighthouse beach), a long, broad bay backed by sand dunes and capped with craggy arched rocks. Immediately north of here is the **Praia do Patacho** (aka Praia Joaquim Marques), where a huge tug lies wrecked on the sand. It is said to be a smugglers' boat that crashed on the rocks in the 1970s while fleeing the coast guards. The beach itself is lovely – a rock pool-encrusted cove sheltered by crumbling sandstone cliffs but sadly blighted by a pipe which at intervals pumps out waste water across the sand. Beaches continue north of here towards Vila Nova's fishing port, where small boats still drag in nets of wriggling mackerel daily. Beyond here lies the broad beach at **Malhão**, which has road access, a campsite and some facilities. The **Praia dos Aivados** immediately to the north is lonelier and more difficult to reach, and even in high season is visited only by a handful of more intrepid tourists and hikers.

Beaches stretch south of Vila Nova, across the Mira River, towards the tiny town of Almograve. **Praia das Furnas** sits on the south side of the river, and when it's not packed with holidaying families it's one of the most beautiful around Vila Nova. It stretches along the bank of the river around a rocky headland, then runs along the open Atlantic for a long, broad, dune-backed stretch. The coast beyond is rockier and more dramatic and the Costa Vicentina path climbs up cliffs covered in low maquis, which watch out over the Atlantic pounding the craggy islets around the **Pedra do Passo**. Between April and October swallows and swifts nest here, swooping around the headlands, and the air is heavy with the scent of wild flowers, rosemary and lavender. Look out for patches of *Plantago almogravensis* – clumps of plants with clusters of yellow conical florets on the end of long stalks. These are among the world's rarest flowers, endemic to this 20km$^2$ patch of southwest Portugal and extant as just one subpopulation. Where the plant grows, the vegetation is wild Mediterranean and the bird and insect life is rich. As you walk along the path you'll notice that where *Plantago almogravensis* has been

## VASCO DA GAMA AND THE FIRST TRADING PORTS

Columbus is remembered for beginning the age of discoveries which heralded the birth of the Renaissance. But in contemporaneous Europe his voyage was of considerably less significance than the voyage made by a sailor from Sines five years later. In 1497 Vasco da Gama achieved what Columbus had failed to achieve – the establishment of a maritime passage to the Indian Ocean. In doing so he opened up the world's most coveted trade route, wresting control of the spice trade from Muslim hands. This would mark a shift in the balance of power away from the Arabian and Ottoman Muslims, who had dominated the Silk Road and Red Sea spice routes, and establish Europe as the new global superpower, with tiny Portugal at its helm, ahead of its rival, Venice.

Da Gama's voyage was an astonishing and perilous achievement. Of the 170 crew members who sailed with him on his two-year quest, only 54 survived the 38,000km journey. But he was heralded as a hero by King Manuel when he returned in 1499. And the monarch wasted no time in seizing the opportunity da Gama had created, dispatching another explorer, Pedro Álvares Cabral, to secure the trade route, carrying the finest European goods. Cabral founded the first European trading connection with the Zamorin of Calicut (modern Kozhikode) on India's Keralan coast and the first trading port at Cochin (modern Kochi). This outraged the Muslim traders, who attacked and murdered 50 of his men. In retaliation, Cabral set fire to their ships, killing some 600. On his journeys, while drifting too far west to avoid the Atlantic doldrums, he discovered Brazil.

In 1502 da Gama set out on his second expedition, this time with a large military fleet of 20 vessels armed with the latest technology, including those firearms that the Portuguese had used to dispel the Moors from the Alentejo. Da Gama literally bombarded his way into Asian ports, destroying Muslim forts and ships and forcing rulers in India to switch their trade to Portugal. In 1511 his compatriot Afonso de Albuquerque conquered Malacca – the strategic centre of the spice routes – for Portugal. Luxury goods like black pepper, cloves, tea, sandalwood, ebony and silk flowed into Europe through Portuguese ports, and through their eastern ports the Portuguese forced the Ottomans and Arabs out of Asia, completely capturing the spice routes for tiny Portugal.

On his return to Portugal from his second trip he retired in Évora, disgruntled at not having received the promised recompense for his voyages from King Manuel. In 1524, at the age of 64, he was dispatched to Goa to serve as the first viceroy of the Indies and to combat the corruption that had overtaken the nascent colony. This time he didn't return, dying in Cochin in December of that year.

trampled and driven out the land is blighted by patches of introduced acacia and intensive stretches of crop monoculture, and there is a substantial drop in bird and butterfly numbers and variety.

The beaches begin again just north of Almograve with one of the region's loveliest, the **Praia do Brejo Largo**, another vast, broad stretch backed by dunes and pocked with rocks and pools. There is car access only along a dirt trail, meaning that but for walkers, the beach is often completely deserted, especially out of season.

**Almograve** Almograve itself is a pocket-sized resort town whose beaches are crammed in around the crashing rocks and very crowded in high season. The town beach – **Praia do Almograve** or Praia Grande – is one of the largest – long and broad, backed by shifting dunes, crowned with low cliffs and pocked with rocks, the largest of which abuts the cliffs right in the centre of the beach, breaking it into two stretches at high tide. It's very popular with families, especially at weekends, and has excellent facilities, including showers, a snack bar and lifeguards. There is access to quieter beaches on trails that run north and south of town. These include, to the north, the **Praia de Nossa Senhora**, a rocky cove reachable by steep steps, and the **Praia da Foz dos Ouriços**, a sandy inlet rippled with rocks set between dunes and cliffs where a stream runs from hills through a narrow valley on to the sand.

**Cape Sardão** South of Almograve the coast is ragged with plunging cliffs, rugged rocks and sea mounts, rising over dunes and capes and dropping into smuggler's bays as it stretches towards the dramatic Cape Sardão. This is capped by a lighthouse, which through a mistake of architectural execution was built backwards, facing inland, with its administrative buildings backing on to the sea. It's a windswept place, with low vegetation clinging to the clifftops, waves pounding the rocks below and storks huddled in untidy nests perched on sharp rocky pinnacles.

**Zambujeira do Mar** The next town south of the cape is the surf mecca of Zambujeira do Mar. Backpackers have been tramping here since the town was a fishing village, and there is still a laidback, hippy feel to the place. Bars sat in the cliff behind the whitewashed pedestrian centre play Ibiza-style chill-out music to post-surf sundowners, and in August the town hosts a big four-day music festival, the **Festival do Sudoeste** (*www.sudoeste.meo.pt*), when big name DJs like Fatboy Slim and performers and bands who have included Emeli Sandé, Oasis, Muse and Black Uhuru play throughout the day and night and the crowds reach their apex.

The beaches around Zambujeira are smaller – bays and coves set beneath rocky cliffs rather than long broad sweeps of sand. The town beach sits immediately south of Zambujeira, below a steep cliff. By Alentejan standards, it's nothing special. Better beaches lie to the south and include the **Praia dos Alteirinhos**, a nudist beach a kilometre south of town, and the **Praia das Bernosas**, a kilometre further on, fringing a tiny bay and reached along a steep trail.

5

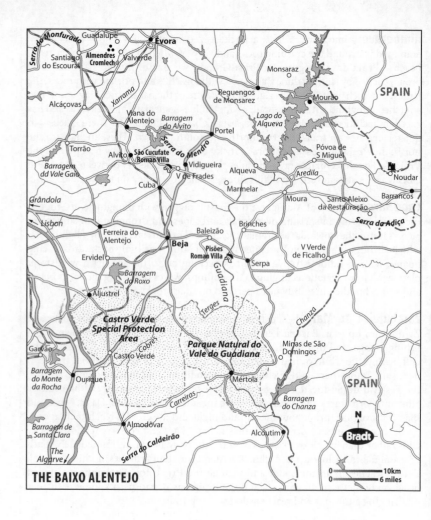

THE BAIXO ALENTEJO

# 6

# The Baixo Alentejo

Lacking the rugged mountains and World Heritage Sites of the Alto Alentejo, the Baixo or lower Alentejo has just one well-visited location – Mértola. Lying within a stone's throw of the Algarve, this fortified town attracts day-trippers and tourists on their way to or from Lisbon. Beyond here the Baixo is empty. Foreigners are an anomaly and even in high season you will share castles and castellated towns only with the locals. And while these towns cannot compare with Elvas or Évora for spectacular sights, they are nonetheless impressive. Beja, the regional capital, huddles around a massive castle keep in flatlands rich with vineyards and olive groves. Its streets are lined with fine mansion houses and churches. Serpa is a criss-cross of winding, whitewashed alleys hidden behind enormous ramparts. Moura has one of the region's best-preserved *mourarias* or Moorish quarters and an upper town filled with stately *azulejo*-covered townhouses. And there's Mértola itself, the prettiest of all the Baixo Alentejo's towns, its castle and jumble of steep streets reflected in the languid water of the Guadiana River.

Between these towns are dozens of sleepy little villages, sprinkled across a flat, arid landscape of cork oak and waving wheat and watered by the vast expanses of the Alqueva, Roxo and Alvito flooded lakes: Moura, Aljustrel, Castro Verde and Cuba are so quiet you can hear widows' dresses rustle as they walk through the narrow streets, and life seems little changed in centuries.

## BEJA

Covering a low hill rising from an expansive plain, Beja is dominated by its enormous castle keep, around which the town's narrow streets gently slope through *praças*, past palaces and monasteries to the town's modern hinterland. As the administrative capital of the Baixo Alentejo and the largest town in the region, Beja feels more local than touristy. There are a handful of sights (they'll take you half a day to visit), but above all Beja is a place to stop, sip a coffee in a streetside café and take in the status quotidian – the old men gossiping in the park, the mothers meeting over prams in the street and the general bustle of Portuguese provincial life unaffected and unconcerned by tourism. It's a cultural centre too, with one of the best theatres in the Alentejo and bars where you can still hear traditional Cante Alentejo, which like the towns of Évora and Elvas is protected by UNESCO, in this case on the UNESCO Intangible Cultural Heritage List.

The countryside around Beja is fertile, with cork oaks and olives, vineyards and wheat, and sprinkled with delightful *adega* hotels, many of them with handsome country estates. Visitors to the region often come here for the rich reds, a short visit to the Parque Natural do Vale do Guadiana just to Beja's south and a whistle-stop tour of the town itself.

**HISTORY** Come to Beja in mid-May and you will find the locals dressed up as Romans, downing wine from terracotta cups and conducting gladiatorial sword fights in the street. For while the hill where Beja lies has been a home for humans since prehistoric times, it was Rome that established a town here. That town was Pax Julia, named in homage of the peace that had been imposed forcibly on Lusitania following Julius Caesar's bellicose campaigns of 60BC. Pax Julia was nominally a *civitas* – or centre of administration – for the dispersed populace who live in the environs. In practice this meant it was a fortress of occupation in an area dominated up until that time by Celtic tribes. It was also the capital of an area of Roman Lusitania the conquerors called Conventus Pacensis, and as such Pax Julia was of greater importance in Roman times than Liberalitas Lulia (Évora) and of equal importance to Emerita Augusta (Mérida) and Scallabis (Santarém), the other two regional Lusitanian capitals.

Roman Beja had imposing walls, a forum (where the Praça da República lies today), baths, an amphitheatre and a temple. Little remains today within Beja itself – just a couple of Roman arches and artefacts preserved in the museum – although there is a ruin of a once magnificent Roman villa in Pisões (see page 161) nearby. The Visigoths swept in from AD415 (and left behind the delightful Igreja de Santo Amaro). After them, the Moors occupied Beja from the 8th to the 12th centuries. Beja's public squares owe much to the Romans, but like so many of the towns in the Alentejo, its streets are entirely Moorish in design.

Despite being the birthplace of the caliph and poet Muhammad ibn 'Abbad al-Mu'tami, however, Beja was not an important place for the Muslims. By the 11th century it had been eclipsed by Évora and Serpa and had begun to fall into decline. This didn't stop the Crusaders violently sacking the city in the 12th century, leaving Dom Afonso III to rebuild it almost from scratch. Scant traces of Moorish Beja remain. Afonso built a new castle and walls, and these were later expanded by Dom Dinis, who is largely responsible for the massive keep you see today. Beja's importance grew from then on. By the mid 15th century it had become a duchy and the Alentejo town of greatest note south of Évora. It was also an intellectual centre – the home of the influential de Gouveia family, whose scions included Diogo de Gouveia, court advisor and tutor to the great explorer priest Francis Xavier, and André de Gouveia, who became chancellor of the University of Paris in the 16th century. During the Portuguese golden era Beja was endowed with a string of fine churches, convents and palaces, some of which remain today.

But the glory lasted but a while. After the expulsion of the religious orders, and most notably the Jesuits, Beja fell into gradual, sleepy decline.

## GETTING THERE AND AWAY

**By car** The N121 highway to Beja runs off the the A2/IP1 Lisbon to Algarve motorway at junction 10, 14km after the turn-off to Grândola. The IP2 motorway connects Beja with Évora to the north and Castro Verde, Almodôvar and eventually Faro to the south. The IP8/N260 motorway runs east to Serpa and the Spanish border at Rosal de la Frontera, eventually reaching Seville. Distances from Beja are as follows: Lisbon 180km, Évora 80km, Serpa 29km, Grândola 70km, Faro 147km, Seville 219km.

**By train** The railway station (*estação de caminho de ferro*) (*Largo da Estação 17; www.cp.pt*) is just over 250m northeast of the centre off Rua General Teófilo de Trindade. Trains run to Lisbon (Oriente station) via Cuba, Alvito and Casa Branca (change here for Évora). A taxi from the railway station to hotels in the historical centre costs €2–3.

**By bus** The bus station (*terminal rodoviário*) (*Praça Antonio Raposo Tavares 284;* \ *284 313620*) is 500m south of the centre just off Avenida do Brasil. Buses run to

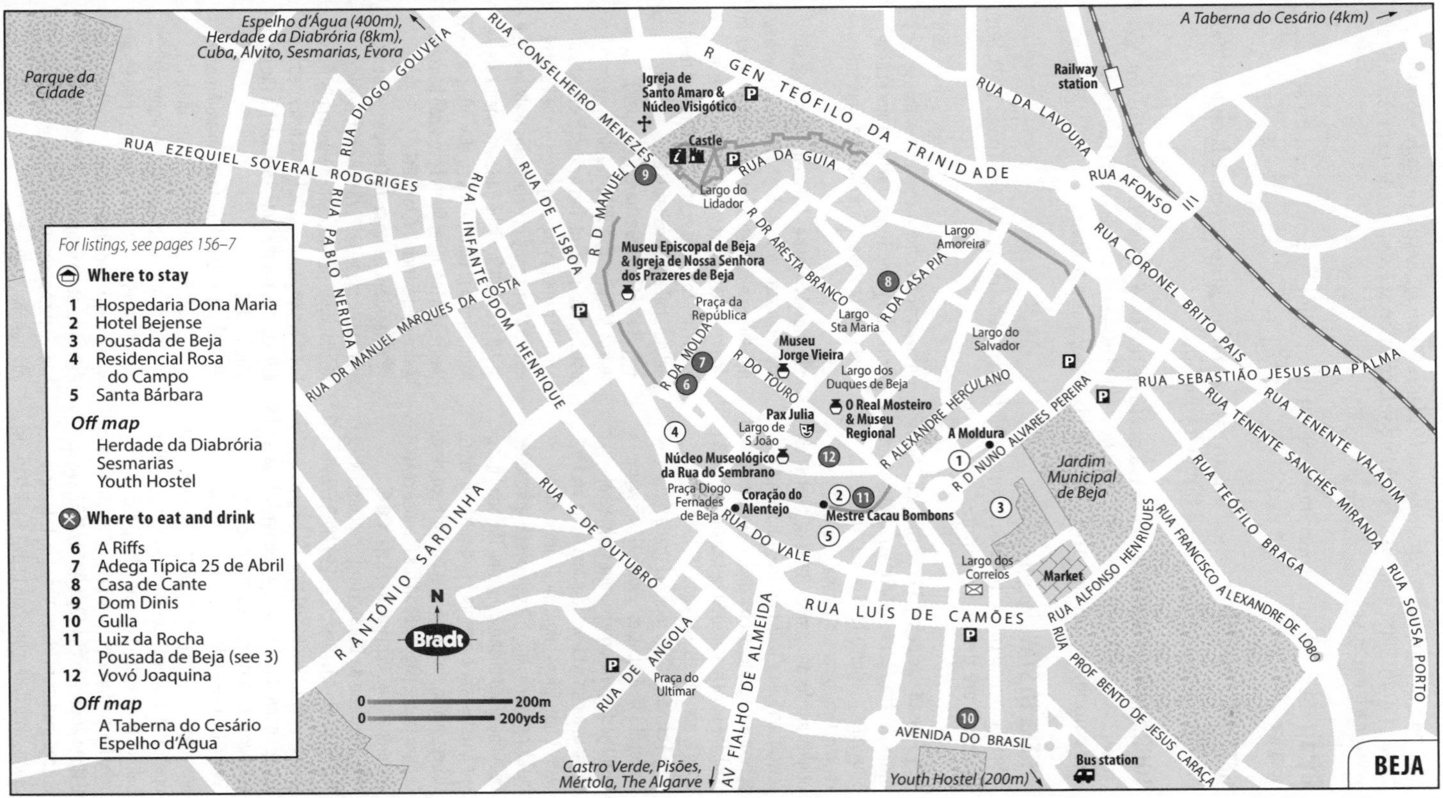

BEJA
Espelho d'Água (400m), Herdade da Diabrória (8km), Cuba, Alvito, Sesmarias, Évora
A Taberna do Cesário (4km)
Castro Verde, Pisões, Mértola, The Algarve
Youth Hostel (200m)
Parque da Cidade
Railway station
Bus station
Igreja de Santo Amaro & Núcleo Visigótico
Castle
Largo do Lidador
Museu Episcopal de Beja & Igreja de Nossa Senhora dos Prazeres de Beja
Praça da República
Largo Sta Maria
Largo Amoreira
Largo do Salvador
Largo dos Duques de Beja
Museu Jorge Vieira
Pax Julia
Largo de S João
O Real Mosteiro & Museu Regional
A Moldura
Núcleo Museológico da Rua do Sembrano
Praça Diogo Fernades de Beja
Coração do Alentejo
Mestre Cacau Bombons
Jardim Municipal de Beja
Largo dos Correios
Market
Praça do Ultimar
RUA CONSELHEIRO MENEZES
R GEN TEÓFILO DA TRINIDADE
RUA DA LAVOURA
RUA AFONSO III
RUA EZEQUIEL SOVERAL RODGRIGES
RUA DIOGO GOUVEIA
RUA PABLO NERUDA
RUA INFANTE DOM HENRIQUE
RUA DE LISBOA
R D MANUEL I
RUA DA GUIA
R DR ARESTA BRANCO
R DA CASA PIA
RUA CORONEL BRITO PAIS
RUA SEBASTIÃO JESUS DA PALMA
RUA TENENTE VALADIM
RUA TENENTE SANCHES MIRANDA
RUA TEÓFILO BRAGA
RUA SOUSA PORTO
RUA FRANCISCO ALEXANDRE DE LOBO
RUA ALFONSO HENRIQUES
RUA PROF BENTO DE JESUS CARAÇA
R D NUNO ALVARES PEREIRA
R ALEXANDRE HERCULANO
RUA DR MANUEL MARQUES DA COSTA
R DA MOLDA
R DO TOURO
RUA DO VALE
RUA 5 DE OUTUBRO
R ANTÓNIO SARDINHA
RUA DE ANGOLA
AV FIALHO DE ALMEIDA
RUA LUÍS DE CAMÕES
AVENIDA DO BRASIL
N
Bradt
0 200m
0 200yds
For listings, see pages 156–7
Where to stay
1 Hospedaria Dona Maria
2 Hotel Bejense
3 Pousada de Beja
4 Residencial Rosa do Campo
5 Santa Bárbara
Off map
Herdade da Diabrória
Sesmarias
Youth Hostel
Where to eat and drink
6 A Riffs
7 Adega Típica 25 de Abril
8 Casa de Cante
9 Dom Dinis
10 Gulla
11 Luiz da Rocha
Pousada de Beja (see 3)
12 Vovó Joaquina
Off map
A Taberna do Cesário
Espelho d'Água

Lisbon (*11 daily, 2½–3hrs*), Évora (*9 daily, 80mins*), Serpa (*3 daily, 35mins*) and Faro (*3 daily, 3hrs 45mins*). For more information see www.rede-expressos.pt and www.rodalentejo.pt

**By air** Beja has an airport, but at the time of going to print it had no scheduled services.

**GETTING AROUND** The best way to get around the historic centre is on foot. Taxis are cheap and can be booked through your hotel.

**TOURIST INFORMATION** There is a **posto de turismo** (*Largo Dr Lima Faleiro;* ↳ *284 311913;* ⏰ *10.00–13.00 & 14.00–18.00 daily*) inside the castle keep. They have maps and pamphlets and can help with hotel bookings and tours.

**WHERE TO STAY** *Map, page 155.*
See also *Serpa* (page 166) and *Parque Natural do Vale do Guadiana* (page 172), both of which are under 20 minutes' drive away.

**Pousada de Beja** (35 rooms) Largo D Nuno Álvares Pereira; ↳ 284 313580; www.pestana.com. Situated in a restored 13th-century Franciscan convent (which has sadly lost almost all of its original interior decoration), Beja's best hotel lies fewer than 5mins' walk from the main sights & is set in a leafy garden with a decent-sized swimming pool. The hotel has the best restaurant in town & is open to non-guests (see page 157). €€€

**Sesmarias** (13 rooms) Estrada Nacional 387, Alfundão; ↳ 965 591197; www.sesmariasturismoruralspa.com. Cloisters of spacious rooms with wood-panel floors, cream walls & lush linens brightened with scatter cushions, overlooking a lovely pool & surrounded by 300ha of woodland & pasture. The hotel has a spa & restaurant & organises birdwatching, visits to Beja, Alvito, the Alqueva lake & the Herdade da Comporta (see page 138) on the Alentejo coast. The property is 30km north of Beja. €€€

**Herdade da Diabroria** (12 rooms) EN 121 Apartado 401, Beja; ↳ 284 998177; www.diabroria.com. Surrounded by a 300ha private estate on the outskirts of Beja, this brightly painted *fazenda* hotel boasts a swimming pool, tennis courts, lawned gardens & modest rooms (the best are suites) situated in long cloisters. Windows don't open. Staff can organise activities including paint balling, birdwatching & quad biking. €€

**Hospedaria Dona Marta** (12 rooms) Largo D Nuno Álvares Pereira 12; ↳ 284 327602; www.hospedariadonamaria.pt. Very simple modern rooms (with little more than beds & work stations)

in an attractive *azulejo*-covered townhouse overlooking a pretty *praça* in the centre of Beja town. The best rooms are the upper floor suites. €€

**Hotel Bejense** (24 rooms) Rua Capitão João Francisco de Sousa 57; ↳ 284 311570; www.hotelbejense.com. Small but well appointed rooms decorated with kitschy floral themes & set in a hotel close to all the sights in the centre of town. Helpful staff & bike rental. €€

**Hotel Santa Bárbara** (26 rooms) Rua de Mértola 56; ↳ 284 312280; www.hotelsantabarbara.pt. This modest 3-star sits off a pedestrianised shopping street in the heart of historical old centre of Beja, 5mins' walk from the castle & a stroll from the museum. Rooms are well kept, furnished with beds & small writing desks, & the best on the upper floors have small balconies. Welcoming & friendly staff. €€

**Residencial Rosa do Campo** (8 rooms) Rua da Liberdade 12; ↳ 284 087066; www.rosadocampo.pt. Simple rooms with polished stone floors & nice chunky rustic furniture housed in an attractive & friendly family-run hotel in the centre of town. €€

**Youth Hostel** Rua Prof. Janeiro Acabado; ↳ 284 325458; www.hihostels.com. The twin rooms & dorms in this little hostel 5mins' walk from the town centre are very simple (the former with a desk & beds, the latter with just beds), but they come at a bargain price, especially when booked through hostel itself, rather than the international HI site. €

# WHERE TO EAT AND DRINK *Map, page 155.*

See also *Entertainment and nightlife* (below), *Serpa* (page 166) and *Parque Natural do Vale do Guadiana* (pages 172–3) for other options.

✖ **Pousada de Beja** Largo D Nuno Álvares Pereira; ☎284 313580; www.pestana.com; ⏰ 12.30–15.00 & 19.00–22.30 daily. Upmarket modern Portuguese cooking served in a hall within the *pousada*, or – when it's sunny – al fresco on the terrace next to the garden. Plates include Serpa cheese melted into an apple and game dishes like rabbit marinated in wine and rosemary and served with sweet potato and spinach. €€€

✖ **A Taberna do Cesário** Rua Venâncio Rosa Gabriel 3–5; ☎284 331383; ⏰ 12.30–15.00 & 18.30–22.30 Tue–Sat & 12.30–15.00 Sun. Hearty Alentejo fare served in a cavernous open-plan dining room, in generous portions at low prices. Excellent *bochechas de porco preto* & reliable seafood & game. €€

✖ **Adega Típica 25 de Abril** Rua da Moeda 23; ☎284 325960; ⏰ 12.30–15.00 & 18.30–22.30 Tue–Sat & 12.30–15.00 Sun. Decorated like an old-fashioned Portuguese tavern & serving traditional Alentejo comfort cooking, from game to *ensopado* stews & the ubiquitous *porco preto*. €€

✖ **Casa de Cante** Rua Casa Pia 26; ☎926 522259; ⏰ 12.30–15.00 & 19.00–22.30 Tue–Sat. Alentejo food, wine & petiscos including *migas*, *bacalhau* & *porco preto*, accompanied by live Alentejo cante. €€

✖ **Dom Dinis** Rua de Dom Dinis 11; ☎284 331383; ⏰ 12.30–15.00 & 18.30–22.30 Wed–Mon. A meat-heavy menu of grills, game & local specialities served in a restaurant opposite the castle keep. €€

✖ **Espelho d'Agua** Rua de Lisboa, Parque da Cidade; ☎284 325103; ⏰ 12.30–15.00 & 18.30–22.30 Tue–Sun. A great spot for lunch or afternoon coffee with tables in a bright glass-fronted dining room, or outside on the terrace, overlooking the largest park in the town centre. Reliable fish & local dishes. €€

✖ **Gulla** Avenida do Brasil s/n; ☎284 361144; ⏰ 12.30–15.00 & 18.30–22.30 daily. A broad menu of international dishes inc sushi & sashimi, pizzas, *bacalhau* & Aberdeen Angus steak. €€

✖ **Vovó Joaquina** Rua do Sembrano 57; ☎284 322140; ⏰ 12.30–15.00 & 18.30–22.30 Tue–Sat. Marble-topped tables, antique mirrors & oil paintings on the walls, Portuguese folk music on the piano, Alentejo cante (on Fri & Sat) & a menu of traditional Portuguese & pan-European dishes inc duck in port wine, pasta & chicken breast cooked with pineapple & banana. €€

✖ **Luiz da Rocha** Rua Capitão João Francisco de Sousa 63; ☎284 323179; ⏰ 08.00–23.00 Mon–Sat & 08.00–20.00 Sun. This traditional café has been serving savouries & cakes since 1893 & is one of the best places in Beja to people-watch over a velvety coffee & *pastel de nata*. Try some of the local specialities like the *empadas de frango*, served in cylindrical puff pastry, or the *porquinhos*, shaped like Alentejo black pigs & flavoured with chocolate, almond & brown sugar. Upstairs is a more formal restaurant serving Alentejo cooking & Portuguese standards like *bacalhau* & *ensopado de borrego*. €–€€

## ENTERTAINMENT AND NIGHTLIFE

♀ **Casa de Cante** Rua Casa Pia 26; ☎926 522259; ⏰ 12.30–15.00 & 19.00–22.30 Tue–Sat. Live Alentejo *cante* from local groups, accompanied by Alentejo food, wine & *petiscos*.

♀ **Riffs Bar and Café Concerto** Rua das Portas de Aljustrel 29; ☎931 616822; Facebook.com/guitariffs; ⏰ 22.00–02.00 Thu & Fri & 18.00–02.00 Sat. A hard rock bar tucked into the ancient stone of Beja's castle & with an upper deck on the battlements itself, affording wonderful views over the town & plains beyond. The bar holds regular jam sessions & live music nights.

♀ **Vovó Joaquina** Rua do Sembrano 57; ☎284 322140. Alentejo *cante* & Portuguese folk music, usually at weekends only.

☞ **Pax Julia Theatre** Largo de São João s/n; ☎284 315090; www.paxjuliateatromunicipal.blogspot.co.uk. Only Portuguese speakers will be able to enjoy the drama, but the theatre doubles up as a cinema showing everything from art house to documentaries (with subtitles) & a concert hall for classical & popular music & dance.

## SHOPPING

**A Moldura** Rua Dom Nuno Álvares Pereira 25a; ☎284 328480. Cluttered with delightful antiques & curios, this corner shop is a good place to pick up traditional tableware, fine decanters & glasses, *azulejos* & early 20th-century paintings, some of them decent & many of them kitschy.

**Coração do Alentejo** Rua Capitão João Franciso Sousa 4; ☎966 551388. Regional wines, olive oils, cheeses & other foodstuffs & a sprinkling of local arts & crafts.

**Mestre Cacau Bombons** Rua Capitão João Francisco de Sousa 33; ☎284 326168. Superior handmade chocolates including some with unusual flavours (Earl Grey, rosemary, Portuguese liqueurs), cocoa powder & juices.

## WHAT TO SEE AND DO

**O Real Mosteiro de Nossa Senhora da Conceição and Museu Rainha Dona Leonor Regional de Beja** (*Largo da Conceição;* ☎ *284 323351; www. museuregionaldebeja.net;* ⏱ *09.30–12.30 & 14.00–17.15 Tue–Sun; admission €2 – includes entry to Santo Amaro church and the Visigoth Museum*) In its heyday this magnificent Gothic-Manueline convent dedicated to Our Lady of Conception and once run by the Poor Clare Sisters was one of the wealthiest in Portugal. Even those with a passing interest in church art and architecture shouldn't miss it. It would be difficult to do so. The building's ornately decorated Manueline tower and elaborately crenellated parapet dominate Beja's skyline, while the building's uniquely Portuguese combination of whitewash and raw stone, Gothic arches and Mudéjar horseshoe windows immediately attract the eye as you walk past. Which you will, for the convent lies in the heart of the old town.

---

### THE SONG OF THE WORKERS

*Cante Alentejano* is a traditional form of a capella singing performed by male voice choirs and based on the songs workers tilling the *latifundio* fields would sing as they worked the soil together. *Cante* is ancient. The melodies are modal, based on patterns of notes more primordial than the major and minor scales that underpin classical music. Modes were used by the Arabs and by the Greeks and Romans before them, suggesting that it is at least as old as Moorish Al-Andalus. Some musicologists have suggested that the people of the Alentejo were singing *Cante* before the Romans invaded. Until the invention of radio you would have heard *Cante* everywhere in the Alentejo, especially in the Baixo, its traditional homeland. Men sang it in the fields, women and children sang it at home, and mixed groups sang *Cante* on religious occasions. It became associated principally with male voice choirs, and increasingly with social protest. Zeca Afonso's anthemic 'Grândola, Vila Morena' is a *Cante*.

After the Carnation Revolution *Cante* began to die out as young people left the Alentejo and their heritage for Lisbon and the larger cities. Nowadays it can be heard only in a few bars in Beja, and at traditional festivals in towns like Monsaraz (see *Festivals*, pages 49–51). But this is slowly changing. In 2014 Cante Alentejano received an enormous boost when it was inscribed as 'Intangible World Heritage' by UNESCO. Together with *fado*, it is one of two Portuguese cultural traditions protected as such. And together with the cities of Elvas and Évora, it is one of the three things in the Alentejo listed as World Heritage. You can hear *Cante Alentejano* on the CD *Cante Alentejano – A Voz de Um Povo* (CNM Music Portugal).

Inside the convent is equally magnificent, especially the nave of the main church, which is covered with swirling 17th- and 18th-century Baroque and Rococo carvings as rich and brightly coloured as a coral reef. Look out for the intricate pietra dura stone inlay on the lateral altars and the portraits of the convent's founders, Dom Fernando and Dona Brites, the first duke and duchess of Beja, who commissioned the building in 1459. There's the tomb of the first abbess, Dona Uganda, whose Manueline style contrasts with the dominant Baroque, and some *azulejos* depicting scenes from the life of St. John the Baptist and dating from the 1740s.

Leaving the church, you will enter the cloisters and a series of further galleries. The convent chapterhouse is particularly striking, covered in Arab tiles from 16th-century Spain. They are among the best preserved and most beautiful in Portugal. Note that every pattern has a small flaw – a sure indication that the artists were Muslim, for only Allah can be perfect.

The rest of the spaces are devoted to housing the eclectic collection of the Beja Regional Museum. This includes a very fine Mudéjar brick screen from the Paço dos Infantes, a palace commissioned by Dom Manuel I in the 1480s when he was the Duke of Beja. Its fusion of Islamic and Western motifs anticipates the Manueline style, which would be named after the king. There's also some very fine Chinese porcelain bowls from the early 16th century, the escutcheons of assorted noble families, the Herdade da Abobada stone (carved with the mysterious script of the ancient Tartessian civilisation – see page 175), Iron and Bronze Age and Roman artefacts, and some very fine Dutch, Portuguese and Spanish paintings. These include a beautiful *Ecce Homo*, a fine early Portuguese *São Vicente* and a portrait of St Jerome holding a skull, attributed to the great Valencian painter and (probable) disciple of Caravaggio, José de Ribera, who together with Zurbarán introduced the Tenebrist (extreme chiaroscuro) style into Iberia.

### Igreja de Santo Amaro e o Núcleo Visigótico (Church of Santo Amaro and the Visigoth Museum) (*Largo de Santo Amaro;* \ *284 321465; www. museuregionaldebeja.net;* ☉ *14.00–17.00 Tue, 09.45–12.30 & 14.00–17.00 Wed– Sun; admission €2*) Beja is regarded as the Visigoth capital of Portugal and is the only town which preserves more than a few remains from the period when Rome had collapsed and Iberia was ruled by Germanic tribes. The Visigoths were the great Germanic tribe who sacked Rome in 410 under King Alaric I. After years of wandering and an attempt to establish a kingdom in Toulouse, they settled in Spain and Portugal in the 5th century. In the late 6th century they converted to Christianity and ruled Iberia for a further hundred years until they were forced to retreat into Asturias after the Berber Muslim invasions of the early 8th century.

Precious few Visigoth churches have survived the Moors and the Crusaders – they remain only in Barcelona, Burgos, Palencia and Ourense in Spain, and in Braga and Nazaré in Portugal. And while Santo Amaro is much altered, it remains at heart a Visigoth church, with characteristic barrel vaulting and low Corinthian columns of a uniquely Visigothic design. It is now home to Portugal's greatest collection of Visigoth art and artefacts. Sadly this amounts to little more than crumbling columns and bits of fragmented carving, but it offers an intriguing glimpse of a civilisation of which we know very little, despite it being the only empire (other than the Roman) to conquer and occupy the whole of Iberia.

### Castelo de Beja (Beja Castle) (*Free admission; tower open to visitors on request – ask in the tourist office*) Dominated by the 40m-high Torre de Menagem tower, Beja's heavyset castle was adapted from an Iron Age fort, a Roman *castrum* and a Moorish

castle. It is probably the oldest castle keep in Iberia. The castle was first constructed by Dom Afonso III shortly after Beja was taken from the Moors in the mid 13th century. Dom Dinis expanded it and João I added the horseshoe arch windows, an interesting fusion of Mudéjar and Mannerist, with exaggerated springers almost meeting beneath the three-quarter circle of the arch and the rectangular opening below.

The castle is best seen from the gardens, which lie immediately outside the ramparts to the north. There's little to see in the castle itself other than an impressive octagonal ogival vault (in the second chamber) and the Casa do Governador, the house once occupied by the *alcaide* and ostensibly built on the orders of King João II to receive his son Afonso on his honeymoon. It now hosts the tourist office and galleries devoted to temporary exhibitions.

### Catedral de São Tiago (Beja Cathedral) (*Sé de Beja, Largo de Lidador s/n;* ⊕ *09.30–12.30 & 14.00–17.30 Tue–Sun; free admission*) The mannerist-Baroque cathedral church of São Tiago next to the castle is worth a brief look-in to see the 18th-century *azulejos* and marble carvings, many of which were recuperated from defunct churches and palaces in Lisbon. Down the hill from the castle is the strangely shaped Mudéjar Hermitage of Santo André (*Rua de Lisboa s/n;* ⊕ *09.30–12.30 & 14.00–17.30 Tue–Sun; free admission*) built – as legend has it – by Dom Sancho I after Beja was taken from the Moors for the first time in 1162, but in reality a 15th-century Gothic-Mudéjar pastiche probably commissioned by Dom Manuel I when he was Duke of Beja. Inside are some remnant 15th-century murals, a Manueline fresco showing the martyrdom of Santo André and some very old *azulejos* rescued from the demolished Convent of Santa Clara.

### Núcleo Museológico da Rua do Sembrano (Rua do Sembrano Museum Centre) (*Rua do Sembrano/Largo de São João;* ✆ *284 311920;* ⊕ *09.30–12.30 & 14.00–18.00 Tue–Sun; free admission*) Take a free guided tour through this small museum and see Beja's long history literally underfoot. Artefacts and archaeological remains recovered through digs on the site are displayed in cabinets and under a floor-level glass case, and include items from prehistoric, Roman, Moorish and Christian eras. Other spaces are devoted to temporary exhibitions.

### Museu Episcopal de Beja e Igreja de Nossa Senhora dos Prazeres de Beja (Episcopal Museum and the Church of Our Lady) (*Largo dos Prazeres 4;* ✆ *284 320918; www.diocese-beja.pt;* ⊕ *10.00–12.30 & 14.30–18.00 Wed–Sun; admission €1.50*) The Museu Episcopal was founded in 1892 to preserve priceless religious objects, sculpture, painting and vestments gleaned from the numerous convents and religious houses that had been vacated after the expulsion of the religious orders under the Marquess of Pombal. The best way to unlock their secrets and places of origin is to take a guided tour (pre-organised through the museum).

The church itself is a very fine Golden Age church dating from the 17th century and enriched with *azulejos*, fabulous gilt woodcarvings (by João de Touro Freitas, Antonio de Oliveira and others), murals and canvases (by Antonio de Oliveira, Pedro Figueira and João Pereira Pagado) and *azulejos* (by Gabriel del Barco). These are devoted to Our Lady and associated with a miracle she performed as patroness of the church. Her life is depicted through the Seven Joys (*Sete Prazeres*) and the Seven Sorrows (*Sete Dores*) of Mary, which you can follow. The Joys are the Annunciation, the Nativity of Jesus, the Adoration of the Magi, the Resurrection of Christ, the Ascension of Christ to Heaven, the Descent of the Holy Spirit upon the Apostles and the Coronation of the Virgin in Heaven, and the Sorrows are the Prophecy of

Simeon, the Flight into Egypt, the loss of the child Jesus in the Temple, Jesus on the way to Calvary, Jesus's death, the piercing of the side of Jesus, Mary receiving the body of Jesus in her arms (*pietà*) and the body of Jesus being placed in the tomb.

**Museu Jorge Vieira (Jorge Vieira Museum)** (*Rua do Touro;* ☏ *284 311920;* ⏱ *09.30–12.30 & 14.00–18.00 Tue–Sun; free admission*) This small museum houses a collection of work by the Lisbon-born Portuguese sculptor Jorge Vieira. While not well known outside Portugal, Vieira (1922–1998), who studied at the Slade in London under Henry Moore and has exhibited at the Tate Modern, is responsible for many public sculptures across his home country, including perhaps most famously the huge statue of *HomemSol* ('Sun-Man') in the Parque das Nações in Lisbon and Monumento ao Prisioneiro Político Desconhecido (Monument to the Unknown Prisoner) on the large roundabout at the entrance to Beja. This museum gives the visitors the chance to see some of his smaller pieces, which are playful and quirky and include delightfully expressive animal and anthropomorphic figurines.

**Roman Villa, Pisões** (*Penedo Gordo, 10km southeast of Beja;* ☏ *266 769450; visits with prior booking only – most easily done through Beja tourist office*) The Roman Villa at Pisões, which is Beja's most significant Roman ruin, looks unimpressive above ground level – a mere jumble of walls and crumbling masonry. They stretch over a large area, indicating that Pisões was the home of an influential Roman citizen. The villa's underfloor heating and sewer system are well-preserved and the peristyle and some of the 40 or so rooms show the fragmented remains of Roman mosaics, featuring a fish and an eel, as well as geometric floral and knot patterns of some intricacy and beauty.

## ALVITO, CUBA AND THE ROAD TO ÉVORA

The E802 and N258 roads running between Beja and Évora have a few places worth stopping off at *en route* and one of the finest hotels and restaurants in the Baixo.

The town of **Cuba**, 21km north of Beja, probably gave its name to the Caribbean island. At least, this is the case according to many Portuguese academics, including the historian José Barreto, who claims that Columbus was from this tiny village, pointing out that it was he who named Cuba, that Columbus uses the words 'my homeland' to refer to Portugal and that contemporaneous court documents refer to his Portuguese origin. The village agrees. A statue honouring Columbus as a local stands in the town square, looking moodily to a distant horizon, and a plaque explains his origins as the son of the duke of Beja and a local woman, proclaiming that his true name was Salvador Fernandes Zarco.

Continue 3km to the north of Cuba to reach the village of Vila de Frades at the crossroads of the N258 Évora road. Turning east here will take you to **Vidigueira**, the town over which Vasco da Gama was appointed count by Dom Manuel I in 1519 after his return from the East, and where Baruch Spinoza's father Miguel, a Sephardi Portuguese Jew, was born and briefly lived before fleeing to Holland from the Portuguese Inquisition in the early 17th century. Spinoza himself was born Benedito de Espinosa in Amsterdam. His ideas led to him being expelled from Jewish society (after being issued a *cherem*) and excommunicated from the Catholic Church. There's a statue to da Gama in the main *praça* and a ruined castle, but little else to see.

Far more interesting is the **Igreja da Vera Cruz** (Veracruz; ⏱ officially 10.00–13.00 & 14.00–18.00 Apr–Sep & 9.30–13.00 & 14.00–17.30 Oct–Mar, although times are not always adhered to; free admission) in the tiny village of Vera Cruz some 10km east of Vidigueira. The church is said to preserve a piece of Christ's cross. The cross itself was reputedly made from wood cut from the Tree of Life which grew in the Garden of Eden. Discovered in the 4th century by Empress Saint Helena after a vision she experienced while on a pilgrimage to Israel, the relics were kept by her son, the Roman emperor Constantine. When Constantinople was sacked by the Saracens, the cross was divided up and sent to different corners of Christendom. This particular piece is still carried around the streets in an annual procession and is said by locals to be used for exorcisms. It's one of four such pieces held in Portuguese churches, and one of many preserved in Europe and the Middle East. Calvin once remarked that 'if we were to collect all these pieces of the True Cross exhibited in various parts, they would form a whole ship's cargo'.

A left turn (west) on to the N258 Évora road at Vila de Frades takes you, after a few kilometres, to the **Roman ruins of the Villa of Áulica and the Convento de São Cucufate (Convent of St Cucuphas)** (⏰ *14.30–18.30 Tue & 10.00–12.30 & 14.30–18.30 Wed–Sun, closes at 17.30 in winter; admission €2*), dating from the 1st century AD and with a villa built in several stages, surrounded by ancillary buildings which once housed grain stores, olive oil presses and servants' quarters. The buildings were occupied over the following centuries, and were at one time used to house a friary. Traces of the medieval frescoes remain. The surrounding meadow landscape is very pretty.

Some 8km west of here is a turning north to the village of **Vila Ruiva**, 3km outside of which is one of the largest Roman bridges in Portugal, spanning 100m over the Ribeira de Odivelas seasonal river. It too dates from the 1st century AD and is one of the few remaining stretches of the old Roman road that connected Beja with Évora.

Back on the N258 and some 7km west of Vila Ruiva is the tiny village of **Alvito**, almost exactly halfway between Beja and Évora and the last village in the Baixo Alentejo. It is replete with pretty Manueline buildings and dominated by a handsome castle, which is now one of Portugal's *pousadas*. In its heyday Alvito was an influential town, founded by Afonso III's chancellor. It was later donated by King João I to one of the most illustrious of his knights, Diogo Lobo, who had distinguished himself in battle and was rewarded by becoming Portugal's first baron, the Baron of Alvito. Like Serpa and Beja, it prospered in the Portuguese Golden Age, when the castle received its Manueline flourishes and many of the Manueline buildings that dot the old centre were built. The castle-*pousada* is the best place for a stay on this route between Beja and Évora (see below) and its restaurant is open for lunch and dinner. Also worth a quick glance are the Hermitage of São Sebastião (whose modest Mudéjar exterior hides some handsome 16th-century frescoes) and the bizarrely stunted fortified church of Nossa Senhora da Assunção.

**GETTING THERE AND AWAY** Bus line 8146 calls at Cuba, Vila Ruiva and Alvito, then continues on to Viana do Alentejo and Évora. Bus line 8232 runs between Beja and Alvito via Cuba and Vila Ruiva. Ask the bus driver to let you off either line at the turn-off to Vila de Frades or São Cucufate. Unless you're prepared to walk or hitch, reaching Ribeira de Odivelas without your own transport is a challenge.

 **WHERE TO STAY, EAT AND DRINK**

**Pousada de Alvito** (20 rooms) Alvito; 284 480700; www.pestana.com. The castle home of the Alvito barons, who were long-favoured by the Portuguese monarchs, is a wonderfully romantic mix of Mudéjar, Manueline, Gothic and modern. Interiors are decorated with priceless antiques from the estate of the House of Bragança, & the *pousada* sits in gardens designed by Gonçalo Ribeiro Telles, Portugal's first post-Salazar secretary of state for the environment, &

later a landscape architect & the winner of the International Federation of Landscape Architects' prestigious Sir Geoffrey Jellicoe Award in 2013. The restaurant (⏰ 13.00–15.00 & 19.30–22.00 daily; €€€) is one of the best in the Baixo Alentejo

serving contemporary Portuguese & regional cuisine, inc *sopa de tomate à alentejana, lombinhos de porco preto com migas de coentro, bacalhau* & the delicious chocolate cake made to a local recipe. €€€€

## VIANA DO ALENTEJO

With a fabulous castle (incorporating one of Alentejo's most striking Manueline buildings) and an interesting Baroque church, this little town merits a short stopover *en route* between Beja and Évora.

**HISTORY** The town was an important early Christian centre with a strong Marian cult. It grew under the Romans as it lay at a crossroads on the trade routes running to and from Roman Ebora (Évora), Pax Iulia (Beja) and Salacia (Alcácer do Sul), but was subordinate to neighbouring Alcáçovas under the Moors. Viana grew after the Reconquest, and was given to one of Dom Afonso's loyal knights, Gil Martins, and subsequently inherited by his son, the Count of Barcelos, who elevated Viana to aristocratic status. The castle was built under Dom Dinis and expanded into the current fortification under Dom Manuel I, after which it became a frequent royal stopover on rides between Évora and Beja.

### GETTING THERE AND AWAY
**By car** Viana, which is officially in the district of Évora, lies 10km north of Alvito, and 32km south of Évora.

**By bus** Bus lines 8052 and 8146 connect Viana with Évora on weekdays, while bus line 8146 connects Viana with Cuba, Alvito, Vila Ruiva and Évora, also on weekdays.

**TOURIST INFORMATION** There's a welcoming tourist information office in the castle, with a gift shop next door (📞 266 930012; ⏰ *Apr–Sep 10.00–13.00 & 14.00–18.00 & Oct–Mar 9.30–13.00 & 14.00–17.30*).

**WHERE TO STAY** The most comfortable rooms, and the best restaurant in the area, are at the Pousada de Alvito (see pages 162–3).

🏠 **Casa de Viana do Alentejo** (5 rooms) Rua Cândido dos Reis 1; 📞 266 953500. Sitting in a Renaissance townhouse with bags of character, this friendly, family-run guesthouse is in the heart of the old town, a stone's throw from the castle. Rooms have little more than a wrought iron bed & a desk but are bright & airy, & the rooftop terrace has good views of the castle & churches. Hearty b/fast. No after-hours service – be sure to arrive early. €€€

🏠 **Monte da Moirana** (4 rooms) Herdade do Barão, Vila Nova da Baronia; 📞 214 142832; www.montedamoirana.net. Cosy duplex family rooms, apartments & dbls in a converted farmhouse with its own flower gardens, in the countryside halfway between Alvito & Viana (both are around 5km away). Swimming pool, warm, personalised service (with help organising excursions to all the sights in the area), bike hire, walks & lots of cats. €€€

### WHAT TO SEE AND DO
**Castelo de Viana do Alentejo e Igreja Matriz (Castle and main church)** (📞 266 930012; ⏰ *Apr–Sep 10.00–13.00 & 14.00–18.00 & Oct–Mar 09.30–13.00 & 14.00–17.30; free admission*) Pentagonal, decorated with Knights Templar symbols

and built by the architect who designed that order's headquarters at Tomar, Viana's castle is a conspiracy theorist's architectural dream. It's fabulously photogenic – rugged and ruddy brown with deep crenellations running to unusual round turrets at each corner. An arched doorway leads to a series of old palace buildings inside (where you'll find a gift shop and the tourist office) and the **Igreja Matriz de Nossa Senhora da Anunciação**, a bone-white church topped with Mudéjar pineapple-top pinnacles. Be sure to see the Manueline door, divided by an elegant mullion and topped with carved ropes and seaweed, armillary spheres and the cross of the Knights Templar. There are faded frescoes inside and 16th century reredos altarpieces. The building is attributed to Diogo de Arruda (see box, page 28), the great Manueline Templar architect and sculptor who also worked on the castle of Evoramonte (page 101) and who with his brother Francisco designed more buildings that have subsequently become UNESCO World Heritage Sites than any other architect in the world.

### Sanctuário Nossa Senhora d'Aires (Shrine of Our Lady of Aires) (*On the outskirts of town in the suburb of Aires, 2km northeast of the castle;* ⊕ *10.00–13.00 & 14.00–18.00; free admission*) This grand Baroque edifice looks almost out of place in little Viana. The architect, Father João Baptista, built it in honour of Our Lady of Piety, the former patron saint of Portugal (she has now been superseded by herself as Our Lady of Fátima and the Immaculate Conception). Our Lady of Piety has been venerated in Viana since pre-Roman times, and a *pietà* in the church is associated with a legend that those who pray to her for succour in the sanctuary always have their prayers answered – as the thousands of votive plaques seem to attest. A procession around the church takes place on the fourth Sunday in September, during Viana's Aires festival.

The sanctuary itself is opulent, replete with Estremoz marble, decorated with *scagliola*, stucco, *azulejos* and mural paintings, and with a huge gilt carved reredos altarpiece with the *pietà* statue at its heart, enclosed in a glass-fronted casket.

### Igreja da Misericórdia (Church of Our Lady of Mercy) (*Largo de São Luís s/n*) Often overlooked by visitors, this beautiful church has a modest Manueline exterior, which hides one of the most impressive interiors in the Alentejo, covered wall to exquisitely painted Baroque ceiling with 16th- and 17th-century *azulejos*. The rear of the nave is flanked with twin magnificent Rococo organs of unknown provenance.

### Alcáçovas The village of Alcáçovas, some 18km from Viana do Alentejo, has an interesting little 15th-century church, the Igreja de Nossa Senhora da Conceição, which is covered in seashells.

## SERPA

The southern Alentejo's most obviously Moorish town sits under a baking summer sun where the expansive southern Alentejo plain meets gently undulating hills. It's a tiny, very pretty town whose streets are barely alleys, laced together in an organic labyrinth of whitewash and cobbled stone, lined with shutters, flowerboxes, gossiping locals and tiny cafés. Bring your sunglasses, for in the noonday sun the old centre – behind the massive ramparts of the Moorish and Crusader walls – is literally dazzling. Serpa competes in an annual 'Rua Mais Branca' competition (look out for the signs as you wander) and is said to be Portugal's whitest town. It's a good alternative to Mértola or Beja as a place to find your base in the southern Alentejo

– sleepy, secluded and very local. What activity there is centres on the castle, set in a stately square at the top of the town, with views out over roofs and turrets to the shimmering heat haze on the horizon, and around the Praça da República, where there's a cluster of bell-towers and administrative buildings and a sprinkling of restaurants and cafés.

The hills and flatlands around Serpa are cut by the limpid Guadiana River, which drifts into the Vale do Guadiana Natural Park to the south. This semi-wild area is surrounded by hectares of vineyards, orchards and wheat fields. As elsewhere in the Alentejo these were once administered by luxurious but cruel *latifundo* country estates, some of whose great houses are now good hotels, devoted to exploring rather than exploiting the beautiful surrounding countryside.

**HISTORY**   Serpa began life as a minor Roman settlement and grew into a town under the Moors. Huddling behind its enormous ramparts, it withstood the Reconquest until 1232, after which it became part of Castile rather than Portugal. It was ceded to Dom Dinis, who in 1295 made it formally a town, crowning it with one of his myriad Alentejan castles.

Serpa's most famous child, Dom Manuel I, was born here in the early 16th century, when Serpa had risen to become one of the most important market towns in the southern Alentejo, exploiting its position on the Seville–Lisbon road and its proximity to the border. Merchants from Spain and Portugal came here to trade woollen garments, iron tools, arts and crafts, dairy products and – once all the Moors had been used up – slaves from the Sahel. In the 16th century Serpa municipality was responsible for an astonishing 27% of Portuguese GDP.

Military pressure in the late 17th century turned Serpa into a strategic frontier town that became increasingly important as a military outpost, watching cautiously across the border into Spain – a mini Elvas to Beja's Évora. It played an active role in the Portuguese Restoration War (1640–1668), the War of Spanish Succession (1701–14) and the Napoleonic campaigns of the Peninsular War (1801–1814).

After the 18th century power in Serpa – as in much of the lower Alentejo – became increasingly concentrated in the hands of the aristocratic *latifundario* landholders, whose serfs struggled under debt peonage. Money earned from their near slave labour was concentrated in aristocratic hands and spent outside the region in Lisbon or beyond, resulting in a wave of chronic underdevelopment (of both land and people) and cultural and educational isolation, whose ripples are felt in Serpa's relative poverty today.

## GETTING THERE AND AWAY
**By car**   Serpa lies just 29km east of Beja on the IP8/N260 motorway. The Spanish border is just over 10km further east. It is possible to drive into the historic centre, but it is not advisable. Streets are very narrow and there's a complex one-way system. There's plenty of parking outside the main castle gates.

**By bus**   The bus station (*terminal rodoviário; Praça António Raposo Tavares 284;* ✆ *284 313620*) is 2km south of the centre and can be reached by walking along Avenida da Paz. Buses run to Lisbon (*4 daily, 3½–4hrs*) and Beja (*3 daily, 35mins*). Bus lines 8607pe and 8607pne run between Beja and Moura via Serpa on weekdays only. For more information see www.rede-expressos.pt and www.rodalentejo.pt.

**TOURIST INFORMATION**   There is a posto de turismo at Rua dos Cavalos 19 (✆ *284 544727;* ⊕ *Apr–Sep 10.00–19.00, Oct–Mar 09.00–18.00 daily*).

## ⌂ WHERE TO STAY

See also the *Where to stay* sections for Beja (page 156) and Parque Natural do Vale do Guadiana (page 172), both of which are under 20 minutes' drive away.

⌂ **Herdade do Vau** (11 rooms) Lugar Monte do Vau, Quintos; ☏ 226 199800; www. herdadedovau.com. Situated close to the Pulo do Lobo falls on the Guadiana River some 10km southwest of Serpa, this is one of the best winery hotels in the Alentejo, with a superb set of grape varieties & vintages & rooms in an old country estate house perfumed by its own herb garden & set in rolling meadows, cork oak woods & vineyards 10mins' drive from Serpa. Activities include bird- & wildlife watching in the Parque Natural do Vale do Guadiana, visits to Beja, Serpa & Mértola, ballooning & excellent wine tours. €€€€

⌂ **Casa da Muralha** (4 rooms) Rua das Portas de Beja 43; ☏ 284 543150; www.casadamuralha. com. In one of the best locations in Serpa, this modest guesthouse sits in a historic building abutting the aqueduct right next to the main Beja gate (making it a stroll from the car parking area & the castle & palaces). Rooms are set around an attractive inner courtyard with orange & lemon trees, & the nicest have views of the aqueduct. The owners organise sports fishing, kayaking on the Guadiana River & visits to the natural park. Generous b/fasts. Best deals through online booking engines. €€€

⌂ **Herdade da Retorta** (5 rooms) Monte da Retorta Apartado 59; ☏ 284 544774; www.

herdade-da-retorta.pt. A gorgeous country house hotel run by the warm & welcoming Dona Gabriela & her husband Carlos, & set in countryside just outside the town. Rooms are simple but elegant – lovely raw wood floors & antique furniture, big, bright windows & quality linens. B/fast is excellent, there's a pool, snooker & table tennis, & Dona Gabriela offers a whole host of activities inc country walks, visits to the nearby Parque Natural do Vale do Guadiana, the Pulo do Lobo waterfall & Serpa itself, paintball & archery. €€€

⌂ **Casa de Serpa** (6 rooms) Largo do Salvador 28; ☏ 963 560624; www.casadeserpa.com. Small, family-run B&B in the heart of historic Serpa near the Igreja do Salvador, with a variety of rooms (the best are bright & airy, the worst have no windows), an attractive back patio & public areas where you can relax with a chilled drink & a book. Bike rental & helpful staff. €€

⌂ **Residencial & Apartamentos Beatriz** (14 rooms) Travessa do Salvador s/n; ☏ 284 544423; www.residencialbeatriz.com. Simple 2-bedroom apartments (in a separate building on the Largo do Salvador 2mins' walk away) & rooms in a whitewashed family townhouse near the Igreja do Salvador right in the town centre. The upper floors have views out over a clutter of roofs to the castle. €€

## ✗ WHERE TO EAT AND DRINK

✗ **A Tradição** Rua Alameda Abade Correia da Serra 14; ☏ 934 238295; www.cm-serpa.pt; ⊕ 12.30–15.00 & 19.30–22.30 Tue–Sat. With a different menu of Alentejo & traditional Portuguese dishes every day, it's hard to recommend a particular dish at this friendly, family-run eatery. Alentejo black pig is almost always on the menu, however, & the restaurant has excellent seasonal game. €€

✗ **Pedra de Sal,** Estrada Circunvalação s/n; ☏ 284 241029; www.restaurantepedradesal.pai.pt; ⊕ noon–15.00 & 19.00–23.00 Tue–Sat. Alentejo & Portuguese dishes & meat grills served in a rustic old farmhouse restaurant, either indoors in the old farm buildings or outside on the bamboo-shaded patio. €€

✗ **Casa Paixão** Praça da República s/n; ☏ 284 544152; ⊕ 09.00–12.30 & 15.00–18.00 daily. Serpa's best café, serving delicious pastries, cakes, ice cream & snacks. Great for a light lunch. €

✗ **Cervejaria Lebrinha** Morada Rua do Calvário 6/8; ☏ 284 549311; ⊕ noon–15.00 & 19.00–23.00 Tue–Sat. This modest little streetside café-bar with formica tables & *azulejos* on the walls serves wonderful, very cold draught Imperial beer which is famous throughout the region, & a menu of excellent *petiscos* & comfort meals, inc octopus salad, black Alentejo pork, the famous local Serpa cheeses & the regional variety of *queijadas*. €

**SHOPPING** Serpa is famous throughout Portugal for its full-flavoured hard sheep's milk cheeses, which taste a little like Spain's famous Manchego, matured over around four months and protected under European Union law as PDO (protected designation of origin) – like Stilton, Champagne and Cognac. Serpa cheeses can be bought everywhere from local grocers to cafés, including at Janeirinho e Filho grocers (*Rua das Portas de Beja 27;* ☏ *284 549182*). The best are officially accredited by the Associação de Criadores de Ovinos do Sul (ACOS). Look for the indication on the label.

**WHAT TO SEE AND DO**   Serpa is a town to wander through. Abandon the car on the Rua dos Arcos (where there is ample parking) and enter through the western Porta de Beja gate. There's a terrific view here. Bisected by an aqueduct, the town's massive walls meet at twin 13th-century turrets, which frame a narrow gate. Through this is a view of a winding alley lined with icing-sugar-white houses and climbing into the old town. Outside the wall a little lawned park is dotted with withered olive trees as old as modern Europe, and when cars aren't passing behind you, the air is so still and quiet that you can hear the chirrup of swifts and swallows as they swoop and whirligig around the crenellations and over the cobbled stone.

In its present form, the aqueduct dates from the 17th century, when it was built to bring water not to the town itself but to the Baroque palace of the Ficalho counts (a title originally created for Philip II of Spain; the palace is not open to the public). Its origins are far older – perhaps dating from Roman times, and at its southern end the structure is straddled by an ancient *nora* or Arabic chain pump, probably dating from the 11th century.

**Castelo de Serpa (Serpa Castle)**   (*free admission*) Streets climb up the low hill from the Porta de Beja to the ungainly and undistinguished Igreja Matriz de Nossa Senhora da Assunção and the castle. The entrance is a little to the west of the church. A giant block of battlement perches precipitously above it, looking as though it might fall down at any moment. It's been there since 1707, however, when the walls were blown up by the Duke of Ossuna in the War of the Oranges. The interior of the castle is little more than a shell, overlooked by a 14th-century tower of obvious Moorish origin, capped by an incongruous bell-gable and equally incongruous clock.

**Serpa's museums**   Serpa has a few small of museums of interest. The **Museu Etnografico (Ethnographic Museum)** (*Largo do Corro s/n;* ☏ *284 549130;* ⊕ *09.00– 12.30 & 14.00–17.30 Tue–Sun; free admission*), housed in the old municipal market, uses old tools, clothing and panel displays to celebrate country crafts and trades slowly dying out. It tells the story of daily rural life in the Alentejo from the point of view of those who grew the crops, tilled the land, shoed the horses and built the buildings.

The **Museu do Relógio (Clock Museum)** (*Convento do Mosteirinho, Rua do Assento;* ☏ *284 543194; www.museudorelogio.com;* ⊕ *14.00–17.00 Tue–Fri, 10.00– 17.00 Sat & Sun; admission €2*) is the sister museum to Évora's and showcases timepieces from the early 17th century to the present day. It includes precious and rare carriage clocks from Napoleonic France, cuckoo clocks and fashionable 20th-century wrist watches collected by Serpa local António Tavares d'Almeida.

At the time of writing, the town's **archaeological museum** (with a collection covering prehistoric to Renaissance times) was closed for refurbishment.

# MOURA

In the far north of the Baixo Alentejo, a stone's throw from the huge (and controversial) Alqueva reservoir and set on the back road between Serpa and

Monsaraz, Moura is a typical Baixo Alentejo town of white alleyways winding around a central castle keep. Its name reputedly comes from a Moorish girl (or *moura* in Portuguese), the princess Salúquia, who was the daughter of the 12th-century *alcaide* of Al-Manijah, as the town was named before the Reconquest.

Salúquia was betrothed to Brafma, the *alcaide* of neighbouring Aroche. Riding to meet her on her wedding day, Brafma was intercepted by Crusader knights and killed. The knights then dressed in the Moorish robes of Brafma's party and continued in his place to Moura. Thinking that her fiancée had arrived, Salúquia opened the gates to the city, only to have it conquered by the Crusaders. In despair she threw herself from the castle tower.

On hearing of her tragic story the Christian conquerors reputedly named the town *Terra da Moura Salúquia*, which over time was shortened to Moura. The dead princess is pictured (fallen at the feet of the castle keep) on the city's coat of arms to this day.

Modern Moura is a pleasant little town which retains vestiges of its Arab past in the castle, the old Moorish quarter, and the municipal museum, which preserves a number of interesting Moorish artefacts.

## GETTING THERE AND AWAY

**By car** Moura lies at the junction of the N255 (the Serpa–Reguengos de Monsaraz road) and the N258, which runs between Évora and the Spanish border. The Rio Guadiana and the Alqueva Lake are 2km north. Distances are as follows: Évora 78km, Lisbon 210km, Serpa 31km, Beja 60km, Monsaraz 52km and Elvas 114km.

**By bus** There is one daily Rede Expressos bus to Lisbon via Évora (*4hrs*). Bus lines 8607pe and 8607pne run between Beja and Moura via Serpa. For more information see www.rede-expressos.pt and www.rodalentejo.pt

**TOURIST INFORMATION** The tourist information office is in the castle (\ *285 251375;* ⊕ *09.00–12.30 & 14.00–17.30 Mon–Fri & 09.30–13.00 & 14.30–18.00 Sat & Sun*).

**WHAT TO SEE AND DO** Salúquia's **castle** (*Calçada do Castelo;* ⊕ *Jul–Aug 10.00–midnight, Sep–Jun 10.00–18.00 daily; free admission*) still stands, albeit having changed greatly over the centuries. The tower from which the princess reputedly threw herself is called the Torre de Salúquia to this day, and you can climb it for views out over the modern town and surrounding plains. Look out for traces of painted ashlars and a stone commemorating the construction of a minaret by al-Mu'tadid in the mid 11th century. The mosque was situated next to the tower before it was demolished by the conquerors.

Moura's **Museu Municipal (Municipal Museum)** (*Rua de Romeira 19;* \ *285 250400;* ⊕ *09.30–12.30 & 14.30–17.30 Tue–Fri, 10.00–noon & 14.00–16.00; free admission*) has an interesting collection of Islamic pieces including an old Arabic well and a chest made of bones.

There's little else to see in Moura, other perhaps than the narrow streets of the old Moorish quarter, the ornamented Manueline door to the **Igreja de São João Batista (Church of St John the Baptist)** (both immediately in front of the castle) and the small **Museu do Azeite (Olive Oil Museum)** (*Praça Sacadura Cabral;* \ *285 250400;* ⊕ *09.00–18.00 Mon–Fri*), which shows how olive oil was once made using wooden presses and huge terracotta jars.

The **Herdade da Contenda** (*Rua Fonte de Aroche s/n, Santo Aleixo da Restauração;* \ *285 965421; www.herdadedacontenda.pt*) near Moura is an important conservation area for wildlife. It is one of the biological corridors for the critically endangered Iberian lynx (see box, page 171) and in 2015 became the first nesting site for the rare Eurasian black vulture in nearly half a century. Visits must be organised in advance.

## Around Moura

*Castelo de Noudar (Noudar Castle)* This ruined Moorish castle is dramatically perched on a rocky hill between the Ardila (which marks the border with Spain) and Múrtega rivers, where they meet to form a single watercourse some 42km east of Moura. The ruins are wonderfully atmospheric and seldom visited, comprising a crumbling walled enclosure covered in grass and flower meadows and extending nearly 13,000m² over the top of the hill. While a Christian citadel occupied the site after the Reconquest, Noudar retains many of its original Moorish features. Access is from the village of Barrancos.

*Lago de Alqueva (Alqueva Lake)* When the vast Alqueva hydroelectric dam opened in 2002 just a few kilometres north of Moura it was the largest in Europe and one of the most controversial. Some 30 environmental protestors dressed in Portuguese mourning clothes and carrying a white elephant paraded as the turbines were switched on, angry at the destruction of a string of villages, wildlife habitats, rocks covered with prehistoric art and a Roman fort. The dam currently provides some 520 megawatts of electricity and irrigates thousands of hectares of arid Alentejo land. The lake has now flooded to become the largest artificial body of water in Europe. Environmentally, at least, it has not been the unmitigated disaster that was forecast by some. It literally teems with fish – throw a breadcrumb into the shallows to see. While habitats further downstream have been damaged by increased aridity, the lake itself has become something of a haven for aquatic life and waterfowl, with healthy stocks of fish, populations of otter and other aquatic mammals and of rare amphibians including the IUCN red-listed gold-stripe salamander. Bird species that were predicted to disappear from the area largely haven't (raptor numbers have if anything increased) and pollution from rotting submerged vegetation has not so far been a major problem. But it's not all good news. Many of the river fish associated with the Guadiana River do not do well in the lake environment of Alqueva, and the reservoir is increasingly a home to invasive species including aggressive fish like pikeperch and European catfish, as well as American crayfish, all of which can damage delicate populations of local wildlife, especially amphibians.

**Getting around and tour operators** Visitors can rent jet skis, water skis and houseboats (complete with GPS and sonar) through the **Amieira Marina** (✆ 266 611173; www.amieiramarina.com) for cruising, fishing and kayaking on the lake, stopping off in the little towns that fringe its shores like Mourão, Juromenha and Aldeia da Luz and in Spain, mooring at the jetties and sleeping under some of the starriest skies in Europe.

**Alqueva Aventura** ✆ 966 482734; www.alquevanatura.com. Nelson Monteiro organises kayaking & fishing on the lake & adventure activities (rock climbing, archery, orienteering) around Alqueva.

**Roteiro do Alqueva** www.roteirodoalqueva.com. Organises all manner of activities around the lake, inc houseboat rental, kayaking, horseback riding, balloon flights & sailing.

6

The southern Alentejo's largest natural park protects some 70,000 ha of wild woodland, semi-wild rural landscapes, meadows, swamp land and Mediterranean heath around the flood plain of the Guadiana River. The park abuts the Castro Verde Special Protection Area (SPA) and is almost contiguous with the artificially flooded Embalse del Andevalo lakes in Spain – the third largest stretch of lakeland in Andalucia.

The Guadiana is a land of extremes, with the highest temperatures and the lowest rainfall in Portugal. The landscape is unique – deep gorges, valleys cut by seasonal rivers, rocky hills and arid steppe are interspersed with man-made landscapes. The high temperatures have led to the colonisation of the area by dozens of aromatic plants, whose essential oils evaporate to protect them against loss of water, and in spring and summer the air is scented with wild rosemary, lavender, myrtle and thyme. Villages dot the park, and the town of Mértola (see pages 175–8) sits right in its centre.

The park and Castro Verde SPA are rich with flora and fauna and together form one of the best locations in Iberia for birdwatching. The flora is particularly beautiful in spring, when wild narcissus (*fernandesii*), oleander, African tamarisk and naked man orchid burst into bloom. And there are a number of rare, threatened and endangered floral species, including bee orchid and the four-leafed aquatic fern *Marsilea batardae*.

Thirteen of Portugal's 17 amphibian species and some 20 reptile species live in the park, among them two species of river turtle, the rare Bedriaga's skink (a little fast-moving brown lizard endemic to Iberia) and the near-threatened Iberian midwife toad, the male of whom carries as many as 180 eggs around with him, stuck to his legs, in search of a suitable body of water in which to deposit them. Mammals include genet, wildcat, garden dormouse and the world's rarest big cat, the Iberian lynx (see box, page 171).

The park is particularly rich in spectacular birds, with healthy numbers of blue rock thrush, Dartford, subalpine and spectacled warblers, rock sparrow and rock bunting to be found here, along with great spotted cuckoo, crag martin, crested tit and golden oriole. The Castro Verde SPA has one of western Europe's healthiest colonies of its biggest flying bird, the great bustard, together with little bustard, short-toed, booted and Bonelli's eagles, stone-curlew, great spotted cuckoo, European roller, European bee-eater, pallid swift, woodlark, short-toed, crested and Thekla larks, tawny pipit, crag martin, black-eared wheatear, rufous-tailed scrub robin, Cetti's, great reed and melodious warblers, woodchat and southern grey shrikes, golden oriole and Spanish sparrow, as well as the omnipresent azure-winged magpies and hoopoes.

Both areas have significant numbers of raptors. These include breeding populations of eagle owl, Bonelli's, Spanish imperial, booted and golden eagle, black-shouldered kite and – in Mértola – the last remaining urban colony of the IUCN red-listed lesser kestrel. Eurasian griffon vultures are regularly seen and in 2015, after an absence of 40 years, a pair of Eurasian black vultures nested just outside the park on an artificial platform established for them by the Liga para a Protecção da Natureza (LPN), a Portuguese conservation organisation.

**GETTING THERE AND AWAY** The only practical access to the park is with your own transport, on an organised tour or a self-guided walk. The park protects the Guadiana River as it runs towards Faro district in the south and the Spanish border to the east, and is cut by numerous small roads and trails. Many hotels can organise guided visits. Base yourselves in Beja, Serpa, Mértola or in the country hotels listed below for access.

**GETTING AROUND** Dozens of little minor roads, not all of them well signposted, run into the park. To reach specific points of interest you will often need to get off road on one of the dirt roads, but if you do so, be careful of hunters in the spring, summer and autumn, when the park is popular for shooting partridge, wild pigeon and boar.

**LOCAL TOUR OPERATORS** Most of the hotels in the park and a number in Serpa and Beja can organise visits (see also *Where to stay*, page 172).

**Algarve Birdwatching** 282 639418; m 912 824053; www.algarvebirdman.com. Manchester-born Algarve resident & professional birder Simon Wates organises wildlife-watching trips into the park either for the day or for several days. Book well ahead as he gets busy.
**Birds and Nature** Avenida do Brasil 112, 2º Dto, Lisbon; 913 299990; www.birds.pt. Bespoke &

pre-organised trips to the park, with or without other locations in Portugal & Spain.
**Visit Portugal Birdwatching** www.visitportugalbirdwatching.com (contact through the site only). Organised & tailor-made trips to Guadiana, some with renowned wildlife author, long-time birdwatcher & professional wildlife photographer Ray Tipper.

## THE IBERIAN LYNX

After the Amur leopard, the Iberian lynx is the most critically endangered big cat in the world. It's a beautiful animal, with a spotted coat, amber eyes and a face framed by black-tipped ears and long, cream-coloured side-whiskers. The lynx is a rabbit specialist. The arrival of myxomatosis in Iberia in 1953 decimated the rabbit population, and that of the lynx followed. In the 1950s there were about 4,000 Iberian lynx in Spain and Portugal, but today the wild population is between 200 and 300 cats. A scientific paper published in 2008 after a six-month study covering over 4,200km$^2$ of Portugal's wildest areas concluded that the lynx was extinct in Portugal. However, in July 2013 a lynx was photographed near Vila Nova de Milfontes. It was identified as a two-year-old male called Hongo, originally from the Doñana National Park in Spain. In December 2014 four lynx were introduced into a large fenced-off area of the Guadiana Natural Park after a National Pact for the Conservation of the Iberian Lynx was signed with some 20 landowners, researchers and non-governmental organisations. A further two were released in 2015, but the female was found dead a few months later after being poisoned, probably by partridge hunters worried about a loss to their game.

Numbers in Spain are gradually increasing, but the number of lynxes being killed on the roads has also soared. Cars are now the biggest threat to the lynx's survival. In 2014 22 lynxes were found dead by the roadside after collisions. The problem has been exacerbated by the economic crisis. According to Ramón Pérez de Ayala, species programme director at the WWF in Spain, the authorities have 'not even carried out the most basic road maintenance works'. It would cost around €6m to make roads safer for lynxes by setting up under-road passages, clearing bush land and providing barriers. For information on how to help protect the lynx see www.projectolynx.com and www.lpn.pt, the website of the Liga Para a Protecçao da Natureza (see ad, page 178).

6

**TOURIST INFORMATION**  Tourist offices in Beja, Serpa, Castro Verde and Mértola (see the town entries on pages 156, 165, 173 and 176) can provide information on what to see and do in the natural park and Castro Verde SPA, and hand out maps.

The Portuguese forestry commission, the **ICNF** (*Instituto da Conservação da Natureza e das Florestas; Avenida da República 16, Lisbon;* 213 507900; *www.icnf. pt;* 09.30–16.30 Mon–Fri) has detailed information on the park on its website (in Portuguese only).

The **Instituto Geográfico do Exército** (*IGEOE; Avenida Dr Alfredo Bensaúde, Lisbon;* 218 505 300; *www.igeoe.pt*) sells accurate scale maps for hiking for around €7 at its shop. The maps can be ordered through the post, although some of them are downloadable from the website.

**WHERE TO STAY**  See also *Beja* (page 156), *Castro Verde* (page 173), *Mértola* (pages 176–7) and *Serpa* (page 166), all of which have town and rural hotels with easy access to the Park, and some of which organise tours.

**Herdade da Malhadinha Nova**  (7 rooms) Albernoa; 284 965432; www.malhadinhanova. pt. One of the southern Alentejo's most luxurious countryside hotels, set in a *fazenda* surrounded by vineyards & cork oak woods on the banks of a tributary of the Guadiana River. It is 23km south of Beja, the same distance north of Castro Verde & just under 10km from the park. There's a good restaurant, a pool & spa, & the owners run a horse stud (offering all manner of horseback excursions) & produce first class wine. The huge menu of activities & themed breaks includes visits to the Vale do Guadiana, cooking classes for kids, wine tours, adventure sports & cultural tours of the region. The best rates can be found on the hotel website. €€€€€

**Herdade dos Grous**  (26 rooms) Albernoa; 284 960000; www.herdade-dos-grous.com. A stately 18th-century country house overlooking a lake & set in a 650ha country estate some 20km south of Beja & 10km from the natural park. The estate produces some of the southern Alentejo's best reds (Herdade dos Grous's Reserva red won the Oenologist Union of Alentejo's top award for 2006) & the owners can organise visits to the park, wine tours & horseback rides (they have their own stud). The hotel has a good restaurant, a large pool & tennis courts. €€€€€

**Herdade Monte da Apariça** (2 rooms) Castro Verde; 937 504089; www. montedaaparica.pt. Set in extensive wild grounds coloured with meadows & pocked with low lakes near the Castro Verde SPA, this beautiful country house turned hotel especially for wildlife lovers & birdwatchers is one of the Alentejo's best destinations for those who want to spend a few days devoted to seeing birds & small mammals. The owners are very knowledgeable about what to see, & when & where, & have full facilities for wildlife enthusiasts, inc scopes, hides & a library of books. They offer day & night tours around the extensive grounds & beyond, by foot, jeep or bicycle, & alongside wildlife watching there's kayaking, horseback riding & fishing on offer. €€€€

**Ecoland**  (4 rooms) Corte Gafo De Cima; 286 611111; www.ecoland.pt. Tucked away in a tiny village in the heart of the park, this rural home-turned-mock Moroccan hideaway has rooms painted in bright reds, blues, greens & oranges & decorated with Moroccan scenes & Arab art. The owners cook delicious berber & North African food (tagines, cous-cous & veggie options) & organise hiking, kayaking & biking trips into the surrounding Guadiana Park (to the Pulo do Lobo falls) & to Mértola & Mina de São Domingos. Peaceful & great value. €€

**WHERE TO EAT AND DRINK**

**Herdade dos Grous**  See above; Albernoa; 284 960000; www.herdade-dos-grous.com; 12.30–14.30 Mon–Sun & 19.30–21.30 Fri–Sun. Alentejo dishes like *lombinhos de porco preto* served with the excellent estate wines in a dining room overlooking vineyards & olive groves. €€€

**Restaurante da Malhadinha**  Herdade da Malhadinha Nova, Albernoa; 284 965432; www.

malhadinhanova.pt. Modern Portuguese cooking with a view out over sweeping countryside & dishes including *bochecha de porco preto* and cream of pea soup with quail's eggs & *presunto*. €€€

**WHAT TO SEE AND DO** The best way to see the park is to hire a guide through one of the tour operators or hotels listed, take to one of the lonelier roads or a trail and drink in the scenery. The Guadiana River is the focus of the park, and roads and dirt tracks run parallel to it out of Serpa (the Estrada de São Bráz) and Mértola (the road to Corte Gafo de Cima). The Pulo do Lobo (Wolf's Leap waterfalls, 37°48′14.83″N 7°38′0.82″W) on the Guadiana River are a set of fast rapids and cascades plunging through a rocky canyon. They can be reached by taking the CM1093 road which branches off the Estrada de São Bráz.

## CASTRO VERDE

This unremarkable but typical little Alentejan town of huddled whitewashed houses scattered across a low hill in softly undulating countryside is famous throughout the country for a decisive battle that made Portugal a nation, and for its summer fête, the Feira de Castro (see *Festivals*, page 51). It's worth a stopover for lunch and a wander in between Beja and the coast, or after a visit to see the great bustards and eagles in the adjacent Castro Verde Special Protection Area (pages 170–3).

### GETTING THERE AND AWAY
**By car** Castro Verde lies at the conjunction of strings of key roads. The IP1-A2 Lisbon–Faro motorway runs past the western edge of town. The IP2-N123 runs west to Ourique (then joins the N263 to Odemira and Vila Nova de Milfontes) and east to the Parque Natural Vale do Guadiana and Mértola. The E802 goes north to Beja, and the N2 runs south to Almodôvar and the Algarve at Faro. Distances are as follows: Lisbon 192km; Faro 80km; Beja 44km; Serpa 73km; Vila Nova de Milfontes 74km; Mértola 43km.

**By bus** There are Rede Expressos buses to Lisbon (*5 daily; 4½hrs*) and Beja (*4 daily; 40mins*), and local buses to Mértola. For more information and other destinations see www.rede-expressos.pt and www.rodalentejo.pt.

**GETTING AROUND** Castro Verde is a small town. The centre (around the huge Igreja Matriz and the Church of Nossa Senhora dos Remédios) is easily manageable on foot and there is ample parking.

**TOURIST INFORMATION** There is a *posto de turismo* on Rua Dom Afonso Henriques ( 286 328148; *www.cm-castroverde.pt*;  *09.00–12.30 & 14.00–17.30 Mon–Fri & 10.00–13.00 & 15.00–18.00 Sat & Sun*).

### WHERE TO STAY
🏠 **Equus Ourique** Rua de Castro da Cola, Fernão Vaz, Ourique; 965 392655; www.equusourique.com. One of the best places in Portugal for a horse riding holiday, with tailor-made luxury or economical riding holidays to suit all levels of rider, accommodation in self-catering holiday cottages surrounded by wooded countryside & full equestrian tuition on Lusitano or Portuguese Cruzado horses. The riding school is BHS-approved & offers riding and jumping up to and including BHSAI exam standard. The school is a member of the Association of British Riding Schools and its Portuguese equivalent, the FEP. €€€€€

## WHERE TO EAT AND DRINK

**✗ Castro Restaurante**  Rua Fialho de Almeida 1, Castro Verde; ✆ 286 322614. José Canário serves generous portions of regional dishes, seafood & grills, inc *bife a Castro*, a sumptuous

fillet of Alentejo beef steak served with potatoes, asparagus & a warm buttery sauce, & *migas* with asparagus, all washed down with fine Alentejo wine. €€

**WHAT TO SEE AND DO**  The **Igreja Matriz de Nossa Senhora da Conceição (Mother Church of Our Lady of the Immaculate Conception)** (*Praça do Municipio;* ⊕ *10.00– 13.00 & 14.00–18.00 Wed–Sun; admission €1*), Castro Verde's monumentally large parish church, has a gilt Baroque chancel, a small sacred art museum and some very fine 18th-century *azulejos* depicting romanticised scenes from the battle of Ourique. Symbolically the most important battle in Portuguese history, this was fought just outside Castro Verde in 1139 by Dom Afonso Henriques against a far larger Muslim army. In the fracas, legend has it that the Crusader king slew five Almoravid kings to become (after the subsequent Treaty of Zamora) the first king of Portugal. The **Igreja de Nossa Senhora dos Remédios** is said to have been founded by the new king, though the current structure dates from the 17th century, having been rebuilt by Philip II through a fund-raising fair, which grew to become the famous Feira de Castro celebrated to this day. The *Milagre de Ourique* (Miracle of Ourique), a painting inside the church by Diogo Magina (1763–67), shows the miraculous vision of Christ Afonso Henriques is said to have been granted prior to the battle of Ourique at the little village of São Pedro das Cabeças near the battlefield. On the Largo da Feira square there is a fully restored **medieval windmill** (✆ *286 328148;* ⊕ *interior open when the windmill is functioning, or the tourist office can organise visits*), one of the finest in Portugal, complete with distinctive Moorish sails and painted in whitewash offset by deep blue window borders.

## OURIQUE

Site of the most important battle in Portuguese history, this little provincial town holds a special place in the heart of all patriotic Portuguese. There's not much to see here, though – a ruined hilltop castle, a few winding Moorish streets and central *praça* filled with sleeping old men in cloth caps. There is an excellent equestrian centre nearby (see page 173).

The **Castro da Cola fort** (*Castro da Cola village, Ourique – access via Ourique and the IC1 highway; free admission*) is a ruined 11th-century Moorish fort on a hill above the Barragem de Santa Clara lake some 20km southwest of Castro Verde. It receives very few visitors. While the fort consists of little more than a skeleton of decrepit walls, it was little altered in Christian times and the most complete structure retains a chicane entrance (common to many post-10th-century fortresses in al-Andalus). There is also a cistern and the remains of an old Islamic village.

## ALMODÔVAR

Sat in flat country where the Alentejo plains wrinkle and rise into the Serras do Caldeirão and Mú mountains, separating the region from the Algarve, Almodôvar is the Baixo Alentejo's last town south. It's worth a pit-stop to see a forgotten museum that preserves a forgotten corner of Iberian history and perhaps to take a hike in the hills and visit the nearby wild boar sanctuary.

### GETTING THERE AND AWAY

**By car**  Almodôvar lies on the N2 road some 10km south of Castro Verde, and just under 6km from the IP1 Lisbon–Algarve motorway.

**By bus** There are Rede Expressos and local buses to Castro Verde and Faro. For more information see www.rede-expressos.pt and www.rodalentejo.pt.

**TOURIST INFORMATION** The *posto de turismo* is in the Convento Nossa Senhora da Conceição (*Rua do Convento;* ☎ 286 660609; ⊕ *09.00–13.00 & 14.00–18.00 daily*).

## WHERE TO STAY

🏠 **Monte Gois Country House and Spa** www. wonderfulland.com. Bungalow cottages & apartments housed in cottages (some of which are large enough for a family), around 2 pretty pools, surrounded by cork oak forests & little lakes. The shady terraces are slung with colourful hammocks & the rooms are painted in thick ultramarines, pinks & yellows, decorated with scatter cushions & draped with mosquito nets. The hotel has a small spa & serves a generous b/fast al fresco. Lots of activities on offer, from hikes & bike rides to visits to Almodôvar & safari trips to the nearby wild boar sanctuary. €€€

## WHAT TO SEE AND DO

**Museu da Escrita do Sudoeste (Museum of the Script of the Southeast)** (*Rua do Relógio;* ⊕ *10.00–13.00 & 14.00–18.00 daily; free admission*) This fascinating small museum is devoted to the ancient southwestern Iberian Tartessian script, a proto-historic language and system of writing developed in Portugal and western Andalucia in the 7th to 6th centuries BC. The people who developed it have vanished from history into myth. Herodotus describes Tartessos as being beyond the Pillars of Hercules. Roman historians claim the civilisation was lost to a great flood, leading archaeologists like Adolf Schulten to suggest that Tartessos was Atlantis. Others thought that the Tartessians were the ancestors of the Turduli people, described by the 1st century BC Greek historian Strabo as possessors of a rich history, poetry and system of law stretching back over some 6,000 years. Discoveries made near Huelva and Seville have led archaeologists more recently to identify Tartessos with Huelva in southern Andalucia or the remains of a settlement uncovered in 2011 in Doñana National Park.

Little is known of the language or script, except that it is probably unrelated to any other Indo-European language other than possibly Basque. The longest known Tartessian text so far discovered is from the Mesas do Castelinho unearthed near Almodôvar, comprising 82 signs, 80 of which have an identifiable phonetic value carved into a flat stone. You can see these in the museum, which (together with the Museu da Rainha Dona Leonor in Beja, pages 158–9) preserves one of the largest collections of Tartessian text in the world.

# MÉRTOLA

Clambering in a clutter of terracotta roofs and whitewash up a steep hill on the banks of the sinuous and sluggish Guadiana River, and surrounded by a natural park, Mértola is the prettiest of the Baixo Alentejo's Moorish towns. And as it's in easy coach reach of the Algarve, it's one of the region's most visited. The town has a long and noble history, but aside from an excellent museum of Islamic art and a fascinating old church built into an original Moorish mosque, there are no outstanding attractions. Like Castelo de Vide in the north, Mértola is a place in which to base yourself, or to visit on a long, languid summer afternoon to soak up the atmosphere and sip a beer or coffee while gazing out over the river.

**HISTORY** The ridge where the town sits was been occupied from prehistoric times by Iberians and later by Carthaginians, Phoenicians (who may have named the town after the son of Hermes, or myrtle plant in honour of Aphrodite, to whom it was sacred), and finally the Romans, who built a fort and a settlement here. While subordinate to Emerita Augusta (Mérida), Scalabis (Santarém) and Pax Lulia (Beja), Roman Myrtillis Lulia was of equal status to Ebora (Évora) and Salacia (Alcácer do Sal), and was the most important economic and military town south of Beja in Roman Lusitania. The town became a river port for the copper mines at Aljustrel and Minas de São Domingos, grew in prosperity and by the 2nd century AD was producing its own coins. It was visited by Christian evangelists and occupied by the Germanic Suebi. A tombstone from Mértola, dating from AD525 and now in a museum in Lisbon, has a horseshoe arch of the kind associated with Muslim Andalucia, suggesting that this architectural style predates the Muslim invasion. This arrived in Mértola in the second decade of the 8th century, when the town fell to the armies of Tariq ibn Ziyad.

It was the North Africans who renamed Myrtillis Lulia Martulah, and the river at its feet the Wadi Anas, latinised as Guadiana. The Moors are responsible for much of the old town you see today. The castle retains many Arabic features, the streets that radiate from it could be Moroccan and the church still has its *mihrab*.

Mértola was conquered by the Knights of the Order of Saint James in 1238 and given to the order thereafter by King Sancho II. The knights did little with Mértola and during the Middle Ages the town gradually lost its economic importance. But for a brief florescence in the 19th century (when mining began again at São Domingos), Mértola remained forgotten, losing 50% of its population during the Novo Estado and only beginning to recover in the late 20th century when tourists from the Algarve began visiting in increasing numbers.

## GETTING THERE AND AWAY

**By car** Mértola lies in the heart of the Parque Natural do Vale do Guadiana at the junction of two major roads – the IC27 (which runs between Vila Real de Santo Antônio on the Algarve coast and Beja) and the N267 (running between Almodôvar, Minas de São Domingos and the Spanish border). Distances are as follows: Minas de São Domingos (14.5km); Beja (53km); Serpa (55km); Vila Real de Santo Antônio (67km); Faro (118km); Lisbon (235km).

Mértola is tiny and easy to get around on foot. It's possible to drive inside the old centre but not recommended. There is ample parking immediately outside the centre.

**By bus** Mértola is not well served by Rede Expressos buses. There are two daily services to Lisbon. Bus lines 8757 and 8768 run between Beja and Mértola on weekdays.

**TOURIST INFORMATION AND TOURS** There is a very helpful **tourist office** at Rua da Igreja 31(✆ *286 610109;* ⏱ *09.00–13.00 & 14.00–18.00*). **Beira Rio Nautica** (*Rua Dr Afonso Costa 108;* ✆ *286 611190; www.beirario.pt*) offers hour-long boat trips on the river, kayak and bike rental.

## WHERE TO STAY

**Convento São Francisco de Mértola** (25 rooms) ✆ 286 612119; www. conventomertola.com. A beautifully situated 400-year-old Franciscan monastery set in a shady garden & with views out over the Guadiana River & the surrounding countryside. Rooms & apts are housed in converted stables & outbuildings.

Wonderfully tranquil. Minimum 2 night stays. Artist in residence programmes. €€€

**Beira Rio** (25 rooms) Rua Dr Afonso Costa 108; ✆ 286 612313; www.beirario.pt. Pleasant, modern rooms with white walls & beds with colourful covers or scatter cushions & great castle &/ or river views from the windows & balconies. €€

**Museu** (25 rooms) Rua Dr Afonso Costa 112; 286 612003; www.hotelmuseu.com. Simple but well-appointed rooms with wooden floors, little workstations & big windows with sweeping views over the river. The hotel is especially good for wildlife enthusiasts & birdwatchers & can organise trips into the adjacent Parque Natural do Vale do Guadiana. €€

**Casa do Funil** (3 rooms) Rua Prof Batista da Graça 19; 286 612056; Facebook: Casa-do-Funil. Small but cosy rooms in a converted family home in the heart of the old town. Rooms are decked out in light wood & whitewash with brightly-coloured little bathrooms & views over the river. €

**Hotel Casa Visconde de Bouzoes** (6 rooms) Rua Dr Antonio José de Almeida 12; 965 351979; www.casa-visconde.blogspot.co.uk. A rustic family house in a terrace in the old centre run by the affable Carlos & his family. Simple but well-located if a little cluttered, & with a decent buffet b/fast. €

**WHERE TO EAT AND DRINK** Mértola has no very good restaurants, just a few small eateries, mostly serving local fare. The two listed below are about the best.

**Alengarve** Av Aureliano Mira Fernandes 20; 286 655133; ⊕ 12.30–15.00 & 19.00–22.30 Thu–Tue. One of the oldest restaurants in town, serving typical Alentejo & Algarve dishes like *lombo do porco preto* and *carapaus alimados*. €€

**O Repuxo** Av Aureliano Mira Fernandes; 286 612563; ⊕ 12.30–15.00 & 19.00–22.30 Sun–Fri. Family-run restaurant specialising in seafood & typical Alentejo dishes. €

**WHAT TO SEE AND DO** Mértola calls itself the museum town, and all of its various museums, the castle and the church are united under the auspices of the **Museu de Mértola (Mértola Museum)** (*www.museus.cm-mertola.pt*; ⊕ 09.30–12.30 & 14.00–18.00 Tue–Sun (an hour earlier in winter); admission €2, tickets available from the tourist office), and with the same opening hours and one combined ticket serving all.

Like many of the Alentejo castles, there is little to see in **Mértola castle** beyond the battlements and crumbling stones. The main reason to climb up to the top of the keep is for the wonderful views out over the town and river. The castle has a long history. Its principal structure is Moorish, but the keep was enlarged by the powerful Order of Saint James, who once had their national headquarters here. Just north of the castle is the **Cemitério de Mértola (Mértola cemetery)**, built over one of the most beautiful parts of the old Moorish town, which was levelled in the 13th century.

Mértola's parish church or **Igreja Matriz de Nossa Senhora da Anunciação**, topped with typical Mudéjar merlons and cylindrical towers, was once a mosque, as its vaulted interior (with later Gothic embellishments) attests. Look out for the horseshoe arches over the doors which once opened on to the *sahn* (interior courtyard of the old Almohad mosque), the two re-used capitals and the original mihrab (a niche in the wall facing Mecca) directly behind the altar. You can still see the remains of the original Muslim decoration at its apex – with three multi-lobed arches topped by a cyma cornice moulded by two cordons symbolising infinity. These are unique in Portugal. The mosque was itself built on top of an earlier Suebin church, which was in turn constructed over a Roman temple.

The **Núcleo Islámico (Islamic Art Collection)** (*Largo da Misericórdia s/n;* 286 610109), housed over two floors of an old granary, is one of the most significant in Portugal, with a wealth of beautiful ceramics from the potteries of medieval Al-Andalus –beautiful *cuerda seca* vases and glazed bowls, oil lamps and spindles made of animal bone, many of them unearthed in and around Mértola, coins, glassware and metalwork. The Centre for Islamic and Mediterranean Studies next door is a research institute which hosts temporary exhibitions of Islamic art and a library of 20,000+ book devoted to Islamic civilisation and culture in the Mediterranean.

The **Núcleo Romano (Roman Collection)** (*Largo Luís de Camões s/n*) shows the remains of a Roman forum, together with a smattering of Roman bric-a-brac excavated from around the town hall. The **Sacred Art Museum** housed in the Igreja de Misericórdia (Largo de Misericórdia) has a collection of Baroque arts and statuary gleaned from abandoned churches in the vicinity as well as three retables depicting the battle for Mértola during the Reconquest.

## Around Mértola

*Minas de São Domingos (São Domingos Mines)* The old Roman copper mines were rediscovered and reopened for business in the mid 19th century by a British firm, which employed almost the entire area around Mértola to work them (7,000 workers; modern Mértola has a population of around 6,500). São Domingos became the first town in Portugal to have telephones and electricity. For a while it boomed and when the British left in the early 20th century it became a ghost town. The mines no longer run but you can still see the rusting buildings, the crumbling chimneys, old steam locomotives and the disused railway as well as a huge quarry gashed from the landscape and filled in part with an evil-looking brown pond polluted with heavy metals and sulphides. The Minas lie 15km east of Mértola.

# Appendix 1

## LANGUAGE

Portuguese is a Latin language that sounds very different to either Spanish or Italian, and to how it is written on the page.

### GUIDE TO PRONOUNCING THE PORTUGUESE ALPHABET

| Letters | Portuguese | Meaning | Pronunciation | English |
|---|---|---|---|---|
| a | abacaxi | pineapple | sounds like [a] | water |
| | maracanã | famous football stadium | nasal sound | |
| b | sala | sitting room | sounds like [b] | ball |
| c | casa | house | **ca/co/cu** sounds like [k] | keep |
| | cebola | onion | **ce/ci** sounds like [s] | civil |
| ç | louça | dish | **ça/ço/çu** sounds like [s] | civil |
| ch | choque | shock | sounds like [sh] | ship |
| d | dama | lady | sounds like [d] | dog |
| e | você | you | sounds like [e] | then |
| | deitar | to lie down | sounds like [ee] at the end, if unstressed | breeze |
| | ferro | iron | sounds like [e] | led |
| f | farofa | flour | sounds like [f] | fork |
| g | gota | drop | **ga/go/gu** sounds like [g] | gang |
| | gente | people | **ge/gi** sounds like [g] | mage |
| gu | guarda | guard | **gua/guo** sounds like [gw] | Nicaragua |
| | freguês | client | **gue/gui** sounds like [g] | gang |
| | bilingue | bilingual | **gue/gui** sounds like [gw] | Nicaragua |
| h | hora | hour | silent | |
| i | menina | girl | sounds like [ea] | seal |
| j | jogo | game | sounds like [g] | age |
| l | lobo | wolf | **la/le/li/lo/lu** sounds like [l] | lip |
| | barril | barrel | **al/el/il/ol/ul** sounds like [w] | crew |
| lh | molhado | wet | sounds like [ll] | grilled |
| m | mesa | table | sounds like [m] | map |
| | bom | good | sounds between **m** and **n**, similar to the French word *bon* | |
| n | nata | cream | sounds like [n] | name |
| | lontra | otter | sounds like [n] | bank |
| nh | manhã | morning | sounds like [ng], the French word *sauvignon* | |
| o | menino, avô | boy, grandfather | sounds like [o] | go |

| | | | | | |
|---|---|---|---|---|---|
| | banco | bank | sounds like a [w] at the end of a word | snow | |
| | loja, bota | Shop, boot | sounds like [aw] | saw | |
| p | prato | plate | sounds like [p] | pipe | |
| q | quanto? | how much? | qua/quo sounds like [kw] | quite | |
| | caqui | persimon | que/qui sounds like [k] | keep | |
| | frequencia | frequency | que/qui sounds like [kw] | quite | |
| r | recordar | remember | similar to [h] sound | hop | |
| | correr | run | similar to [h] sound, if preceded by n | hop | |
| | curto | short | sounds like soft [r] | storm | |
| | claro | clear | similar to [r] sound | fair | |
| rr | burro | donkey | similar to [h] sound | hole | |
| s | sapo | toad | sounds like [s] | sail | |
| | insano | insane | like [s] | sail | |
| | três | three | after vowels sounds like [s] | grass | |
| | camisa | shirt | sounds like [z] | zebra | |
| sc | piscina | swimming pool | sce/sci sounds like [s] | sail | |
| ss | passado | past | sounds like [s] | sail | |
| t | chiclete | chewing gum | sounds like [ch] | chip | |
| | uma | one | sounds like [w] | boom | |
| | voz | voice | sounds like [v] | viper | |
| x | axé | joy | sounds like [sh] | shape | |
| | baixa | lower | after ai/ei sounds like [sh] | shape | |
| | táxi | taxi | sounds like [ks] | taxi | |
| | maximo | biggest | sounds like [s] | symbol | |
| | excelente | excellent | exce/exci sounds like [s] | symbol | |
| | exato | exact | exa/exe/exi/exo/exu sounds like [z] | zebra | |
| z | zebra | zebra | before a vowel sounds like [z] | zebra | |
| | vez | turn | after a vowel sounds like [s] | sail | |

## FOOD AND DRINK

| | | | |
|---|---|---|---|
| abacate | avocado | carne | meat |
| abobrinha | courgette | cenoura | carrot |
| açúcar | sugar | cerveja | beer |
| agua mineral | mineral water | chá | tea |
| alface | lettuce | colher | spoon |
| almoço | lunch | faca | knife |
| arroz | rice | feijão | beans |
| atum | tuna | frango | chicken |
| azeitona | olives | frutos do mar | seafood |
| bacalhau | cod | garfo | fork |
| bacon/toucinho | bacon | gelo | ice |
| batata | potato | jantar | dinner |
| bebida | drink | lance | snack |
| bife | steak | laranja | orange |
| café da manhã | breakfast | leite | milk |
| café | coffee | limão | lime |
| camarão | shrimp/prawn | lula | squid |
| caranguejo/siri | crab | maçã | apple |

| | | | |
|---|---|---|---|
| *manga* | mango | *queijo* | cheese |
| *manteiga* | butter | *robalo* | bass |
| *maracujá* | passionfruit | *sal* | salt |
| *pão* | bread | *salada* | salad |
| *peixe* | fish | *sanduíche* | sandwich |
| *pepino* | cucumber | *sopa* | soup |
| *peru* | turkey | *sumo* | fruit juice |
| *pimenta do reino* | black pepper | *tomate* | tomato |
| *pimenta* | chilli | *vinho* | wine |
| *presunto* | ham | | |

## GENERAL WORDS AND PHRASES

| | | | |
|---|---|---|---|
| bad | *mau* | I don't understand | *Não compreendo* |
| big | *grande* | I'm on holiday | *Estou de férias* |
| Could you help me, please? | *Pode me ajudar, faz favor?* | I'm sorry | *Desculpe* |
| | | later | *mais tarde* |
| closed | *fechado* | May I/Can I? | *Posso?* |
| Do you speak English? | *Fala inglês?* | My name is ... | *Meu nome é…* |
| enough | *suficiente* | No | *Não* |
| good | *bom* | now | *agora* |
| Good morning | *Bom dia* | open | *aberto* |
| Good afternoon | *Boa tarde* | Please | *Por favor* |
| Good evening/night | *Boa noite* | See you later | *Até logo* |
| Goodbye | *Tchau* | small | *pequeno* |
| Excuse me | *Com licença* | Thank you | *Obrigado(a)* |
| Hello, pleased to meet you | *Olá, prazer em conhecê-lo(a)* | there | *ali* |
| | | When | *Quando* |
| Here | *aqui* | Where | *Onde* |
| How | *Como* | Who | *Quem* |
| How are you? | *Tudo bem?* | Why | *Porquê* |
| I don't speak Portuguese | *Não falo português* | Yes | *Sim* |

## BUYING AND SELLING

| | | | |
|---|---|---|---|
| bakery | *padaria* | I'd like ... | *Queria ...* |
| bookshop | *livraria* | grams please | *gramas, por favor* |
| change | *troco* | | |
| cheap/er | *barato/mais barato* | I'd like a kilo of ... | *Queria um quilo de ...* |
| chemist | *farmácia* | I'm looking for ... | *Preciso de ...* |
| clothes | *roupa* | I'm just looking, thank you | *Só estou olhando, obrigado(a)* |
| Do you accept credit cards? | *Aceitam cartões de crédito?* | | |
| | | market | *mercado* |
| Do you have a bag for this? | *Tem um sacola para isto?* | money | *dinheiro* |
| | | supermarket | *supermercado* |
| | | This one | *Este(a)* |
| expensive | *caro(a)* | | |
| How much is this? | *Quanto custa?* | | |

## HEALTH AND DIFFICULTIES

| | |
|---|---|
| accident | *acidente* |
| Can you call a doctor? | *Pode chamar um médico?* |
| dangerous | *perigoso* |
| diarrhoea | *diarréia* |
| emergency | *emergência* |
| I don't feel well | *Não me sinto bem* |
| I have been robbed | *Fui assaltado* |
| I've got a fever | *Tenho febre* |
| help | *socorro* |
| medicine | *remédio* |
| police | *polícia* |
| Where is the nearest hospital? | *Onde é o hospital mais próximo?* |

## SLEEPING

| | |
|---|---|
| bathroom/toilet | *casa de banho/toalete* |
| Do you have a room? | *Têm um quarto?* |
| Do you serve evening meals? | *Servem jantar?* |
| double room | *quarto de casal* |
| guesthouse | *pousada* |
| hostel | *albergue* |
| Is the room air-conditioned? | *O quarto tem ar?* |
| How much each night? | *Quanto é por noite?* |
| May I see the room? | *Posso ver o quarto?* |
| Please can I pay my bill? | *Posso pagar a conta?* |
| single room | *quarto individual* |
| swimming pool | *piscina* |
| twin room | *quarto duplo* |
| with bath/shower | *com banheira/choveiro* |
| When do you serve breakfast? | *Quando servem o pequeno almoço?* |

## NUMBERS

| | | | | | |
|---|---|---|---|---|---|
| 1 | *um* | 11 | *onze* | 21 | *vinte e um* |
| 2 | *dois* | 12 | *doze* | 30 | *trinta* |
| 3 | *três* | 13 | *treze* | 40 | *quarenta* |
| 4 | *quatro* | 14 | *catorze* | 50 | *cinquenta* |
| 5 | *cinco* | 15 | *quinze* | 60 | *sessenta* |
| 6 | *seis* | 16 | *dezasseis* | 70 | *setenta* |
| 7 | *sete* | 17 | *dezassete* | 80 | *oitenta* |
| 8 | *oito* | 18 | *dezoito* | 90 | *noventa* |
| 9 | *nove* | 19 | *dezanove* | 100 | *cem* |
| 10 | *dez* | 20 | *vinte* | 1000 | *mil* |

## DAYS OF THE WEEK

| | |
|---|---|
| Monday | *segunda-feira* |
| Tuesday | *terça-feira* |
| Wednesday | *quarta-feira* |
| Thursday | *quinta-feira* |
| Friday | *sexta-feira* |
| Saturday | *sábado* |
| Sunday | *domingo* |

## MONTHS

| | | | |
|---|---|---|---|
| January | *janeiro* | July | *julho* |
| February | *fevereiro* | August | *agosto* |
| March | *março* | September | *setembro* |
| April | *abril* | October | *outubro* |
| May | *maio* | November | *novembro* |
| June | *junho* | December | *dezembro* |

## SEASONS AND FESTIVALS

| | | | |
|---|---|---|---|
| spring | *primavera* | winter | *inverno* |
| summer | *verão* | Easter | *Páscoa* |
| autumn | *outono* | Christmas | *Natal* |

## OTHER TIME PHRASES

| | | | |
|---|---|---|---|
| morning | *manhã* | yesterday | *ontem* |
| afternoon | *tarde* | tomorrow | *amanhã* |
| evening | *fim da tarde* | day | *dia* |
| night | *noite* | month | *mês* |
| today | *hoje* | year | *ano* |

# Appendix 2

## GLOSSARY OF PORTUGUESE, ARABIC AND TECHNICAL TERMS

| | |
|---|---|
| *alfiz* | rectangular surround to an Arabic arch |
| *alcaide* | governor/lord (of a castle) – the chief authority in a town. From the Arabic - al-qā'id (the one who gives orders) |
| *cuerda seca* | a method of separating different coloured glazes on a ceramic object during firing using cords greased in fat |
| *latifundio* | landholding run through slave or indentured labour, often established in Roman times |
| *latifundario* | landholder |
| Mannerist | late Renaissance artistic style using exaggerated perspective, movement or specific architectural motifs to express emotion |
| Manueline | specifically Portuguese form of Gothic which fused Mudéjar with elaborately carved nautical motifs and which was associated with the reign of Dom Manuel I |
| Mudéjar | a Christian architectural style that was heavily influenced by Islamic design |
| mullion | the vertical element that forms a division between units of a window, door, or screen |
| *pelourinho* | pillory/whipping post |
| *pietra dura* | polished stone inlay – western antecedent of Parchin Kari |
| *scagliola* | imitation *pietra dura* marble inlay or marble facing |

### FOOD AND DRINK

| | |
|---|---|
| *açorda* | a thick bread-based sauce |
| *ameijoas* | clams |
| *ameijoas à bulhão pato* | clams in white wine and fresh herbs |
| *arroz* | rice |
| *arroz de pescada/tamboril/lingueirão* | a mix between a stew and risotto, with hake/monkfish/razor clams |
| *arroz de lebre* | hare risotto flavoured with laurel and rosemary |
| *bacalhau* | salt cod |
| *bacalhau dourada* | salt cod in olive oil |
| *bacalhau com espinafres* | salt cod with spinach |
| *bochechas de porco preto* | black pork cheeks |
| *camarão/camarões* | prawn/s |

185

| | |
|---|---|
| *carapaus alimados* | horse mackerel in lime and parsley sauce |
| *cebolada* | an onion-based sauce used for fish and game |
| *codorniz* | quail |
| *choco* | cuttlefish |
| *coentro* | coriander |
| *costelas/costelatas* | ribs |
| *cozido de grão com vagens à alentejana* | lamb and chick pea stew |
| *dourada* | gilt head (sea) bream |
| *empada* | Portuguese pasty but made with puff pastry |
| *ensopado de borrego* | goat meat broth |
| *espargos* | asparagus |
| *farofas* | beaten egg whites and sugared hazelnuts |
| *frango* | chicken (juvenile), also a synonym of *galinha* |
| *galinha* | chicken (adult), also a synonym of *frango* |
| *gamba/s* | shrimp/s |
| *gila* | pumpkin |
| *lombo de porco com amêijoas* | pork chops with clams |
| *lombinhos de porco preto* | mini pork chops from Alentejo black pigs |
| *migas* | olive oil and puréed breadcrumbs, flavoured with herbs – a little like a thick Rouille sauce; served as an accompaniment |
| *pão de rala* | sweet cake made with breadcrumbs and eggs and flavoured with almonds, lemon peel and pumpkin |
| *pastel de nata/Belém* | Portuguese custard tart, often called just *nata* |
| *pescada* | hake |
| *petisco* | Portuguese equivalent of tapas |
| *porco preto* | Alentejan pasture-grazed black pig |
| *presunto* | Portuguese dried ham (like parma ham) |
| *queijada* | a sweet tart made from cream cheese, eggs, milk and flavoured with condiments |
| *robalo* | European sea bass |
| *sopa de tomate a alentejana* | thick tomato and vegetable soup served cold with a poached egg |
| *tamboril* | monkfish |

# Appendix 3

## PORTUGUESE MONARCHS AND PRESIDENTS

### HOUSE OF BURGUNDY

| | |
|---|---|
| 1128–1185 | Alfonso Henriques I (from 1139) (*o Conquistador* – the Conquerer) |
| 1185–1211 | Sancho I (*o Povoador* – the Settler) |
| 1211–1223 | Alfonso II (*o Gordo* – the Fat) |
| 1223–1245 | Sancho II (*o Capelo* – the Pious/Hooded) |
| 1245–1279 | Alfonso III (regent until 1248) |
| 1279–1325 | Dinis (*o Lavrador* – the Farmer) |
| 1325–1357 | Alfonso IV (*o Bravo* – the Brave) |
| 1357–1367 | Pedro I (Peter) (*o Justiceiro* – the Lawman) |
| 1367–1383 | Ferdinand (*o Formoso* – the Handsome) |
| 1383–1385 | Interregnum |

### HOUSE OF AVIS

| | |
|---|---|
| 1385–1433 | Joao I (regent 1383–1385) (*o de boa Memória* – of Good Memory) |
| 1433–1438 | Duarte (Edward) (*o Eloquente* – the Eloquent) |
| 1438–1481 | Alfonso V (*o Africano* – the African) |
| 1481–1495 | João II (*o Príncipe Perfeito* – the Perfect Prince) |
| 1495–1521 | Manuel I (*o Venturoso* – the Fortunate) |
| 1521–1557 | João III (*o Piedoso* – the Pious) |
| 1557–1578 | Sebastião (*o Desejado* – the Desired, or sometimes the Regretted) |
| 1558–1580 | Henrique (Cardinal) (*o Casto* – the Chaste) |

### SPANISH RULE

| | |
|---|---|
| 1580–1598 | Filipe I (II of Spain) (*o Prudente* – the Prudent) |
| 1598–1621 | Filipe II (III of Spain) (*o Pio* – the Pious) |
| 1621–1640 | Filipe III (IV of Spain) (*o Grande* – the Great) |

### HOUSE OF BRAGANÇA (BRAGANZA)

| | |
|---|---|
| 1640–1656 | João IV (7th Duke of Bragança) (*o Restaurador* – the Restorer) |
| 1656–1667 | Alfonso VI (*o Vitorioso* – the Victorious) |
| 1667–1706 | Pedro II (regent until 1683) (*o Pacífico* – the Pacific/the Peaceful) |
| 1706–1750 | John V (*o Magnánimo* – the Magnanimous) |
| 1750–1777 | Joseph (*o reformador* – the Reformer) |
| 1777–1816 | Maria I (*a Piedosa* – the Pious) joint reign with Peter III until 1786 |
| 1816–1826 | João VI (regent, 1792–1816) (*o Clemente* – the Clement) |
| 1826 | Pedro IV (*o Libertador* – the Liberator) |
| 1826–1828 | Maria II da Glória (Maria Leopoldina of Austria) |
| 1828–1834 | Miguel II (regent from 1827) (*o Usurpador* – the Usurper) |
| 1834–1853 | Maria II da Glória (2nd time) (*a Educadora* – the Educator) |

| 1853–1861 | Pedro V (*o Esperançoso* – the Hopeful) |
| 1861–1889 | Louis (*o Popular* – the Popular) |
| 1889–1908 | Charles (*o Diplomata* – the Diplomat) |
| 1908–1910 | Manuel II (*o Desventroso* – the Unfortunate) |

## REPUBLIC OF PORTUGAL (PRESIDENTS)

| 1910–1911 | Teófilo Braga (provisional) |
| 1911–1915 | Manuel Jose de Arriaga |
| 1915 | Teófilo Braga |
| 1915–1917 | Bernardino Machado |
| 1917–1918 | Sidónio Pais |
| 1918–1919 | João do Canto e Castro |
| 1919–1923 | António José de Almeida |
| 1923–1925 | Manuel Teixeira Gomes |
| 1925–1926 | Bernardino Machado |
| 1926 | provisional government |
| 1926–1951 | António Oscar de Fragoso Carmona |
| 1951 | António de Oliveira Salazar (Prime Minister, but *de facto* acting head of state between 1932 and 1968) |
| 1951–1958 | Francisco Craveiro Lopes |
| 1958–1974 | Américo de Deus Rodrigues Tomás |
| 1974 | António de Spínola |
| 1974–1976 | Francisco da Costa Gomes |
| 1976–1986 | António Ramalho Eanes |
| 1986–1996 | Mario Soares |
| 1996–2006 | Jorge Sampaio |
| 2006– | Aníbal Cavaco Silva |

# Appendix 4

## FURTHER INFORMATION

### BOOKS
### History

Crowley, Roger *Conquerors: How Portugal seized the Indian Ocean and forged the First Global Empire* Faber 2015. A long overdue popular history of how Portugal explored and conquered the world's most lucrative trade routes.

Disney, A R *A History of Portugal & the Portuguese Empire* Cambridge, 2009. By far the best history of the country available in English. In two volumes, the first dealing with Portugal, the second with the Portuguese Empire.

Hourani, Albert *A History of the Arab Peoples* Faber, 1991. The definitive short history of the Arab peoples from the time of Muhammad to the present day, with accounts of the history and culture of al-Andalus.

Newitt, Malyn *Emigration and the Sea: An Alternative History of Portugal and the Portuguese* C Hurst & Co, 2015. The history of the Portuguese diaspora including stories of those who left mainland Portugal and the islands, the Sephardic Jews, the African slaves imported into the Atlantic islands and Brazil and the Goans who spread across the globe from East Africa to the UK.

Russell, Peter *Prince Henry 'the Navigator': A Life*, Yale University Press, 2001. A well-researched biography of the half-English prince who sponsored shipbuilding, technological innovations and voyages of discovery in 15th century Portugal.

Saraiva, José Hermano *Portugal: A Companion History* Carcanet, 1997. The liveliest outline of the country's history from the Lucy Worsley of Portugal.

### Art, culture and food

De Castro e Silva, Miguel *Recipes from My Portuguese Kitchen* Aquamarine, 2013. One of a series of books from the best-selling writer and former Portuguese Chef of the Year.

Levenson, Jay (ed.) *The Age of the Baroque in Portugal* Yale University Press, 1994. Comprehensive illustrated review of Portuguese Baroque art and architecture.

Mendes, George *My Portugal* Stewart, Tabori & Chang, 2014. Portuguese recipes and cooking techniques from the Michelin-starred chef and owner of the Aldea restaurant in New York.

Vieira, Edite *The Taste of Portugal* Grub Street, 2013. A gastronomic journey through Portugal, its culture and its history.

### Literature and travel

Beckford, William *Recollections of an excursion to the monasteries of Alcobaça and Batalha* 1835. Gloriously descriptive accounts of travel in late 18th-century Portugal from one of the first Gothic novelists.

Cornwell, Bernard, *Sharpe's Enemy: The Defence of Portugal* HarperCollins. The 15th instalment of the rip-roaring historical series, set in Portugal during the Napoleonic Peninsular War.

De Queirós, Eça *The Maias* Carcanet Press, 1965. The 19th-century naturalist novelist's magnum opus, chronicling the decline of an aristocratic Portuguese family at the end of the monarchical era, and written when the writer was living in Newcastle and Bristol.

Macaulay, Rose *They Went to Portugal* Jonathan Cape, 1946. A wonderful mixture of history, biography and travel literature, charting the impressions and stories of foreign visitors to Portugal from Roman times until the 20th century and including writers like Fielding and William Beckford.

Pessoa, Fernando *The Book of Disquiet* Penguin Classics, 2015. The melancholy musings of Pessoa's heteronym, Bernardo Soares, and a meditation on the alienation and futility of modern working life that stands shoulder-to-shoulder with *Prufrock*.

Plutarch tr. John Dryden *Lives* The Modern Library, 2001. Rip-roaring Roman lives from the 2nd-century Greek, translated by Dryden and including (in the second volume) a wonderful account of the life of the Lusitanian Hannibal, Sertorius.

Saramago, José *Journey to Portugal* Vintage, 2002. Saramago's desultory and whimsical wanderings through the country includes a long chapter on the Alentejo.

Saramago, José *Raised from the Ground* Harvill Secker, 1980. One of the Nobel prize-winning writer's earlier novels telling the story of generations of indentured workers in the Alentejo. Harrowing, humorous and masterfully written. A modernist, rural *Germinal*.

Saramago, José *The Year of the Death of Ricardo Reis* Harvill Secker, 1984. Arguably Saramago's greatest novel tells the story of Fernando Pessoa's literary heteronym who lives on after Pessoa's death.

## General

Saramago, Alfredo *Livro-Guia do Alentejo* Assirio & Alvim, 2007. Lovingly researched and very detailed cultural and gastronomic guide to the Alentejo, published in Portuguese.

Salvador J A *ABeCedário dos Vinhos* Guias de Enoturismo, 2010. A comprehensive guide to wine in Portuguese with extensive information on Alentejo bottles.

## Natural History

Aarnio and Saarinen *Butterflies of Europe: A Photographic Guide* A&C Black, 2009. A field guide to all the 440 species of Europe with photographs of the species with opened and closed wings.

Arnold & Ovenden, Nicholas *Reptiles and Amphibians of Britain and Europe* Collins 2002. Descriptions of every species found in mainland Europe.

Chinery, Michael *Insects of Britain and Western Europe*: 3rd edition, A&C Black, 2012. An excellent and expansive book covering many key European species.

Davies & Gibbons *Field Guide to Wild Flowers of Southern Europe* Crowood Press, 1993. This volume describes 1,200 species from Spain, Portugal, southern France, Italy and Malta with information on habitat, distribution and flowering time, and coverage of the more conspicuous species of orchids.

De Juana & Garcia, *The Birds of the Iberian Peninsula*, Bloomsbury 2015. The most comprehensive guide to birds in Iberia, with detailed range maps and migration, distribution, habitats and breeding and wintering information, but very few illustrations.

Elias, G *Birds of Portugal: An Annotated Checklist*, CreateSpace Independent Publishing Platform, 2013. As the title suggests, this is a comprehensive Portuguese species list, not a field guide.

Gosney, Dave *Finding Birds in South Portugal* Easybirder 2013. Maps and indications of where to find particular species, but with no illustrations.

Grey-Wilson & Blarney *Wild Flowers of the Mediterranean* A&C Black 2004. The most comprehensive guide to 2,500 wildflower species from the Mediterranean, covering most species found in the Alentejo.

Mitchell-Jones & Moutoull *Mammals of Europe, North Africa and the Middle East* A&C Black, 2009. Illustrated accounts of all the European terrestrial mammal species from North Africa (north of the tropic of Cancer) to the Arctic Circle and the shores of the Portuguese Atlantic to the western shores of the Caspian Sea.

Moore, Elias & Costa *A Birdwatchers' Guide to Portugal, the Azores and Madeira* Archipelagos Prion, 2014. The most comprehensive location guide for birdwatchers visiting Portugal. In black and white. You'll need a companion species guide for identification.

Svensson & Mullarney, *Collins Bird Guide* Collins 2010. Perhaps the best of the birding field guides, covering all of the species and with accounts accompanied with sharp, clear photographs and illustrations.

Thorogood, George *Field Guide to the Wild Flowers of the Algarve* Kew Publishing, 2014. Also useful for the Alentejo, with illustrations and species coverage which, while far from comprehensive, is extensive.

## WEBSITES
See the main sections of the guide for websites for tour operators, hotels and so on.

**visitportugal.com** Official website for the Portuguese tourist board
**visitalentejo.pt** Official regional website for the region
**evora-portugal.com** Comprehensive information on the city of Évora and its surrounding attractions

# Index

Page numbers in **bold** refer to main entries and those in *italics* to maps.

## INDEX OF ADVERTISERS